D1756897

The Song of the Distant Dove

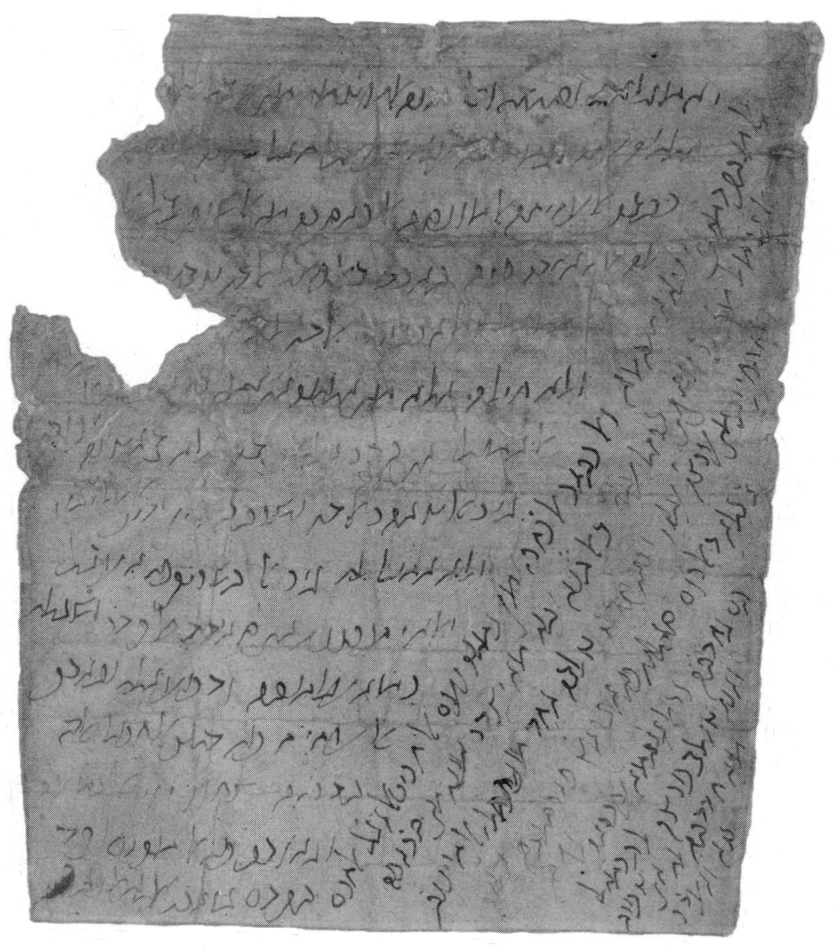

A letter by Judah Halevi to Ḥalfon ben Nethaniel Halevi in Arabic language and Hebrew script (ENA NS 1.5r, reproduced courtesy of the Library of the Jewish Theological Seminary). The document is discussed below, pp. 100–102.

The Song of the Distant Dove

Judah Halevi's Pilgrimage

RAYMOND P. SCHEINDLIN

2008

OXFORD
UNIVERSITY PRESS

Oxford University Press, Inc., publishes works that further
Oxford University's objective of excellence
in research, scholarship, and education.

Oxford New York
Auckland Cape Town Dar es Salaam Hong Kong Karachi
Kuala Lumpur Madrid Melbourne Mexico City Nairobi
New Delhi Shanghai Taipei Toronto

With offices in
Argentina Austria Brazil Chile Czech Republic France Greece
Guatemala Hungary Italy Japan Poland Portugal Singapore
South Korea Switzerland Thailand Turkey Ukraine Vietnam

Published by Oxford University Press, Inc.
198 Madison Avenue, New York, New York 10016

www.oup.com

Library of Congress Cataloging-in-Publication Data
Scheindlin, Raymond P.
The song of the distant dove : Judah Halevi's pilgrimage / Raymond P.
Scheindlin.
p. cm.
Includes bibliographical references and index.
ISBN 978-0-19-531542-4
1. Judah, ha-Levi, 12th cent. —Travel. 2. Judah, ha-Levi, 12th
cent. —Translations into English. I. Title.
PJ5050.J8Z825 2007
892.4'12—dc22 2006038504

9 8 7 6 5 4 3 2 1

Printed in the United States of America
on acid-free paper

To Janice
in love and gratitude

Preface

My theme is poetry; specifically, the poetry of Abū l-Ḥasan Ibn al-Lawī, generally known as Judah Halevi, the best-known and most admired Hebrew poet of the Judeo-Arabic age. This book is an attempt to create a complex picture of Halevi's poetic imagination and religious spirit by examining his poems both as independent literary artifacts and as products of the cultures and the literary traditions that nourished him.

The discussion is so organized as to build toward the poems that Halevi wrote in connection with his famous pilgrimage, undertaken toward the end of his life—poems that, like the act itself, bring to focus a wide range of religious ideas and literary motifs that had engaged the poet since the beginning of his writing career. These eighteen poems are presented in part III in Hebrew, accompanied by new literary translations and a few pages of explanation and discussion for each. By way of preparation for the pilgrimage poems, twelve poems are presented and given similar full treatment in part I, making a total of thirty key poems. They are numbered consecutively from the beginning of the book to the end; they are referred to elsewhere in the book by their opening words in translation and their number. Between the preparatory poems of part I and the pilgrimage poems of part III comes a detailed narrative of Halevi's pilgrimage in part II. The narrative is built out of a group of letters written in Arabic, presented here only in translation.

In the course of the discussion and narrative, I have quoted lavishly from Halevi's other poems and from texts written by him and others in Arabic. The Hebrew poems embedded in the discussion and narrative appear only in translation and are printed in italics to distinguish them from quotations of Arabic texts. Also printed in italics are translations of Hebrew epistles and extended passages of elegant Hebrew salutations embedded in Arabic documents. Translations from documents written in Arabic and translations of quotations from the Bible and rabbinic literature are printed in roman type. All translations are my own, and all but three are new.

The Arabic documents translated here suffer from textual and interpretive problems due to the damaged state of the manuscripts and shortcomings in the present knowledge of their medieval nonstandard Arabic idiom. I have smoothed out their wording a bit; marked the places of indecipherable, illegible, and unintelligible passages with ellipses; and bracketed words supplied by conjecture. Also in brackets are occasional summaries of material from the documents omitted as irrelevant to my purposes.

I normally cite only one source for each poem, which for Halevi's poems almost always means the edition by Ḥayim Brody. For the documents, I normally cite only the recent book by Moshe Gil and Ezra Fleischer in which they are all collected, relying on its full bibliographies to direct the researcher to the places where the documents were originally published. The index of Hebrew first lines at the end of this volume lists every poem in the book, including the many poems that appear in whole or in part in English only.

Monorhymed poems in quantitative meter (the dominant form of medieval Hebrew nonliturgical poetry) were written in long verses, each composed of two lines (the technical term is "hemistich"). Strophic poems consist of stanzas, which in turn are made up of individual lines. When citing poems in the course of the discussion, I have tried to avoid referring to verses or lines by number, so as not to have to place numerals in the margin; but when a passage from a monorhymed poem in quantitative meter is cited by verse number, the number is based on the Hebrew original, in which each verse corresponds to two lines of English. For monorhymed poems, "verse 4" therefore usually means "lines 7 and 8" in the translation. Because the process of translation has expanded some verses into three lines of English and contracted others into one, this calculation will often give only an approximate idea of where a particular quotation can be found in the translation, but this should only rarely present a problem.

In transliterating Hebrew, I have used a very simplified system in which ʾ represents the noninitial consonantal *alef*; "ḥ" represents *ḥet*; "kh" represents *kaf* after a vowel; ʿ represents *ayin*; "q" represents *qof*; "ts" represents *tsadi*; "e" represents both *segol* and *sheva naʿ*; and "ei" represents *tseirei*. Long vowels and the doubling of consonants are not indicated. The transliteration represents the pronunciation used in Israel today, not that of Halevi and his contemporaries. In transliterating Arabic, I use a modified version of the system employed by the *Encyclopaedia of Islam,* with "q" instead of "ḳ," "j" instead of "dj," and no underlining. Hebrew and Arabic words found in English dictionaries are given their standard English spellings. For Hebrew proper names, I use the common English equivalents, when they exist. I refer to Jewish festivals by their English equivalents except for Sukkot, Hanukkah, and Shavuot.

I have attempted to write a book that could be read by anyone interested in poetry or religion, and therefore, in the text, have stuck strictly to the story, the poems, and the information that a general reader needs in order to understand them. Supporting arguments, commentary, and dialogue with other specialists may be found in the notes, along with bibliographical references.

It is a pleasure to acknowledge the help of friends and institutions that made this book possible. My wife, Janice Meyerson, has helped not only in the large ways—by being my perfect companion and partner in life and letters—but also by so enthusiastically throwing herself, while in the midst of her own career, into the time-consuming and tedious task of preparing a manuscript that would rise to her own supreme level of perfection.

Colleagues who have helped with advice, information, and critical reading are Mark Cohen of Princeton University; Angel Sáenz-Badillos of the Universidad Complutense of Madrid; Yosef Yahalom of the Hebrew University of Jerusalem; Mordechai Friedman of Tel Aviv University; Michael Sells of the University of Chicago; Jonathan Decter of Brandeis University; and Michael Rand of the Academy of the Hebrew Language. Professor Sáenz-Badillos was instrumental in my receiving a research grant from the Universidad Complutense, where I spent a delightful and productive period drafting a significant portion of the book.

The last of the research and the bulk of the writing was done during a sabbatical year when I had the pleasure and honor of holding a fellowship at the Dorothy and Lewis B. Cullman Center for Scholars and Writers at the New York Public Library. The Cullman Center provided a perfect environment in which to finish the research and writing of this book, as well as warm and interesting colleagues in fields remote from my own with whom to discuss it. It is a pleasure to thank the Center itself; Jean Strouse, its director; Pamela Leo, its assistant director; the staff members of the Asian and Middle Eastern Division and of the Dorot Jewish Division, who were so assiduous in locating the materials that I needed; and Paul LeClerc, president of the library.

I would also like to thank my student Danielle Witherspoon Kranjec for her work as my research assistant over several years when this book was in preparation; Leslie Rubin, for preparing the subject index; and Itay Zutra for preparing the Hebrew index. I also wish to take this opportunity to acknowledge my friend and colleague of more than forty-five years standing, Stephen A. Geller, from whom I have learned, in our near-daily telephone conversations, more than from years of reading and note-taking.

The Jewish Theological Seminary of America, on whose faculty I have served for more than three decades, has supported my work both intellectually and materially—intellectually, by providing me with students sufficiently advanced in the study of Hebrew language and Jewish culture that I could try out my interpretations of Halevi's poetry and career on them; and materially, with grants from the Abbell Research Fund and the Shalom Spiegel Institute and with leaves of absence in which to write. My thanks are due also to the Seminary library for providing the scan of the autograph letter by Halevi that serves as the frontispiece of this book and for permission to reproduce it. I wish to thank Jack Wertheimer, former provost of the Seminary, for his help. I will always be indebted to Ismar Schorsch for his friendship and support during his twenty-year tenure as chancellor the Seminary.

Contents

The Song of the Distant Dove

Introduction

Judah Halevi lived most of his life in the country now known as Spain, at the time when it was an Arabic-speaking, predominantly Muslim, territory known as al-Andalus and was linked more tightly to North Africa and the rest of the Islamic world than it was to Europe. A member of the Jewish social and intellectual aristocracy that flourished throughout the Muslim world during the age of Islamic ascendancy (750–1300), Halevi was a physician, theologian, merchant, religious scholar (though not, as far as is known, a rabbi), and a prominent figure in public affairs. He may be regarded as a representative figure of the so-called Golden Age of Hebrew letters.

Halevi's story stands out from among those of the other members of the medieval Judeo-Arabic elite because of his decision, taken in late middle age, to withdraw from his conventionally successful life and end his days in the Land of Israel. After much debate with himself, family, and friends, he sailed from al-Andalus in the summer of 1140, intending to settle in Palestine and die there.

Arriving in Alexandria on September 8 of that year, Halevi was acclaimed as a celebrity by the local Jewish community. Instead of proceeding immediately to his destination, he remained in Alexandria, hosted by friends and admirers, into the winter. He then traveled to Cairo, where he spent several months with a prominent member of the Jewish community of Egypt, Ḥalfon Halevi (not a relative, despite the name), and called on Samuel ben Ḥanania, head of the Jews of Egypt. Halevi may have contemplated continuing his journey across the eastern desert so as to approach Palestine from the same direction as the ancient Israelites, but he returned to Alexandria, and at last boarded a ship that set sail on May 14, 1141.

Did Halevi reach Jerusalem? According to a late tradition, he arrived at the gates of the city and was kneeling there to recite his great Ode to Jerusalem, when an Arab horseman, enraged at this display of Jewish piety, charged and trampled him under the hooves of his steed. This story is probably a legend. All that we know is that Halevi died during the summer of 1141. But the legend of Halevi's violent death embodies a higher sort of truth, for the devotion to the Land of Israel expressed in his poetry emits a whiff of martyrdom. Furthermore, the legend's depiction of Halevi dying in the embrace of the stones and the soil of the Holy Land echoes a particular recurring image in his poetry that expresses his principled quest for concreteness and certainty in religious experience. It was this quest, pervading his poetry and religious thought, that led him to the East.[1]

Halevi's journey was not a typical pilgrimage. To go on pilgrimage normally means to travel to a shrine, to pray there and offer respects to the relics or tomb or sacred object, and to return home feeling religiously uplifted through the encounter with the sacred. In classical Judaism and Islam, pilgrimage is an obligatory mass ritual performed at a particular time of the year at the religions' holy cities. Pilgrimage in this sense was practiced in both religions in the Middle Ages: the Islamic rite has had a continuous history since its origins, and the Jews, too, held a communal annual pilgrimage to the Mount of Olives until the practice was discontinued in the 1070s. In both religions, lesser pilgrimages were made to the tombs of saints, some being communal pilgrimages held at particular times of year, others being of an individual nature, when a person felt the need to obtain the blessing that is conferred by attendance on the saint. All three types of pilgrimage exist in Christianity as well.

Halevi's journey was of a different kind. He did not go to Palestine in order to visit Jerusalem and the other holy sites and return, but rather to die there and mingle his body with the stones and soil of the Land of Israel. His behavior is so different from that of others that the word "pilgrimage" hardly seems like the right word for his journey, and is used here for lack of a more exact term.

Halevi is the first Jew we know of in the Middle Ages who traveled to the Land of Israel not as part of a religious community and not in order to join an existing religious community, but as an act of individual piety, with a view toward ending his days there. There are plenty of references to Jewish pilgrims to the Land of Israel in the Middle Ages, but mostly in the form of groups that intended to establish permanent communities in Palestine, such as the Karaite Mourners of Zion movement in the tenth century and the groups led by Ashkenazic rabbis in the thirteenth century. Such individual pilgrims as we do hear of were already traveling, anyway, and made use of the opportunity to visit a holy site. Halevi is the first known Jew who went to the Land of Israel out of a desire to mend his worldly ways and live out his last days as what Muslims call a *jār allāh*—a neighbor of God. His is a unique case that cries out for an explanation.

Three kinds of sources have come down to us for understanding Halevi's pilgrimage.While still in al-Andalus, Halevi wrote a book explaining his religious thought, commonly known as the Kuzari. It is in the form of a dialogue between a rabbi and a pagan king, embedded in a narrative framework. In the opening episode of the frame, the king, motivated by a dream, asks a philosopher, a Christian, and a Muslim to explain their systems of belief; dissatisfied with their expositions, the king seeks out a rabbinic scholar to explain his beliefs. The conversations between the king and the rabbi—which induce the king to convert to Judaism—occupy the bulk of the book. In the closing episode of the frame, the rabbi announces his decision to leave the land of the Khazars and to settle in the Land of Israel. This conclusion suggests that Halevi's decision to make the pilgrimage emerged from the religious system propounded in the Kuzari, and implies that we can arrive at an understanding of the pilgrimage by studying that work.

The second source is Halevi's poetry. Throughout the age of Islamic ascendancy, especially from the tenth century on, Jewish intellectuals wrote and sponsored the writing of poetry in Hebrew both for liturgical and nonliturgical purposes. They had acquired their taste for nonliturgical poetry from Arabic culture, which in many ways was their own culture, and from Arabic poetry, which they knew and admired. From the time of his youth, Halevi was one of the most fluent and productive of the Hebrew poets, writing great quantities of poetry both for liturgical functions and for entertainment, and exchanging complimentary poetry with some of the most important Jewish leaders of al-Andalus. In later life, he also wrote poetry of a more personal kind, exploring his religious experiences, arguing his principles with imaginary interlocutors, and exposing his doubts and fears in gorgeous Hebrew verse.

Some of Halevi's liturgical poetry found its way into the prayer rites of various Jewish communities. Selections of his poems were assembled as booklets in his lifetime, and soon after his death, an Egyptian scholar assembled his *dīwān,* a large corpus of his Hebrew poetry, both sacred and secular. The *dīwān* also contains several literary epistles, formal letters written in rhetorically styled Hebrew rhymed prose, a customary courtesy among the medieval Jewish literary elite; such epistles are to be distinguished from ordinary letters, which were usually written in Arabic and in a colloquial register of that language. Halevi's *dīwān* is not only a magnificent record of his mind and sensibilities, but one of the greatest Hebrew literary works of premodern times. Many of the poems it comprises refer to Halevi's pilgrimage. Some of the poems in it were addressed to people he encountered in the course of the pilgrimage. And many of the poems in it deal with themes that are related to his decision to make the pilgrimage.

The third source is a group of medieval letters in Arabic, thanks to which we are now able to tell the story of Halevi's pilgrimage in considerable detail. The letters were found in the remains of the Cairo geniza, a cache of manuscripts preserved in a medieval synagogue that still stands in the old city of Cairo. The geniza manuscripts were mostly brought to Europe in the 1890s and were scattered among various libraries, many eventually reaching the United States. The manuscripts had been thrown haphazardly into a storage room in the old synagogue for centuries. Most were discarded because they were no longer needed, but many were discarded because they were damaged; under the conditions of their storage, all have deteriorated further, some to the point of illegibility. Most are fragmentary. Most are in the Arabic language but in the Hebrew script; many, especially those of Andalusi provenance, employ a difficult cursive script. For these reasons and because of the paucity of specialists in geniza studies, the process of sifting through the manuscripts has been slow and disorganized.

About sixty years after the geniza manuscripts were brought out of Egypt, Professor S. D. Goitein discovered among their remains in Cambridge and New York some letters in the handwriting of Judah Halevi and others written to him; he also discovered letters by and to other twelfth-century figures in which Halevi and his activities are mentioned. An additional letter by Halevi has come to light in recent years. These documents provide precious information about Halevi's life in al-Andalus and Castile, and they shed particularly bright light on the eight months that Halevi spent in Egypt on his way to the Land of Israel. The poems and literary epistles that Halevi wrote during this period are also a usable source of biographical information, but, as products of strict conventions of form and genre, they have to be used with caution and should be trusted more for Halevi's personal attitudes than for historical facts. The documents and the poems acquaint us with a whole cast of characters and, through them, with a whole social class: the Jewish business elite of Fatimid Egypt. Like the Jews of al-Andalus, they spoke Arabic as their native language, and their customs and habitual ways of behaving and thinking were virtually the same as those of their Muslim neighbors, except for modifications necessitated by their adherence to the Jewish community and Jewish religious traditions. The letters provide tantalizing glimpses of their manners, customs, and speech.[2]

In telling the story of Halevi's pilgrimage, we will draw mostly on the geniza letters, while in our attempt to understand the religious impulse behind it we will draw mostly on Halevi's poems. The Kuzari will for the most part be kept in the background because it is not a confessional work but a work of theory, while what interests us is not his religious system but his religious sensibility. The Kuzari's theoretical system may have provided Halevi with a solid intellectual foundation for the course he chose, but that course itself—the wrenching decision to overthrow his apparently normal existence—must have had its origins not in an intellectual system but in an inner religious state. This would be especially true of a thinker like Halevi, whose very system gives priority to experience over philosophy. The poetry offers a window on his inner state, not just by what it says—the paraphrasable content that could just as well have been expressed in prose—but by how the poetry employs and manipulates formal structures and literary traditions to express something that cannot be expressed in abstractions. Even when the poetry and the Kuzari echo each other, the poetry is not merely a decorative version of the theory expounded in the Kuzari but has a perspective of its own.

The Kuzari will not be neglected, for to refuse to attend to Halevi's own words would be merely willful. But when the poetry pulls in a different direction from the Kuzari, we will read the Kuzari in the light of the poetry rather than the poetry in the light of the Kuzari. In principle, there is no reason to assume that the Kuzari is Halevi's sober, authoritative word and the poetry merely a decorated formulation of his real thought. We will allow the poetry to lead the discussion and make the Kuzari follow. This ordering of priorities occasionally necessitates a new reading of certain passages of the Kuzari, but it will enable us to see the pilgrimage more clearly.

This procedure has another advantage. The Kuzari expounds Halevi's religious thought as a complete and rounded system (though its compositional strata may betray the stages in the development of Halevi's thought), and its central figure, the rabbi, speaks with certainty and authority from beginning to end. But the poetry shows that Halevi's religion was not a static state of being. It drives toward a religious fulfillment glimpsed from a distance, to a contact with a divine world that is striven toward. In the Kuzari, everything is settled in the rabbi's mind; but in the poetry, everything is in process, the outcome unsure, the devotee trembling. The poetry preserves the religious sensibility of a Halevi who is more human and more vulnerable, perhaps more congenial than the Kuzari's unflappable rabbi.

Remarkably, few of the poems are regularly brought into scholarly discussions of Halevi's pilgrimage, and those that are used are nearly always quoted merely as snappy renditions of ideas stated abstractly in the Kuzari, not as testimonies in their own right. It is past time that the poetry was recognized as an indispensable tool for understanding Halevi's pilgrimage.[3]

By foregrounding the poems and the geniza documents, we gain an additional benefit. The geniza documents are snapshots of everyday life in a great commercial and intellectual society. They speak of ships, cargo, and travel arrangements; of friends and hosts; of business transactions and lawsuits; and of personal satisfactions and complaints. The words that they contain are frozen conversations among people Halevi knew, written down without any thought that they would be of interest in the distant future. They enable us to visualize the lives and manners of real people and, above all, to hear them speaking in their natural voices. Likewise, the Hebrew poetry and formal epistles of the Judeo-Arabic age, though written in accordance with strict literary conventions, represent the voice of a real person, a voice that is especially compelling when it speaks, as do so many of Halevi's poems, in the confessional mode. Letters, poetry, and epistles enable us to hear medieval people speaking—in their vernacular voices in the letters, in their eloquent public voices in the poems and epistles. In the writings that they left behind, these people, now dead nearly a thousand years, continue to murmur to us from the grave.

This book takes every opportunity to preserve and display Halevi's voice and the voices of his contemporaries. Part I sketches Halevi's world, life story, and religious development leading up to the pilgrimage. Each of its chapters includes a mini-anthology of his poems, presented in Hebrew with English verse translations and brief explanatory essays to illustrate this development and to lay the foundation for the study of the pilgrimage by highlighting the religious and literary motifs that are central to it. Part II tells the story of the pilgrimage through selections from the geniza documents and from Halevi's poems and literary epistles written in Egypt; much of this material is appearing in English for the first time. Part III begins with a close look at one of Halevi's epistles written in Egypt in order to clarify his motives in making the pilgrimage, and goes on to present all the extant poems in which Halevi dealt directly with his pilgrimage.

Part I

A Portrait of the Pilgrim

I

Halevi's Religious Development

Halevi's World

In Halevi's time, Islam was still the dominant power in the Mediterranean region, though no longer a single political entity. By the end of the eighth century, the Abbasid Empire, with its capital at Baghdad, ruled in theory over territory that reached from Persia to the Atlantic, but its component regions were already functioning more or less independently. The Iberian Peninsula, known to Arabic speakers as al-Andalus, was conquered for Islam in 711, but was free of Abbasid control after the establishment of the Umayyad dynasty in Cordoba in 756 and constituted an independent caliphate after 929. But unified Muslim rule of al-Andalus broke down, in turn, early in the eleventh century and was replaced by miniature states known as the *taifa* kingdoms. These were continually making war on one another and on the rising Christian kingdoms of the peninsula's north.

By the eleventh century, Christendom was encroaching on Islamic territories throughout the Mediterranean world. In the East, the First Crusade established the Kingdom of Jerusalem in 1099 and imposed Christian control over territory that had been subject to the Egyptian Fatimid Empire and smaller local principalities. This territory was eventually retaken by Islam, but only after two centuries of intermittent warfare. Christian pressure against Islam was successful also in the central Mediterranean, with the Normans putting an end to Arab rule over Sicily and southern Italy in 1071.

The West was the theater of the so-called Reconquista, the gradual conquest of al-Andalus by the Christian kingdoms of the north, beginning the process that would lead to the unification of most of the peninsula as a Christian country called Spain in 1492.

Halevi was probably born around the time of one of the milestone events of the Reconquista, the conquest of Toledo by Alfonso VI of Castile, which occurred in 1085. In the decades following his birth, the *taifa* kingdoms were increasingly threatened by the Christian kingdoms, and eventually the Muslim rulers solicited the help of the Almoravids, a Berber military-religious sect that ruled what is now Morocco. Together, they scored a resounding victory over the Castilians in 1086, but the Almoravids returned in 1090 to swallow up the *taifa* kingdoms and incorporate them into their own empire. The Almoravids would dominate al-Andalus until the 1140s. They would, in turn, be replaced by the Almohads, another Berber military-religious sect that began its takeover of al-Andalus in 1146, a few years after Halevi's departure for Palestine. The arrival of the Almohads was fateful for Jewish culture, since this fanatical group abrogated the tolerance of mainstream Islam toward the monotheistic minorities, forcing Judaism underground and resulting in the flight of the Jewish leadership class to Christian territories, which, in this period, were more hospitable.

Jews had been present in the Iberian Peninsula since Roman times (the oldest known synagogue to be excavated, in Elche, dates from the fourth century). Subject to intense persecution while the peninsula was under Visigothic control, the Jews welcomed the arrival of the Muslim conquerors in 711, especially since Islam guaranteed the security of the minority monotheists, Christians and Jews, and their right to maintain their ancestral ways.

Throughout the territories ruled by Islam, especially in Iraq, Palestine, Egypt, North Africa, and al-Andalus, the Jews thrived along with the Muslim majority. Throughout the Islamic world, Jews enjoyed communal autonomy, prosperity, and freedom from persecution; some were able to acquire real wealth. Jews played prominent roles in Muslim courts, held positions in the Muslim bureaucracy, and engaged in discussion with Muslim intellectuals. A distinctive Judeo-Arabic culture emerged, as Jews behaved like their Muslim neighbors in nearly every way not actually at variance with their religion: they spoke the same language, wore the same clothes, ate the same kinds of foods, lived in the same kinds of houses, and earned their livelihood plying the same trades and crafts.

Judeo-Arabic culture flourished particularly in al-Andalus under the Umayyad caliphate, the *taifa* kingdoms, and even under the Almoravids. During most of this period, members of the Jewish elite engaged in such lucrative businesses as the manufacture of silk and international trade; some obtained positions at court as physicians, tax and duty collectors, and all-purpose courtiers. This elite class produced a cadre of rabbis, philosophers, poets, and men-of-many-parts, who exercised leadership in the autonomous Jewish community while serving in the court, managing their businesses, and, in a few cases, maintaining literary careers.

The intellectual horizons of these men were broad, for many had been educated in both the Jewish and the Arabic curricula. As children, they studied the Jewish religious tradition (the Bible, the Talmud, and the associated works of religious law and lore) and then went on to acquire a formal knowledge of classical Arabic through the study of grammar, poetry, belles-lettres, and sometimes even the Qur'an and other Islamic religious texts. The Arabic language afforded them access not only to Arabic literature and Islamic religious writing but also to the Hellenistic scientific and philosophical tradition. Members of the Jewish elite who held positions in the bureaucracy or at court were thrown together with Muslim courtiers; Jewish businessmen traded and formed partnerships with Muslim businessmen. The style of life, forms of expression, and intellectual interests of the Jewish and Muslim elites largely merged.

In this rarefied society, poetry was an important vehicle of social cohesion as well as a popular form of entertainment. The Jewish elite acquired its taste for poetry from the Muslim courts, in which panegyric, lampooning, and funeral odes were vital political tools, where poetry on love and wine drinking was the most popular form of entertainment, and where the improvisation of poetry was a much relished amusement. At least since the tenth century, Jews in Iraq, Palestine, Egypt, and al-Andalus had adopted the typically Arabic literary institutions of panegyric poetry and rhymed prose epistles, using Hebrew as their linguistic medium. The poets of al-Andalus expanded this range of genres to include many new themes, including love and wine drinking, and developed a new prosody that lent Hebrew verse the rhythms of Arabic. In the work of these tenth-century poets, the rhetorical manners and the thematic repertoire of Hebrew poetry came more and more to resemble that of Arabic. By Halevi's time, the taste for the new Arabized Hebrew poetry had spread to other Jewish communities of the Arabic-speaking world, and several Hebrew poets of genius had emerged.

Coming of age after a century and a half of this new kind of Jewish literary productivity, Halevi contributed prolifically to all the themes and genres that were by now standard, writing panegyric and funeral odes for many leading members of the Jewish community. He excelled in love poetry and expanded the repertoire of this popular genre to include wedding songs, some of which are surprisingly sensuous, considering their quasi-religious function. He also composed literary epistles in elaborate rhymed Hebrew prose, corresponding to the elaborate rhymed-prose epistles in Arabic that were a standard feature of courtly relations among the Muslims.

The Arabization and secularization of Hebrew literature did not meet with universal approval in the Jewish community. In the eleventh century, Samuel the Nagid's son felt it necessary to defend his famous father's love poetry by claiming that it was not meant literally but was only an allegory of the Jewish people's love for God, in the tradition of the biblical Song of Songs. Late in the twelfth century, Maimonides would object vigorously to the singing of Hebrew love songs at wedding feasts, on the grounds that they created an atmosphere of lewdness and degraded the holy language. Halevi himself came to question the propriety of some kinds of Hebrew verse. The Hebrew poetry of the age itself hints, here and there, at a certain degree of discomfort with its own subversiveness. To moralists, secular poetry was a symptom of the decadence of a worldly Jewish aristocracy in thrall to their own love of luxury, power, and prestige, devoted to Arab ways, and forgetful that they were members of an exilic community that by rights should be devoted not to pleasure but to doing penance for the sins that, it was generally assumed, had induced God to exile them in the first place.[1]

Even their intellectual pursuits were suspect, for Greek philosophy in its Arabic garb was seen by many as competing with Jewish religious teachings. The analogous problem had arisen in Islamic society, especially in the twelfth century, when Aristotle's ideas became more widely disseminated, especially in the Islamic West. Greek thinking, based on strict logic applied to universally observable data, tended to reduce the revealed religions' sacred texts to mere metaphors for philosophic truths, and their religious law to the status of mere political systems with no absolute validity. As a pursuit common to intellectuals across the lines of the religious communities, philosophy threatened also to blur communal distinctness. Religious leaders of both communities labored to exploit the methods and materials of philosophical analysis in order to defend their revealed and traditional religious doctrines, thereby creating Islamic and Jewish theology. In the East, the Muslim thinker Abū Ḥāmid al-Ghazzālī (d. 1111) wrote a vehement polemic against philosophy, vindicating absolute claims of Islam, and his work was quickly disseminated throughout the Muslim world. In the West, Halevi took a similar, though not as extreme, position against philosophy in the Kuzari. We shall hear the echoes of this conflict in Halevi's poetry.

But rich and sybaritic or philosophically relativistic, the Jewish aristocrats did not fully deserve the moralists' reproaches. They were, on the whole, generous in their financial support to the community, devoted to their synagogues, faithful in their observance of religious rituals, commands, and prohibitions, and enthusiastic in their intellectual pursuits. And their poetry was not all worldly, for they saw to the continued embellishment of the synagogue service with new liturgical poetry, both by patronizing liturgical poets and by composing liturgical poetry themselves, just as they did for secular poetry. While Andalusi Hebrew poets continued to write synagogue poetry in the old genres and styles inherited from their predecessors in Islamic Iraq, they also developed new kinds of liturgical poetry employing the Arabic-style meters and rhetorical techniques and reflecting the more complex intellectual concerns of a religious elite that was learned in the sciences and steeped in Arabo-Islamic culture.[2]

A Portrait of the Poet

Halevi was born into this Jewish leadership class either in Toledo or Tudela (the evidence is inconclusive), probably about 1085.[3] Even in Christian Toledo, he would have acquired a Judeo-Arabic education, for the city retained its Arabic character for some time after the Christian conquest. As a young man, he went south to Granada, the heartland of Arabized Jewish culture, where he fell in with the circle of intellectuals and communal leaders around Moses Ibn Ezra.

We know next to nothing specific about Halevi's mature life. He was a physician in Toledo for at least part of his career, possibly a court doctor, but he also lived part of his adult life in Cordoba. He may have engaged in business as well; that could have been the reason for his visit to North Africa with Abraham Ibn Ezra.[4] He had some connection with the chief rabbinic leader of al-Andalus, Joseph Ibn Megas; apart from his early panegyric on Ibn Megas's ascension to the headship of the academy of Lucena in 1103, one of his epistles shows him to have Ibn Megas's ear and one was written on Ibn Megas's behalf. But there is no evidence that he studied at Ibn Megas's academy in Lucena or that he had a regular position as his secretary, as has been said, nor does he seem to have been a rabbi. That Halevi was involved in community leadership can be inferred from three extant letters that he wrote as part of a campaign to raise money to redeem a captive woman. His family is mentioned only in his pilgrimage poetry, where he mentions a daughter and a grandson whom he left behind; this implies that there was also a wife, but we do not know whether she died before his voyage or whether she, too, was left behind.[5]

The esteem in which Halevi was held by his contemporaries may be judged by the honorifics that they attached to his name. It is true that the manners of the age dictated the lavish use of titles and praises, but the encomium "the heart and soul of our land" used of him in a letter written in 1130 is unique or, at least, rare. Halevi is often called "the pious man" and "the poet," both specific terms not used of people of conventional piety or occasional versifiers. Particularly extravagant are the praises of a writer from Burgos who, besides stressing Halevi's piety and poetry, parades his own knowledge of philosophy in hopes of getting an audience with the great man.[6]

Halevi wrote poetry from his youth onward—panegyrics, eulogies on the dead, liturgical poetry, wedding poems, riddles, and epigrams. It is not known whether he ever wrote poetry to earn his livelihood, but his enormous productivity as a liturgical poet and author of laments for the dead in verse suggests that he wrote it in some official capacity. (A few of his liturgical poems have found their way into traditional Jewish prayer books; one is sung at the dinner table on the Sabbath by traditional Jews to this very day.) He wrote many poems of courtesy to friends and associates, including some of the most prominent men of al-Andalus in his time. The *dīwān* also shows Halevi's lighter side in its numerous love poems to or about young beauties, both female and male; wine-drinking poems; poems describing nature; and wedding songs, epigrams, and riddles in verse. Bursting with quantity and variety, his *dīwān*, the largest of any of the great Hebrew poets of the Golden Age of Hebrew literature, affords a picture of a well-rounded, balanced, personable, and successful man.[7]

Yet Halevi's *dīwān* also affords glimpses of dissatisfaction. In an epistle that Halevi addressed to Rabbi Ḥabīb of al-Mahdiyya we hear the voice of a middle-aged man complaining about being past his prime and too engrossed in his responsibilities as a doctor to engage much in literary activity:

> *I call this place "Busy," for it keeps me on the run. It makes me the watchman of others' vineyards while I neglect my own, makes me have dealings with healing, diverts me from the prophets' words. . . .*
>
> *I wish, I wish, I wish the Merciful One would restore me to what I was before and bring back my youth! I would go back to studying [what I failed to study] and achieve a wisdom I failed to achieve before. I would stay among the columns and listen like the students. . . . But what can I do, now that the white hairs have overwhelmed the black, tender youth has turned to tinder, and dawn has turned to sunset? Now that the turn of years has altered me and the seasons made me falter and set me on coals? I have aroused myself and shaken out my clothing and rowed hard to get back to the dry land, yet I have failed. I have searched out my conscience and laid bare my hidden self; but no vision came, and my meditations brought no revelation from God.*[8]

Halevi takes up these themes again in his epistle to a certain Rabbi David of Narbonne, citing the burdens of his work as a doctor as his excuse for not answering a letter from a third party, and complaining of those unwanted honors that he would later abjure:

> *I have not even had time to respond to his letter, much less to do what he asked. Great deeds are ascribed to me. People exaggerate about me and make great claims about me, and many falsely sing my praises, while the multitude, who will believe anything, look to me for the wisdom of Kalkol and Darda, though I have neither culture nor learning. The result is that I am caught up day and night and in between with the foolishness of medicine, though it can never heal them. This is a great city inhabited by powerful men, hard masters whom I can only satisfy by wasting my days on their whims and using up my years healing their ills. "We have tried to cure Babylon, but she has not been cured."*
>
> *All I ask of God, my only petition to Him, is that He bring about some favorable turn of events of the kind He has in infinite number; that He save me speedily, proclaim my freedom from slavery, find me a place of rest, and exile me to the place of the living waters that surge from your spring, to the fountains of your age's sages whose waters emerge from a sacred source.*[9]

He again complains about being too busy in an epistle to his friend Solomon Ibn Ghiyath.[10] It was a common complaint, then as now. Like others of his successful contemporaries and like many of us moderns, Halevi was feeling that his worldly and religious pursuits, in themselves good and beneficial, made life too hectic to permit a man to devote sufficient attention to matters of ultimate importance.

At the stage of his religious development represented by the two epistles quoted above, Halevi is most troubled by his neglect of religious scholarship; he imagines fleeing to a place where he can devote himself to the words of the sages—presumably, meaning study of traditional rabbinic texts. Later, the contents of his religious aspirations would change, and this fantasy of flight would be concretized in his famous pilgrimage.

When Halevi prayed, in the epistle to Rabbi David of Narbonne, that God proclaim his freedom from that slavery, he may have been expressing exasperation with the pressures of his career and public role, but the conflict between servitude to God and servitude to man came to be one of the central themes of his poetry and of his religious thought. Celebrated is his epigram:

> *The slaves of Time are slaves of slaves;*
> *the slave of God alone is free.*

And so when others seek their lot,
I say, "No lot but God for me."[11]

"Time," as often in Arabic and Hebrew poetry, represents all things that are subject to time, all mutable things, hence, the things of this world—possessions, honors, position, and even family. "Slave of slaves" is a superlative (like "Song of Songs"), but it also implies a hierarchy, saying very concisely that Time and Time's things are in God's hands, so that to be their slave is to be twice removed from God. Paradoxically, freedom from Time through servitude to God is the only true freedom.[12]

The theme of servitude to God has a long history in Jewish literature. The Bible describes the people of Israel being rescued from bondage to the Egyptians in order to enter the service of God; it refers to the offering of sacrifices as *ʿavoda,* literally meaning "service"; and it uses the expression "slave of God" to express the worshiper's dependence on God. Rabbinic tradition spoke with contempt of an individual who would voluntarily accept servitude to another man, since the people of Israel are supposed to be servants to God alone, and it considers the institution of public prayer to be just as valid a "service" as the sacrificial system itself. But Halevi's epigram about servitude is not about Israel's covenant with God, about ritual, or about the specific needs and desires of the worshiper; it is about the individual who is caught between the demands of the temporal world and the demands of the eternal. It says that the man who submits to God, the master of Time, frees himself from the temporal and thereby achieves the only true freedom available to man.[13]

Halevi's use of images of slavery to denote piety has less to do with the Bible than it does with the Islamic usage according to which man is seen as completely subject to God's will, religion is described as submission to God, and the pious man is defined as one who recognizes and gladly accepts his servitude. Halevi uses the unqualified Hebrew substantives *ʿeved* and *ʿoved,* which traditionally meant only "slave," and "worker," respectively, like their Arabic cognates *ʿabd* and *ʿābid,* meaning a person who is devoted to the service of God—a pious man, and especially an ascetic.[14]

Yearning for servitude to God, as a purely personal religious theme, is pervasive in Halevi's poetry. It is explicit at the beginning and end of a strophic meditative poem:

If only I could be a slave
to my God, Who made me!
Then my friends might shun me,
but He would bring me near.
O Maker and provider—

You own my soul and body.
You penetrate my mind,
You see into my thoughts,
and You encompass me,
when I lie down, when I walk out,
whatever path I take.

....

Incline my heart to do
the service of Your kingdom;
purify my thoughts to know You
in Your true divinity;
and when I ache, do not delay
to heal me in Your mercy.
Answer me, O God! Do not
punish me with silence.
Acquire me a second time,
and to Your slave say, "Here am I!"[15]

The delight of this poem is the reversal of the image of the slave in the closing word, *hineini,* which means "here I am," the Hebrew equivalent of "at your service." The speaker begs to be made God's slave, confident that God's slave is in a reciprocal relationship with God, each knowing and doing the other's will, a paradox similar to the statement that only God's slave is truly free. This daring placement of the language of an inferior into the mouth of God shows that the image of servitude is to be taken seriously in interpreting the poem.[16]

We find the theme of servitude also in a poem dealing with the national problem, the challenge faced by the Jewish people living as a tolerated minority in the domains of Islam and Christianity. Here, the "I" is the Jewish people. The language of slave and king relates only to Israel's condition—slave to the nations when she would be slave to God.

Benighted people, slaves to idols
torment me on Your account.
I say to them, "I'd rather serve
the God that your gods stand in need of.
When He is angry with me, I'm a slave to slaves;
when He is pleased, He makes me king to kings."[17]

But Israel speaks here in the first-person singular, so that, as so often in the religious poetry of this period, the voice of the individual and the voice of the community merge. The poet could be making use of a public genre for the expression of individual piety, speaking of the challenge of Christianity and Islam to Judaism when he is really thinking of the challenge of the worldly to the pious. Something analogous often happens when Israel's exile and redemption are used in poetry as an allegory for the fate of the human soul. Perhaps, then, this poem is not too different in meaning from the epigram on the slaves of Time, which was quoted above.[18]

In another poem, written in the voice of a synagogue precentor introducing the morning prayer, synagogue attendance prefigures attendance at the Temple in Jerusalem, thus anticipating the ultimate direction of Halevi's personal religious thought:

Lord, I yearn to visit Your abode,
and ache to throw myself down before You.
Accept me as Your slave forevermore,
for none but You do I desire to serve.
All souls belong to You, their form and matter:
I cannot even speak but by Your leave.[19]

Halevi often uses this theme of his desire to be a slave of God in order to express his frustration with what we call the world of getting and spending, with being out of tune with eternity. Where the Romantic poet regrets being too caught up in commerce to feel at one with nature, where the moralist regrets being too caught up in pleasure to attend to the welfare of his soul, Halevi complains of being too caught up in the service of men, especially through medicine—a religiously suspect activity from which he derives guilty accolades—to devote himself to the service of God. In the two epistles with which we began, his fantasy of resolution is shaped in the mold of rabbinic Judaism, which identifies the service of God with the study of religious texts. But in its mature form, Halevi's conception of service to God ceased to be purely rabbinic.

Reading Halevi's religious poetry, we often feel that he is trying to convert the religious cliché "servant of God" into a serious ideal of religious life, that he is trying to go beyond the mere conscientious observance of religious duties and to subordinate worldly concerns to divine ones. In this ascetic tendency, much of Halevi's poetry apparently contradicts his assertions in the Kuzari that asceticism is not a preferred form of piety. Yet the ascetic aspect of his religious poetry is too persistent not to be taken seriously. The rejection of asceticism in the Kuzari (2:45–50 and 3:1–7) is part of a specific argument that is important to Halevi's system. He characterizes asceticism merely as a kind of service to God that men have arrived at through the application of their reasoning and personal opinions, but Jewish ritual, being based on the revelation of God's specific demands, is a higher system that cannot be arrived at by mere reason.

Yet even the rabbi is forced to admit that the prophets sometimes spoke in the same terms as ascetics (2:48), and he speaks with admiration of the rare individuals for whom unworldliness is natural and appropriate: mystics; philosophers, such as Socrates; and the prophets of ancient Israel. The servant of God may love life and length of days, as the rabbi says; but what he really wants is to be like Enoch and Elijah—to be free of worldly necessities so as to be alone with God (3:1). Such a way of life is appropriate for those who have devoted themselves to spiritual perfection and thereby transcended material concerns. Thus, while Halevi does not think asceticism is in itself the ultimate form of the service to God, even in the Kuzari he sees it as a natural outcome of an intense religious life.

Halevi's poetry sometimes even seems to toy with a vision of a Jewish monasticism. He describes the pious ideal in lines that would have been congenial to any Sufi:

Go out at midnight, follow the paths
of the pious men of olden times.
Their mouths were filled with praise of God;
their souls were empty of deceit.
Their days were for prayer,
their nights for fasting.
In their hearts were paths to God,
and on His throne, places for them.[20]

In his desire to overcome worldliness, Halevi must have come to be disgusted by the materialism and worldliness of the wealthy, cultured, and learned leadership class to which he himself belonged. He was undoubtedly familiar with a moralizing work of the late twelfth century, the *Guide to the Commandments of the Hearts,* by Baḥya Ibn Paquda. (Like most Jewish books of the time, it was written in Arabic; it is often known as *The Duties of the Hearts,* after the title of the medieval Hebrew translation.) Baḥya wrote in acute consciousness of the hypocrisy that threatens to undermine a religious system that is as concerned with outward behavior as is Judaism; among his aims was to encourage readers to clarify and refine their inner lives so as to achieve consistency and becoming modesty in their behavior. Critical of the obsession of the Jewish leadership with worldly concerns, he preached moderate asceticism for ordinary people, which he describes as a normal life of work, family, and social intercourse, but with worldly desires under tight control and the thought of God constantly in mind. Baḥya also envisioned a more severe degree of asceticism for individuals especially endowed with the religious spirit, as would Halevi in the Kuzari.[21]

Baḥya was no extremist in his ascetic preaching, and he certainly wrote within a Jewish framework. But the religious attitudes that he stressed in his writing, while present in the Jewish tradition—indeed, in all Western monotheism—are considerably more prominent in Islam than they were in standard rabbinic Judaism. It is now well established that the overall framework, the technical vocabulary, and the long passages in Baḥya's book were adapted from Islamic works on pietism and mysticism. Halevi, too, was familiar with Islamic pietistic writing. The abrupt prominence of the theme of submission to God and of the motifs of slavery in his poetry reflects a religious environment in which these themes were far more prominent than they had been in traditional Jewish preaching.[22]

Among Baḥya's contributions to the repertoire of Jewish piety was a chapter that he devoted to trust in God, a concept that, while present in rabbinic teaching, was never strongly stressed until Judaism came into contact with Islam. The weakness of this concept in rabbinic Judaism is evidenced by the fact that it did not even have a name until Baḥya introduced the Arabic term *tawakkul* into Jewish religious writing. The term comes from the Qur'an's teaching, "Let those who put their trust put it in God." Its root conveys the element of trust found in the secular word *wakīl*, meaning "trustee" or "agent." A person who confidently puts his trust in God is called a *mutawakkil*. The slogan "I place my trust in God" is uttered routinely by Muslims when beginning any undertaking.[23]

As developed in Islamic preaching, *tawakkul* came to imply far more than a vague sense of being in God's hands; it was understood to mean that a person should accept whatever befalls as being God's will and that one should be satisfied with whatever God decrees for him. This notion was particularly applied to sustenance, which was regarded as predetermined, as the Qur'an says:

> He feeds them from a source of which they have no expectation.
> He who places his trust [*yatawakkalu*] in God,
> God will suffice him.
> God makes His command take effect.
> God has fixed a measure for everything.[24]

It was held that one can no more change his sustenance by his own industry than add a limb to his body, and that striving to increase one's livelihood evinces weakness of faith. Some doubted the religious propriety, or even the efficacy, of medicine; there is an echo of this attitude in Halevi's epistle to Rabbi David of Narbonne quoted above. The attitude is that one ought to give his fate up to God.

For the larger public, the principle of *tawakkul* was balanced by traditions encouraging engagement in useful and lawful business when conducted in a moral manner, so that Islam did not turn into a people of wandering mendicants. But the ascetic, mystical, and hagiographical literature of Islam lauds individuals who made *tawakkul* the basis of their lives, and while some sources try to impose limits on its practice, others celebrate its more extreme manifestations. Within the realm of religious normalcy, the principle was evoked to encourage the believer to achieve a tranquil state of mind, equanimity in the face of reverses, and a mild indifference to material things.[25]

Baḥya's chapter on the subject led to the concept acquiring a name in Hebrew, *biṭaḥon*, which is first used in Jewish literature to denote a religious value in Judah Ibn Tibbon's Hebrew translation of Baḥya's classic (after 1161). Jews acquired this religious theme from their environment. Even the Arabic letters of Jews, like those of Muslims, frequently include among their closing formulas the Islamic maxim "God is sufficient for me, and He is the best to be trusted" deriving from two passages in the Qur'an and constantly in the mouths of ordinary Muslims (we shall see examples in the documents quoted in part II). This practice shows that the concept had seeped into popular piety. We occasionally encounter a Jew with the Arabic name al-Mutawakkil, "He who puts his trust in God."[26]

Halevi occasionally uses the equivalent Hebrew verb *bataḥ*, "to trust," in this particular religious sense, but the religious posture of the *mutawakkil*, the person who puts his whole trust in God, is the inspiration behind many passages in which Halevi does not actually use the term. The theme is expressed not so much by means of terminology as by the stance of passivity in God's presence characteristic of his religious verse, an attitude of pious quietism that, among the poets of al-Andalus, he made his own.[27] Here is an example, a poem designed to be recited publicly to introduce the morning prayers in the synagogue:

Before I came to be, You did select me,
and while Your breath is in me You protect me.
Where can I stand steady if You shake me?
How can I find my way if You deflect me?
What can I say?—My very thoughts are Yours.
Whatever can I do if You neglect me?
I come to You in time of favor—hear me!
Shield me with Your grace, do not reject me.
Rouse me at dawn to come into Your temple
to bless Your great and holy name direct me.[28]

The poet says that his course was chosen for him before his birth and that his very breath depends upon God's constant providence; he can neither stand nor move without God's care, cannot even think a thought that was not put into his head by God. What can prayer mean when man can take no initiative, can conceive no words of thanksgiving, praise, or petition, that are not already known to God? He can only approach God at the time pleasing to Him and at God's instigation, and pray the words that God has put into his mouth.[29] Completely Jewish in its language, this poem reflects the trend in Islamic piety that tends to reduce the pious man to a completely passive object in God's hands. A person who has achieved true *tawakkul* is said by the Muslim pietists to be "like a corpse in the hands of the washer."[30]

If the poem just quoted directs the thoughts of pious passivity inward to the poet's self, other poems convey the same message outward to an implied congregation. In the medieval manuscript of the following poem by Halevi, the Arabic heading reads: "About trust in God [*tawakkul*], he said":

God's hands will provide you shelter,
if in truth you huddle there.
He will steady your step to walk,
give your hand the strength to act.
So seek peace, and peace pursue;
the Lord of peace, He will make peace.[31]

But even in poems couched in a preaching voice, Halevi's treatment of *tawakkul* can take a decidedly inward-directed tone. The following poem is in the second person, so that in English it might seem to be a public harangue. But the Hebrew original takes advantage of the distinction, not available in English, between masculine and feminine pronouns of the second person. These pronouns signal that the poem speaks to a female addressee, which the reader can easily identify as the poet's own soul. (Many Arabic poems use the same procedure.)[32]

If you will put your hope in God alone,
why worry at the troubles Time can bring?
If you would truly trust in God's own name,
the things that Time can do
would make you neither glad nor sorry.
You've made your home among the graves of lust,
and turned your back on right behavior,
lived in mindlessness,
pent in such darkness that you cannot
even see the place of light. How then can you tell
the good from bad?

Soon you must travel on. Choose the right path—
why wander to the right or to the left?

Time will betray you; better if you
betray her first!—Then you'll do well.
Go for a treasure you
can keep forever; spurn the one
you must bequeath to those who follow.

The rabbinic tradition says that one should bless God for the good and the bad, and the semi-mythical rabbi Nahum of Gamzu is said to have found comfort for his sufferings in the belief that God does everything for the best. But the source of Halevi's language in this poem is not the rabbinic tradition but Arabic poetry on asceticism and the preaching of *tawakkul*. We have already encountered Time as a manifestation of the worldly and the mutable. The Stoics preached indifference to life's constant shift of good and bad fortune, pleasure and pain, because they thought that one should keep one's gaze fixed on eternal, indifferent reason; the Islamic and Jewish preachers taught contempt for the things of this world because one should trust the will of God, a will that derives from His perfect knowledge. How can man, who lives in darkness, know what is good or bad for him? The course of wisdom is trust.

The epistles discussed above show Halevi in a state of restlessness that we moderns naturally identify with our own theme of midlife crisis. In the modern version of this pattern, observed in real life, analyzed by psychologists, and canonized in journalism, one comes to regret having spent half one's years in bondage to career and family, and erupts into a new vision of self-discovery and freedom. The Middle Ages had an analogous, but converse, standard life pattern, a common subject of preaching, poetry, biography, and, occasionally, of real life. The change occurred in old age and was occasioned by contemplation of death. The signs of old age—gray hair, failing strength—were viewed as a summons to reevaluate a life that had been lived in godless materialism and libertinism. What medieval men now sought was not more freedom, as do we moderns, but a return to God's control. This religious return is called *tawba* in Arabic.[33]

Arabic has a genre of poems on repentance called *zuhd* poetry. Pioneered by the Abbasid court poet Abū l-ʿAtāhiya in the early ninth century, it is not limited to themes of asceticism, as the Arabic word would suggest. Rather, it consists of versified sermons, in which the speaker admonishes a listener or himself to reflect that life is short, and death is certain; the world is a whore, seducing us with destructive pleasures, so beware! Our mundane concerns are trivial in light of what Islamic tradition calls "the promise and the threat"—the thought of paradise and hell. One should take charge of his soul (called *nafs* in Arabic, cognate with the Hebrew word *nefesh*) before it is too late. The soul, in this tradition, is understood not as the divine spark trapped in the temporal body (as in the Neoplatonic tradition, so influential in other aspects of the Islamic and Jewish literary traditions) but as a force for sin, the equivalent of what is called in Hebrew the *yetser hara*ʿ; in this context, perhaps the word is better understood to mean "appetite." *Zuhd* poetry preaches that one should strive to suppress this "soul" and crush it into submission. The poet or the listener has reached an age when he can expect death at any moment:

> How long, O soul, will you deceive yourself with lying hopes?
> O soul, repent before you are unable to repent!
> Seek forgiveness for your sins from the Merciful One, who forgives sins.[34]

Of course, this convention also has roots in the Jewish tradition, such as in the famous admonition: "Repent one day before your death." The Arabic genre influenced the *tokhaḥa,* poems of rebuke written to supplement the liturgy of fast days, and inspired the creation of nonliturgical poems of the same type.[35]

Zuhd poems are sometimes directed inward to the poet's own self, as embodied in the personified soul. In this case, the preaching voice is softer and addresses the soul in sympathetic tones, as a father might admonish a daughter. Occasionally, the poet speaks of his own age:

> At the age of sixty, should I be sleeping in my comfortable spot,
> when the urgers-on-to-death are calling to break up camp,
> when Time has unfurled the banner of my white hair?[36]

You are fifty, haven't you learned to be serious? You are sixty, won't you repent? You are seventy! You are eighty! Such poems reinforce the idea that there is a right age for repentance, that a young person can be indulged in a certain amount of freedom but that it behooves an older person to behave more prudently and to get himself right with God.

Islamic religious literature is replete with characters who took this advice seriously, not by merely doing penance for particular sins, nor by merely repenting inwardly, but by changing their lives—in our terms, undergoing conversion—often accompanying the change by a dramatic gesture: becoming a wandering mendicant, retreating to a Sufi community, going on jihad, or settling in Mecca to become a "neighbor of God." Whole treatises were devoted to anecdotes about people in high positions who abandoned their wealth and embraced asceticism.[37] The motif is especially marked in the case of poets and literary figures, because poetry, for all its popularity and ubiquity in Arabic, was always considered religiously somewhat suspect by Islam. We shall see the reflection of this attitude in Halevi's story as well.

The pattern of late-life repentance and piety is not strongly marked among the Jews of Judeo-Arabic society (or, for that matter, in rabbinic Judaism), but there are hints of it. Hebrew moralizing poetry is full of Islamic-sounding admonitions to abandon worldly concerns and return to God.[38] Moses Ibn Ezra, an older contemporary of Halevi's, captured the motif very well in an impressive and moving poem that employs many of the standard motifs of Arabic preaching poetry and ends by declaring his intention to turn away from the seductions of this world and devote his old age to scholarship and poetry. He sounds this note also in his Arabic treatise on poetry. But Moses Ibn Ezra's turn to wisdom was not expressed in the language of religious conversion and did not take the form of dramatic action. Baḥya's chapter on *tawba* speaks mainly of repentance for particular sins; it does not seem to contemplate an extreme life change.[39]

A sensational act of *tawba* occurred in the Muslim world in Halevi's youth: the case of Abū Ḥāmid al-Ghazzālī, whom we have already met. Al-Ghazzālī, a Persian, was a distinguished scholar of Islamic religious law holding a government-sponsored professorship in the great academy in Baghdad, the Nizamiyya. He was an academic celebrity who lectured regularly to three hundred students until, at age thirty-seven (in 1095), a religious crisis induced him to resign his professorship and abandon Baghdad. Traveling first to Damascus, he went to Jerusalem and spent some time there. At last, he made the pilgrimage to Mecca and Medina by way of Hebron and returned to his hometown of Tus. There he lived in ascetic seclusion until, under government pressure, he resumed his post in Baghdad and taught there until his final retirement.

In his spiritual autobiography, *The Deliverer from Error*, al-Ghazzālī describes his lifelong yearning to know and understand the competing religious systems of his time. Years of study showed him the flaws in the systems of the theologians, of the Ismailis, and of the philosophers, and he came to realize that religious law, his life's work, was no adequate guide in man's pilgrimage to the hereafter. Only Sufism, with its stress on religious experience, its demand for religious sincerity, and its cultivation of a simple life stripped of show and hypocrisy offered the certainty that he was aiming for. The call of these demands on his spirit was exigent, but his way of life held him back—his fame, his government position, and those three hundred disciples—so he vacillated until an attack of aphasia took the choice out of his hands. Suddenly unable to teach, he went into a decline that we might call a breakdown. In this extremity, he experienced what we would call a religious conversion, and it was this that led to his turn to asceticism and his departure from Baghdad.[40]

Al-Ghazzālī's *Deliverer from Error* was read throughout the Muslim world; his works were brought to Spain in his own and Halevi's lifetime, and fragments of them, transcribed in Hebrew letters, are found in the geniza, proving that they were studied by Jews.[41] Just as Baḥya was inspired by the writings of Muslim pietists, so other religiously sensitive Jews must have been impressed by al-Ghazzālī's story. Perhaps we can detect a hint of that influence in the structure of Halevi's Kuzari, which resembles al-Ghazzālī's *Deliverer from Error* in that the protagonist examines and rejects three religious systems before reaching the final solution: in the case of al-Ghazzālī, Sufism; in the case of Halevi's fictional king, Judaism. And indeed, al-Ghazzālī's own story—a man reaches the pinnacle of success in the religious and intellectual spheres, comes to realize that even his religious practices and teachings are tainted, and consequently abandons everything, going on an extended pilgrimage in order to devote himself to God—is structurally similar to that of Halevi. Despite important differences between Halevi's life and that of al-Ghazzālī, there are so many points of similarity that it is hard to believe that Halevi had not contemplated al-Ghazzālī's life with admiration.[42]

Halevi's embarrassment at his own reputation and at being engaged in the service of mortals is similar in spirit to al-Ghazzālī's self-accusation of hypocrisy in professing religious law for the sake of worldly fame and prestige. Halevi does not say what it was that impelled him to begin thinking this way; the two epistles do not dwell on the theme of aging or personal guilt, though these themes do come up in some of his penitential writing and in his pilgrimage poetry. Al-Ghazzālī's spiritual autobiography suggests that the Muslim scholar was impelled to his act of *tawba* as an outcome of his intellectual engagement in the study of religious systems: the intellectual crisis occasioned by his rejection of the three dominant systems led him to embrace Sufism, which in turn occasioned a religious crisis, forcing him to choose between a "normal" life and a life of ascetic seclusion.[43] Halevi's conversion could have been related to his meditations on aging, in accordance with the common topos, for themes of aging are prominent in his poems. His conversion could also, like that of al-Ghazzālī, have been in part the product of his intellectual development.

The Development of Halevi's Religious Thought

Although the great majority of Judah Halevi's poems cannot be dated, the differing patterns of religious thought found in them suggest that his outlook developed over time. The proposed reconstruction that follows is based on the assumption that Halevi started out with the attitudes and assumptions typical of his class as we know them from the works of his predecessors, especially the poets. There is much evidence that his most important model was Solomon Ibn Gabirol, who was both a philosopher and poet of first rank. The kind of religious thought expressed in Ibn Gabirol's poetry was common to poets of Halevi's circle, especially his mentor, Moses Ibn Ezra, and his contemporaries Joseph Ibn Tsadiq and Levi Ibn al-Tabban.[44] We may assume that poems of Halevi's that deviate from the common assumptions of his age came later in his career, and that poems dealing specifically with his own pilgrimage came latest. Of course, other reconstructions are possible and should be considered.

Such philosophically minded Jews were not simple believers, as were the Jewish masses and average rabbis. Educated not only in classical Jewish texts, but also in Arabic literature and in what were called the "Greek sciences" (especially medicine, logic, astronomy, and metaphysics), they had sufficient mental agility to have assimilated their Jewish learning to their humanistic learning. Their outlook was dominated by views on life, the cosmos, and God that derived from Jewish sources and from a complex of philosophical ideas, widely current among the intellectual elite of the Muslim world, which today is called Neoplatonism. Al-Andalus even produced a major Jewish Neoplatonic metaphysician, Solomon Ibn Gabirol (d. ca. 1058), the author of *The Fountain of Life*. Ibn Gabirol was also a poet of force, originality, and great influence on Halevi. In his synagogue poetry, Ibn Gabirol pioneered the incorporation of Neoplatonic religious ideas in the liturgy; in this respect, Halevi began his career as Ibn Gabirol's disciple.

Neoplatonism developed in late antiquity among the successors of Plato and Aristotle.[45] By Halevi's time, it was actually a religious system parallel to and deeply embedded in the religious thought of sophisticated Muslims and Jews. Two closely related aspects of this system, its theories of Creation and of the human soul, were particularly influential on sophisticated Muslims and Jews.

Contrary to what has come to be accepted as orthodox Islamic and Jewish doctrine, Neoplatonism holds that the world was not created after having been nonexistent but is the product of the overflow of divine potency from a perfect being known as the All or the One. The One is imagined as a high, perfect, eternal source, but the emanations from it become ever more contaminated with matter as they descend, until, at their lowest reaches, they form the four elements of the material world, including our bodies and the earth that our bodies inhabit. The products of emanation at the higher reaches of this eternal process, such as the spheres that constitute the heavens, are pure and eternal, but the world and our bodies, inferior by-products of emanation, are inherently corrupt and perishable.

As heretical as this theory of Creation sounds in light of settled orthodox Islamic and Jewish doctrine, in Halevi's time it was maintained by many mainstream religious thinkers in both religions. In classical Judaism, the best-known adherent of this theory was Abraham Ibn Ezra (d. 1164), who incorporated it into the interpretation of the Creation in his famous and much-studied Bible commentary. The theory of the eternity of the universe was rejected by such a foundational figure as Saadia Gaon (d. 942); but though both Judah Halevi and Maimonides argued against it, both admitted that they could not absolutely refute it.

In Neoplatonic theory, body and soul, like everything else, are products of the series of emanations. The body, as a product of the combination of the four elements, is low on the scale of emanated things. However, the soul of a person, deriving directly from the world-soul, is eternal, an individual manifestation of the Universal Soul that has become separated from its source, and a link between the superior and inferior realms. Imprisoned in the body against its will, it yearns to break free and return to its source, there to lose its individuality and blend back into the Universal Soul. This return is only possible when the body has died, and then only if the soul has kept itself uncontaminated by worldly things. But the rare soul that has kept itself aloof from the mundane world and has refined itself by cultivating its intellectual powers sufficiently can achieve moments of such union, ecstatic moments when it is briefly out of the body (from Greek *ek-stasis,* "standing outside"). Those souls that have not kept themselves pure will not achieve this union even after death; thinkers differed on what their fate would be, but all agreed that it was an unhappy one.

Neoplatonism is not just a philosophy but, like a religion, offers a spiritual goal and a way of life. The goal is eternal bliss through the return of the soul to its source; the way of life consists of moral purity and philosophical contemplation. For intellectuals, both were easily merged into Islam and Judaism. Neoplatonism's notion of the One was identified with the God of scripture. The essential difference between God and the One—God is an anthropomorphic figure who acts, like men, in time and in accordance with His will, while the One is featureless and does not act at all but merely overflows automatically and eternally—was resolved by skillful exegesis; the Bible and the Qur'an were reinterpreted and understood as figurative expressions of Neoplatonic ideas, a way of bringing complex truths home to ordinary people who are in need of images and concrete expressions. (A modern analogy is the way in which liberal Christians and Jews have assimilated the theory of evolution into the biblical account of Creation.)

The monotheistic religions also easily assimilated the Neoplatonic view that the soul is the divine core in man that one must cultivate and perfect; this doctrine provided a philosophical foundation for ethics in general and especially for the principle of repentance. It also provided a rationale for the observance of religious law and rituals. For the Muslim and Jewish masses and average religious teachers, religion meant mostly obedient assent to traditional doctrines and practices, including ritual as well as ethical precepts, the purpose being to avoid divine punishment and to achieve divine rewards. But for the philosophically minded, religious law was a tool for moral and intellectual perfection, leading to salvation in the form of eternal spiritual life. Thus, when Ibn Gabirol, in his confessional poems, laments the difficulty of realizing his spiritual ambitions, his goal is not the perfect observance of the commandments or knowledge of the Torah but the flash of enlightenment, the moment of ecstasy, believed to come to those who have achieved intellectual perfection.

The theme of the soul's return to its source has a commanding presence in the Hebrew liturgical poetry of the eleventh and twelfth centuries, especially in the *tokhaḥa*. As mentioned above, in Halevi's time, this was a kind of sermon of repentance in verse, reinforced with motifs deriving from Arabic *zuhd* poetry; it was also enriched by the Neoplatonic literary tradition. Halevi inherited this way of writing from Ibn Gabirol, his greatest predecessor, but he shared it with all the great synagogue poets of the age.[46]

The theme of the soul's return to its source appealed to Jews not only because it provided the religious theme of repentance with a philosophical rationale but because it happened to coincide with another theme of return that was already present and deeply embedded in the Jewish tradition. Medieval Jews were conscious of their status as an exilic community in a way that is unimaginable to Western Jews today. This consciousness was not merely an aspect of historical memory but an aspect of their daily life. While Islamic rule during the great age of Islamic ascendancy (eighth to thirteenth century) was mostly benign, Jews in the Islamic domains, like Christians, were regarded and regarded themselves as a separate self-governing community. These autonomous communities were protected by the Muslim state in exchange for payment of a special tax and for abiding by certain restrictions that, if completely enforced, could make their lives quite uncomfortable. (A person enjoying this protected status is called a *dhimmī*.) That the restrictions were, on the whole, but laxly enforced during the age of Islamic ascendancy was some comfort, and there is much evidence that the protection of the Jews actually was enforced. But against this must be weighed the difference between the attitude of the authorities, who usually acted to uphold the law protecting minority communities and who had a strong interest in maintaining order, and the attitude of the masses of ordinary Muslims, who far outnumbered the Jews and the Christians and who could easily be whipped up by any small incident or by demagogic preaching to violence against the minorities.[47]

As *dhimmīs*, Jews lived very much as did their Muslim neighbors at every level of society, yet they prayed constantly for rescue from their second-class status and for the restoration of their identity as a nation among nations. The theme of national redemption and the many motifs associated with it—the coming of a messiah, the rebuilding of the Temple, the restoration of the Davidic monarchy, the judgment of the wicked nations—were a constant in preaching and liturgical poetry until modern times, when the extension of full citizenship to Jews in the Western countries reduced their importance in Jewish life.

On the level of history, sophisticated and simple Jews alike prayed for redemption from exile. But for the former, the exile that mattered was the exile of the soul, and for this theme, the core of their religious outlook, they turned the exile of the nation into a mere worldly symbol. As Jews, they shared the national dream of redemption; but as individuals of philosophical-religious sensibility, they dreamed of their own souls' redemption from the transience of flesh to eternal, disembodied bliss. In their liturgical poetry, the themes are thoroughly intertwined, so that it is sometimes impossible to say for sure which theme is the one that the poet intended. Ibn Gabirol pioneered the technique of writing synagogue poems that lament the national exile and pray for national restoration but that the philosophically trained congregant could understand to be speaking about individual salvation through the ascent of the soul to its source.[48]

The trajectory of Halevi's religious poetry is, in part, a motion away from this allegory toward a renewed focus on the specifically Jewish in the literary tradition. The fictional king and the rabbi in the Kuzari reject the universalizing claims of the philosopher, who believes that because the cultivation of the intellect is the true purpose of life, it makes no difference whether one is pagan, Muslim, Christian, or Jew. Through his fictional spokesmen, Halevi argued that philosophy cannot satisfy the heart that longs for religious certainty; he relegates philosophy to a secondary role in his scheme of life and replaces it with his vision of Judaism as the one path to contact with the divine. Likewise in his liturgical poetry, Halevi replaced the universalizing tendency of his model, Ibn Gabirol, with concretely Jewish references.[49]

Like Ibn Gabirol, Abraham Ibn Ezra, and other poets of the age, Halevi wrote liturgical poems that are clearly about the exile and redemption of the soul but that end with references to the Jewish national exile and redemption theme, rendering them suitable for synagogue use.[50] Halevi also wrote poems unambiguously, passionately lamenting the national exile and praying for national restoration. But in a small third group of poems on national redemption, he mimics the language of individual salvation, thereby suggesting that he is turning away from the latter and from its Neoplatonic outlook. These different ways of writing about exile and redemption presumably reflect the difference between his earlier,

Neoplatonic orientation and his later, nationalistic thought. We may observe the shift by comparing two poems that we will meet later in this chapter: "My Soul Is Yearning" (poem 3); and "Your Bride Is Coming out to Meet You" (poem 4). Though these are similar in language and phrasing, the former is entirely about the exile and return of the soul, while the latter is unambiguously about the exile of the Jewish people and their longing to return to the Land of Israel.

We can take the measure of the distance that Halevi traversed in the course of his career by considering the following lines of his, from a presumably early liturgical poem:

At the mountain of God I ask my prophet,
"Does He appear in the bush?"
I pass through the land of my footstool and throne—
there is no answer.
Perhaps in my bondage, my prison,
perhaps within me He dwells?—
I found Him dwelling
within my own home,
like a friend or a brother.
He came, sorrow fled,
pain and heartache passed.
I find healing for my ailment,
for He keeps me in bondage.
I do not ask for dominion
or to inherit the Lovely Land,
only for love drawn to me,
the company of my friend.[51]

In this passage speaks a forgotten Judah Halevi, a believer of a different kind from the one who made the pilgrimage and wrote the pilgrimage poetry that we will be reading—a Halevi who declares that in his quest for God, it does not matter where he is, for he can find God within his heart. This statement is so radically Neoplatonic that we would not have been surprised to find it in Ibn Gabirol. The poem, taken as a whole, embraces the patient acceptance of the Jewish exile, pending an eventual messianic restoration contemplated without urgency. This poem thus says the exact opposite of what Halevi would proclaim with such passion in the pilgrimage poetry of his later years: that God is revealed only in the Land of Israel.

Halevi tells us about the shift in his thinking in his Kuzari, which is largely an attempt to define the limits of philosophy. Like al-Ghazzālī, Halevi came to the conviction that not only could philosophy not provide the warmth and comfort of concrete and intense religious experience but that it could not even provide intellectual certainty about the larger questions it dealt with. Halevi's disillusionment with philosophy may have been triggered by personal causes such as the malaise depicted in the epistles quoted earlier or by midlife reflections on old-age decrepitude and death; perhaps he would have continued to be satisfied with his conventional Neoplatonic version of Judaism until the rising trend of Aristotelian philosophy, more radical than Neoplatonism and less susceptible to harmonization with the Jewish tradition, soured him on all philosophical systems.

Given the differences in their cultural and communal background, Halevi's solution to the problem of philosophy was not identical to that of al-Ghazzālī. Al-Ghazzālī was a Muslim theologian, mystic, and jurist who had studied philosophy and devoted significant effort to a vigorous refutation of its claims to truth, while Halevi, as a doctor, was a philosophically oriented Rabbanite Jew who merely had come to see philosophy's limitations; it was not in his makeup to reject philosophy altogether. But Halevi resembled al-Ghazzālī in demanding an almost tangible sense—a taste, as he so often puts it—of the reality of religious experience, not merely proofs for the existence of God and the createdness or non-createdness of the world. Despite all the differences in detail between the writings of the two, there is a similarity in their quests. And, like al-Ghazzālī, Halevi concretized his quest by leaving home and going on pilgrimage.

Halevi made the late-life shift, traditional in the Islamic world, from worldliness to piety, or, as he put it, from being a slave to men to being a slave to God. As with many who underwent this kind of conversion, he was partly motivated by a generalized sense of guilt. He hints at it in the Kuzari and in one of his epistles, and speaks briefly but passionately on the subject in one of the pilgrimage poems:[52]

I tremble for my early sins,
all recorded in God's book,
and even more for recent sins,
sins of my old age,
new sins every day.
No way
to repent my waywardness—
what to do in this distress?

We do not need to imagine a dramatic biographical event, a particular sin in his earlier life that made him burn with the need for expiation at its end. Late-life conversion is nearly always described in Islamic literature as a generalized expression of regret for a life devoted to worldly pursuits—the commonplace sin of people of ordinary piety—and less commonly as expiation for particular sins. Like many elderly people of his time, Halevi may have felt that he needed to atone for a life that attempted to strike a compromise between dutiful attendance to the requirements of religion with worldly accomplishments and pleasures—the kind of balanced life that we moderns consider healthy and well-rounded but that to medieval pietists seemed merely hypocritical. Perhaps, like many, he felt that he had worked too hard at directing the course of his own life, not trusting in God to take care of his needs in accordance with the demands of *tawakkul*. Perhaps he felt that only in the proximity of the Temple, and only by dint of hardships undergone in the process of getting there, could he achieve expiation.[53]

Guilt and repentance were an element in Halevi's pilgrimage, but repentance alone is not enough to explain Halevi's decision, for he could have repented in other, more conventional ways. He could have turned to Talmud study, as he had fantasized in his epistle to Rabbi Ḥabīb of al-Mahdiyya. He could have retreated inward, as recommended by Baḥya, while externally going about his normal life. He could have turned his literary gifts to writing moralistic treatises. Halevi's midlife change involved two elements: the turn from worldliness to piety, so typical for his age; and the turn away from the Neoplatonic spiritualizing and toward a vision of religious fulfillment through a renewed embrace of the spirit of prophecy.

I

אֲדֹנָי, נֶגְדְּךָ כָל תַּאֲוָתִי
וְאִם לֹא אַעֲלֶנָּה עַל שְׂפָתִי.
רְצוֹנְךָ אֶשְׁאֲלָה רֶגַע וְאֶגְוַע--
וּמִי יִתֵּן וְתָבוֹא שֶׁאֱלָתִי--
וְאַפְקִיד אֶת שְׁאָר רוּחִי בְּיָדְךָ
וְיָשַׁנְתִּי, וְעָרְבָה לִי שְׁנָתִי.
בְּרָחְקִי מִמְּךָ מוֹתִי בְחַיַּי,
וְאִם אֶדְבַּק בְּךָ חַיַּי בְּמוֹתִי.
אֲבָל לֹא אֵדְעָה בַּמָּה אֲקַדֵּם,
וּמַה תִּהְיֶה עֲבוֹדָתִי וְדָתִי.
דְּרָכֶיךָ, אֲדֹנָי, לַמְּדֵנִי,
וְשׁוּב מִמַּאֲסַר סִכְלוּת שְׁבוּתִי,
וְהוֹרֵנִי בְּעוֹד יֶשׁ-בִּי יְכֹלֶת
לְהִתְעַנּוֹת, וְאַל תִּבְזֶה עֱנוּתִי,
בְּטֶרֶם יוֹם אֱהִי עָלַי לְמַשָּׂא,
וְיוֹם יִכְבַּד קְצָתִי עַל קְצָתִי,
וְאִכָּנַע בְּעַל כָּרְחִי, וְיֹאכַל
עֲצָמַי עָשׁ, וְנִלְאוּ מִשְּׂאֵתִי,
וְאֶסַּע אֶל מְקוֹם נָסְעוּ אֲבוֹתָי,
וּבִמְקוֹם תַּחֲנוֹתָם תַּחֲנוֹתִי.
כְּגֵר תּוֹשָׁב אֲנִי עַל גַּב אֲדָמָה,
וְאוּלָם כִּי בְּבִטְנָהּ נַחֲלָתִי.
נְעוּרַי עַד הֲלוֹם עָשׂוּ לְנַפְשָׁם,
וּמָתַי גַּם אֲנִי אֶעְשֶׂה לְבֵיתִי?
וְהָעוֹלָם אֲשֶׁר נָתַן בְּלִבִּי
מְנָעַנִי לְבַקֵּשׁ אַחֲרִיתִי.
וְאֵיכָה אֶעֱבֹד יוֹצְרִי בְּעוֹדִי
אֲסִיר יִצְרִי וְעֶבֶד תַּאֲוָתִי?
וְאֵיכָה מַעֲלָה רָמָה אֲבַקֵּשׁ
וּמָחָר תִּהְיֶה רִמָּה אֲחוֹתִי?
וְאֵיךְ יִיטַב בְּיוֹם טוֹבָה לְבָבִי
וְלֹא אֵדַע הֲיִיטַב מָחֳרָתִי?

I

O Lord, all my desire is plain to Thee
although I do not even speak the words:
to please You just one moment, then die.
If only this one wish were granted me!—
Then I would put my last breath in Your hands
and drift to sleep, and sweet that sleep would be.

I know that, far from You, my life is death,
and when I cling to You, my death is life.
But still I do not know what gift to bring,
what service to perform, or how to live.

Teach me Your ways, O Lord, and turn
me back from being folly's captive.
Teach me while I still have strength
to bear my penance, one You will not scorn,
before I turn into a burden to myself,
my limbs too weak to hold each other up,
my bones like cloth moth-eaten,
too frayed to carry me—
when piety is all that's left to me—
before I go the road my fathers traveled,
and make my camp where they encamped before.

For I am but a traveler here,
lingering briefly on this surface—
my real home is within.
Till now, the youth in me looked out for its own needs.
The time has come to look out for myself,
seek my eternal home.
And yet this world is present in my heart,
preventing me from tending to the next.
How can I serve my Maker—I,
prisoner of urges, slave to desire?
Why do I seek honors, when I know
that soon I will have worms for company?
How can I enjoy a day of pleasure,
not knowing what that everlasting day to come will be for me,

וְהַיָּמִים וְהַלֵּילוֹת עֲרֵבִים
  לְכַלּוֹת אֶת שְׁאֵרִי עַד כְּלוֹתִי,
וְלָרוּחַ יְזָרוּן מַחֲצִיתִי,
  וְלֶעָפָר יְשִׁיבוּן מַחֲצִיתִי.
וּמָה אֹמַר, וְיִצְרִי יִרְדְּפֵנִי
  כְּאוֹיֵב מִנְּעוּרַי עַד כְּלוֹתִי?
וּמַה לִּי בַּזְּמָן אִם לֹא רְצוֹנָךְ?
  וְאִם אֵינְךָ מְנָתִי, מַה מְּנָתִי?
אֲנִי מִמַּעֲשִׂים שׁוֹלָל וְעָרֹם,
  וְצִדְקָתְךָ לְבַדָּהּ הִיא כְסוּתִי.
וְעוֹד מָה אַאֲרִיךְ לָשׁוֹן וְאֶשְׁאַל?
  אֲדֹנָי נֶגְדְּךָ כָל תַּאֲוָתִי.

The speaker is conscious that he has reached the midpoint of life. Looking back, he sees that he has wasted his youth in pursuit of material things; looking ahead, he foresees the deterioration of his body. But he is still in his full strength, his heart is still full of "the world,"[54] and he is still "a prisoner of urges," a "slave to desire." The day when he will have to travel the road taken by his ancestors still appears far off.

In identifying middle age as a turning point in religious life, Halevi modifies the convention of Hebrew and Arabic moralizing poetry, with its emphasis on old age as the time for repentance. Here, the ominous thought that impels one to repentance is not death but decrepitude. *Now* is when repentance is meaningful, when one is old enough to grasp the vanity of mundane satisfactions, but before the delight in them is gone; now, while the world is still tugging at one's heart, and resisting it costs a struggle. When the appetites are gone, there is no virtue in renouncing pleasures. As a Muslim moralist put it, "O you old men, who do not abandon sin until sin abandons you, and who think that your abandoning it is repentance! If only, when it leaves you, you did not wish so ardently for it to return!"[55] Moreover, now the speaker still has the strength to bear the mortifications he deserves; later, he will be too frail to repent other than in mere words. This moment, at the brink of old age, is the last chance to repent meaningfully and to suffer condign punishment.

The poem begins and ends by stating that God sees and knows all the speaker's desires. Speech is superfluous. The speaker does express his desires in the poem, as a petitioner must if he is to say anything at all; but he manages

heedless that my days and nights have conspired
to wear my flesh out, use me up,
leave half of me to float off with the winds,
return the other half back to the dirt.

How can I even speak to You,
when worldly urges have pursued me,
been my foe since I was young,
and will be till I die?
What can Time offer me except to please You?
But if not You, what can my portion be?
I stand before You now, a naked man,
with nothing but Your grace to cover me.
What point is there in speaking longer, begging,
when, Lord, all my desire is plain to Thee.

---

to use no more than three imperative verbs in the entire poem, all in the short passage, "Teach me Your ways, O Lord, and turn / me back from being folly's captive.// Teach me while I still have strength / to bear my penance." These verbs ask no more than that God help him to see His way clearly enough to be able to follow it; far from begging God not to punish him, he actually urges God to do so, and sooner rather than later. The entire petition is geared toward God's will and the effacing of the speaker's own.

This theme of God's will is adumbrated in the opening, where the poet speaks of God's *ratson* ("will," or "pleasure," in v. 2). Several possible emphases vie for attention. God's *ratson* in Jewish prayer often means God's satisfaction with a person or with his act of worship; accordingly, the most obvious meaning here is that Halevi prays that God be pleased with him. But the Hebrew word also means "wish," or "desire," so that Halevi might also be asking not for the gift of God's favor but to know what it is that God desires. Thus in the extreme economy of two Hebrew words (*retsonekha esh᾽ala*), Halevi manages to express two complementary petitions: "I seek Your favor"; and "I seek to know Your will." But we readers do not need to choose between the two petitions, because, combined, they make a single petition: to please God is to accept God's will; to live in accordance with God's will is to live in God's favor.

The speaker in Halevi's poem reduces his own will to the smallest conceivable compass: "to please You just one moment and then die." Not his desires, but only God's desires should control his life. To satisfy God, even for a moment, would be the fulfillment of his life's desires, and if it were granted him, he would be ready to die on the spot, content with his life's achievement.[56]

Defining life and death in terms of God's will, Halevi gives new force to an old motif. "I know that, far from You, my life is death, / and when I cling to You, my death is life" is the ancient paradox that physical life is spiritual death, but physical death is an awakening to true life. The admonition to die to the world in order to live for the spirit goes back to Plato, has a parallel in the Talmud, and was adopted from the Greeks by Muslim philosophers and mystics and by Jewish pietistic writers and poets; but Halevi, atypically, puts it into the mouth of a speaker who has already internalized the admonition and who begs God for help in applying it rigorously to his life.[57]

Halevi's poem's true theme and the religious attitude that dictates its prevailing mood is the suppression of the speaker's selfhood, the trusting subjugation of his will to God's. Halevi also shows us how difficult this self-suppression is. His argument is that he cannot help having a self and that only with God's help can he suppress it; like the king in the Kuzari, he wants to do God's will but does not know exactly how, and wants to know exactly what is demanded of him. Halevi's contrition derives not from fear of the punishment in the afterlife but from the belated desire to renounce the ego and abandon one's self to God's power and mercy.[58]

We are close here to the themes of *tawakkul,* which we have already met, and two others closely related to it: *qunūʿ,* being satisfied with what one has; and *riḍā*—the loving acceptance of God's will, even if what God decrees is *not* to provide for one's material wants, or even if what God decrees is suffering. These concepts often lead to paradoxes, such as the opinion that a person should not even care whether God has decreed paradise or hell for him.[59]

The term *riḍā* can function in two directions.[60] The Qur'an says of the righteous: "God is pleased with them and they are pleased with Him," meaning that God rewards the righteous (in paradise) for their obedience, and the righteous are delighted with God for providing the reward. But Sufi writers used the reciprocal formulation to bring out different values: some interpreted it to mean either that God is pleased with man when man is pleased with God; and others, that man can only achieve the state of being pleased with God when God has already bestowed His pleasure on man.[61]

But the ideal of matching one's will to the will of God turns petitionary prayer into a theological problem; indeed, it renders it practically impossible. Logically, the religious stance of one who has reached perfect *tawakkul* and *riḍā* would be never to pray for any specific outcome.[62] Normal Islam encourages the pious to pray for their needs. But how does one pray when one is striving to shape one's religious life around the triad of *qunūʿ, tawakkul,* and *riḍā*? The prayer of such a person would not be a petition but an expression of submission; at most, it would ask for God's help in so submitting. This is the kind of prayer that Halevi composed in "O Lord, All My Desire Is Plain to Thee."

This becomes clearer when the opening line is repeated at the poem's end. At the beginning, all it seemed to mean was that the speaker's heart is transparent to God. But at the end, the meaning is modified by the context:

> *What can Time offer me except to please You?. . . .*
> *I stand before You now, a naked man,*
> *with nothing but Your grace*[63] *to cover me.*
> *What point is there in speaking longer, begging,*
> *when, Lord, all my desire is plain to Thee.*

The speaker is no longer merely asserting God's omniscience or expressing a desire to please Him. He is saying that, since all he wants is for God to do God's own will, there is, logically speaking, nothing left to pray for but the strength to accept that divine will and thus to live in God's favor—to please God by being pleased with Him alone.

2

יָהּ אָנָה אֶמְצָאֲךָ?   מְקוֹמְךָ נַעֲלֶה וְנֶעְלָם.
וְאָנָה לֹא אֶמְצָאֲךָ?   כְּבוֹדְךָ מָלֵא עוֹלָם.

הַנִּמְצָא בַקְּרָבִים   אַפְסֵי אֶרֶץ הֵקִים.
הַמִּשְׂגָּב לַקְּרוֹבִים,   הַמִּבְטָח לָרְחוֹקִים.
אַתָּה יוֹשֵׁב כְּרוּבִים,   אַתָּה שׁוֹכֵן שְׁחָקִים.
תִּתְהַלֵּל בִּצְבָאֲךָ,   וְאַתְּ עַל רֹאשׁ מַהֲלָלָם.
גַּלְגַּל לֹא יִשָּׂאֲךָ,   אַף כִּי חַדְרֵי אוּלָם.

וּבְהִנָּשְׂאֲךָ עֲלֵיהֶם   עַל כֵּס נִשָּׂא וָרָם,
אַתָּה קָרוֹב אֲלֵיהֶם   מֵרוּחָם וּמִבְּשָׂרָם.
פִּיהֶם יָעִיד בָּהֶם   כִּי אֵין בִּלְתְּךָ יוֹצְרָם.
מִי זֶה לֹא יִירָאֲךָ?--   וְעֹל מַלְכוּתְךָ עֻלָּם.
אוֹ מִי לֹא יִקְרָאֲךָ?--   וְאַתָּה נוֹתֵן אָכְלָם.

דָּרַשְׁתִּי קִרְבָתְךָ,   בְּכָל לִבִּי קְרָאתִיךָ,
וּבְצֵאתִי לִקְרָאתְךָ   לִקְרָאתִי מְצָאתִיךָ,
וּבְפִלְאֵי גְבוּרָתְךָ   בַּקֹּדֶשׁ חֲזִיתִיךָ.
מִי יֹאמַר לֹא רָאֲךָ?   הֵן שָׁמַיִם וְחֵילָם
יַגִּידוּ מוֹרָאֲךָ,   בְּלִי נִשְׁמָע קוֹלָם.

הַאֻמְנָם כִּי יֵשֵׁב   אֱלֹהִים אֶת הָאָדָם?
וּמַה יַּחְשֹׁב כָּל חוֹשֵׁב   אֲשֶׁר בֶּעָפָר יְסוֹדָם?
וְאַתָּה קָדוֹשׁ יוֹשֵׁב   תְּהִלּוֹתָם וּכְבוֹדָם.
חַיּוֹת יוֹדוּ פִּלְאֲךָ   הָעוֹמְדוֹת בְּרוּם עוֹלָם.
עַל רָאשֵׁיהֶם כִּסְאֲךָ,   וְאַתָּה נוֹשֵׂא כֻלָּם.

2

Where can I find You, Lord?—
Your place is high and hidden.
But where can I not find You, Lord?—
Your glory fills the world!

You created the world, yet reside in man's heart.
Protector of men, refuge of angels,
You dwell in the Temple, yet dwell in the heavens.
Praised by Your hosts,
yet far above praise;
too great for the spheres,
yet contained by a chamber.

And when You ascend to Your throne on high,
You are closer to them than their breath or their bodies.
Their mouths proclaim that none but You made them.
Who does not fear You?
They bend to Your yoke.
Who does not call on You,
You their provider?

I longed to be near You, I called You sincerely,
went out to seek You, and found You *me* seeking!
Your wondrous Creation I saw as Your temple.
Who has *not* seen You?—
The stars and the heavens
resound with Your glory,
resound without words.

Yet, can God make His dwelling in man?
What can earth-mortal thinkers imagine?
Yet You, Holy Lord, have Your throne on their praises!
The angels above us
acknowledge Your wonders.
Your throne is yet higher,
Yet You support them.

The first step in Halevi's pilgrimage is the uneasy recognition that God is somewhere else and needs to be sought. The solution, in this poem of paradoxes, is in the dialectic of immanence and transcendence, culminating in the compact, memorable, and untranslatable line in the heart of the third stanza, which, literally rendered, means: "When I went out to greet You, to greet me I found You." The Creator-God, whose heavenly throne is exalted over the very angels, may be found right here on earth, in human hearts and on the golden cherubim in the Temple; He comes looking for the person who seeks Him. There is indeed comfort for the God-seeker in the thought that God is inside us already; that He is revealed in nature and in the Temple; and that He has a dwelling place on earth. Why, then, is this poem so full of expressions of unease?

The notion that God is at all times mysteriously present inside a person reflects the philosophical view that the soul is a spark of the divine world, trapped in the material body and longing to return to its source. To adherents of an emanationist view of the universe, the ancient words of the liturgy "His glory fills the world" (based on Isa. 6:3 and quoted in line 4 of the poem) no longer meant merely that God is so great as to dwarf the world and its inhabitants, as in Isaiah, but that the divine presence pervades everything, and is particularly present in the soul. Though ordinary experience shows us that God is not accessible to the human eye, and though the Bible teaches that "no man shall see Me and live" (Exod. 33:20), to many medieval thinkers, God is indeed visible to one who sees with the philosophical eye, for to contemplate God's creative acts is to see God indirectly, and to contemplate the soul is to contemplate God in miniature. Thus, in the most thrilling of the poem's paradoxes, Halevi can reverse the biblical and liturgical commonplace and exclaim: Who can say he has *not* seen You?[64]

The notion that God is found in His works and inside individual persons should not be confused with blind faith or with a mere warm and comforting sense of God's presence. It is not even the passive sense of awe at the contemplation of nature that we call the sublime. Only the active application of reason to the external world permits us to understand the complex operations of the natural world and to grasp a part of the divine reason that operates in it. Many medieval thinkers pointed out that this is the closest that we can come to apprehending God. They called this kind of apprehension "seeing God with the eye of the intellect." As the seat of the intellect, the soul is imagined as a lamp that lights the soul's way.[65] It is this inner vision that Halevi has in mind when he says, "Can God indeed make His dwelling in man?" The consensus of the philosophical poets was that, by implanting the soul in human beings, He could; but the rhetorical question in our poem—can God make His dwelling in man?—implies uncertainty.

The problem of God's transcendence—how can we know and worship God when He is beyond our sight, beyond our comprehension?—is expressed by the ancient liturgy in a passage that describes the angels asking, as they praise God, "Where is the place of His glory?," as if even these celestial servants of God are unsure of His place, unsure that their hymns of praise will reach Him. The liturgical passage brings together two biblical verses: "Holy, holy, holy the Lord of Hosts; the whole earth is full of His glory" (Isa. 6:3), the angels' hymn to God, sung in His presence, stating that that presence is everywhere; and "Blessed is the Glory of the Lord from His place" (Ezek. 3:12), which was understood as implying that even the angels are uncertain as to where He may be found ("from His place" was interpreted as meaning "wherever that place may be").

Halevi's poem belongs to the genre of *ofan,* a poem designed to be inserted into the liturgy between these two prophetic verses when they are recited as part of the morning service. In the four-line leading strophe that may also have served as a refrain, Halevi begins his poetic embellishment of this moment in the liturgy by reformulating the two phrases from the liturgy so as to bring out the paradox: "Where can I find You, where can I not find You." The rest of the poem is a congeries of variations on this paradox. In the first full strophe, each line offers a variation on the theme "God is near, God is far," climaxing with the thought that the cosmos is too small to contain God, yet a chamber suffices. That chamber, in traditional Jewish terms, is the Temple, which has already been mentioned (the word translated "Temple" in v. 5 actually refers to the two golden cherubim that stood on the ark in the innermost chamber of the Temple; in the poem, they function as a synecdoche for the Temple). But the chamber could also represent the heart, which is sometimes portrayed by poets as a miniature Temple.[66]

The poem has generally been read as a mystical testimony, a breathless statement of the poet's adoration of God's presence in the world and in himself. It is that, but it is something else besides. If we look only at the poem's motifs in the abstract, all we will see is the affirmative mood. But paradox, as a form, lays stress on both members, and, in a poem that contains little *but* paradoxes, this means that the uncertainty is at least as strong as the certainty. Furthermore, many of the poem's paradoxes are formulated as rhetorical questions: "Who has not?" "Who does not?" "Who can say?" Such formulations, from the point of view of logic, imply certainties; but in their reiteration and combination with the paradoxes, they cast a penumbra of doubt around the ecstatic mood.

Paradoxes and queries parade by and uncertainties accumulate, becoming explicit in the last strophe, which asks (literally translated), "Does God indeed make His dwelling with man?" This question could elicit the answer "Yes, indeed He does" or "No, indeed He does not"; we almost expect the assurances of the preceding three stanzas to be revoked. This feeling is reinforced by the next sentence (again, literally translated): "What can any thinker think whose element is earth?," putting the mind's powers in their place. In the last lines of the poem, we find ourselves not on earth or in the heart but at the highest, most inaccessible, reaches of the cosmos, in the world of angels, who, bearing the throne of God, are at the same time borne by Him. This final paradox seems to place God and mortal at an infinite remove from each other.[67]

The theological content and language of the poem are fairly conventional for Halevi's time and place. Even the idea of asking about God's location is biblical and traditional. What is new and specifically Halevian is the poem's

(*Commentary continues on the next page*)

3

נַפְשִׁי לְבֵית אֵל נִכְסְפָה גַּם כָּלְתָה,
גַּם בַּחֲלוֹמוֹת לַחֲזוֹתוֹ עָלְתָה.
עָלְתָה וְלֹא מָצְאָה אֲרוּכָה, כִּי חֲלוֹם
לֹא יַחֲלִים נֶפֶשׁ בְּהָקִיץ חָלְתָה.
חָלְתָה בְּיוֹם לֹא חִלְּתָה פָּנִים אֲשֶׁר
לוּלֵי יְקָרָם וַהֲדָרָם בָּלְתָה.
בָּלְתָה לְהִתְחַדֵּשׁ, וְיָגְעָה לַעֲלוֹת,
כִּי לֹא לְתֹהוּ גָּלְתָה יוֹם גָּלְתָה.
גָּלְתָה וְדַלְתֵי מַעְיָן פָּתְחָה, וְעוֹד
עֵינָהּ אֱלֵי מַיִם עֲמֻקִּים תָּלְתָה.
תָּלְתָה עֲלֵי יָחֵד וְאִסָּר אָסְרָה
בַּל תַּעֲזֹב חָכְמָה, וְאָלָה אָלְתָה.

---

delicate balance of certainty and uncertainty, a distinctive anxiety about God's location; we imagine the poet saying, "Despite philosophy, God is *not* exactly here. I must go *out* to find Him; only then will He come to find me." He may have experienced intimations of God's nearness—in nature, in his soul, in philosophical contemplation—but Halevi, at some point in his religious development, could not remain satisfied with the compromise of philosophical immanence. Though he probably never abandoned the notion of the soul that was the common property of serious thinkers of his time, he came ultimately to conceive of finding God as seeking Him somewhere other than in the self, and of having found Him as meaning the concrete experience of revelation. In this poem, these notions are still inchoate, but they would become clearer and more concrete as his thinking developed.

3

My soul is yearning, longing for the House of God,
  in dreams she tries to rise to see Him—
rises, finds no comfort. How can dreams
  bring healing to a soul in sorrow?—
in sorrow since the day she first was barred
  from visiting the Presence
  without Whose splendor she would fade away.
She fades away to be renewed,
  and struggles upward—
  not for no purpose was she exiled.
Exiled, she opened a fountain's door,
  lifts her eye to deeper waters;
lifts herself onto a solid perch, makes solemn vows
  never to abandon wisdom,
binds herself with solemn oaths.

Here, too, the speaker—or rather, his soul—longs to be somewhere else, but where it longs to be depends on which of two manuscript readings we prefer—"the House of God," the version adopted in the translation; or "the father's house"—a difference of only one letter in Hebrew! Both readings are useful to us.

The soul is separated from its divine home and imprisoned in a human body; only in death can it be restored. Since "soul" is feminine in Hebrew, it can be imagined as a woman unhappily married and longing for her father's house, the place to which a divorced woman in premodern times would naturally return. This poem is about the yearning of the soul for this return. Sleep, a simulacrum of death, affords it a glimpse, albeit an unsatisfactory one, of its redemption.

But the word "exiled" in verse 4 and "rise," in verses 1 and 2 would make a reader think that the poem is speaking about the national exile and its hoped-for redemption (for the verb translated "rise" is often used of making a pilgrimage, literally "going up" to Jerusalem). These terms associated with the national problem might seem to support the reading "House of God," i.e., the Temple. Indeed, the whole first line is reminiscent of Ps. 84:3, in which the psalmist speaks of his intense desire to see the Temple. In this poem, as so often, language and imagery deriving from the Jewish national predicament are put into the service of the philosophical theme of the redemption of the individual soul through reunion with its divine source. Both readings are satisfactory, for the return to the Temple and the return to the father's house amount to the same thing.

The route of the soul's return is upward, through the celestial spheres to the One. The poem imitates the upward way by repeating the last word of each verse at the beginning of the next, forming a verbal ladder for this spiritual ascension. The bottom rung is provided by the word "rise," linking the first two lines; the series continues through the succeeding pairs of linked verses until the soul reaches the "fountain," an image used since Plotinus to denote the One in its aspect as the source of emanations that, in their descent, form the cosmos and all its contents.[68] The key to this restoration, it was believed, was the cultivation of the intellect, and that is the object of the vow mentioned at the poem's end.

The soul's ascent is blocked by the body. When the body sleeps, the soul can escape by means of dreams, but each morning finds her back in her prison, still not cured of her longing. Yet the soul is not completely without spiritual resources in this life. For though the divine world is blocked to the eye of flesh, the divine within us can be glimpsed through contemplation of the soul. When the soul contemplates herself, she is contemplating her source, a paradoxical lifting of the eye through a downward gaze at the "deep waters." In this self-contemplation, she not only approaches but also resembles God, and gets some relief for her longing. The poem's biblical vocabulary hints at the philosophical concepts underlying it, for the term "deep waters" in our poem comes from a passage speaking of human intellect: "The council of man's heart is deep water; a wise man will draw it" (Prov. 20:5). The poem implies a Neoplatonic interpretation of the verse: the wise man contemplates the divine nature of his own soul, thereby preparing it in life for its ultimate restoration to its source after death.[69]

We are reminded that the poem is not about the actual ascent of the soul but about the philosopher's dream of the soul's ascent (v. 1). In its temporary freedom from the body in sleep, the soul ascends until it finds itself, a discovery that becomes the starting point of the sleeper's waking meditation. This is as far as it can go, but it is a taste of what is in store. The soul—the poet—vows never to flag in his lifelong devotion to philosophical wisdom, which brings him this temporary relief in sleep and which promises redemption after death.

The Judah Halevi who composed this poem, like the author of "Where Can I Find You, Lord?" (poem 2), is impelled to seek the ultimate divine experience apart from the self; but unlike the author of "Where Can I Find You, Lord?," he accepts philosophy as a substitute, pending the soul's ultimate release in death. This poem has none of the anxiety of "O Lord, All My Desire Is Plain to Thee" (poem 1); rather, it rings with confidence about the nature of the quest and about the speaker's ability to see it through. As with many of the poems of Halevi's early period, its spiritual yearning is closer to the spirit of his Neoplatonic predecessor Solomon Ibn Gabirol than to that of the mature Judah Halevi of the pilgrimage poetry or the anxious Halevi in between.

Yet for all the poem's confidence, it bespeaks a yearning spirit and ends on a note of incompleteness. The vow at the end of the poem again reminds us of Ibn Gabirol's vow to cling to philosophy as the key to redemption.[70] It also foreshadows a very different vow that will figure in Halevi's later poetry when Halevi's physical pilgrimage to the Land of Israel came to replace the philosophical pilgrimage represented by "Where Can I Find You, Lord?" and many other poems of his early life.

4

יָצְאָה לְקַדֶּמְךָ כַּלָּה לְךָ כָּלְתָה,
מִיּוֹם אֲשֶׁר לֹא חִלְּתָה קָדְשְׁךָ חָלְתָה.
הִשְׁתּוֹמֲמָה מִדֵּי עֲלֹתָהּ לְהַר קֹדֶשׁ,
כִּי רָאֲתָה זָרִים עָלוּ וְלֹא עָלְתָה.
וַתַּעֲמֹד רָחוֹק מִשְׁתַּחֲוָה נֹכַח
הֵיכָלְךָ מִכָּל מָקוֹם אֲשֶׁר גָּלְתָה.
דִּבְרֵי תְחִנָּתָהּ שָׁלְחָה לְךָ מִנְחָה;
לִבָּהּ וְעֵינֶיהָ מוּל כִּסְאֲךָ תָּלְתָה.
הַשְׁקֵף וְהַאֲזִינָה, וּשְׁמַע לְשַׁוְעָתָהּ,
קוֹרְאָה בְּמַר לִבָּהּ וְנַפְשָׁהּ אֲשֶׁר כָּלְתָה.

The poem shares with "My Soul Is Yearning" (poem 3) the central image of a yearning female who seeks to go outward and upward to find God. There are also a number of similarities in wording, some of which even survive translation. But the woman spoken of here does not represent the philosopher's yearning soul; she stands for exiled Israel, yearning to "go up" to perform the festival pilgrimage. This poem affords us our first view of Halevi's writing on the national theme.

The poem presupposes an occasion. It is a festival, and the people of Israel, here represented by the bride, are assembled in the synagogue, unable to greet God by performing the obligatory pilgrimage to Jerusalem stipulated in the Torah: "Three times in the year, all your males shall visit the presence of Yahweh your God in the place that He will choose" (Deut. 16:16). The bride Israel is heartsick, or, as we would say, feels guilty, at her inability to perform the rite. She is also ashamed, because she sees others thronging to the Holy Land while she remains at home.

Who are these throngs? Christians had long made the pilgrimage to the Holy Sepulcher and Muslims to the Dome of the Rock—Islam's greatest architectural monument—and the al-Aqsa mosque.[71] Halevi must also be thinking of the Crusades, in which Christians and Muslims battled in the Holy Land to contend for control over the Jewish holy sites, while the Jews themselves could only look on from the side. All the world seems to have made the pilgrimage except the people who are actually obligated to do so. Israel must be content to watch

4

Your bride is coming out to meet You, longing,
heartsick since the day she first was barred
from visiting Your sanctuary.
Each time of pilgrimage, she gazes, shamefaced,
at the strangers who have made the journey,
while she has not.
She stands far off
in all the places of her exile,
bowing toward Your Holy Temple,
sending prayers instead of sacrifices,
lifts her heart and eyes toward Your throne.
Look down at her from heaven, hear the cry
she cries with bitter heart and yearning soul.

from her substitute temples, the synagogues of her scattered communities, as strangers pay homage to her true sanctuary. Unable to bring her festival offerings, as in biblical times, she sends her prayers in their stead, and lifts her eyes in silence to the site. Perhaps in the background of Halevi's poem is the recent cessation of the nonbiblical Jewish pilgrimage to the Mount of Olives that was held during the festival of Sukkot until the late eleventh century.[72]

To feel the force of this poem, we have to imagine it in its original setting as part of the festival service, for the point it makes works against its liturgical function. Traditionally, the precentor prays that God restore Israel to the Temple service, for which the synagogue ritual is considered merely a substitute. But our poet is troubled by the congregation's complacency. By comparison with the way the nations of the world are drawn to the site of the sanctuary, with Christians and Muslims actually dying for possession of the site, the anodyne rites performed so dutifully by the poet and his coreligionists appear as mere lip service. The Jews pride themselves in retaining their identity and their religion in spite of all temptations to give it up, yet they remain in places of their exile—lamenting their exile but doing nothing about it. This insight lends ironic force to the plea for redemption; its implicit demand for sincerity would contribute both to the argument of the Kuzari and to Halevi's pilgrimage.

Halevi undoubtedly wrote traditional synagogue poetry praying for an end to the exile throughout his career, so the contents of this poem alone do not justify our assigning it a specific place in his religious development. What may justify our doing so is the relationship between it and "My Soul Is Yearning," because it makes the impression of being a Judaized rewriting of the rather universalizing "Your Bride Is Coming out to Meet You."[73] Halevi may be doing here with one of his own poems what he sometimes does to poems by Ibn Gabirol: replacing the philosophical tendency with a particularistic Jewish theme, striving to relocate the spiritual within the physical reality of the Jewish experience. This tendency will occupy us more when we come to the pilgrimage poetry.

2

The National Problem

Political Plight

The political conditions of Halevi's times undoubtedly nourished the thinking that led to his pilgrimage. Halevi lived through the collapse of the *taifa* kingdoms and the coming of the Almoravids; important events of the Reconquista; the First Crusade; and the rise of the Almohads in North Africa.[1] Castile, which had been notably hospitable to Jews when it first returned to Christian control in Halevi's youth (1085), became less so in the course of his lifetime, with the murder of the Castilian Jewish courtier Joseph ben Ferruziel in 1108 and the anti-Jewish riots that broke out upon the death of Alfonso VI, conqueror of Toledo, in 1109. In al-Andalus, the Almoravid takeover beginning in 1190 displaced Jewish courtiers formerly in the service of the *taifa* rulers and introduced a more austerely Islamic regime. Halevi must also have observed the religious fanaticism of the Almohads as their movement burgeoned in northwest Africa beginning in 1130; given their religious extremism and dynamism, he might well have anticipated their expansion into al-Andalus and the disruption it might cause, events that actually came to pass a few years after his death. Within Iberia, the wars between Christians and Muslims must have contributed to a general feeling of instability and uncertainty. Perhaps this situation is what led Halevi to write:[2]

Between the Christian and Muslim troops,
my own troops perish,
for they go out to battle each other,
and in their defeat, it is we who fall—
so it has always been for Israel.

The fall of Jerusalem to the crusaders in 1099, when Halevi was probably in his teens, must also have had an emotional impact on him and other members of his generation. Besides their anxiety on behalf of the Jewish community of Palestine itself, they must have felt that the Holy Land, by being largely removed from the Islamic *oikoumene,* had become even more inaccessible than formerly. The wars in Palestine made Halevi and his contemporaries feel like bystanders in the duel for power between the other two monotheistic religions. This last feeling is prominent in Halevi's poetry.

The back-and-forth fortunes of Christians and Muslims in Iberia made it hard for Jews to assess where they would be best off. Some have even maintained that it was the deterioration of the status of the Jews in Halevi's time that led him to believe that the best course was to head for their original homeland, which, though not particularly hospitable or even safe, was at least, in some sense, the Jews' natural place. But it is hard to imagine that Halevi thought of his pilgrimage as a practical course that would enhance his people's immediate physical security.

Religious and Cultural Competition

The Jews' inferiority weighed on them for religious reasons as well. They believed themselves to be the recipients of divine revelation and partners in a covenant with God, yet found themselves subjugated to Muslims in one part of the world and Christians in another, two competing religions that also claimed to be the sole bearers of divine truth. In the quarrel between Judaism and the two rival monotheistic religions, world history mattered religiously, for the political reality of Israel's subordinate status seemed to confirm the rivals' claim that Israel had been superseded as the sole bearers of the divine word. This claim was demoralizing for Jews, even in the absence of active persecution.

Jewish writers compensated by claiming superiority. Jews, they said, were the originators of the sciences and the founders of philosophical schools; their language was the source of all other languages. Halevi went even further in the Kuzari, claiming that that the Jews' unique talent for prophecy sets them apart from and above all mankind in the hierarchy of earthly creatures. The theme of competition with the other monotheistic religions abounds in Halevi's liturgical poetry. In a poem on God's love for Israel, he describes the competition between Israel and the nations of the world as embodying the kind of tension that might exist in a harem, in which wives quarrel over their status in the eyes of the husband.[3] In a poem on the Sabbath, he mocks the pretenses of Christians and Muslims for their claim of having their own divinely ordained day of rest:[4]

They compare—it's just lip service!—
their day to my holy day.
Christians push it up to Sunday,
Muslims put it back to Friday.
How can Arab and Christian lies
fool the folk who have the truth?

The competition theme even occurs in a personal poem, along with a hint that in a part of Halevi's soul he was capable of admiring Islamic piety. We are to imagine him waking at the call of the muezzin and reproaching himself for sleeping so late:[5]

Lazy Levite! Aren't you ashamed
to be asleep and silent, though it's morning?
Listen to the Gentiles calling,
worshiping the Lord with all their hearts.
They do not know Him, yet they worship—
how can Jews, who really know Him, be so heedless?
How can you sleep? Up!
See those strangers steadfast on their watch,
while you lie dreaming!

This defensiveness is evident in the Kuzari's promoting of Jewish intellectual attainments and religious institutions at the expense of those of Christianity and Islam. It is evident in the pilgrimage as well, which represented in part a rejection of the Andalusi Jewish courtiers' admiration for and engagement in Arabo-Islamic culture.[6]

The feature of Judeo-Arabic culture at its height that makes it so attractive to us moderns is the extent to which Jews were acculturated to Arabo-Islamic ways. It is natural for us to applaud both the relative openness of Islamic society in this period and the Jews' adaptability, which together permitted them to function smoothly as a part of that society. But from the perspective of many a medieval observer, Jews who spoke Arabic, resembled Muslims in most respects, aspired to the same kinds of success as did Muslims, and circulated easily among Muslims—whose very Jewish practices were Arabized—were all too susceptible to slipping into apostasy.

Jewish participation in the common intellectual life was particularly risky for the community because it offered an intellectual basis for assimilation. Philosophers of the three religions were more or less in agreement that the truth about God, man, and the universe was taught by the ancient Greek sages, and that the prevailing religions were merely fables designed for the establishment and maintenance of social order among the uneducated and uneducable masses.[7] To the philosophers, it hardly mattered whether a person was a Muslim, Christian, or Jew, or, for that matter, whether he made up his own religion, if he could persuade enough people to follow him so that a stable society would result. We moderns find this relativism and the concomitant tolerance of members of minority groups most congenial.

Muslim religious leaders had no tolerance for philosophical discussions in which Islam was merely one system among many; for them, it was only a question of heresy versus true religion. Jewish religious leaders had a more concrete social problem to worry about, because philosophical relativism could loosen ties to the Jewish tradition and entail the erosion of the Jewish leadership class. The king in the Kuzari points out how easy apostasy was for the Jews and that only a single sentence—the declaration of faith in God and the authenticity of Muhammad's prophetic mission—stood between them and complete acceptance. Indeed, opportunistic conversion to Islam was not uncommon among intellectuals in this period.[8]

As against his coreligionists' reflexive admiration for Arabic culture, Halevi elaborated both a theory of the superiority of Jewish religious and cultural institutions and a critique of philosophy. Yet even he could not escape the Judeo-Arabic culture that had nourished him. We have seen in chapter 1 how the very act of repentance that culminated in his pilgrimage was consistent with a pattern of life and literature that prevailed in his Arabo-Islamic world. We may observe a similar inconsistency in his changing attitude toward poetry.

The adoption of Arabic verse forms by Hebrew poets in the tenth century had been one of the most productive developments in premodern Jewish literary history, and Halevi was one of the greatest masters of their use in Hebrew. He nevertheless included in the Kuzari a critique of the use of Arabic prosody in Hebrew on grammatical and ideological grounds, and he laments that Jewish poets had chosen this alien form in favor of the native prosodic tradition found in the Bible.[9]

But Halevi never stopped writing Hebrew poetry in quantitative meters. He even wrote a two-page guide to Hebrew metrics in which he provided verses of his own composition as models of the Arabic meters that work well in Hebrew. The treatise includes a summary of the grammatical objections to the use of Arabic metrics in Hebrew that he raised in the Kuzari and concludes with a liturgical formula begging forgiveness for sins. But since his purpose in writing the treatise (as he explicitly says) is to show which quantitative meters work well and sound beautiful in Hebrew, the treatise cannot be considered the major cultural critique that it is sometimes made out to be. Halevi did experiment with verse forms not derived from Arabic, but there is no certainty that he did so because of his belated objections to Arabic verse forms. What Halevi never did—as far as we know—was to write Hebrew verse using the biblical verse forms that he promoted in the Kuzari as the only ones suitable for Hebrew.[10]

Halevi is traditionally alleged to have vowed to stop writing Hebrew poetry altogether. This tradition derives from a statement by Solomon Ibn Parḥon, a younger contemporary of Halevi's, in his Hebrew lexicon. Ibn Parḥon recapitulates the Kuzari's grammatical critique of the effect of Arabic metrics on Hebrew. He cites Halevi as his authority and climaxes with the statement that Halevi gave up poetry as an act of repentance (*teshuva,* the equivalent of Arabic *tawba,* not a vow) before his death. But Ibn Parḥon's statement is manifestly false; in our account of the pilgrimage in part II of this book, we shall see him writing poetry throughout the last year of his life, even on the deck of the ship that carried him on its last stage a month or two before his death. In Ibn Parḥon's eagerness to reinforce his point about the problematic status of Arabic metrics in Hebrew, he must have assimilated Halevi to the familiar Islamic topos of the poet who gives up poetry as a late-life act of *tawba.*[11]

Halevi frequently speaks in his pilgrimage poetry of having made a vow, but with one exception, this vow always refers to the pilgrimage itself. That exception occurs in his ode and epistle to Nathan the Associate in Cairo, both of which will be reproduced and discussed in chapter 5. In the ode, Halevi says that he has sworn off not metrical poetry, but panegyric poetry, which now seems to him to be inconsistent with his determination to stop being a servant of men and to serve God alone. In the epistle, he describes himself as having come to see poetry as an activity suitable only for the young, as something inappropriate for one who has reached the time in life when one's thoughts should be devoted to repentance alone. Again, not nationalism but the sobriety associated with late-life repentance is the motivation.

Halevi's remarks on poetry in his correspondence with Nathan remove the subject from the sphere of cultural protest and return us to the theme of midlife repentance. For poets in the Islamic world frequently turned against poetry in old age or were said to have turned against it. This trend is a poet-specific variation on the standard theme of *tawba* in the Muslim biographies. Despite the enormous popularity of poetry in the Arabic-speaking world, a streak of ambivalence, even of negativity, toward it was always present in Islamic civilization. Preachers objected to poetry on the grounds of its sensuality, its association with wine drinking, and the whole network of worldly life that surrounded it as a phenomenon of court culture.[12] We are constantly reading of poets who performed dramatic acts of *tawba* by destroying their works or swearing off poetry, and of poetry collectors who destroyed their collections. An early connoisseur of poetry burns his houseful of notes on the language and poetry of the pre-Islamic age. An early poet and critic vows to stop composing poetry, and then recants. A prominent court poet on his deathbed asks to have his lampooning poetry burned. Yet another court poet throws notebooks of his verses into the river. An Andalusi poet swears off poetry, backslides into it, and quickly resolves to do penance by going on jihad. Writers of secular strophic poetry compose penitential poems to atone for earlier secular poems.[13]

What these examples show is that even if Halevi intended his occasional disparagement of poetry as part of a cultural critique directed against the Judeo-Arabic synthesis, the very fact of his turning against it shows him to be a true son of that synthesis.[14] In his conscious life, Halevi may well have blamed himself for his past devotion to philosophy and poetry and criticized his friends for not seeing what was wrong with these things. But this social and cultural critique cannot provide a complete description of his mentality and certainly not a complete explanation for the pilgrimage.

Messianism

All medieval Hebrew poets wrote extensively of Israel's suffering in exile and longing for redemption, and many wrote passionate prayers for the coming of the messianic era. The uncertainties of the times, discomfort over the Jews' subordinate status, and dissatisfaction with the synthesis that permitted the smug elite class to enjoy it were processed by Halevi's literary imagination and verbal genius into messianic poetry more powerful than that of any of his predecessors in the genre. Much of his work in this vein is sufficiently vivid to suggest that at some point in the course of his career, he was convinced by calculations that placed the messianic redemption in his own lifetime or that he placed serious hope in one of the messianic movements or messianic pretenders of those decades.[15]

Halevi himself sometimes speaks in the voice of the Messiah, summoning his people to abandon their homes and return to the Holy Land, as had so many false messiahs in the past and as so many would in the future. The summoning voice is particularly prominent in a poem that begins with these lines:[16]

O doves who dwell apart from men
in a land of steppe and ruin,
rise! For this is not your resting place
while your homeland lies abandoned.
Return to your delightful home,
to Ḥamat and Yanoḥa.
May God grant that you find rest.

This summoning voice led some readers to suppose that in the poems in which it occurs, the historical Judah Halevi was summoning the Jews of his time and place to take the problem of exile into their own hands by going to the Land of Israel and thereby bringing about the redemption through their own efforts. This reading implies that Halevi believed that the Jews actually had it in their power to go to the Land of Israel en masse and thereby force the coming of the Messiah, that it was their duty to do so, and that in making his own pilgrimage, Halevi was setting an example that he intended others to emulate.[17]

In evaluating this reading, we must first recall that Halevi was not the first Hebrew poet to write poetry that imagined the redemption as already under way. The genre was pioneered, like so many others, by Solomon Ibn Gabirol (ca. 1021–1058), who lived in the early *taifa* period before the Almoravid takeover, before the Crusades, before the persecutions in Toledo, and before the rise of the Almohads; when Jewish life was undisturbed and a Jewish vizier stood close to the top leadership of Granada, one of the more powerful states of the Iberian Peninsula of the time. Yet he, too, indulged in writing fantasy poems of the onset of the messianic era, such as these lines, addressed to the Messiah:[18]

Draw your sword, my love radiant and ruddy;
make my enemies a footstool for my feet
Night has passed, day has come;
Rise! Mount! Ride! Do not go on sleeping!

Or these, addressed by the Messiah to the Jewish people:[19]

Return, O girl, to the Holy Land.
I am gathering your scattered folk
in song and joy,
rebuilding your Temple,
with turquoise stones,
bringing news of consolation
to the ruined one.

From Ḥabor and Ḥalaḥ
I will assemble them—

scattered from their nest,
torn by passersby.
Your Messiah has come
to the tower of your rest.

Or these, also addressed by the Messiah to the Jewish people:[20]

O you who dwell in the fields among the tents of Ishmael—
stand on top of Carmel, look out on Bashán.
Gaze, O bride, at your ruined garden,
observe how your furrow has put forth lilies.

Admittedly, Halevi's poems take this messianic fantasy to a higher degree of intensity, and his summoning voice is more exigent. But most of Halevi's more extreme poems of messianic fantasy cannot be taken as manifestos for a program for imminent redemption, since every such fantasy is disavowed by the context. The quotations that appear to express a messianic program are only snippets taken out of whole poems. The messianic fantasy is momentarily so vivid that we readers almost imagine ourselves about to depart for the Holy Land ourselves; but within a few lines, the tone of summons abates, and the poem ends merely with the lame hope that the vision will someday become a reality. Students of poetry, who have been trained to attend not only to the individual line but to the structure of a poem as a whole and who are used to thinking of a poem as an integrated literary unit making a unified statement rather than as a congeries of individual lines, will not be misled by such moments; we will ask, rather, what the effect of the buildup of intensity in the beginning is on the poem's anticlimactic ending.[21]

Thus the poem "O Doves Who Dwell Apart," quoted above, follows up its passionate summons to return to Ḥamat and Yanoḥa with a conditional clause in the third strophe that bursts the fantasy bubble of the first:[22]

If only I had the wings of a dove!
I'd fly and alight,
abandon south and the north
aspiring for Zion.
In the end God would establish
seven kings, eight shepherds, as at first,
and against the oppressor's sword,
unsheathe a sword, a sword!

The nation—which is the real speaker in these lines, not Judah Halevi the historical person—is only metaphorically a dove. It does not have wings, cannot fly upward to redemption, can do no better than "tread the heights of hope" (line 13), an earthbound attainment at best.

As for the conclusion of the Kuzari, which is also sometimes cited as evidence for Halevi's messianic summons: while the book ends—as do so many traditional Jewish books—with thoughts of national redemption, nowhere does the book proclaim that the messianic era is at hand, nowhere in the book does Halevi issue a call for a return to Zion, and nowhere in the book does Halevi have his rabbi recommend that the king of the Khazars abandon his kingdom and depart with him for the Land of Israel. The end of the Kuzari does look forward to the ultimate redemption but not as an immediate expectation and certainly not as a call to action. (The relevant passages in the Kuzari will be examined more closely and these assertions defended in chapter 7.) Since the last part of the Kuzari was probably written shortly before Halevi's departure for the Land of Israel, its avoidance of the summons probably reflects Halevi's final thoughts on the subject.

Nor is the messianic summons at all present in Halevi's pilgrimage poetry, which would be a remarkable omission if the summons theory were correct. Its absence from his pilgrimage poetry suggests that any thoughts that he might have had for an imminent redemption and any messianic enthusiasm that he may have experienced at an earlier stage were depleted by the time of his pilgrimage. It is likely that at one point in his life, Halevi was swept up by messianic enthusiasm. At least two messianic movements occurred in al-Andalus in Halevi's lifetime; the leader of one, Moses Darʿi (mid-1120s), was a disciple of Joseph Ibn Megas and could well have been personally known to Halevi. Perhaps enthusiasm for this or some other such movement is reflected in the intensity of Halevi's redemption poetry, especially in the special glow lent to his few poems that contain the summons motif. But as computed dates came and went, as one by one messianic pretenders failed in their missions, Halevi must have become disenchanted with calculations and pretenders alike. The following passage seems to document a specific disappointment of this kind:[23]

O God, grant Your pleasure's bounty to a hoping folk and me,
on the day my children, nursed on misery, come to plead with You,
for all my redeemers have failed. And so I come before You saying,
"If but my way were clear before the Lord,
that He might see how my redeemers failed."

Such a disappointment could have been the impetus for a late-life inward turn in Halevi's religious yearning, leading him to seek a more personal solution to the religious problems of the age and his religious yearnings. In any case, the pilgrimage poetry proves that if Halevi had ever entertained notions that the messianic era was at hand, if he was ever swayed by a calculation or a pretender, any thoughts of rallying the Jewish people to take their fate into their own hands had already passed by the time he came to write his pilgrimage poetry.[24]

We might go so far as to say that Halevi's pilgrimage bespoke a definitive embrace of quietism on the national level, signifying that he had despaired of all attempts to force a resolution to the Jewish problem. The people either can-

(*Commentary continues on the next page*)

5

הֵיכַל אֲדֹנָי וּמִקְדַּשׁ הֲדֹמוֹ--
גָּלָה כְבוֹדוֹ וְנִפְזַר עַמּוֹ,
וּמִמֶּרְחַקִּים יִדְרְשׁוּ שְׁלוֹמוֹ,
וְיִשְׁתַּחֲווּ לוֹ אִישׁ מִמְּקוֹמוֹ.

גּוֹלִים בְּמַעֲרָב בְּכוּשׁ וּמִצְרָיִם
מְגַמַּת פְּנֵיהֶם יְרוּשָׁלָיִם
אֶל אֲבִיהֶם אֲשֶׁר בַּשָּׁמָיִם,
לַעֲמוֹד לְשָׁרְתוֹ וּלְבָרֵךְ בִּשְׁמוֹ.

אוֹבֵד בְּעֵילָם וְנִדָּח בְּשִׁנְעָר
לְדֶרֶךְ אַרְצוֹ פִּיהוּ יִפְעַר
מִבֵּין שְׁנֵי זְאֵבֵי יָעַר,
וּמִתּוֹךְ צַעַר יַחֲזִיק בְּתֻמּוֹ.

גָּלוּת צִיּוֹן אֲשֶׁר בִּסְפָרַד
בַּעֲרָב מְפֻזָּר וּבֶאֱדוֹם מְפֹרָד
לִפְאַת מִקְדָּשׁ יִתַּר וְיֶחֱרַד.
לְבָבוֹ כְּגָמוּל עֲלֵי אִמּוֹ.

שָׁפַךְ תְּפִלָּה וְצוּר מִתְעַלֵּם,
וְשָׁמַע חֲרָפוֹת וַיְהִי כְאִלֵּם.
בְּשׁוּב שְׁבוּת צִיּוֹן הָיָה כְחוֹלֵם,
וּבַהֲקִיצוֹ אֵין פּוֹתֵר חֲלוֹמוֹ.

מָתַי אֶקְרָא וְאַתָּה תִרְצֶה,
וְאֶת מִשְׁפָּטִי לָאוֹר תּוֹצֵא,
וְיִוָּדַע יוֹם תַּצִּיל וְתִפְצֶה:
אֱמֶת כִּי רוֹצֶה אֲדֹנָי בְּעַמּוֹ!

not bring an end to the exile or, as he hints in the Kuzari, lack the passionate desire and strength of will to do so. The best thing to do is to wait for God to settle matters in His own time. Not only is this the prevailing message of Halevi's poetry on the theme of redemption, but it is a message very much in harmony with the themes of trust in God and acceptance of His will that are so prominent in Halevi's personal religious poetry. If Halevi preferred to spend the time waiting in the Land of Israel, that was a consequence of his own particular religious orientation, as we shall encounter it in chapter 7, and of the heightened inwardness in evidence throughout his pilgrimage poetry.

5

The palace of God and the Temple, His footstool—
gone is its glory, its people are scattered.
Yet from afar they all send their greetings,
bowing toward it, each man from his place.

Exiles in Egypt, Morocco, and Yemen—
all keep their faces turned toward Zion,
facing their Father far off in His heaven,
standing and serving, blessing His Name.

Lost in Persia, in Babylon straying—
all yearn to find their way to God's land,
to escape the fangs of the wolves of the forest.
Yet in their sorrow, they hold to their faith.

The remnant of Zion residing in Spain
here among Arabs, there among Christians—
trembling, ready to leap toward the Temple,
yet trusting and calm, like a child at the breast.

They pour out their prayers, but God does not listen.
They put up with insults, but never complain,
dream of themselves returning to Zion;
waken—but none can interpret their dream.

When will I call, when will You answer,
when will You demand justice for me?
When comes the day when You will redeem us,
when all will know that God loves His people?

This poem transfers to the national level the anxiety of direction that Halevi developed so subtly in "Where Can I Find You, Lord?" (poem 2). But here, there is no ambiguity about where God is to be found. God is to be found far away: in the Land of Israel, where the Temple lies in ruins, and in heaven, aloof from His people's prayers. Scattered in exile and politically helpless, the Jewish people are limited to futile gestures of reverence, each immobilized in an isolated community.

For four strophes, Halevi enumerates these exiled communities, and in the fifth he dreams, or rather, he describes Israel's collective dream. Meditating by day on the theme of redemption, at night the personified nation dreams the biblical verse "When God restored the exile of Zion, we were like dreamers" (Ps. 126:1). The poem's redemption is a dream of a dream; there is no one to interpret it, no one to assure the people upon waking that the redemption is actually imminent.

A dream's interpretation was considered just as important as, and perhaps more important than, the dream itself, for, according to rabbinic tradition, "the dream follows the mouth," that is, a dream takes effect not in accordance with its actual content but in accordance with the meaning attributed to it.[25] We find the idea in love poetry, as in the following delicious epigram by Halevi:[26]

Wake up, lover, from your sleeping,
let me see your face in waking.

(*Commentary continues on the next page*)

6

יוֹנַת רְחוֹקִים, נַגְּנִי הֵיטִיבִי,
וּלְקוֹרְאֵךְ טוּב טַעֲמֵךְ הָשִׁיבִי!
הִנֵּה אֱלֹהַיִךְ קְרָאָךְ. מַהֲרִי,
הִשְׁתַּחֲוִי אֶרֶץ וְשַׁי הַקְרִיבִי,
וּפְנִי אֱלֵי קִנֵּךְ לְדֶרֶךְ אָהֳלֵךְ,
צִיּוֹן, וְצִיּוּן בַּעֲדֵךְ הַצִּיבִי.
דּוֹדֵךְ אֲשֶׁר הֶגְלֵךְ לְרֹעַ פָּעֳלֵךְ
הוּא גוֹאֲלֵךְ הַיּוֹם, וּמַה-תָּרִיבִי?
הִתְיַצְּבִי לָשׁוּב לְאֶרֶץ הַצְּבִי,
וּשְׂדֵה אֱדוֹם וּשְׂדֵה עֲרָב הַכְאִיבִי.
בֵּית מַחֲרִיבַיִךְ בְּאַף הַחֲרִיבִי,
וּלְאוֹהֲבֵךְ בֵּית אַהֲבָה הַרְחִיבִי.

Did you dream that we were kissing?
I can tell you what that dream meant!

In the epigram, to interpret the dream is to fulfill its promise of a kiss. In "The Palace of God," Israel awakes to find herself unkissed, unredeemed.

This poem bespeaks the anxiety of distance from God that seems typical of Halevi's pre-pilgrimage period as well as a powerful sensitivity to the plight of the Jewish people, but it does not yet display a Halevi who is thinking of pilgrimage. Intense the poem surely is: its central image of Jews converging upon the Land of Israel from the four corners of the earth *without taking a step* anticipates the greetings from the four corners of the earth that Halevi would develop in his great Ode to Jerusalem (poem 16). But unlike the Ode, with its fantasy of traversing specific holy sites in the Land of Israel, "The Palace of God" does not dream about the topography of the Land of Israel, and it contrasts strongly with the Ode's personal character and intimate tone, being focused on the nation and the national problem. It certainly does not offer the slightest hint that the redemption is imminent or that it is the job of the people to bring it about. It represents a stage in Halevi's development when the content of his poems on Israel's plight and thoughts of redemption were identical with those of his fellow poets, when the idea of actually going to the Land of Israel had not yet taken shape in his mind.[27]

6

Distant dove, sing your song well,
and give good answer to Him who calls you.
Your God it is Who calls, so hurry,
bow low to the ground, and make your offering.
Back to your nest! Retrace your steps
to Zion, where your tent awaits you;
set clear way-posts along the road.

Your lover turned you out because you sinned—
today He redeems you! Why do you complain?
Arise, return to the Lovely Land.
Ruin the fields of Edomite and Arab!
Destroy the home of your destroyers,
but make your love a wide and loving home.

No medieval Hebrew poet used the image of the dove or of birds in general with such frequency or in such varied ways as did Judah Halevi. Birds figure often in his poetry as images of the people Israel and of the soul; they also figure in his pilgrimage poetry.[28] These avian images originate, for the most part, not in nature but in the Bible or in the Arabic literary tradition. The dove of the distance in our poem's first line comes from the mysterious heading of Psalm 56, which might be translated: "For the leader, on the dove of silence of distance." We do not know what the author of the psalm had in mind when he wrote these words, but to Halevi, who referred to them frequently, the combination of the dove with "silence" and "distance" meant Israel in exile, silent in the face of her persecutors and mockers, distant from her homeland.[29]

In this poem, Israel and God play their accustomed roles in liturgical poetry. Israel, the dove, is singing a complaint, as doves traditionally do in secular love poetry.[30] The speaker urges her to change her tune to joy, for the moment of redemption is at hand; it is time for the dove to return to its nest

(*Commentary continues on the next page*)

7

מֵאָז מְעוֹן הָאַהֲבָה הָיִיתָ--
חָנוּ אֲהָבַי בַּאֲשֶׁר חָנִיתָ.
תּוֹכְחוֹת מְרִיבַי עָרְבוּ לִי עַל שִׁמְךָ;
עֲזָבֵם--יְעַנּוּ אֶת אֲשֶׁר עִנִּיתָ.
לָמְדוּ חֲרוֹנְךָ אוֹיְבַי, וָאֹהֲבֵם,
כִּי רָדְפוּ חָלָל אֲשֶׁר הִכִּיתָ.
מִיּוֹם בְּזִיתַנִי בְּזִיתִנִי אֲנִי,
כִּי לֹא אֲכַבֵּד אֶת אֲשֶׁר בָּזִיתָ.
עַד יַעֲבֹר זַעַם וְתִשְׁלַח עוֹד פְּדוּת
אֶל-נַחֲלָתְךָ זֹאת אֲשֶׁר פָּדִיתָ.

---

in Jerusalem, like the dove in Ps. 84:4, which nests so gladly on the altar in the Temple.

The speaker in this poem speaks in the imperative mood; the voice is the longed-for voice of Elijah or of the Messiah declaring an end to Israel's exile. The poem provides the auditor with a moment of fantasy; it urges him to imagine vividly that the moment of redemption has come and to meditate how that moment might feel. The purpose of such an exercise was consolatory. Through the intensive application of imagination, preachers and poets tried to help the members of their communities to keep hope alive.

The message is delivered so directly and the poem's commanding voice is so exigent that it is tempting to interpret it as an actual messianic summons by which Halevi urged his fellow Jews to set sail for Palestine in order to force the messianic redemption. If that is the case, Halevi must have given up this kind of thinking before he left al-Andalus, for the theme is completely absent from his pilgrimage poetry.

7

From time's beginning, You were love's abode:
my love encamped wherever it was You tented.
The taunts of foes for Your Name's sake are sweet,
so let them torture one whom You tormented.
I love my foes, for they learned wrath from You,
for they pursue a body You have slain.
The day You hated me I loathed myself,
for I will honor none whom You disdain.
Until Your anger pass, and You restore
this people whom You rescued once before.

Halevi knew Arabic love poetry well and even translated a few Arabic love poems into Hebrew; he was himself a prolific author of secular love poetry in Hebrew. The first four verses of this poem read like a secular love poem in which the lover boasts of his submissiveness to his beloved. But the fifth verse, with its promise of a future redemption and its allusion to an earlier one, turns the poem away from the torments of secular love to the problem of the Jewish people among the nations.

The enemies turn out, in retrospect, not to be the conventional lovers' enemies of love poetry—persons who have been spying on the lovers or trying to talk the lover out of his obsession—but the nations of the world that subjugate Israel and punish her for her loyalty to her own religion. The beloved turns out not to be a girl who torments the speaker by refusing to yield to him, but God, who has His own reasons for punishing His people through exile. The lover speaks with equanimity: not only does he endure his suffering gladly; he has adopted the beloved's own attitude of contempt toward himself. This is the true measure of a lover: to love what the beloved loves and to despise what the beloved despises. Such sentiments are commonplace in Arabic love poetry; by applying them to exiled Israel, Halevi has captured an aspect of a subjugated nation's psyche in a way that no other medieval Hebrew poet even attempted to do.[31]

As was pointed out by a medieval copyist, the first four verses of this poem actually *are* a secular love poem, a four-verse love poem by an Abbasid court poet of the early ninth century.[32] But the secular Arabic poem had an afterlife in Islam as a religious poem, for it was adopted by a Sufi master to illustrate the principle of love of God. Asked by a disciple, "What does it mean to love God?" the master replied by asking, "What was the song you were singing last night?" The disciple repeated the four verses, and when he finished, the master commented: "To love God is to love what He loves and to hate what He hates—even yourself." Halevi could have known the poem from his general familiarity with Arabic poetry, the familiarity of a man of letters. But more intriguing is the possibility that he knew it from his reading of Sufi writings, that it was the teaching of the Sufi master that gave Halevi the idea of adapting the Arabic poem to the use of the Jewish liturgy. That such were the channels is suggested by the fact that the poem was also used by an Andalusi Sufi, a contemporary of Halevi, in his own discussion of love of God; it is entirely possible that his book gave Halevi the idea of using the poem for religious purposes.[33]

The Muslim teacher converted the poem from secular to sacred; Halevi converted the Muslim (now-)sacred poem into a Jewish one, while shifting the point of view from that of an individual to that of the Jewish community. But the underlying religious attitude in Halevi's version derives from the Muslim mystic's interpretation of the poem as exemplifying the acceptance of God's will to the point of adopting God's point of view vis-à-vis one's self. Halevi's most elaborate expression of this ideal on a personal level is in "O Lord, All My Desire Is Plain to Thee" (poem 1); the present poem is an extreme expression of the ideal on the national level. The right attitude of Israel toward her exile is the same as the right attitude of an individual toward God: identification with God's will, passive acceptance of His decree—*tawakkul* leading to *riḍā*. Halevi's application of these themes to the national plight is also evident in the Kuzari.[34]

When raised to the national level, the demand of *tawakkul* is that Israel accept exile as God's will and await the redemption passively, contrary to the messianic summons in the preceding poem. Perhaps this theme rose to prominence in Halevi's thinking as a result of the failure of various messianic movements; or perhaps it is simply a spiritualizing of the quietism that was the dominant position of rabbinic Jewry throughout the Middle Ages.

3

The Visionary

Visual experiences are a prominent feature of Halevi's poetry. True, we cannot expect any medieval Hebrew poet to describe things from nature, for literary conventions and the self-imposed limitation of their language to biblical Hebrew ensured that all of their descriptions would be stylized. Yet within the latitude that medieval poets permitted themselves, Halevi tends to speak of abstractions and imagined things as if they were visible and to concretize the objects of religious longing in visual images. The examples that we shall see in this chapter strongly prefigure the kind of writing that we will encounter in some of the pilgrimage poems.

An example of the tendency to give visual form to abstractions is found in an unusual ballad-like passage within an otherwise conventional penitential poem in which Halevi describes a nocturnal encounter with his own sins:[1]

I saw my sins in a dream
and I said, "Have you come
in a dream to lie with me?"
I cried aloud:
"You have laid siege to me,
bound me, limbs and guts
from head to foot!
What a high mountain you are!"
Sages explained the dream.

They said, "All is well.
Only come forward and say,
like Cain to God, 'My sin is great.' "

Using phrases taken from the stories of the encounter of Joseph with Potiphar's wife and of Samson with Delilah, Halevi imagines his sins confronting him in the form of a voluptuous woman who binds him helpless to the bed, a concretization of conscience in the form of a dream vision. Noteworthy, too, is the dreamer's consultation with an interpreter upon awaking, a feature of dream poems that we have encountered in a poem on the national redemption and that we shall encounter again in this chapter.[2]

In Halevi's work, as in both the rabbinic and the philosophical tradition, dreams are a lesser form of prophecy.[3] The dreams in his poetry are not idle fancies but are of the essence of his religious orientation, part and parcel of his penchant for direct, visible, and tangible contact with the divine world and word.

A dream sets the entire book of the Kuzari in motion, when the Khazar king is roused to seek the true religion by means of a dream. The rabbi whom the king eventually consults demonstrates to him that the criterion of the true religion is revelation. Halevi teaches that the Jews have a succession of prophets and an irrefutable tradition that the entire folk witnessed the revelation at Mount Sinai. The Jewish people, he maintains, are heirs to a faculty for prophecy that distinguishes them from humanity in general in the way that humanity is distinguished from the lower orders. Prophecy occurs only when divine light falls upon the divine nation in (or about) the divine land; it comes only to a descendant of Jacob of perfect piety, in the Land of Israel. Prophecy was suspended when the Jewish people went into exile, but it will be restored at the time of their ultimate restoration, not only for individuals but for the entire redeemed folk, as the prophet says: "For they will behold eye to eye when the Lord returns to Zion" (Isa. 52:8, quoted in Kuzari 5:23). The entire course of the discussion of the Kuzari makes it clear that the prophet represents the religious ideal and that prophecy is the ideal religious experience, the goal to which religion ultimately strives.

In the absence of full-fledged prophecy, minor forms of revelation such as dreams are to be taken very seriously. They are not necessarily random events but can be generated by spiritual exercises. In the Kuzari, Halevi recommends the use of the imagination as part of religious discipline; specifically, he recommends meditating on the revelation at Sinai, the binding of Isaac, the tabernacle erected by Moses in the wilderness, the Temple service, and the divine presence (*Shekhina*) resting on the Temple.[4] In some of Halevi's poems, these subjects are dealt with not merely as traditional themes of liturgical poetry but as dream visions, suggesting that the nocturnal vision was an outcome of daytime meditation.

Thus, in a liturgical poem describing a dream vision, Halevi envisions himself standing at Sinai as the glory of the Lord descends upon him, as it descended upon Moses:[5]

My heart beheld You and was sure of You
as if I stood myself at Sinai mountain.
I sought You in my dreams; Your glory passed
before my face on clouds descending, landing.

In "O God, the Joy of Being near You!" (poem 12), which we will soon be reading, Halevi envisions himself observing and participating in the Temple service.

But even in poems that do not mention dreams, Halevi treats biblical scenes suitable for meditation with the peculiar vividness that is his signature. In the following poem, he describes an ordinary congregation at worship as if it were in the midst of a theophany. In reading this poem, remember that it is not a freestanding poem meant to be read in private from a book but is a liturgical poem designed to be recited in the synagogue by the precentor as the introduction to a public religious service:[6]

The spheres of heaven once beheld
Your glory and were terrified;
the Red Sea's waves fell silent,
torn in two, when You went forth.
How then can men withstand Your presence,
You who dwell in boulder-melting flames?
And yet, they have the strength, if You will grant it,
to join the angels who behold and serve.
And so all souls sing praises to You ever,
O God, to Whom all praise and song is due.

Many poems confirm that Halevi, in the maturity of his religious life, aspired to, or at least focused his religious attention on, the vision of God such as the prophets of Israel beheld, as described in the Bible. In yet another poem referring to Moses by the epithet "one of His household" (derived from Num. 12:7), he expatiates on the experience of this man whom "God knew face-to-face" (Deut. 34:11):[7]

When He was pleased
with one of His household
He set His Presence

in His tent,
where there were mirrors
for prophecies,
by which His image could be seen.
No shape or dimension—
unbounded His essence—
only His appearance
in the eyes of His prophets,
like a king high and exalted.

An earlier passage in the same poem seems to say that the speaker himself has had a visual encounter with God—if not an actual vision of His face, at least a visual experience of His light:[8]

I sought Him, encountered Him—
a tower of strength, a rock of protection,
bright as shining light—
without mask, without cover.

But that the divine presence has a corporeal nature that can be seen—that, indeed, has been seen by the prophets and patriarchs of Israel—is a point firmly made in the Kuzari.[9] Halevi's poetry, too, is suffused with the aspiration for a vision of the divine presence, the divine light, or the divine command.

Some of this poetry carries on the literary tradition of the *merkava* texts, ancient writings that describe the angels praising God in His presence. The religious experience of imagining one's self in the company of the angels and participating in their worship underlies important parts of the Jewish liturgy. What stands out in Halevi is not the raw fact that he wrote poems in this tradition, for it was customary to embellish those parts of the liturgy with poems in the *merkava* spirit; we saw an example in "Where Can I Find You, Lord?" (poem 2). But in the following selection, he turns a rather stylized genre, in which the people Israel are normally depicted as collectively praising God in tandem with the angels, into an evocation of individuals who have been blessed with the privilege of standing in the divine presence:[10]

He has created prophesying souls
summoned to come before Him,
and given them the strength to encounter
the awful vision.
They behold His royal train
and walk among His angels.
They pour His generous spirit

over those who are true to His covenant
For they draw rivers of prophecy
from the sources of His wisdom;
for they are familiar with mysteries and prophecy,
both in dreams and visions.
In quest of the face of the King
they crowd around the gate of their Lord.

Halevi, like his predecessors, often speaks of seeing God with the eye of the heart or of the intellect. This ancient expression was used metaphorically, sometimes meaning to grasp the existence and wisdom of God intellectually through the study of His Creations, and sometimes to represent the soul's ascent from the contemplation of individual things by means of the senses to the contemplation of universals:[11]

Behold the splendor of His works
with the eye of your heart
in the sight of the sky and inside yourself,
and you will see the image of your Lord's glory.

Here, the language of vision is probably being used metaphorically. When Halevi is thinking in this philosophical vein, he is capable of denying man's ability to see God literally:[12]

When my love calls You,
my heart and my insides find You;
but my thoughts do not carry You,
nor do my dreams and imaginations conceive You.

It is natural to suppose that when Halevi uses the expression to refer to these intellectual means of apprehending God, he is following the inherited philosophical traditions and has not yet come into his own, more literal, conception of the meaning of this figure. Yet the longing for a divine vision is ever present:[13]

The soul of Your handmaid's son
sought to behold You,
and though it did not see You,
it saw something other than You:
Indeed, I see You in your miracles and signs.

In other words, God may not be literally accessible to sight, but the contemplation of His miracles—the wonders of His Creation—gives us something "other than" God that brings us as close to the vision of God as is possible for humans.[14]

One of God's signs that is particularly effective in bringing about this metaphorical vision of God and particularly accessible to human contemplation is the human soul itself, which, with its rational faculty, is a spark of the divine present in the world:[15]

The eye yearns to see Him,
but He is revealed by my flesh to my heart:
I see the Lord in my body.

The last line quoted is an allusion, typical for poets of Halevi's background, to Job 19:26, "From my flesh I shall see God." For philosophically inclined readers, this verse was understood to allude to the idea of the microcosm. The soul is an image of God; therefore, knowing God necessitates the study of one's own soul. The verse was thus understood as the Jewish equivalent of the Delphic maxim in the form: "Know thyself and thou wilt know thy Lord."[16]

But in the Kuzari and in some of his poetry, Halevi also uses the expression "eye of the heart" to signify not the inference of God's existence from His miraculous works in the world, and not the disembodied bliss of union aspired to by the philosophers but the visual experience of God as "a real objective entity, spiritual in nature . . . a spiritual form that in the prophetic state becomes tangible."[17] In such cases, the seeing is meant not metaphorically but literally, except that the seeing is not of a material object with the material eye but of a spiritual object with the inner eye. We have already observed Halevi toying with this notion in "Where Can I Find You, Lord?" (poem 2). He must have a similar experience in mind when he describes God's true devotees by saying:[18]

They could not see His light with their eyes, but searched
their hearts and saw His glory and were terrified.

Or:[19]

Pure souls have seen You,
but have no need for luminaries;
they heard You with the ears of their thoughts,
though their ears are deaf.

God is accessible to the elect through the inner sense of sight and sound.

The theme of the vision of God is particularly prominent when Halevi touches on the ultimate redemption. In one poem, he expresses the idea of redemption almost entirely in visual images:[20]

Lord, how long will You conceal
Your consoling vision?

....
My thoughts despair
of seeing Your face,
for my time is delayed
as times come and go.
....
When, O Rock, will I come
and be seen before God,
to haunt Your Temple
and behold Your delights?

This conception of the redemption is strengthened by allusions to Isa. 52:8: "For they will behold eye to eye when the Lord returns to Zion," already quoted in this connection.[21]

My eyes are lifted up to You,
whence comes my help:
When will You bring me
to the house of wine [i.e., the Temple]
and show me Your glory
eye to eye?

Several religious traditions known to Halevi laid stress on the visual experience of God. We have already considered the *merkava* tradition of the vision of God's chariot, which figures in some of Halevi's liturgical poems in its traditional form and from which Halevi drew his language of divine vision in the Kuzari. But the poems in this chapter and the others like them belong to a more philosophically tinged religious mode. Muslim and Jewish Neoplatonists also wrote of the divine vision as the culminating religious experience.[22]

Sufi writers also laid stress on the visual experience of God. A recent study has shown abundant evidence of the impact of Sufi writing on the Kuzari, especially this visual aspect of Sufi writing.[23] Wolfson downplays the possibility that Sufi sources may account for Halevi's emphasis on the visual experience of God,[24] and he is undoubtedly right in saying that not all the language in Halevi's poetry that has a parallel in Sufi writing necessarily reflects Sufi religious thought. We do not find in Halevi's poetry such provocative declarations of the mystic's merging with the God as we do in a famous poem by the Sufi martyr al-Hallaj:

I saw my Lord with the eye of my heart.
He asked, "Who are you?" I answered "You."

Nevertheless, it is necessary to explain why the theme of seeing God is so much more prominent in Halevi than in earlier Hebrew poets who also were heirs to *merkava* mysticism, such as Ibn Gabirol and Ibn Ghiyath. We cannot call Halevi a Jewish Sufi; but it is also hard to deny that just as his religious orientation and vocabulary were touched by general Islamic piety, so he must have been somewhat touched by the Sufi religious sensibility. This seems a certainty, given his interest in al-Ghazzālī, his Sufi terminology identified by Lobel, and the near-certainty that he was familiar with the treatise by Ibn al-ʿArīf, as pointed out in chapter 2.

Confirmation of Halevi's interest in Sufism seems to come from his frequent use of imagery of taste in both the Kuzari and his poetry to represent sensible contact with the divine world. The value of this evidence can be minimized by considering it merely a medieval extension of the psalmist's call: "O taste and see that God is good" (Ps. 34:9). But in the case of taste, as in the case of trust in God, the ancient language of the Bible got a boost and a twist from the language of Islamic piety. Taste (*dhawq* in Arabic) is a technical term in the vocabulary of Sufis; it did not merely signify a person's pleasure in his consciousness of divine care and protection, as it did to the psalmist; it was a stage in the personal experience of contact with God, an intimation of the ecstatic union with the beloved. While Halevi's religious aspirations did not take him that far, the Sufi term appealed to him as a way of expressing his sensual conception of contact with the divine; it is found several times in the Kuzari in the same passage as the one in which he discusses visions of God.[25]

Halevi brilliantly identified taste as the hallmark of personal experience of the divine presence in a biblical passage that he exploited for his own purposes in a short poem. Crowded with images of divine light and revelation, the poem ends: "When I tasted His Torah I said, 'Come, see how my eyes are shining.' "[26] In the biblical passage (1 Sam. 14:29), Saul's son Jonathan is explaining that eating a bit of honey has restored his strength. But the first four verses of Halevi's poem set up such a strong connection between light and revelation that the poem cannot be resolved merely into a sense of physical well-being; the speaker's eyes shine not with physical strength but with the afterglow of God's presence. This mystical aspect of taste may be at play in the frequent mention of the taste of the Land of Israel's soil in the pilgrimage poetry.

Perhaps the internal drive for concreteness in religious experience explains why Halevi came to be dissatisfied with the Neoplatonic aspirations of his predecessors. Driven by his temperament and his early philosophical studies to seek direct contact with the divine world, he retained the Neoplatonic longing for the soul's reunion with a divine source outside the body, while abandoning the philosopher's intellectualized approach to that goal. Focused as he was on achieving the sensory experience of God, Halevi came to place his hopes in revelation and prophecy, as holding greater promise. These, at least, were known to have achieved results, as recorded in scripture. Returning to what he regarded as this distinctively Jewish approach to religious perfection, Halevi focused on the sensory experience of God through revelation and prophecy as the meeting point of all these trends and the goal of religious aspiration.

The poems that follow have an ecstatic or visionary element. In poems 8 and 9, the vision is of a material place that is elsewhere: the Land of Israel. But poem 10 also speaks of yearning for the face of God, and poems 10, 11, and 12 speak of dreams. This last poem takes Halevi in a dream vision to the Temple in Jerusalem—in other words, to the Land of Israel, leading us to the very threshold of Halevi's pilgrimage.

8

אֵלֶיךָ אֵלֵכָה   וְעֵינַי לִמְעוֹנֶךָ
בְּלֵב נִשְׁעָן עָלֶיךָ   מְשַׁכְתִּיו אֶל רְצוֹנֶךָ.
גֵּר וְתוֹשָׁב בְּאָהֳלֶךָ   לִמְצֹא חֵן בְּעֵינֶיךָ
הֲבִיאֹתִיו אֵלֶיךָ,   וְהִצַּגְתִּיו לְפָנֶיךָ.

דְּלָקוּנִי אֲהָבֶיךָ,   וְאַחֲרֶיךָ דָּלָקְתִּי.
הֱיוֹתִי מִקְּרוֹבֶיךָ   מִקְּרוֹבַי רָחָקְתִּי.
וְאֵצֵא בַעֲקֵבֶיךָ   קַל וְלֹא הִתְאַפָּקְתִּי.
זְעָמוּנִי עוֹזְבֶיךָ,   וַאֲנִי בְךָ הֶחֱזַקְתִּי.
חוֹסֶה בְּצֵל שִׁכְנֶךָ,   לֵאוֹר בְּאוֹר פָּנֶיךָ.

טוֹב יוֹם עַל אַדְמַת אֵל   מֵאֶלֶף בְּאַדְמַת זָר;
יְדִידוֹת חָרְבוֹת הַרְאֵל   מֵאַרְמוֹן כָּל מִנְזָר,
כִּי בְאֵלֶּה אֶגָּאֵל,   וּבְזֶה אֶעֱבֹד אַכְזָר.
לְךָ לְבַדְּךָ אֲנִי שׁוֹאֵל,   וְלֹא בְּבִלְתְּךָ אֲנִי נֶעֱזָר.
מָעוֹז בִּימִינֶךָ   וּמַחְסֶה לְמַאֲמִינֶיךָ.

8

To You I come,
my eyes on Your home,
drawing my trusting
heart to Your will—
I, a stranger
here in Your precincts,
eager to please You—
bring it to You, lay it before You.

Your love has pursued me,
and I have pursued You;
abandoned my dearest,
all for Your nearness.
Light-footed, freely
I followed Your footsteps,
hated by people
who scorned and abandoned You.
Your shade is my shelter, Your face is my lantern.

A day in God's land,
not a lifetime with strangers!
More joy in God's ruins
than in any palace—
the one means redemption,
the other spells bondage.
Only to You
do I pray, and no other.
Your hand is a fortress, protection for the faithful.

נַפְשִׁי כְּחֹרֶב בְּצָיוֹן אֶל טַל חוֹרֵב וְצִיּוֹן.
סִתְרִי סֵתֶר עֶלְיוֹן לָגוּר לְבָנוֹן וְשִׂרְיוֹן.
עֵינַי כְּעֵינֵי אֶבְיוֹן לַחֲזוֹת גֵּיא חִזָּיוֹן.
פָּנַי אֶל הַחֶבְיוֹן, מְקוֹם לוּחוֹת וְגִלָּיוֹן.
צְרוֹר גִּנְזֵי אֲרוֹנֶךָ סָבִיב לְשֻׁלְחָנֶךָ.

קוֹרֵא לָאוֹר וְגוֹלֵל עֲרָבִים מִפְּנֵי בְקָרִים--
רַב מֵהְיוֹת מִתְחַלֵּל שִׁמְךָ בְּפִי דוֹבֵר שְׁקָרִים,
שֵׁם אֲשֶׁר בּוֹ נִתְהַלֵּל מְחוֹלָלִים מְדֻקָּרִים.
תִּמְכֹּר יָקָר לְזוֹלֵל, בְּנֵי צִיּוֹן הַיְקָרִים.
הַבָּנִים בָּנֶיךָ וְגַם הַצֹּאן צֹאנֶךָ.

To the congregation assembled in the synagogue, it would have been obvious that the "I" who announces that he has arrived at the synagogue and is standing in God's presence was speaking for them; but we, who read the poem in a manuscript or in a book, remain in the dark about the speaker's identity until the last stanza, where the poet's reference to the suffering of the Jewish people and his prayer for redemption show us that that the poem originally had a public function. It was a common practice of synagogue poets to begin a liturgical poem in the singular, as if the precentor is speaking to God on his own behalf and to bring the public into the poem only later; we saw an example in "From Time's Beginning" (poem 7). But precisely because Halevi's original audience understood from the beginning that the poem's "I" represented them and not the speaker as an individual, they must have been startled by the intensely personal style of this poem.

The poem could be understood as a conventional prayer for redemption from exile. It opens with the declaration that the precentor and the congregation are assembled in the synagogue and goes on, in the second strophe, to speak of the people's eager pursuit of God and of their being hated by the nations that do not know Him. The third and fourth strophes describe the people's longing for

Thirsting for dew
from Zion and Sinai,
I long for the shelter
of God in Hermon,
hungry to see
the Valley of the Vision,
my face toward the place
of the fragmented tablets,
that lie hidden alongside Your ark and Your altar.

God, who brings day on
and rolls away evenings!
Long enough
has Your name been disgraced,
the name we take pride in
though slain and stabbed.
Turn shame to glory
for the dear sons of Zion.
"The sons are Your children, the sheep are Your sheep."

---

redemption from exile and restoration to the Land of Israel. In the final strophe, the voice of the speaker shifts from declaration to petition: God is addressed as the creator of dawn, in phrases that echo a specific passage in the daily liturgy, suggesting that the poem may have been intended for the morning service. A poem in this form and with these themes could have functioned as a penitential poem or as an embellishment to the morning service. There are hundreds like it.

But the poem is suffused with motifs and images that belong to Halevi's personal vision. It opens with a passionate declaration of submissiveness to God's will, couched in the astonishingly visual image of the speaker laying his heart before God.[27] In the second stanza, the theme of pursuing God somewhere else, especially in its paradoxical formulation ("Your love has pursued me, and I have pursued You"), recalls the paradoxes of "Where Can I Find You, Lord?" (poem 2), while the theme of abandoning one's own to be nearer to God and therefore of being in conflict with others anticipates Halevi's pilgrimage poetry.

The third and fourth stanzas most uncannily anticipate Halevi's pilgrimage poetry, with its themes of longing for the land, preferring service to God to servitude to man, and trust in God alone. The pilgrimage poetry is prefigured particularly strongly in the fourth strophe, where the speaker names particular sites and artifacts in or near the Land of Israel that are connected with revelation—Mount Sinai, Mount Zion, Mount Lebanon, Jerusalem (the prophetic "Valley of the Vision"),[28] and especially the remains of the Temple and the broken fragments of the Ten Commandments, buried somewhere under the rubble of Jerusalem.

Halevi's personal concerns are sufficiently strong in this poem that ambiguity of public and private must have been present even when it was recited in its original congregational setting. Halevi expresses his congregation's yearning to behold the presence of God in His Holy Land with a concreteness that they might well have found disturbing, especially when he speaks of his pur-

(*Commentary continues on the next page*)

9

אַחֲלַי יִכּוֹנוּ לִפְנֵי אֵל אֳרָחַי,
כִּי יֵצְרוּ עָלַי מַעֲרָבַי וּמִזְרָחַי
לִרְאוֹת מְקוֹם נְבִיאַי וּמְקוֹם כִּסְאוֹת מְשִׁיחַי
צָמְאָה נַפְשִׁי לֵאלֹהִים לְאֵל חָי.

אֶל גִּבְעַת הַלְּבוֹנָה   מְגַמָּתִי נְכוֹנָה.
לָלֶכֶת צִיּוֹנָה   מִי יִתֵּן מִמְּעוֹנָה
לִי אֵבֶר כַּיּוֹנָה?--   אָעוּפָה וְאֶשְׁכֹּנָה.
אֵלֲךְ לִי אֶל הַר הַמֹּר   וְאֶל גִּבְעַת הַלְּבוֹנָה.

אֶשָּׂא עֵינַי לִמְרוֹמֵי גְבוֹהִים--
מֵאַיִן יוֹפִיעוּ עָלַי גַּלְגַּלֵּי נְגוֹהִים?
לִקְרַאת מַלְכֵּי אָרִיד וְאָהִים.
מָתַי אָבוֹא וְאֵרָאֶה פְּנֵי אֱלֹהִים?

---

suit of contact with the divine, rejection of life in exile, and the specific sites in the Land of Israel. By the time this poem was composed, Halevi must already have been brooding deeply on the idea of the pilgrimage.[29]

But the pilgrimage in this poem takes place only in the mind's eye; the last strophe returns us to the synagogue, where the poet is leading the congregation in prayer, duly expressing their yearning for national redemption. It is pleasant to imagine that Halevi brought this poem with him to Jerusalem and recited it there on his own behalf; how apt would have been the opening words "To You I Come" and how satisfying to declare, in the midst of those ruins: "A day in God's land, not a lifetime with strangers!"

9

If but my path to God were clear
(for west and east are too narrow for me)
to see the place where prophets lived
and my kings had thrones.
"My soul is thirsting for the Lord, the living God."

My goal is set to the Fragrant Hill—
to Zion, if it be God's will.
If I had dove's wings,
to fly and alight—
"I would go to the Mount of Myrrh, the Hill of Frankincense."

I lift my eyes to the lofty heights—
Whence will the shining spheres be revealed to me?
I long and yearn
to go to my king.
"When will I go and see the face of God?"
....

Only three stanzas remain of a longer poem, and an intriguing one at that: like "To You I Come" (poem 8), this is a synagogue poem in which Halevi has permitted his personal fantasy of pilgrimage to obtrude upon the poem's public function.

More than in most of the poems in this book, the fabric of the poem consists of biblical phrases, in addition to the longer biblical quotations that close off each of the stanzas. The sources from which these quotations are taken reinforce the meaning sometimes directly, and sometimes by contrast. The first line in the Hebrew original is a verbatim quotation of Ps. 119:1, in which the psalmist entreats God at great length to "make his way straight before God" by teaching him His commandments and enabling him to observe them. Though Halevi was a perfectly observant Jew, his great theme was not the virtue of observing the commandments but the joy of directly experiencing God's presence. When the psalmist spoke of "a straight way before God," he intended a metaphor of righteousness and obedience, but Halevi uses it literally, converting the metaphor into the pilgrim's route.

The poem's first stanza concentrates several of Halevi's themes. Line 2, with its merism "west and east" (meaning "everywhere"), describes the poet's feeling of being hemmed in by every place that is not the Land of Israel. Line 3 compactly names the two elements of the Land of Israel that make it so important

(*Commentary continues on the next page*)

10

לִקְרַאת מְקוֹר חַיֵּי אֱמֶת אָרוּצָה,
עַל כֵּן בְּחַיֵּי שָׁוְא וָרִיק אָקוּצָה.
לִרְאוֹת פְּנֵי מַלְכִּי מְגַמָּתִי לְבַד--
לֹא אֶעֱרֹץ בִּלְתּוֹ וְלֹא אַעֲרִיצָה.
מִי יִתְּנֵנִי לַחֲזוֹתוֹ בַחֲלוֹם?--
אִישַׁן שְׁנַת עוֹלָם וְלֹא אָקִיצָה.
לוּ אֶחֱזֶה פָּנָיו בְּלִבִּי בַיְתָה
לֹא שָׁאֲלוּ עֵינַי לְהַבִּיט חוּצָה.

to him: revelation and sovereignty. And line 4 is a quotation from Ps. 42:3, which in its original context speaks of a pilgrimage to the Temple. The phrase at the end of this quotation—the living God—is one that Halevi returns to in other poems;[30] for him, it meant the God Who can be experienced, as opposed to the abstract concept of God dreamed up by the philosophers.

In the second stanza, we again meet the dove. This particular dove comes from Ps. 55:7, a passage in which Halevi found precedent for his own longing; but whereas the psalmist wishes for the wings of a dove so that he might flee his enemies, Halevi's dove is one on whose wings he might soar away to the distant Holy Land. Perhaps Halevi conflated this dove with the swallow from Ps. 84:4 that we have already met, the bird that longs to reach the Temple and its altar. The stanza concludes with a verse from the Song of Songs, where the lover describes his anticipation of a dalliance with his beloved as going to the mountain of myrrh and the hill of frankincense; in citing this verse, Halevi followed the midrash in taking these fragrant places as referring to the Temple Mount.[31]

The fragment breaks off at a pregnant moment: the mention of the poet's desire to see the face of God. This phrase in its source in the Psalms was traditionally understood to have the innocuous meaning of appearing before God in the Temple on the pilgrimage festivals. But given the visual bent of Halevi's religious aspirations, we can hardly escape the echo of its literal meaning.

10

Toward the fountain of true life I run,
disgusted by this life of emptiness,
my only goal to see my sovereign's face.
None other do I fear, none else revere.
If only I could see Him in a dream—
O then I'd sleep forever, never wake.
If I could see His face within my heart,
my eyes would never bother looking outward!

The poem opens with an antithesis, routine in Arabic *zuhd* poetry and in the writings of moralists and Sufis, between the transient world of appearances that we inhabit in our everyday life, and the real, unchanging, eternal world of God's presence. The image of God as a fountain, of course, is Neoplatonic, but the goal of the poet's religious aspiration as formulated in this poem is described in the language of Islamic and Jewish mysticism.

The Bible warns that "no man shall see my face and live"; yet even the Bible offers a few cases of prophets who did see God. The vision of Moses is the most elaborately narrated; Isaiah and Ezekiel also had visions of God, which served as models for later Jewish mystics. The Qur'an promises that on the Day of Judgment, the elect will see God's face, and while some theologians and all philosophers would deny that this statement can be understood literally, Muslim mystics pondered the expression and its implications.

Neoplatonists such as Ibn Gabirol, Moses Ibn Ezra, and the younger Judah Halevi often said that man sees God with the eye of the intellect. In "Toward the Fountain of True Life," Halevi aspires to a more concrete vision, to an internal visualization of that which cannot be grasped with the mind, an inner experience that is as palpable as seeing with the eyes, whether in waking or in dreams. He is, in effect, aspiring to prophecy.

Now, the biblical threat directed at the person who would see God's face is converted into an aspiration. If the speaker could see God in a dream, he would indeed die—not as punishment for thrusting himself, all unworthy, into the divine presence, but rewarded with the fulfillment of his life's purpose. Death holds no terror if what it promises is bliss. And since death is merely an extension of sleep, the dream of God would endure to eternity. Likewise, if the speaker could see God in an inner vision and live, his eyes would no longer be of use to him, for after what he had experienced internally, what value would there be in mere external vision?

The poem begins as a conventional poem of asceticism, but by the end it professes a readiness to discard not just the worldly things that an ordinary ascetic rejects, but life itself. The passionate language of the poem's second half transcends worldly piety and carries us into the realm of martyrdom—not martyrdom in defense of the religion against disbelief or persecution, but the kind of martyrdom that lies in the background of much Sufi poetry, the martyrdom of love. We have already seen Halevi thinking along these lines near the beginning of "O Lord, All My Desire Is Plain to Thee" (poem 1), when he said that he would be prepared to die for a moment of God's pleasure.[32]

II

נַמְתָּ וְנִרְדַּמְתָּ וְחָרֵד קַמְתָּ--
  מָה הַחֲלוֹם הַזֶּה אֲשֶׁר חָלַמְתָּ?
אוּלַי חֲלוֹמְךָ הֶרְאֲךָ שׂוֹנַאֲךָ
  כִּי דַל וְכִי שָׁפֵל, וְאַתָּה רַמְתָּ.
אִמְרוּ לְבֶן הָגָר: אֱסֹף יַד גַּאֲוָה
  מִבֶּן גְּבִרְתֶּךָ אֲשֶׁר זָעַמְתָּ!
שָׁפָל רְאִיתִיךָ וְשׁוֹמֵם בַּחֲלוֹם;
  אוּלַי בְּהָקִיץ כֵּן כְּבָר שָׁמַמְתָּ,
וּשְׁנַת תַּתַ"ץ תַּתֵּץ לְךָ כָּל גַּאֲוָה,
  תֵּבוֹשׁ וְתֶחְפַּר מֵאֲשֶׁר זָמַמְתָּ.
הַאַתְּ אֲשֶׁר נִקְרָא שְׁמָךְ פֶּרֶא אֱנוֹשׁ?
  מַה כָּבְדָה יָדְךָ וּמֶה עָצַמְתָּ!
הַאַתְּ מְקֹרָא פֻּם מְמַלֵּל רַבְרְבָן
  וַאֲשֶׁר בְּקַדִּישֵׁי זְבֻל נִלְחַמְתָּ.
הַאַתְּ חֲסַף טִינָא בְּרַגְלֵי פַרְזְלָא
  בְּאַחֲרִית בָּאתָ וְהִתְרוֹמַמְתָּ.
אוּלַי נְגָפְךָ אֵל בְּאַבְנָא דִי מְחָת
  צַלְמָא, וְשִׁלֵּם לָךְ אֲשֶׁר הִקְדַּמְתָּ.

Halevi may not have been granted the mystical dream of God's face that he wished for in "Toward the Fountain of True Life" (poem 10), but in the present poem he describes an internal religious event that is impressive enough, a prophetic dream. Focused on worldly events, this earthbound poem lacks the ethereal quality of "Toward the Fountain of True Life" and even turns violent toward the end. It is unusual in containing the date of its own composition and in its shift in the last three verses from Hebrew to Aramaic.

Like "From Time's Beginning" (poem 7), the present poem emerges out of Halevi's obsession with the exiled state of the Jewish people. It reports on a dream, presumably a product of the poet's waking preoccupation with the Jewish exile. The first two verses describe the poet's waking with only the memory of having dreamed, unable to remember more than that his dream had to do with the collapse of Muslim rule. But as the poet reflects, fragments of Nebuchadnezzar's dream vision in the second chapter of Daniel come to his mind, permitting the inference that his dream resembled the one ascribed to the Babylonian king.

II

You dozed and fell asleep and rose in fear;
What was this dream you dreamed, already unclear?
Perhaps your dream revealed to you your foe—
You the master; he humbled and low.

Tell Hagar's son, "Let down your haughty hand
from Sarah's son, the rival you have scorned.
for I have seen you in my dream, a ruin;
Perhaps in life, you really are undone.
Perhaps this year, eleven-hundred thirty
will see your pride thrown down, your thinking thwarted.

Yes, you who now are known as 'desert ass':
how mighty is your hand, how puissant.
Yea, thou are cleped the haughty-speaking mouth,
who warrest with the holy ones of heaven—
yea, thou the clay mixed with the iron feet,
come at the end of days, in pride uprisen—
haply He hath hurled the stone, smashed
The effigy, requital for thine ancient misdeeds given."

Nebuchadnezzar is said to have seen a great statue in the form of a man, with its parts made of different materials, each representing one of the empires that would rule the world. The statue was imposing, but unstable because the toes on its iron feet were made of mixed iron and clay, materials that cannot be combined. As Nebuchadnezzar contemplated the statue, a hurled stone struck the clay and toppled the statue. Daniel interpreted the statue as representing the succession of four kingdoms that would rule over Israel from the destruction of the Temple in 586 BCE until the restoration of the Davidic dynasty; for the book's author, writing in the second century BCE, those four kingdoms were Babylonia, Media, Persia, and Macedonia. As political realities changed in the centuries after the book's composition, the interpretation of the dream kept shifting. Commentators of Halevi's time identified the statue's iron feet and toes as the Muslim and Byzantine Empires.[33] The "clay mixed with iron feet" and the hurled stone toward the end of the poem thus represent a Jewish dream for the speedy collapse of Muslim rule and the present political order.

Whether the poem reports a dream Halevi actually dreamed or whether it is a fiction, it captures the mental state of a medieval Jew who had scoured the Bible for clues to the date of the messianic redemption; Daniel was one of the main sources of such clues, for much of the book is devoted to visions of the end of Israel's suffering and enigmatic hints about the time remaining. Perhaps Halevi had been meditating on the second chapter of Daniel during his waking hours, causing the image of the statue and its collapse to come to him in his sleep. On waking, he must have thought that he had been given a sign, and he would naturally have attempted to decode any hint that the dream contained.

We can plausibly retrace Halevi's effort to interpret his dream. The collapse of the statue representing the nations that subjugated Israel must have made him think of the Hebrew verb *natats* (to pull down) and a famous biblical verse containing that verb: "See, I appoint you this day over nations and kingdoms to uproot and to pull down, to destroy and to overthrow, to build and to plant" (Jer. 1:10). Seeking a foothold for interpretation, he would naturally have realized that this verb, in the form *titots* (= you will pull down), spelled the number of the current year, 4890, corresponding to 1129/30 in our calendar, for the Hebrew letters have numerical value, and the letters designating a year often also spell a word.[34] Such number exegesis comes naturally and automatically to the rabbinic mind. Halevi was undoubtedly aware that the word *titots* and its numerical equivalent had long figured in attempts to calculate the date of the onset of the messianic era. We do not need to seek any special historical event that occurred in that year to explain Halevi's dream; the number itself is the dream's explanation.[35]

(*Commentary continues on the next page*)

12

אֱלֹהַי! מִשְׁכְּנוֹתֶיךָ יְדִידוֹת,
וְקִרְבָתְךָ בְּמַרְאֶה, לֹא בְחִידוֹת.
הֱבִיאַנִי חֲלוֹמִי מִקְדְּשֵׁי אֵל,
וְשַׁרְתִּי מַלְאֲכוֹתָיו הַחֲמוּדוֹת,
וְהָעוֹלָה וּמִנְחָתָהּ וְנִסְכָּהּ,
וְסָבִיב תִּימְרוֹת עָשָׁן כְּבֵדוֹת.
וְנָעַמְתִּי בְּשָׁמְעִי שִׁיר לְוִיִּם
בְּסוֹדֵיהֶם לְסֵדֶר הָעֲבוֹדוֹת.
הֱקִיצוֹתִי, וְעוֹדִי עִמְּךָ אֵל,
וְהוֹדֵיתִי, וְלָךְ נָאֶה לְהוֹדוֹת.

Other motifs in our poem confirm that Halevi is thinking of the Islamic hegemony. He calls the Muslims "Hagar's son," meaning Ishmael, the progenitor of the Arabs in both the Jewish and Muslim tradition. The "desert ass" also refers to Ishmael, deriving from the words of the angel (Gen. 16:12) who predicted that he would become a nomad. The "haughty-speaking mouth" derives from the vision of the terrifying fourth beast of Daniel 7, which commentators in the Muslim world such as Abraham Ibn Ezra identified as representing Ishmael and the rule of Islam.

Daniel's book is full of dreams, dream visions, and mysterious hints about the end of the exile. These hints were drawn upon by myriad preachers and poets as sources of consolatory hope. But Halevi does something in this poem that not one of the other preachers and poets who evoked Daniel's prophecies did. He put Daniel's words in his own mouth. And he calls attention to his doing so by not simply quoting the book, but by shifting languages, so that like the book of Daniel itself, the poem is both Hebrew and Aramaic. (Among the Aramaic chapters of Daniel are chapter 2, recounting Nebuchadnezzar's dream; and chapter 7, describing the horned beast.) The shift occurs in verse 7. The poem is crafted so as to make the Aramaic voice of Daniel emerge smoothly out of the Hebrew voice of Halevi, so that poet and prophet seem to have completely merged.[36]

The poem shows more than Halevi's concern with the Jewish exile. Other medieval Hebrew poets dreamed and wrote about the end of the exile, but Halevi is the only one who used his dream to turn himself momentarily into a prophet.

12

O God, the joy of being near You!—
for being near means seeing,
not mere speculation.
I dreamed that I was in God's Temple
watching every lovely, holy rite:
the whole-burnt sacrifice, the meal and wine,
the thick smoke twisting upward,
Levites singing, me among them, blissful,
as they did their service.
I woke, but still with You, O Lord,
offering my gratitude.
How good to give You thanks!

If the dream of "You Dozed and Fell Asleep" (poem 11) arose out of Halevi's meditations on the problem of Jewish exile, the dream of "O God, the Joy of Being near You" arose from his meditation on experiencing God's presence. "You Dozed and Fell Asleep" is about Halevi's national aspirations; "O God, the Joy of Being near You" is about his personal aspirations. In the former, the poet's dreamed role is prophetic; in the latter, sacerdotal.

The dream of "You Dozed and Fell Asleep" had partly dissipated on the poet's waking, leaving him with only an impression, but on awaking from the dream in "O God, the Joy of Being near You," the poet still feels himself to be in the presence of God and is able to describe his vision in detail. We must consider what daytime meditations brought on such a vivid dream of the Temple service in Jerusalem, something that the poet had never actually seen, that no one had actually seen for centuries, but that is described in detail in Jewish sacred writings.

In the opening line, the phrase "the joy of being near You" might be translated "Your dwelling place is a delight," for the word *mishkan* is used in the Bible for the shrine built by Moses to house the Ten Commandments, and later it was sometimes used as a metonymy for the Temple; the phrase is adopted from Ps. 84:2, where the psalmist exclaims at the thought of making pilgrimage to the Temple. I believe that, while Halevi intends for the word *mishkan* to mean the Temple, he is also thinking of it as a verbal noun signifying "to dwell in or near a place": not only "How delightful is Your dwelling place" but also "How delightful is dwelling with You," as confirmed by the parallel verbal noun *qirvatekha,* "being near you," in the parallel clause.

So the poem is about being near God, and the phrasing of the opening tells the prepared reader that the Temple is the site of this proximity.

As we have seen, Halevi had come to believe that God must reveal Himself plainly, as He once did to the entire people of Israel at Sinai, not in the theoretical speculations of the philosophers—here called *ḥidot* ("dark speech," "riddles")—but in clearly perceptible visions that leave no ambiguity or room for doubt. In "Toward the Fountain of True Life" (poem 10), Halevi expresses his religious ambition as a desire to see God. Here, that aspiration is transformed into a dream of being in the presence of God as the Jewish tradition conceived it: of visiting God in the Temple and of participating in its biblically ordained rituals. Never in all Halevi's poetry does he write of having actually been granted the vision of God; but in this poem, he associates his vision of the Temple service with that ultimate religious goal. Halevi's dream of the Temple gives him religious clarity by transporting him through space and time to the place where, as he believed, God's presence formerly was regularly made manifest. He joyfully watches the priests killing the sacrificial animals, sprinkling the blood, and pouring the libations; he sees the smoke rising from the altar to God. This, according to the Torah and the Jewish tradition, is the means prescribed by God Himself for achieving the closeness for which Halevi yearned, now foreclosed by the destruction of the Temple and Israel's exile.

Halevi prefaces his vision by saying that God appears to man "in seeing, not mere speculation"; the wording comes from the biblical description of the prophecies of Moses; in the narrative, God says: "Mouth to mouth I speak to him; in visions, not in dark speeches; he sees the image of God" (Num. 12:8). The contrast intended by Halevi is not the biblical antithesis between clear and unclear visions but the antithesis, so important to his own religious thought, between direct experience and philosophical speculation. My translation of the word meaning "unclear speech" as "speculation" is designed to make Halevi's intention explicit. It is in utterances of this type that we glimpse the mystical character of Halevi's religious aspirations, and in this poem we can also get an inkling of how that aspiration would eventually lead him to the Land of Israel.[37]

Being a poet and a Levite, Halevi found the singing of the Levites even more intense as a religious experience than the rites performed by the priests. In the time of the Temple, the Levites were not priests but secondary officiants, among whose duties was to sing the psalms that accompanied the sacrifices. Halevi identified strongly with his ancestral tribe. Like Samuel Ibn Nagrella, a great political figure and poet of the preceding century, Halevi saw himself as fulfilling this Levitical duty, even in Israel's exiled state, by virtue of being a poet and a composer (and presumably, singer) of hymns in the synagogue, a Levite for his own age.

Thus once more, we have found Halevi's fantasy of finding God in a place outside himself. But here, the place is a particular one and the anxiety is gone. We can infer that by the time this poem was composed, Halevi's thinking had fully matured and he knew what he had to do, whether or not he had yet made up his mind to do it. In the following chapters, we shall see how he transported himself physically to the Temple's site.

Part II

The Pilgrimage

4

Alexandria

Amram b. Isaac was a Jewish businessman in the Mediterranean port city of Alexandria. On Sunday, September 8, 1141, he wrote to a colleague in Fustat, the old city of Cairo that was home to most of the city's Jewish inhabitants:[1]

> To our honorable, splendid, glorious, great, and holy master and teacher, Ḥalfon Halevi of the clan of Kehat, the wise, sage, and respected nobleman who has feared heaven since he was a youth, the son of our master and teacher, the respected elder Nethaniel Halevi, who in life was pious and in memory, a blessing; from one who is grateful for his kindnesses, Amram son of Isaac, may he rest in paradise.
>
> [Several paragraphs about various business arrangements follow.]
>
> A few of our associates arrived on the general's ship and told us that Master Judah Halevi is to arrive on the sultan's new ship, expecting me to inform you, but I was afraid to worry you. We waited and waited for him to arrive. I became particularly frantic, and I prayed to God, the great and exalted, that he might be safe and that you might get what you had so long been hoping for. Then God graciously granted that the ship did arrive on Sunday, Elul 24. Mansūr Abū Furūgh disembarked, but *he* did not disembark today, Sunday, Elul 24, the day I am writing these lines. I am hastening with

> these lines in order to get word to you . . . the best I can to serve that great man. God, Who knows all hidden things, knows how I am writing these lines, when I am all swollen, as God is my witness, and my eye is in the worst possible state so that I cannot see what I am writing. . . .
>
> And I congratulate your honor on the arrival of our wise, sage, and distinguished master Judah Halevi, may his honor be established forever; and with him, as we were informed, arrived the masters, the sons of Master Abraham Ibn Ezra, may God preserve him. . . .
>
> I have already written much, and it is evening, besides which, my eyes are dim.
>
> From what I have written, you can learn my condition. I am today what our master Moses Ibn Ezra—may his soul be bound up in the bond of life!—described in his poem about how brothers and sons change:
>
> *When a man is dead, he has no power,*
> *no use for the wealth he's won—*
> *expelled from his house by his closest friends,*
> *even his darling son.*[2]

The man addressed by the unhappy writer of this letter, Abū Sa'd Ḥalfon ben Nethaniel Halevi, was one of the most prominent Jews of Fatimid Egypt in the first half of the eleventh century. (He was not related to Judah Halevi; Halevi is not a family name but a title claimed by all descendants of the biblical tribe of Levi.) Though Ḥalfon was a scholarly man with a serious interest in books and even wrote some poetry, he was primarily a businessman, and a large-scale one at that, active in the India trade and traveling up and down the Red and Mediterranean Seas. Ḥalfon had visited Spain a number of times and had met Halevi and other members of his circle there.

As Halevi's closest contact in Egypt, Ḥalfon probably would have liked to welcome him upon his arrival in the port of Alexandria. But that year, the two-day New Year festival fell at the end of the week of Halevi's arrival, on September 14 and 15. Other holidays followed in close succession: the Day of Atonement on September 23; and the Festival of Sukkot, on the nine days from September 28 to October 6. This was a time when even inveterate travelers tried to be at home with their families. Ḥalfon lived in Fustat; unable to be present himself, he had deputized Amram to make arrangements for the distinguished traveler, and Amram's letter has the nature of a report on this and other business matters with which Ḥalfon had entrusted him.

Some details of Amram's report help us imagine the scene in port. The two ships called the "general's ship" and the "sultan's new ship" must have traveled part of the way together or met in some port along the way, after which they became separated and reached Alexandria several days apart. The intervening days were filled with anxiety for those awaiting the sultan's new ship. Would Halevi's party actually be on this second ship? Had it been captured or wrecked along the way? Would the elderly Halevi arrive in good health after the rigors of the journey? Amram must have inquired anxiously after the identities of the disembarking passengers as they scrambled onto the dock out of the boat that had carried them from the ship anchored in the harbor. Perhaps the disembarking passenger Mansūr Abū Furūgh, whom we cannot identify but who seems to have been known to Amram and Ḥalfon, was the one who relieved Amram's anxiety by informing him that Halevi and his companions were indeed on board.

It is not surprising that Halevi and his companions did not disembark on the day of their ship's arrival, for arriving travelers were often detained until customs inspectors could interrogate them, assess their duties, and release them. This procedure particularly affected members of the officially protected religious minorities, called *dhimmīs*—Jews like Halevi and his companions, as well as Christians—who had to produce evidence that they had paid the year's *dhimmī* tax in their home countries.

Halevi traveled with two companions, but Amram was misinformed when passengers disembarking on Sunday told him that they were both sons of the famous poet and scholar Abraham Ibn Ezra. One of Halevi's companions was indeed Abraham's son Abū Saʿd Isaac ben Abraham Ibn Ezra al-Qurṭubī, known as Isaac Ibn Ezra.[3] The other was Abū l-Rabīʿ Solomon ben Joseph Ibn Gabbai. They remained by Halevi's side throughout his stay in Egypt, either out of personal loyalty and family duty, or because Halevi was in a position to introduce them to powerful people, or both. But they did not sail with him when Halevi resumed the journey eastward the following spring.

Amram intersperses his letter with complaints about his poor health and eyesight, and he concludes with a gloomy verse by a distinguished Andalusi-Hebrew poet, Moses Ibn Ezra (1055–after 1135), another intimate of Halevi's. That Amram concludes his letter with a quotation from his verse shows that Hebrew poetry from al-Andalus was circulating in Egypt and that it was appreciated even by harried businessmen like Amram and Ḥalfon. Although Egyptian Jewry had not yet produced great Hebrew poets of its own, its Judeo-Arabic culture was similar to that of al-Andalus, and Egyptian Jews, like their Andalusi coreligionists, seem to have been avid consumers of poetry.

Etiquette dictated that Halevi pay a call even before he was fully settled in. We learn this and other details of Halevi's activities during the first weeks of his stay in Alexandria from a letter written to Ḥalfon on October 23, presumably by Abū Naṣr b. Abraham, another business contact and frequent correspondent of Ḥalfon's, who also suffered from an affliction of the eyes (the letter's first page is lost):[4]

> [...] he had no opportunity to visit anyone but the sheikh on the day of the New Year before the prohibition came into effect and also a man known as Kirām the wax-man, who arrived with him on the ship. He gave him his word from there that he would be with him, so on the day of his arrival he went there for a little while and returned.
>
> Sometime later, the sheikh Abū l-Karam Ibn Matrūḥ worked hard to get him to visit, partly by ingratiating himself with him, partly by pressuring him through the judge and a messenger from the governor, until finally he visited him on the night of the Sabbath, and nobody was there but he himself and the judge and the son of Master Abraham. But on the festivals and the fast day and most of the Sabbaths, he stays with the Elevated Master. As for the rest, we will speak of it when we are together, God willing. "A hint is enough for a wise man."
>
> I have written these lines while stuck in the house on account of an attack of ophthalmia. God is the One Who is asked for cure. I am embarrassed before my master and lord, the son of the great sheikh Abū l-Munā, may he rest in paradise, your brother, because of an excuse that you are aware of. So far, no one has entered my house. When I have wanted to be together with our master Judah Halevi, may his Rock protect him, I carry my dinner each night and visit and spend the night there. My intention was to put a stop to the talk of those who wanted him, so that no one would be able to say to him, "You were with So-and-So but never came to him."
>
> I am awaiting your honor's arrival (God protect you) every single instant, hoping that I will be able to meet him in your presence. I am surprised at your delay, for it is high time that this headache be ended. You have the tact and the skill that inevitably resolve such crises, this one in particular. May God relieve your heart and undo your sorrows. This prayer we have in common, for I am one with you in joy and trouble. . . .
>
> As for the account, it is in the shop and I am at home, so I cannot go over its details so as to be able to inform you. I am concerned that if

> your honor delays, you will miss the canal and the goods will remain blocked in Alexandria. My opinion is that you should not delay any longer, God willing. . . .
>
> I beg your honor to continue making use of my services and that you graciously forgive me, for God knows that I have to write with bandages dangling over my eyes. "God is sufficient for me, and He is the best to be trusted." 10 Marheshvan

Most of this letter deals with the people whom Halevi saw socially during his first six weeks in Alexandria. We hear about a man named Kirām the waxman, who had been on the ship with Halevi and whom Halevi had promised to visit the very day of his disembarking. Then there is an unnamed sheikh—this Arabic honorific was used by Arabic-speaking Jews to refer to any person with some seniority or dignity in society, especially a merchant—whom Halevi visited on Rosh Hashanah, the Jewish New Year festival, which occurred that year only a few days after Halevi's arrival; the reference to a prohibition coming into effect that day is, for the present, unclear. Finally, there was Abū l-Karam Ibn Matrūḥ, who moved heaven and earth to get a visit from Halevi, who was joined by "the son of Abraham," probably Halevi's companion Isaac Ibn Ezra, and "the Elevated Master," probably Aaron Ibn al-ʿAmmānī the judge, of whom we shall be hearing more presently.

The social obligations that fill the first part of Abū Naṣr's letter, written only about six weeks after Halevi's arrival in Alexandria but reflecting the events of Halevi's first week there, would plague Halevi throughout his stay in Egypt. Halevi was a dignitary whom everyone wanted to know and who bestowed status on everyone who could claim to be his intimate. Look at the lengths to which Abū l-Karam Ibn Matrūḥ went in using his influence with two of Alexandria's highest officials, one Jewish—the highest official of the Jewish community—and the other Muslim—the highest official of the city itself—to induce Halevi to spend the Sabbath in his house.

Given these pressures, Halevi could not evade the obligation, but Abū Naṣr wants Ḥalfon to know that he is doing his utmost to help Halevi keep to himself. Abū Naṣr points out that he was successful in keeping the party at Abū l-Karam's house small. He points out also that he has not even invited Halevi to his own home because, if Halevi accepted, he would have a hard time turning down invitations from others. Instead, Abū Naṣr has been going to Halevi's lodgings, bringing his own dinner with him.[5] He implies that the tension over the hosting of Halevi had already involved more people than those mentioned in the letter and, using the familiar rabbinic maxim "A hint is enough for a wise man," implies that he has more to tell Ḥalfon in private. Later in the letter, he calls the competition for Halevi's attentions a headache and urges Ḥalfon to come to Alexandria and use his diplomatic skills to allay it. But Ḥalfon lingered in Fustat.

Rosh Hashanah occurred on the weekend following Halevi's arrival, and Halevi would have attended New Year services in the synagogue in the company of the dignitaries of Alexandria. The appearance of a foreigner of Halevi's dignity, fame, and high connections in the synagogue would have been a noteworthy, perhaps even a sensational, event. Halevi's reputation as a poet had preceded him; it would have been a fine courtesy if one of Halevi's own liturgical poems had been inserted into one or more of the services of the New Year festival, since the medieval precentor had some freedom in selecting poems that would be inserted into the regular liturgy. To this day, one of Halevi's penitential poems is sung in congregations of Middle Eastern origin on the New Year festival; it is pleasant to imagine that on his first attending a holiday service abroad, Halevi recognized his own words:[6]

May the memory of Your folk
ascend and come before You.
They bow toward Your Holy Ark.
They sound the horn: its call recalls
the bells that hung upon the hem of Aaron's robe.
They pray to draw Your time of pleasure
down upon themselves;
they blow the horn to quell Your anger.
In their grateful prayers they bring
their blood, their tears, their souls,
that they may be remembered.
They offer prayer as long as they have breath,
as long as through their throats their voices pass.

But as he stood in this strange synagogue celebrating his first festival away from home, Halevi could well have called to mind one of the poems that he had written in anticipation of the very kind of nostalgia he was experiencing, containing the lines:[7]

I'll soon be forgetting the house where I worshiped,
where sacred books were once my refreshment;
the pleasure of Sabbaths, the splendor of festivals,
Passover's dignity, all are forgotten.
I now turn my dignities over to others;
let idols enjoy the praises once mine!

Among the dignities that Halevi may have been thinking of in writing the strikingly ambiguous last lines of the quoted passage were those that he enjoyed in the synagogue back home. There, too, he would regularly have sat with the community dignitaries at the east wall, alongside the Holy Ark. Everyone else sat facing the Holy Ark—necessarily, facing the dignitaries as well.[8] As the religious sensitivities that impelled Halevi to the pilgrimage intensified, he must have become ever more uncomfortable with this sort of worldly glory being indulged in a place better suited to humility and social equality. It was just such contradictions built in to conventional religious life that Halevi had come to Egypt to escape. Halevi's entire stay in Egypt was a struggle, both internal and external, to balance his engagement with the Egyptian Jewish elite and his stance as a pious pilgrim.

Even if this picture of Halevi's predicament in the synagogue is complete fantasy, it is clear from Abū Naṣr's letter and other sources that in Alexandria, Halevi was not passing through Egypt as an anonymous ascetic making his humble way to the Holy Land, but as a public figure who was treated as such. Yet he was conflicted about his role. In a letter that Halevi wrote to Ḥalfon, probably soon, but not immediately, after his arrival, he complains of the attentions showered on him; with remarkable candor he also acknowledges his own weakness in not resisting these attentions. The letter, one of several extant letters in Halevi's own hand, is so tattered and its writing so cursive that for stretches, only isolated words and staticky phrases can be deciphered; yet it yields a fairly clear idea of what was troubling him.[9]

> To the distinguished sage, the exalted prince, master and teacher Ḥalfon Halevi, may God protect him, the son of the honorable master and teacher Nethaniel Halevi, may he rest in paradise.
>
> O master and lord, pillar and support, may God make your glory endure and give length to your days. . . . The note that I sent to you about your coming to . . . in which I mention to you that your letter arrived . . . with your customary kindness and attention to every manner. I was . . . after the entanglement, but . . . with God's grace and yours. The community showed me so much kindness and acceptance, acclaim, thoughtfulness, courtesy, and honor that I was embarrassed. I participated outwardly. . . . Inwardly, it was very burdensome for me. For I did not come for any of this, and all I want is its opposite—isolation and solitude—as appropriate for one who is near to expecting death any minute. But being of such an emotional character, as you know, I have no choice but to accept anyone who intends to do me kindness and to devote myself to him.

> As for the chief, the rabbi and judge, my master and lord, he is devoted to it.[10] He has made me his slave and his bondsman [so that I have neither . . .] nor tongue to thank him. Do me the favor you have done in the past of writing a noble letter to him on my behalf . . . whom I have given your letter to read. . . . I shall copy . . . his intellect that this . . . and that soul. . . . God knows . . . my nature . . . with you in every calamity, all the more, to the point that . . . for the things that have befallen you . . . contempt for this world . . . I have concerned myself . . . the soul I have occupied my mind with . . . the soul . . . open, on account of the quickness of the coming to light of as. . . .
>
> I adjure you by the strongest oath . . . to favor me by sending your solid judgment . . . our merchandise there. This merchandise . . . in silk . . . part of the silk . . . will benefit . . . if Ibn Barukh gets . . . Abū l-Majd. . . .

For all its lacunae, and despite the commercial tone struck at the end, this letter contains an important confession. One of Halevi's motives in undertaking the pilgrimage was to fight the strain of worldliness in his own makeup, to crush his worldly desires into submission, as recommended by moralists; undoubtedly, he felt that he would achieve this once he reached the Holy Land, where he imagined that he would be alone with God. But asceticism went against the grain of his personality, and therefore his behavior along the way to the Holy Land via an important Jewish community was inconsistent. If Halevi had adopted mendicancy and social isolation, the kind of tension reported in the letter by Abū Naṣr quoted earlier, and in others that we shall be reading, probably would not have arisen. But Halevi was determined to maintain his financial independence, so he continued to engage in business. And he could not isolate himself, partly because he was dependent upon the goodwill of others, but also because of his own outgoing personality.

Nor were all the people with whom Halevi socialized in Alexandria a burden to him. He seems to have been genuinely happy in the company of Aaron ben Yeshuʿa Ibn al-ʿAmmānī the judge, the man who had accompanied him and Isaac Ibn Ezra to the home of Abū l-Karam Ibn Matrūḥ on the New Year and who was his main contact during his stay in Alexandria. When Halevi says, in the letter just quoted, that Ibn al-ʿAmmānī has made him his slave and bondsman, he is not complaining, but rather praising the judge for overwhelming him with kindness. But note the language of servitude that he uses toward the judge, and recall how passionately Halevi had written of his desire to be independent of men, to be the slave of God alone.

Halevi was not sparing in his praises to Ibn al-ʿAmmānī. During the months he spent in Egypt, he wrote an extraordinary number of poems to this dignitary, who was about the same age as he and who was one of the chief grandees of the Alexandrian Jewish community, perhaps its official head. Soon after arriving in Alexandria, Halevi sent a poem to a friend in Morocco, mentioning Ibn al-ʿAmmānī's hospitality:[11]

God has brought me up
and out of the ocean depths,
those cursed, bitter waters,
and here I am in Alexandria,
among twelve wells, amid seventy palms—
a lovely house with lovely fragrances,
with nard and henna blossoms in its garden,
and a spring of water flowing cold and clear
direct from God's own house.
Here, the staff of Aaron
blooms with almond blossoms
for a Levite, new ones blooming every day.

The poem speaks of a landscape, but it is actually a tangle of biblical allusions. Like the Israelites after crossing the Red Sea, Halevi has miraculously crossed the ocean and come to an oasis, like the one at which the Israelites encamped, with its twelve wells and seventy palms (Exod. 16:27). The image of the desert refuge is conflated with a brief description of Ibn al-ʿAmmānī's urban palace with its patio and fountain, standard equipment for the home of a Middle Eastern grandee; we shall see it described in detail in another poem by Halevi to Ibn al-ʿAmmānī. To enhance the compliment to Ibn al-ʿAmmānī and to complicate the picture, Halevi imagines the water of Ibn al-ʿAmmānī's fountain as flowing from Jerusalem (a reference to Ibn al-ʿAmmānī's Palestinian origin) and fructifying his household so that it pours benefactions on the visitor like the almond blossoms that miraculously flourished on Aaron's staff in the Bible.[12]

While in Alexandria, Halevi may have lived in Ibn al-ʿAmmānī's house, but even if he occupied his own rented quarters, he was certainly a regular visitor, for in several short poems he laments his own or Ibn al-ʿAmmānī's absence on a Sabbath or a festival. To an unnamed friend in al-Andalus he wrote:[13]

Bring my greetings, mountains, deserts, oceans,
to my sorrowing friends, and tell them this:
your hearts need not be anxious
for my lot has fallen in a pleasant place.

I'm being cared for in a palace here in Alexandria,
a golden place, a mine of precious ore—
Aaron's house, a place of holiness and song,
of gardens, wells, and pools—
the dwelling of a scholar and a sage,
a rabbi and a judge, a righteous, pious man;
a man of Jerusalem, the heir to holiness
bequeathed him by his ancestors.
They were holy people from a holy place—
the Temple's site.
Their birthplace was the Mount of Fragrances.
He bears the Law of God, wields power over men
in splendor, just as Aaron
bore the Urim and Tumim before God.

Ibn al-ʿAmmānī is often called the *dayyan* (judge); this Hebrew term, corresponding to the Arabic title *qāḍī*, refers to Ibn al-ʿAmmānī's position as the chief Jewish judge of Alexandria. Since the tolerated religious minorities operated their own legal systems under their own religious leaders and legal traditions, and since the Jewish community of Alexandria was large and wealthy, the chief judge of the Jews of a large city was a powerful man. He held his office by the appointment of the head of the Jews, the chief of the semiautonomous Jewish community of the Fatimid Empire, who resided in the capital and who held his appointment directly from the Fatimid caliph. We shall meet this even loftier dignitary when we follow Halevi to Cairo.[14]

Halevi was impressed with Ibn al-ʿAmmānī's origins in Jerusalem, given his own obsession with the Holy Land; he mentions the fact in nearly all his poems to and about Ibn al-ʿAmmānī, including the two that we have already seen. Perhaps Halevi felt that merely by virtue of his being Ibn al-ʿAmmānī's guest, some of the holiness of the Holy Land was already rubbing off on him. Halevi also found in Ibn al-ʿAmmānī a man whose education, style of life, and manners resembled in every important way those of the Jewish elite back home in al-Andalus; a man who, like the Andalusis, appreciated Hebrew poetry in the Arabic style and was receptive to panegyrics in his own honor. Even his home and manner of entertainment would have been familiar: Halevi's most important poem to Ibn al-ʿAmmānī describes Ibn al-ʿAmmānī's palace and wine-drinking practices in terms similar to those of the Hebrew poets of Spain. He depicts Ibn al-ʿAmmānī's palace and its patio as an artificial paradise rivaling nature; the patio's fountains are described as competing with the very clouds of heaven:[15]

I know a man who is the best
of henna blossoms, finest nard,
the first in fragrances and every tasty thing;
and that man has a garden
with its beds arranged just so
around a pool—
a well of generosity
inside a vale of plenty.

This paradise has a pebble floor,
a surface ringed with columns,
and all inlaid with gold.
From below the water flows,
gushing upward, sprinkling the sky,
spraying upward, dripping downward,
determined to outdo the clouds,
flying, soaring,
heavy though it be.

There's a shelter in that garden,
made of willow branches
with doves and swallows on them,
and below, dear friends and fellows—
henna blossoms, rose blossoms,
new ones, old ones—
more than enough delights
to satisfy your appetite;
other delights, too,
served in cups and pitchers,
brought round eagerly by Jupiter and Mars.

You sit there facing
the Great Bear's five stars—
the five sons of Aaron,
a holy man of God—
five sons, marvels all, invited to the occasion,
all ripe for the throne,
awaiting their kingdoms,
doing each his very best
to reach their father's rank.

Halevi enjoyed Ibn al-ʿAmmānī's hospitality during the autumn months. But he was anxious to continue his journey eastward, as he says in a letter to Ḥalfon that was probably written about this time:[16]

> To the great sage and most excellent leader, Master Ḥalfon Halevi, may God protect him, son of the honorable Master Nethaniel Halevi, may he rest in paradise; from one who longs for him and is devoted to his service.
>
> O master and lord, O you who are the greatest of God's favors to me! May God extend your greatness forever and bring us together under the best of circumstances. Your dear, warm letters reached me . . . which no one has the craft to bring about but God: that He graciously grant that we meet . . . if God so determine. I have no secret wish, only the open one that I made plain to you and that I laid out before your lofty presence—to go eastward as soon as possible, if it is God's will to assist me.
>
> How I am occupied, you yourself know. Your dear letter was handed to me at the gathering you know about on Friday morning, and I replied on the spot. I have already replied to the two earlier letters, in obedience to your command.
>
> The book about the Khazars—among the favors that the physician and rabbi, Master Joseph Ibn Barzel, has done for me was to praise this bit of foolishness that I wrote; otherwise, I would hesitate to show it to you. It came about because a certain heretic in the Christian territory asked me about several things, and I sent it to him, but then disavowed it. When we are together, you, too, will see it. I am looking for the opportunity to complete what I have resolved upon, if I can manage.
>
> I am writing with people standing over me because I have been told that the messenger who is to carry my reply is in a hurry. Longing makes me fly to you in spirit, and I sing:
>
> *Love is my guarantor and not my feet.*[17]
>
> Peace to my master—peace as great as my longing—and God's mercy.

This letter tantalizes us with its hints of Halevi's activities in Alexandria that were known to Ḥalfon, its addressee, but not to us. We can imagine Halevi being interrupted in his conversation at some Friday morning gathering by a messenger with a letter, reading the letter and writing a quick response while the messenger waited; but there is no way to know what the nature of the gathering was. We have some idea of how Halevi was occupied—with business and with socializing—but we do not know what it was that he was looking for the opportunity to complete; this phrase in the letter could be referring to a writing project or a business transaction; it could refer to the pilgrimage itself. What we would like to know is what was detaining him in Alexandria, and why he did not take the first ship leaving after October 6, the last day of the holiday season, for Acre.

This question is part of the larger question of why Halevi spent so long in Egypt. It has been suggested that he may simply have been detained because there was no shipping between Alexandria and the ports of Palestine during the winter months. But more substantive considerations suggest themselves. Halevi probably did not want to leave Egypt without seeing Ḥalfon. When he insists so forcefully in his letter to Ḥalfon that his only intention is to go east as soon as possible, he might mean that he has no intention of traveling to Cairo, and that Ḥalfon should come to Alexandria as soon as possible so that Halevi can continue on his way. But Ḥalfon could not easily get away, and, given the etiquette of the age, Ḥalfon must have wanted Halevi to be his guest in Cairo. Halevi may have found it more difficult to turn down a learned and powerful benefactor than he did the grandees of Alexandria. When Halevi writes, in a poem to Ḥalfon, "Ah me, what can I do? Canaan is my destination, but Cairo is his residence," he may be saying that he has decided to yield to Ḥalfon's entreaties and to defer his departure for Palestine for the sake of the detour upriver.[18]

Other reasons began to present themselves for Halevi to go to Cairo. Samuel ben Ḥanania, head of the Jews of Fatimid Egypt, who resided in Fustat, sent word to Halevi through Ḥalfon expressing an interest in meeting him. It would have been discourteous of Halevi to turn down such an invitation, besides, perhaps, being embarrassing to Ḥalfon. Halevi himself would have been flattered to have an audience with a man of Samuel's stature, and Aaron Ibn al-ʿAmmānī seems to have looked forward to having Halevi put in a good word for him with the great man.

There were religious satisfactions, too, in the prospect of visiting Cairo. There, Halevi would be able to visit the site of the events of the Exodus, as related in the Bible, for Cairo was known to have been built near the ruins of the ancient capital of the Pharaohs. Furthermore, it may have occurred to Halevi that by going to Cairo he could turn his pilgrimage into a reenactment of the Exodus, beginning at the Israelites' starting point and traveling overland through the Sinai, perhaps even standing at Mount Sinai before entering the Holy Land. He devoted a short poem to imagining the overland journey:[19]

Detour me through Cairo,
past the Red Sea, then by Sinai;
take me the long way round to Shiloh
only then to reach the ruined Temple's mound.
Let me take the ark of the covenant's route
to where it now lies buried
and lick that soil—so sweet!—
see the lovely maiden's nest she long ago forgot—
the place from which the doves were driven,
settled now by ravens.

Thus, Halevi's need and desire to visit Ḥalfon and Samuel, head of the Jews, in Fustat were quite in line with the religious nature of his itinerary. Even if not his original intention and even if the overland route proved impracticable, he would surely not have felt any religious compunctions about a detour to Cairo, where the *Shekhina* had once, if briefly, alighted, to set Jewish history in motion.[20]

Why, then, did Halevi not proceed immediately to Cairo? Very likely, the etiquette of the age required Ḥalfon to come to Alexandria in person to fetch him home. But Ḥalfon was delayed, first, undoubtedly, because of the holidays, and then because of business affairs. For his own part, Halevi would state, in his epistle to Samuel ben Ḥanania (below), that he regrets not being able to get to Fustat sooner but that he is being detained by the hospitality of Aaron Ibn al-ʿAmmānī and by his own business affairs. So Halevi, caught up in business once again and waiting for Ḥalfon, lingered in Alexandria, enjoying the hospitality of Aaron Ibn al-ʿAmmānī; and Ibn al-ʿAmmānī, proud to have Halevi as an intimate, made it easy for Halevi to linger.

We are much better informed about the other item mentioned in Halevi's letter, the Kuzari, which Halevi modestly refers to as a "bit of foolishness." This expression should not be taken as a serious disparagement of the book's literary or theological content. Self-deprecation, the counterpart of the exaggerated praise of the addressee, was considered becoming modesty and was a persistent feature of the manners of the age.

The Kuzari, ending with its account of the rabbi's departure for the Land of Israel, was completed shortly before Halevi's own departure from Spain. To judge from the letter, Ḥalfon must have heard about its existence only recently. Halevi would certainly have brought a copy with him to Egypt, but since books in the age of manuscript were unique objects, he would not have been expected to give Ḥalfon a copy, as an author of our time would naturally do. Rather, Halevi says that he will gladly "show" it to Ḥalfon; it would be up to Ḥalfon to commission a copy if he wanted one.

While Halevi lingered in Alexandria, pressure was building for him to leave for Cairo in the form of the interest shown in him by Abū Mansūr Samuel ben Ḥanania, head of the Jews in Egypt. Poems and formal epistles preserve a partial record of Halevi's relations with him.

Samuel ben Ḥanania (d. after 1159) was a Jewish physician in the court of the Fatimid caliph al-Ḥāfiẓ (r. 1131–49), as Maimonides would later be in the court of the Ayyubids. He was a figure important enough to be mentioned by Muslim historians, but their tale of his rise to prominence sounds like a bit of folklore. As reported, the caliph, faced with a civil war over which of his two sons should succeed to the caliphate, asked two physicians—Samuel and a Christian physician named Ibn Kirfa—to poison one son. Samuel decided that it would be wiser not to cooperate, but the Christian physician did as he was told. When the caliph—predictably—repented, he had Ibn Kirfa killed and rewarded Samuel by appointing him chief physician and bestowing upon him the Christian physician's property.[21] Thus Samuel ben Ḥanania became a courtier.

Under the system whereby Jews and Christians were considered members of self-governing religious communities, the head of the Jewish community was usually a wealthy Jew who had some function—or, at least, connections—at court. As the most prominent Jew in the Fatimid kingdom, Samuel became also head of its Jewish community—in effect, the minister of Jewish affairs in the Fatimid court—with the Arabic title *ra'īs al-yahūd* (head of the Jews) and the Hebrew title *nagid* (prince). He stood at the apex of a bureaucracy that functioned as a miniature but quite real government over a significant part of the population of Egypt, collecting funds, maintaining order, administrating justice, providing social services, and appointing judges and other local officials such as Aaron Ibn al-ʿAmmānī, head of the Jewish community of Alexandria. This pattern obtained throughout the Islamic world.

Samuel sent word to Halevi through Ḥalfon of his desire for a meeting, and Halevi replied with a supreme example of medieval Hebrew epistolary art, studded with expressions of praise and deference that go far beyond even the most fulsome of the panegyrics in the personal letters that we have been reading. But when the epistle's elaborations are stripped away, its description of Halevi's progress from his home in al-Andalus to the present moment and his anticipation of an audience with Samuel is quite straightforward. Halevi begins by identifying himself as "Judah Halevi, whose land is Spain, Jerusalem his aim." He explains his motives for making the pilgrimage and relates how he lingered in Alexandria as the guest of Aaron Ibn al-ʿAmmānī, where word reached him, through Ḥalfon, of Samuel's greetings to him, followed by a written communication from Samuel, to which the present epistle is a reply. Halevi's epistle confirms some of what we know of his circumstances in Egypt and provides some details that we would not otherwise know. It is also a rare opportunity to hear him speaking about his pilgrimage in his own voice. For the present, we will read parts of the epistle that deal with his travels and relationships with other people.[22]

Like many formal epistles, Halevi's to Samuel begins with a poem:

Deck yourself in splendor, glory, ornaments, and finery,
O light in the land of darkness,
O lofty angel anointed with a goodly name
who reigns aloft on the throne of Jehoiachin,
whom God, the strength of Jacob, sent to lead
and tend His few remaining flocks,
O lord who gives commanders their command,
the Lord's nagid—Samuel, Ḥanania's son.

The epistle goes on, in rhymed prose:

Greetings, greetings of peace from the servant of God and of my master, from Judah Halevi, whose land is Spain, Jerusalem his aim. Let me speak of my lord's exploits and his kindness as I stand hopefully before him to see what he will say to his servant.

Halevi opens using language that goes beyond ordinary courtesies, addressing Samuel in terms traditionally associated with Jewish royalty. Jehoiachin, on whose throne he says that Samuel sits, was the penultimate king of Judea. Exiled to Babylonia in 597 BC, as recounted in the Bible, he was later elevated to courtly dignities, and subsequently came to be thought of as the ancestor of the line of exilarchs. Halevi's language is meant to suggest that Samuel, as *nagid* of Egypt, is *de jure* king of the Jewish people. This idea is also implied by the Hebrew term *nagid,* used by Halevi in addressing Samuel in the epistle. Such royal terminology had been applied to the exilarch, the head of the Jewish community in Iraq, in Abbasid times.[23]

The first part of the epistle concludes with more panegyrics. In the second part, Halevi identifies himself and sketches the religious ideas that impelled him to the pilgrimage. This important material will be presented and discussed in chapter 7. In the third part of the epistle, Halevi turns to the events of his stay in Egypt thus far. He starts by making it clear that he is financially independent:

God has blessed me and has not made me needy; I need nothing, only to cross with my feet. I have brought all I need with me and left bounty behind besides. My intention was to be treated with dignity and not to be a burden to anyone.

This declaration was necessary to assure the addressee that he would not be asked for money, for pilgrims were often without resources, and it was considered a communal obligation to help them. Moreover, since ordinary paupers often used the pretense of pilgrimage in order to lay claim to charity, a letter from a pilgrim to a public official was very likely to be a begging letter.[24] Halevi is going out of his way to distinguish himself from the ordinary run of pilgrims. He goes on:

> *I thought to make Alexandria a place of transit. I would not have restrained the pounding feet of my chariot-steeds but that I encountered someone mightier than I, a man who works in the service of God: the outstanding scholar and most eminent colleague of the rabbis, our master and teacher Aaron the judge, my lord, may he be remembered for good, who holds office under your authority. He greeted me with his favors and the gifts of his hands, delicious food and restful lodging, secure residence and spacious chambers—a dwelling, a house, a table, and lamp. His generosity overwhelmed me, his food surrounded me. He countered my irritation with pleasure and my refusal with temptation. He tempted me successfully; he brought me food and I ate, I and my friends and relatives and all who are accompanying me. We take shelter in his shade, and camp by his standard, in chaste beds restfully stretched, pampered with his bread, drunk with his delights. He has not yet unbuckled his belt or untied his shoes.*[25] *My praises fall short of all he has wrought for me—he and his sons and all those who stand in attendance upon him. Associating with him has elevated me to the highest status and has made me everyone's favorite guest of honor. He has treated me, his disciple, his child, with the respect due to his own teacher and father. What can I offer him, when my praises are not commensurate with him?*

Thus, Halevi puts in a good word for Ibn al-ʿAmmānī, an essential act of gratitude for the latter's hospitality, stressing that Ibn al-ʿAmmānī is Samuel's appointee, and mentioning that Ibn al-ʿAmmānī had extended hospitality to Halevi's companions, Isaac Ibn Ezra and Abū l-Rabīʿ. Halevi also mentions, somewhat indirectly, that he has duly celebrated his host by writing poetry in his honor. Halevi goes on to describe his relations with Ḥalfon ben Nethaniel as the second stage in a rising ladder of dignitaries he has encountered:

> *But all this was merely the gently flowing waters of Shiloah, compared to the overflowing Jordan that has swept over Judah in its course,*[26] *when the word of my lord reached the hand of my lord, the distinguished sage, the fortress and tower, the pure and righteous father of justice, the all-capable*

and all-knowing master and teacher Ḥalfon Halevi, my protector and beautiful ornament, who has overwhelmed me with his favor these past two years and multiplied it seven times over and over again. He is a covering for my eyes,[27] *for I have been thrown into his care. I am counting on him to kindly serve as an eloquent mediator between me and my lord, trusting that he has the power to correct my neglect and to bring my declaration to the ears of my lord in the way I desire.*

The neglect that Halevi refers to must be his delaying his response. This passage strongly suggests that Halevi's acquaintance with Ḥalfon went back no further than 1138, presumably when Ḥalfon visited al-Andalus.[28] Now comes the fourth and final part of the epistle, in which Halevi turns his attention to Samuel:

Then your letter arrived, girded in all might and containing all splendor. It was nearly sent to an ear that was shut tight and locked. It was far too hard for me to understand, so far above me that I couldn't make it out, full of wisdom and elegantly formed; how lovely was its surface, how profound its content. No one could design a setting for such pearls or compound such fragrant perfume. Who can even understand it, let alone that I should answer it!

Samuel's letter to Halevi must have been a formal epistle in Hebrew. It was customary to praise a letter for being both a beautiful physical object—referring to the calligraphy, the paper, and the ink—and an elegant literary production. Respondents often compliment writers on the difficulty of their style, for obscurity arising from a display of erudition, considered a defect in our writing, was exactly what elite writers strived for in a culture that was founded on widespread knowledge of a uniform body of classical texts. As one of the age's greatest Hebrew writers, Halevi could not really have been at a loss to understand Samuel ben Ḥanania's epistle; and Samuel must have been aware that Halevi was speaking hyperbolically; this style was dictated by protocol.

Now Halevi reaches his main point:

When your messenger arrived and delivered his speech, my soul yearned to be in your resting place, and my heart was sick with longing to behold the light of your moon and the gleam of your sunrise.

I tell a lovesick heart
licked by passion's flame:

Cairo has the cure—
thither will I send you.

So I said to the messenger: "Lead me and go, do not prevent me from riding, but take me to his place. . . . Let there be no delay in greeting the presence of him who grants wisdom with delight and gives joy to the sight in the garden of the lord, in Cairo. He will give me his hand in aid so that I reach Jerusalem, with the help of God, after I embrace the place that his sole has trodden and covered myself with the dust of his feet."[29] *I beg my lord the Nagid to forgive the freedom I have taken with his dignity in delaying a bit and moving so slowly, refraining from the road in spite of myself, through being preoccupied with a business affair. "They called the place 'busy' for they did business with him there."*[30] *I linger, but my letter goes on ahead to be my ransom and to appease my master with the gift that precedes me. Accept this small thing from the least of your servants, the youngest of your disciples. May your honor accept the greetings in this reply to your splendid letter, which is my crown and splendor. The ears heard and the hands wrote; the eyes became jealous and consulted the feet, and said: "Come, let us go, appear and be present, know and proclaim, tell and make heard." All my insides were longing and trembling, hoping for the spirit to pour over us and carry us that we might be seen before you, may that time be near and soon to arrive. Amen.*

Echoing his complaint of being too busy in the epistle to Rabbi Ḥabīb of al-Mahdiyya, Halevi apologizes for his delay in responding to the Nagid's letter and in coming to Cairo. He must have been certain that his excuse—that he was being detained in Alexandria by a business affair—would be perfectly well understood and accepted, even by a lofty official like the Nagid, who presided over a supremely mercantile society, most of whose most powerful constituents owed their wealth to business rather than to landowning, agriculture, or professions.

Halevi sent with the epistle the customary lengthy panegyric poem. It is organized as a series of apostrophes: the speaker summons, one after the other, the heavens, the leaders of Israel, the Levites, and even the dead, to go to do honor to Samuel, the wise leader and life-giving physician. At last, he addresses the clouds and the Nile, asking them to convey his own greetings to the Nagid. This leads him to reflect on his own status as a wanderer in a strange land and as a poet facing a great challenge in praising a man of the Nagid's stature. In order to understand the address to the Nile, it is necessary to know that many medieval Jews thought that the Nile was the same as the biblical river Pishon, one of the four rivers said to emerge from the Garden of Eden:[31]

O Nile stream, behold my streams of tears,
and judge if you have wept as much as I.
You, who come from Eden's river,

you, who watered Eden's trees:
Pour, Pishon, and weep for one
who left a paradise, as you did.
You know the wanderer's lament,
for you have been a stranger too.
As you rise every year in spring,
we have come up from the West,
to visit Samuel. You have traversed
the lands of gems and gold,
but nothing like him have you seen.
O inspiration, hand of God!—
why do you hold back when I call?
O wings of thought!—
why have you suddenly gone slack?
O lines of verse!—you spoke so eagerly when I lied,
but now that I have truth to speak, are mute!
You all conspire against me, traitors,
refuse the reins I want to put on you.
I used to take you in as you ran my way
like animals to Noah's ark,
but now when I want to gather you,
you've scattered like a flock without a shepherd.
Come, gather round and let me make a diadem
of you. Then see how splendid you can be!

It is tempting to interpret these lines as a complaint about some sort of writer's block, even to try to connect them with the notion that Halevi intended to quit writing poetry when he became a pilgrim, but in the context of the panegyric, they mean something quite different. They are a play on a topos, familiar to medieval readers, that poetry is the art of falsehood. "The best of poetry," says the famous Arabic maxim, "is its falsest part," but to praise the Nagid is to speak the truth. When the poet was writing conventional poetry in praise of conventional grandees, when his poetry was all exaggeration and falsehood, it came to him easily. To praise Samuel ben Ḥanania is a task to which the poet is unaccustomed, for words of truth are not inherently poetic and do not come with the same ease. The poet tries to beguile the words to do his will by promising them that in crowning Samuel with praise, they will be crowning themselves: this man is so great that he makes poems immortal instead of the other way around.

The plan was for Ḥalfon to come to fetch Halevi home to Fustat, but he only managed to get away from Cairo a few weeks before Hanukkah. Ḥalfon must have felt uncomfortable in making Halevi wait so long, but business was pressing, and even when he did get away, he left an important transaction pending. One of his brothers, Abū ʿAlī Ezekiel, lived in Qalyub, twelve miles north of the capital, and from a letter that he sent Ḥalfon in Alexandria on November 17, we learn that Ḥalfon had visited him on his way north; when Ḥalfon continued his northward journey, Abū ʿAlī made a quick trip to Fustat to handle this business affair on Ḥalfon's behalf. Since now Abū ʿAlī would be unable to join Ḥalfon in Fustat on the latter's return home, Ḥalfon was planning to pay him a visit, with Halevi, in Qalyub on their way south; Abū ʿAlī asks for exact information about the date of the intended departure so that he would be able to meet them partway, an act of courtesy to the distinguished visitor. He sends Halevi his apologies for not being able to attend him in Alexandria. It is interesting to observe, besides the lofty titles that he attaches to Halevi's name, this businessman's deference to Halevi's renown as a writer:[32]

> To my honorable brother and master, the pupil of my eye, our master and teacher Ḥalfon Halevi, the sage and the wise, the son of my father and master Nethaniel Halevi the pious, may his memory be a blessing, of Damietta. . . .
>
> I left my master and brother in distress for having permitted him to embark in the boat alone with no other traveler or merchant, and I experienced a great sense of danger. God grant it end with your welfare and safety, and may He bring us together soon in the happiest way, with your business successfully concluded, God willing![33]
>
> [A detailed explanation of the business transaction in Fustat follows.]
>
> Let me know soon that you have arrived safely in Alexandria (may God protect it) and when you will depart for your return trip so that perhaps I can go to meet you. And I beg you, my master and brother, to employ all diplomacy in representing me in the service of my master, the splendid lord, the scholarly, learned, distinguished, glorious, great, and holy master Judah Halevi, the humble, God-fearing sage, may God help him and fulfill all his heart's desires. Tell him that my tongue lacks the eloquence to write to such a person as he; that I am determined to stand before him and to meet him and serve him; that I am determined, but that the circumstances of time, of which you know, are still preventing me from doing so.
>
> Your servant Mukārim and all his brothers are my master and brother's servants. They send their greetings and kiss your feet. May my master and brother be well forever and ever. Sunday, 5 Kislev.

Hanukkah began on December 7 that year. It would seem that Halevi was still in Alexandria during the holiday but that Ibn al-ʿAmmānī had gone away, leaving Halevi to celebrate the holiday with others. Who could have been these people with whom Ibn al-ʿAmmānī spent the festival and at whom Halevi hurled the dart in the last line?[34]

Unhappy are my thoughts this Hanukkah;
they sigh, my lord, because you are away.
How can I enjoy your company
if you're not in my bed? What joy is there in drinking?
My thoughts were happy on Sukkot, with you;[35]
but now, on Hanukkah, they're dead.
When you were near, this was a watered garden,
but now that you're away, a dust-land.
Swear by your friendship, friend, swear by
the Hasmonean priest and by his sons,
to keep your friends in mind while you're away
and keep them ever in your heart, so wise.
Remember, lions are not lambs,
or roses the same as thorn-bush cuttings!

The poem's allusion to the Hasmonean was intended as a compliment to Ibn al-ʿAmmānī. Mattathias the Hasmonean was the first leader of the rebellion of the Judeans against Antiochus IV in 167 BCE, the success of which is celebrated on the festival of Hanukkah; Mattathias had five sons, known as the Maccabees, who founded a dynasty of kings of Judea. The reference to him is intended to imply that Ibn al-ʿAmmānī, likewise a leader of his people who had five sons, was a man of similar stature. Halevi was not so complimentary about the people with whom Ibn al-ʿAmmānī spent the holiday. He calls them lambs and thorn-bush cuttings, while calling himself a lion and a rose. This indiscreet remark would be thrown back at Halevi a few months later.

5

Cairo

O God, each age narrates
Your wonders to the next,
fathers tell their children—
truth incontrovertible.
Witness this Nile here before me,
which You turned to blood—
not by magic, charms, or sorcery,
but just Your name in Moses' mouth,
with Aaron at his side,
and in his hand, the staff You turned into a serpent.
O, be with me, Your trusting slave, as I make haste
to see the places where Your miracles took place.

As Halevi and Ḥalfon, accompanied by Isaac Ibn Ezra and Abū l-Rabīʿ Solomon Ibn Gabbai, moved up the Nile, Halevi was already approaching the first of the goals of his pilgrimage, for he was entering the territory where, according to tradition, the biblical narrative of the Exodus had taken place.[1] He now beheld the sites where, according to the Torah, miracles occurred that, he had argued in the Kuzari, were authenticated by the unbroken Jewish tradition going back to the age of Moses. It was in this kind of certainty that he had sought to ground his faith, rather than in the illusions of rational argument.

Halevi and Ḥalfon set out for Cairo during or just after Hanukkah. A letter from Amram to Ḥalfon suggests that they spent a

Sabbath en route in Abyar, not far from the midpoint; Amram—as usual, full of complaints about his personal troubles—again wryly quotes a famous line of poetry, this time taking the opportunity to quote Halevi himself:[2]

> I was in a state of continual worry until someone told me that you had spent the Sabbath in Abyar. If I had known that the feet of our master and teacher Judah would tread that room, I would have rubbed my face in the dust that his feet have trodden;[3] but there is no escaping the decree of God. Nothing else has occurred except that I am caught up in my illness and the illness of the one with me,[4] in misery such that no one has ever heard or seen the like. . . . Indeed, I am in the state that our master (may he be established forever!) described about reaching the decade of one's seventies, when no one listens to what he says and his opinions are not taken seriously. . . . "He returns to his native soil." And if I were to describe to you what has happened since the two of you left. . . .

Amram's gloomy "There is no escaping the decree of God" refers to his own illness and his inability to pay sufficient homage to Halevi. The poem that he quotes is a famous one by Halevi on the ages of man.[5]

From Abyar, they proceeded up the Nile, stopping at Qalyub, where Halevi at last met Ḥalfon's brother Abū ʿAlī Ezekiel. Our only information about this visit is a poem that Halevi wrote by way of farewell, the last line of which suggests that they were treated to a hearty meal:[6]

Curses on this crooked Nile!
It squirms in its course like a twisty serpent,
but straightens out to help me leave you,
clears the way for separation,
sweeps the very pebbles
from a traveler's path.
God strengthen my distended belly
as I bid farewell
to a cousin-Levite of Kehat,
the Prince Ezekiel—
the pride of princes, boast of the bountiful,
chief of chiefmen, best of scribes and merchants.
I still can taste his manna and the rain
his clouds poured over me—
manna that does not melt, and never spoils.

Halevi connects every aspect of the visit with Abū ʿAlī to some aspect of the Exodus. In his facetious irritation with the twisting Nile for facilitating his departure from Qalyub, he implicitly compares it to the pillar of cloud in the desert, which, according to the midrash, cleared the serpents and stones ahead of the column of wandering Israelites.[7] In thanking Ezekiel for his bountiful meal, he recalls the manna with which God sustained the Israelites in the desert. And he cannot resist calling attention to their common descent from Levi through Kehat.

If Ḥalfon and Halevi left Alexandria right after Hanukkah (Sunday, December 22), their Sabbath in Abyar would have fallen on the day before the fast of the Tenth of Tevet, and they would have reached Ḥalfon's home on the fast day. This fast commemorates the beginning of the siege of Jerusalem in 587 BCE that ended with the Temple's destruction in 586. There is a poem by Halevi that was written on the Tenth of Tevet in the presence of Ḥalfon, mentioning Halevi's planned pilgrimage and thanking Ḥalfon for his help in accomplishing it. In the present state of our knowledge, it is impossible to tell whether the poem was written at this point in our narrative, on the day of their arrival at Ḥalfon's home in December 1140; more likely, it was written during Ḥalfon's visit to Spain two years earlier. But Halevi and Ḥalfon could not have helped bringing it to mind now, and Halevi would have sung the refrain with considerable satisfaction now that he was so much closer to completing his journey.[8]

My heart is urging me
to go up to my Temple, see my city.

The high and radiant God
Whose wonders stun men's hearts,
Whose word has made
the sundial go backward,

Who made the Nile
wash the peaks of Spain—
He will strengthen me
to stand in the Holy Sanctuary.

Who will help me,
if not the best man of my fathers' tribe?
My lot has fallen
among the best of Jewish clans—
the Levites,
who sing my Temple's hymn;

Yet but for him,
Kehat would be bereft.

The poets spell
each other singing Ḥalfon's praise.
His friends all find
welfare and peace on every side;
his enemies
encounter scorpions on their path.
He is my lion when I need
his help, my song on days of joy.

My garden of delight,
of nard and henna he.
My seeds have flourished
for Ḥalfon's hands are light.
My plants are thriving,
yielding luscious fruit—
the fragrance of my harvest,
of henna clusters I have plucked.

His name, Ḥalfon, means "changer,"
for he changes woe to joy,
has turned this day of sorrow
into a day of feasting.
Thanks and song today
present their gifts to him;
O fast day of the Tenth—
You now are Ḥalfon's feast!

My heart is urging me
to go up to my Temple, see my city.

The two conceits of miraculous reversal of direction in the opening strophe probably mean that Ḥalfon's visit to al-Andalus and offering to help Halevi in his pilgrimage are wonders comparable to the sun's shadow reversing course on the face of a sundial or the Nile's waters washing the hills of Spain. "He will strengthen me" formally has God as the subject, but since the focus of the strophe has been on Ḥalfon, it could just as well refer to the latter, especially since the poet will dwell on Ḥalfon's help in the second full strophe. Halevi stresses Ḥalfon's status as a fellow Levite. The turning of days of mourning into days of feasting in the last stanza refers to a messianic promise in the Bible;[9] in accordance with the penchant of Golden Age poets for applying sacred language to secular uses, Halevi here plays on Ḥalfon's name, making him the agent through whom the fast day turns into a feast, thereby indirectly calling Ḥalfon his savior.

In Cairo, Halevi was geographically farther from the Land of Israel than he had been in Alexandria, but in the logic of the sacred journey he was actually nearer, for although Alexandria was twelve hundred years older than Cairo, it had no special associations with Jewish sacred history, while Cairo was the biblical heartland of Egypt. As the Muslim pilgrim, on reaching the environs of the holy cities of Mecca and Medina, replaces his secular clothing with the white garments of pilgrimage, so Halevi might have been expected to clothe himself in a mood of heightened religiosity as he approached the capital. This would have been especially true if, indeed, his intention was to begin his journey where the ancient Israelites began theirs and to retrace their steps. We sense this change of mood in some of his poems.

Gazing over the landscape around Cairo, Halevi saw places that he identified as Goshen, Pitom, and Raamses, where the biblical Israelites lived and labored, places named in the Torah readings that, by coincidence, were the very ones being read in the synagogue, pursuant to the annual lectionary cycle, around the time of Halevi's arrival. He mentions these three sites in the great panegyric poem addressed to Nathan ben Samuel that we will be reading later, but short poems of this period also give us a taste of his excitement and awe at being on biblical territory:[10]

Look! Cities, countryside
that once belonged to Israelites.
Tread Egypt lightly, give her deference;
don't pound her soil or crush the streets
that God once walked
seeking doorposts daubed with blood of paschal lambs—
where fire and cloud once rose in pillars
and people stopped and gazed.
This land is the very quarry
out of which the Lord once hewed
the people of the covenant, from which He cut
the leaders of the people of the Lord.

Gazing at the desert surrounding Cairo, he reflected on the roundabout course that was his preferred route to the Holy Land:[11]

Now Time has led me by its twisted ways
to Egypt's wilderness. To Time I say:
"Just keep on twisting me, till I behold

Judea's wilderness, until I reach
the northern slope, that lofty, lovely place.
There I will robe myself in God's eternal name,
and twist a turban of His holiness around my head."

The poem is governed by the rare verb *tsanaf,* which means "to wind" or "to twist." Time—inexorable fate and its vicissitudes, a traditionally sinister figure from the stock of literary traditions that Halevi inherited from Arabic poetry—has exiled Halevi to Egypt. But Halevi has no complaint about this kind of exile—bring on more exile, he says, because this is an exile that is a return; when he once reaches his goal, the twisting course of his journey will be twisted into a turban of dignity.[12]

Perhaps the sight of the desert that he planned to traverse put him in mind of Moses gazing from the peak of Mount Nebo in the wilderness of Moab at the land he would never reach and gave him the idea for his poem "Hail, Mount Avarím!" (poem 13).

These connections between Egypt and the early history of the Jews, felt so strongly by Halevi, were used against him by friends who tried to persuade him to give up his pilgrimage and remain in Egypt on the grounds that Egypt itself was full of holy sites. In response to their arguments, Halevi wrote an angry poem, "Praise to Egypt!" (poem 19), acknowledging the role of Egypt in the history of Israelite revelation and peoplehood, but insisting on the primacy of the Land of Israel.

The poems quoted until now show that, in a sense, his pilgrimage really began in Cairo; but his other writings of the time show that even there he did not stop living in the world. The most striking evidence comes from one of the richest and most famous of the poems that he wrote in Egypt, a poem that, more than many, shows how mixed in him were the sacred and the secular. It is a panegyric ode addressed to Rabbi Nathan ben Samuel, the secretary of the Nagid of Egypt, written in response to a letter from the secretary, who was undoubtedly the Nagid's gatekeeper.[13] At the beginning of the epistle, not included in the part translated above, Halevi implies that Nathan had taken the initiative in the correspondence. It affords us a precious glimpse of Halevi as an individual and the complexities of his commitments, for though it begins with a secular description of the Egyptian spring, it ends with religious scruples:[14]

Has Time thrown off its robes of terror,
dressed itself in garb of pleasure?
Nature here is dressed in white and colored garments,
sits on cushioned mats of gold brocade,
and every plot of planted ground along the Nile

is wearing checkered cloth. The Land of Goshen
sports a breastplate like a high priest's
(set with flowers, though, not precious stones).
Oases, too, are spread with colored matting;
Raamses and Pitom
have draped gold chains of office on their chests.
Beside the Nile are girls, and not just one or two;
gazelles, yet different from gazelles, for not as fleet—
their arms weighed down with heavy bracelets,
golden anklets heavy on their legs.
They steal your heart, make you forget your age;
your mind goes back to youths and girls
from other times and places.
Meanwhile, in this Eden that is Egypt,
in gardens by the Nile's bank, in the fields,
the greenish, reddish grain stands tall
as if in colorful dresses, rippled
by a western breeze; it makes you think
of people bowing, giving thanks to God,
or paying homage to a prince,
a man of princely speech, to Master Nathan,
the man who made their land
resemble a pavilion in a garden
or a bridegroom's many-colored chamber. . . .

Blessed are the ships that brought me here,
and blessed, too, their stork-wing sails
that carried me to where he lives in splendor
to see how lovely are his dwelling places,
while on my way to my ancestral land,
which I intend to measure with my feet.
My lord, you crown me with the crown
of your own glory—glory yours by nature,
to others, affectation;
glory that comes and goes with them, but is with you always.

Take this poem, take this best of songs
(best, because your accomplishments are its theme),
intended as a lyric chain of honor,
but honored by the very name it sings.
By singing it, I steal a bit from God,

to Whom alone my songs are promised.
I have devoted, dedicated, put aside
my songs to Him alone, the only God.
But I permit myself this one exception:
to honor and to thank His sons and scholars.
I trust His clemency—it suits Him to forgive—
and give Him thanks, as due to Him from me.

The poem is a classic Andalusi *qaṣīda,* or formal ode, constructed in accordance with a literary tradition that goes back to the pre-Islamic Arabic tribal poetry, refined and regularized by the poets of the court of Baghdad in the eighth century and adopted by Arabic-speaking Hebrew poets (as well as poets writing in Persian, Turkish, and most other languages of the Islamic world). In accordance with the conventions of the genre, it begins with no obvious indication that it is a panegyric. The opening lines are devoted to nature description and the evocation of sensual pleasures—in this case, the Nile, described as paradise—girls on the riverbanks, and Egypt's bounteous grain swaying in the breeze. Then a pivot verse links the descriptive material in the first part to the poem's addressee. This is done here by comparing the swaying grain to people praying or bowing in homage to Nathan, named here for the first time. Now comes the poem's second part, containing the actual panegyric; here, the image of Egypt-as-paradise slides into the praise of the addressee, suggesting that all this delight is somehow Nathan's doing. The poem ends with an *envoi*—"Take these poems"—an optional type of conclusion.

The panegyric (abridged in the translation provided here) praises Nathan as a scholar and religious teacher, which must have been pleasant enough to the recipient's ears. But it contains a surprise, as Halevi modulates from the panegyric to the autobiographical mode. Arabic panegyric poets often included in their odes an account of their journey to the patron, and in this vein, Halevi praises the ship that brought him to Egypt and into the presence of Nathan. But he also points out that his goal is not Nathan, worthy as he is, but the Land of Israel. This autobiographical twist prepares the way for the astoundingly original turn in the *envoi,* where Halevi outdoes himself in the play of sacred and secular, and praises Nathan in terms extravagant even for panegyric. This occurs in the lines in which he claims that he has given up writing panegyric poetry, having decided that no mere mortal but only God should be the object of his praises. (Halevi thus hyperbolically subsumes panegyric under a religious transgression known by the technical term *meʿila,* the misappropriation of cultic objects.) This theme is consistent with Halevi's repeated remarks disparaging the service of men, whether his own service to others or the homage of others to himself. Halevi justifies making an exception for Nathan on the grounds that as a scholar of Torah, Nathan deserves some of the honor normally due to God. This factitious renunciation of panegyric is the only extant statement in Halevi's own words (besides the remark in the accompanying epistle to be discussed next) of an intention to limit his writing of poetry. It is not a blanket renunciation of poetry, and it is brought up only to be broken; Halevi's renunciation of panegyric turns out to be merely a strategy of panegyric.

But Halevi the pilgrim did not stop writing panegyric verse; he remained caught up in ordinary human relationships. We have seen him bursting with poetry throughout the period of his pilgrimage, poetry that deals with all the conventional themes and forms—serious poetry and frivolous poetry, public poetry and private poetry, secular poetry, and now, even panegyric. There were grumblings about the inconsistency of Halevi's behavior, as we shall see, but he does not hesitate to call attention to it.

The poem to Nathan accompanied a formal epistle, a writing swimming in expressions of adulation for the recipient and of humility on the part of the writer. We have encountered such extreme rhetoric in Halevi's epistle to Samuel ben Ḥanania and even to his friend and host, Aaron Ibn al-ʿAmmānī, though in a slightly lower key. We should assume that the language of each of these formal epistles represents the exactly appropriate degree of deference for the recipient's status. As respected and honored as were men like Ibn al-ʿAmmānī and Ḥalfon, they were merely businessmen and professionals; but the Nagid was the nearest thing the Jews had to royalty, and the members of his staff were his courtiers. The Nagid conferred more dignity on the people around him than could any ordinary rabbi or merchant, no matter how learned or rich.

But amid the rhetoric, the letter contains some of Halevi's additional reflections on his position as a man devoted to the religious life, yet still caught up in ordinary human relationships; a man who has sworn off panegyric but who can revert to it when pressed by social obligation.[15]

> *. . . to the marvelous sage and loftiest crown, a man whose name is greater than all others, our master and teacher Rabbi Nathan the Associate, the crown of the rabbis, the son of our honorable master, the righteous Rabbi Samuel the Associate (may his memory be a blessing) from one who is but a particle of his light, a mere branch of his river, Judah Halevi, his inferior, a leftover from his harvest and a gleaning of his vine, who sends his heart ahead of this letter, fearful and fainthearted, to reply to the substance of what he has written. Armed with plough and spade, how can I contend with real warriors, the Cherethites and Pelethites, the mighty host, who fight for Nathan, he, a Benaiah for command, an Ethan for council?*[16] *Who am*

I, what is my life, what are my longings and what are my desires, I who am cinders and ashes, a man ruined and sickened, preoccupied with my sins, the transgressions of my youth and old age, I who have set my face to attend my God with my prayers, I, a stranger passing for the night, a Levite here for a brief sojourn.[17]

How can I approach or consort with the majesty and grandeur, not to mention the golden tongue? I have summoned counsel from afar and taken up my instruments and come and gone hither and yon, but found nothing better than silence. In shame and humiliation, I despaired of answering; I was too weak to go forward to meet him. I fumbled at the wall in the dark like a blind man and sought somewhere to hide.

Then I encountered stern taskmasters from the marvelous sage pressing and urging; from the prince, the exalted captain, our master and teacher Ḥalfon Halevi, calling in your name and rousing me to cling to you; my lord and splendor, lofty, exalted, and great, who mediates between us, joining our hearts by sending our letters and openly declaring our love. He pressed me and urged me and pressured me and roused me; he hurried me out of the prison of inanition and helped me unstintingly, saying, "Come, let me try you; complete your labor, and fill the quota of the bricks of quality as if you had been given the straw of wisdom. Act the young man in your old age, know to whom you are responsible, on whose account you are writing, and on whose account your work is sealed."

His charmers pushed me forward, his magicians did their work, so that finally I broke my vows and undid my oaths; my bonds melted away, my youth was restored; my poems came rushing, and my lyres assembled. My fears were forgotten, and so were the long years I have dwelled in this world. I put aside the knowledge that the day has come near to setting, the inn is nearby. But the labor is great. I mixed myself in with massy multitude, roused myself to youthful activities, and did the things expected of men whose hair is still black, hid my white hair like stolen property, though my denial itself protests against me. Then I poured forth my speech, struggling doughtily; I wrestled with the lion and prevailed, wresting an ear-tip out of his grip; I treated my own life lightly, making myself to be like the scribes of the king, men who have the strength to stand in his palace.

May my lord in his kindness forgive his servant, and not examine his words too carefully or weight them with scruples. Judge me leniently and bring me not into the strict judgment dictated by your wisdom.

This is the fruit of my thoughts, the hymn of my love, the best of my speech, the most my hand and tongue can do, to mark my place until I can come to my master and attend at his gates to gather his crystals and to sing his praises, which are only a bit of his ways and a small part of the gleaming of his moon. May He who makes peace in His heavens give you much peace, security to your friends, war to your enemies, and fulfill your plans so that you may pass your days in welfare, and I close with "peace." Amen.

The rhetoric is not devoid of specifics. When Halevi calls himself too inept to write, it is the expression of modesty appropriate for a man known to the recipient as a master of the written word. When he calls himself a sojourner in the land, that is plainly true. When he calls himself a humble Levite, we recall that he often boasts of his Levitical pedigree; but here, he turns the boast to an expression of humility by using biblical quotations that describe the Levites not as glamorous celebrants of the Temple ritual but as mere sacred menials; he also throws in a passage that speaks of a down-on-his-luck Levite who came to a bad end. Thus, the apparently ready-made formulas contain much specific content. They become even more specific when he calls himself a man ruined and sickened, "preoccupied with my sins, the transgressions of my youth and old age, I who have set my face to attend my God with my prayers," phrases that relate specifically to his pilgrimage. The theme of guilt as a motivation for the pilgrimage, touched on here, will come up again in the pilgrimage poetry.

Halevi brings up again in the epistle the theme of the propriety of poetry that was such a striking feature of the accompanying poem. He says that he has broken a vow in order to write the epistle but does not say exactly what the vow was. Having read the accompanying poem, we might conclude that he is speaking of the vow to stop writing panegyric poetry to ordinary mortals, but the formulation is a bit broader. By saying that in order to write the epistle and the poem he has had to behave like a young man again, he associates the writing of poetry with youth, and old age with the abandonment of poetry. In this way, he ties the vow to the classic motif of the poet who gives up poetry in his old age, discussed above in chapter 2. But, like the passage about panegyric poetry in the ode, it does not seem like a serious autobiographical statement. It makes the impression, rather, of using the familiar motif as a vehicle for expressing deference to Nathan, as if to say: I have gone so far in honoring you that I have even dispensed with my dignity as an elderly pilgrim and written poetry again like a young man.

The youthful spirit of Halevi's ode to Nathan, with its opening invocation of the lushness of nature and the luxuriousness of sexual attraction, is indeed astonishing in a man like Halevi. Some of Halevi's contemporaries may have thought it incongruous for a pilgrim to write in such a worldly vein. But Halevi's point at the end of the poem and in the epistle is that for any man of his age and condition, secular poetry is inappropriately worldly; and besides, from a religious point of view, even socially appropriate panegyric comes near to idolatry, being tantamount to the worship of man by man. Not for Nathan such religious niceties; this rabbi and courtier of the Egyptian Nagid, like his Andalusi peers, took such conventions for granted. We may assume that he received Halevi's poem and epistle with pleasure and gratitude.

Halevi's correspondence with Nathan was undoubtedly related to his planned audience with the Nagid. After the audience, Halevi reported on it to Aaron Ibn al-ʿAmmānī in an epistle that was partly intended to assure the latter that Halevi had not missed the opportunity of the audience to advance his affairs. The epistle begins with the usual opening compliments, in the course of which Halevi writes of his longing for Ibn al-ʿAmmānī. Do not be shocked at the erotic language that he employs: in the epistolary conventions of the Hebrew Golden Age, as in those of the Elizabethan Age, expressions of friendship, especially expressions of friendship at a distance, often adopt the language of lovers:[18]

> *On my bed at night, I sought him who my soul loveth. I said to my heart, "Let me go unto the mount of myrrh." And while I was still speaking, before I had concluded, God brought to my hand an epistle sent to me on the wings of the wind, perfumed with the myrtle of peace and taken from the stores of the spice merchants, anointed with holy oil, spreading the fragrance of the apple tree spreading in all directions, disseminating free-flowing myrrh and the fragrance of frankincense, having no peer. . . .*

There follow many lines of panegyric to Aaron that need not detain us. Halevi again seems to be apologizing for not having written sooner. His excuse is simply that his inspiration had fled until he thought about Aaron, whereupon it came rushing back:

> *My deeds are diminished, my thoughts are lost and find no vision from God. I cannot find the children of my mind. I regret ever having begotten them, for they have gone rebellious on me like the house of rebellion, setting their faces hard, closing their eyes, and stopping their ears. . . . I spread my net and drew my bow, when no one was with me, meaning to draw them to do my will and to bring them into the folds of my rein. I summoned them in your name, set riders on them and, lo! They came running, one after one, for now the divine vision was everywhere: Who could not prophesy?*

Halevi professes to regret having left Ibn al-ʿAmmānī to come to Cairo:

> *Thus I have come today to send you greetings, to attend you in your place, and to proclaim to my lord how sorry I am that I ever left you, since I love you. When I think of you, I seek you, but do not find you. My days have turned to haze, my nights to blights, my times to terrors; demons attack me, devils harass me; they roll me like a ball, assay me as in a furnace, and almost burn me to cinders, after having expelled me, pursued me, ripped me like a lion, washed me away like a river. If I did not have your epistles for my delight as a planted garden or an orchard in flower; as my brethren and friends, my kin and my companions; as the sweetness of my goblet and the pleasure of my bed; if I could not read them at all times so that they strengthened my limbs; were they not like sixty warriors surrounding my bed, extinguishing the fires of my suffering and restoring my soul, I nearly would have regretted and repented and said, "What possessed me to go to Cairo to drink the black waters of the Nile?"*[19]

Halevi now introduces his meeting with the Nagid:

> *I came to Egypt and my eyes saw many multiples of what my ears had heard in the circle of his honor, the prince of princes, the nagid of negidim, the home of nagidship and the tabernacle of friendship. I saw it directly, not in hints and riddles: a man true to the sacred and good to men, who combines greatness and learning, who partakes of the two tables.*[20] *But he, in his humility . . . uses up his days seeking the welfare of his people. To see him is to see the face of God, and to ask his counsel is to ask an oracle. His messengers brought word from him, filled me with his delights, bore me his treasures, and proclaimed his friendship to me, so much so that my hands are tired from counting and my praises exhausted with telling. So now, if I have found favor in your eyes, lend me your tongue and your princely conceits; lend me your pearls and push forward your clouds so as to emit some word of praise to requite him partly for his favors and for a little of his generosity. May his crown blossom*[21] *and God be by his side.*

At last, he comes to the part of such importance to Ibn al-ʿAmmānī:

> *Your status with him is great, and you are dear to him; he elevates you in his sacred opinion, and does not lower you.*[22] *The slanderer's word has no effect on him for better or worse; it does not put you in bad odor and should not shake your trust; does not part you from allies and should not trouble your sleep. You can take rest without fear. How can anyone not know your greatness when it is he who tests silver, he the assayer's crucible for testing*

> *gold. You are all gold with no blemish. Who of the elders of your generation are like you or can be compared to you? They have the title "judge" but you have the substance.*[23] *They are the cisterns, but you are the fountain. Not all that flows is water; not every tent is the heavens; not every birth yields an Aaron; not every pine tree can be made into a mast.*[24] *He deserves dominion and you deserve to be vice-regent and captain of his camp. The golden altar can only be sanctified with the holy incense.*[25] *Your praises derive from his dominion, and his praises come from your eloquent songs. May God keep you together in office, and may He preserve your wisdom forever.*

At the epistle's conclusion, we can see that Halevi is still troubled by the clash between his spiritual aspirations and his worldly self. Delightfully for us, he reverts to the secular themes that we have already encountered in his letter and poem to Nathan:

> *And may the two of us return to the delights of wine and the delusions of the eye . . . for you and I both remember the poems we used to compose in the days of our youth, so fine, now flown. You ask, "Can it be done when the heart is youthless and no longer feckless, when one looks around and sees no gleam of light, and when spring rains fall no longer?" One day, your friends were busy drinking and firing the brazier of love. They gave me something to drink, too, and we talked of old times. I awoke speaking verses, uttering words fit for princes, poems of friendship, with a particular delightful man in mind. So now, in your kindness, take this offering, cense yourself with its fragrance, and forgive its shortcomings.*

Thus the epistle ends with the promise of a poem, one written in a youthful spirit; and indeed the attached poem takes up, both at the beginning and the end, the erotic themes hinted at in the letter's close. The erotic opening of this poem is even more elaborate than that of "Has Time Thrown off Its Robes of Terror?," the ode addressed to Nathan the Associate, and shows definitively that Halevi was still willing to devote significant effort to composing full-length panegyric *qaṣīdas*:[26]

Sweet singers, bring your lyres to lovelies!
Singers, players, spell each other
singing to those girls secluded,
peering, gazing through the lattice;
all true daughters of Rebecca,
pure of heart and pure of body
but for this: they draw their bows—
all innocence—to murder men!

They do not need swords for warfare,
for they have those bare white arms.
They can hardly lift their eyelids;
how then do they manage bangles?
If they raised their faces sunward,
they would leave the sun sun-burnt!
With white faces and black tresses,
they command the light and dark,
with tunics bright as days of meeting,
hair as dark as nights of parting.
They are stars, my heart the sphere
where they will revolve forever.
Easy it is to fall in love
with girls who're delicate, yet ample,
with red mouths that complement
their brilliant rows of crystal teeth.
Don't be hard on them for flirting,
for they're bearing weighty burdens:
apples, pomegranates, roses,
roses that have healing powers.
What to say about a woman
tall and noble as a palm,
yet blown about by any wind?
See!—the hearts they stole are ruined;
should they pay the damages?
Or was this their just revenge
on us for gazing at their cheeks?
Ask a rabbi, ask a judge
who's mastered every legal topic.
A capital case?—Ask Ben-Zion!
He will tell you what God's law is.
Aaron wears the high priest's Urim
and the Tumim on his body.
Dignity selected and
anointed him with finest chrism,
left the leftovers to his colleagues.
They may be his peers in fame, but
when you need them, they're just blowhards.
Knowing that his sheaves are full ones,
who'd want others' withered sheaves?

Aaron challenges death's angels,
draws his sword and holds his own,
halts a plague, like Aaron in the
desert and revives the dead
with his drugs and herbs but also
with the wisdom of his lips.
When I think of him, my heart
is like a dove that flees the hawk,
and when I write of him, his memory
makes my heart's blood flood my face.
To Zion and her sons my heart
thirsts for water like a desert.
He has five sons, like the Bear—
the very Pleiades bow before them!—
shall I not go, show my face
before their presence, sow my longing,
which I thought would end or fade,
but which I now find ever growing?
Can Cairo contain me, when
my soul is rushing toward Zion?—
My heart will scorch her very stones,
my tears will wash away her soil
when at last I go bareheaded
and unshod to comfort her.
My tears rushed out before I wrote,
for my sighing pressed them forward,
tears that surge continuously
like gifts raining from your hand.
Your bounty is like harem girls,
like lyres, fountains, singing birds,
rewarding you with pleasures doubled,
tripled, thousanded, O master!

Thematically conventional but brilliantly executed, the poem opens with a play on words too elaborate to reproduce in translation, summoning the singers to praise the beautiful girls of a harem. These beauties are said to slay men by making off with their hearts. Is this culpable behavior, or can the metaphorical crime be excused on the grounds that the women were merely avenging themselves on the men for stealing glances at their cheeks? A weighty conundrum; in verse 19, the poet suggests bringing it for adjudication to Aaron Ibn al-ʿAmmānī, the judge, thus effecting the transition to the panegyric, which occupies the rest of the poem.

As in the poem to Nathan, Halevi introduces a personal statement into the panegyric. After praising Ibn al-ʿAmmānī as a wise rabbi and an effective doctor, and after mentioning his sons, as he had done in some of his other poems to Ibn al-ʿAmmānī, Halevi uses Ibn al-ʿAmmānī's epithet Ben-Zion (son of Zion) to connect the poem with his journey. His longing for this son of Zion reminds him of his longing for Zion itself; his longing for Ben-Zion will draw him to Alexandria, but his greater longing for Zion will draw him out of Egypt entirely. As we shall see often in Halevi's pilgrimage poetry, he speaks of his longing for stones and the dirt of the Holy Land, and imagines himself walking bareheaded and barefoot in mourning over its ruins. But Halevi cannot leave this panegyric poem to end on such a sorrowful note; he ends by returning briefly to the opening evocation of song and beautiful women, and borrows their voice with which to send his greetings to Ibn al-ʿAmmānī.

There is nothing in the letter or the poem to hint at the irritation that Halevi must have felt toward Ibn al-ʿAmmānī after receiving a letter from a friend named Abū l-ʿAlā a few weeks before Passover. In it, Abū l-ʿAlā raises a question that permits us to make some inferences about the status of Halevi's pilgrimage. He also reports some disturbing news involving Halevi's reputation in Alexandria, information sensitive enough to prompt Abū l-ʿAlā to end the letter with the instruction that it be read and then burned:[27]

> In Your Name.
>
> My longing for my master—may God grant you long days of happiness, make your high rank and greatness endure, protect you and keep you!—has intensified. News of you was delayed longer than expected. May God bring me together with you as is desired, for He is the One Who is capable of doing so, if He be willing.
>
> I had already written two letters about the tax but could not reach the travelers in time with this third, for they left at dawn, so I am sending these few lines after them to inform your honor and his honor, my master Abū l-Rabīʿ—may God bring us all together, if He be willing!—what I had explained in the previous two letters. I also want to let you know that your servant my father has not purchased any provisions, whether of east or of west. He greets you and awaits word from you regarding the journey. We long for you to be so good

as to write us about your intentions. If you wish, he will come up to you, and if you wish, he will wait for you here.

As for me, your servant Abū l-ʿAlā, I swear and God knows that if I were not tied up with Gentiles (in fact, with some of the most prominent of this city) and if there were someone here who could take my place, I would substitute myself for this letter. Perhaps that will be during the week of Passover, for I do not care about the kind of worldly things that others do.

As for the news here: the judge took all the poems and made them into a *dīwān,* with headings such as, "This is the poem that Master Judah recited about a pool and a fountain" and "This is what he said in reply"; "This is what Master Judah (may his Rock protect him) recited about chickens" and "This is his reply"; and what he said about this, that, and the other person, and "What he said in a dream."[28] People who saw them [the poems] and hadn't seen that sort of thing were saying, "How can a man who has declared himself a pilgrim be speaking such nonsense?"—especially when he saw what he saw. I was told these things by several witnesses. One incident was only reported by a single person of the judge's circle, according to whom he [Ibn al-ʿAmmānī] said, "One of the top men of the community offered Halevi bread in his house, and he refused to eat it; but he has been with us and does not stop writing panegyrics about us." This caused a great uproar among people who were angered that this had happened to him. I swear, I gave everyone the answer that he deserved, though I am really displeased with the one in the circle of the judge who was the cause of all this because he caused people embarrassment.

In addition, [he was criticized for] the phrase "thorn-bush cuttings" in his poem with the first line "Unhappy Are My Thoughts This Hanukkah." . . . The only thing that led me to mention this, by God, is pure friendship for you, not anger at anyone else, and my caring for your dignity (may it ever be great!). Do not task me with thoughtlessness or frivolity. This is not my nature. I have only one face and I do not conceal a thing, either in religious or worldly affairs.

Special greetings to you for your best welfare. Also the best of greetings to my master the Ṣāhib al-Shurṭa, my master Abū l-Rabīʿ, and my master Isaac.

Put your healing on my heart's wound,
for your love lives deep inside me.

When I'm sad because you're absent,
looking at your writing heals me.

Read and burn immediately. Peace.

Despite the deferential rhetoric at the beginning and end, this letter was evidently written in exasperation. Abū l-ʿAlā begins by explaining that he is writing soon after already entrusting two letters for Halevi to a pair of Cairo-bound travelers. He now finds that he has something to add, but it too late to send this letter with the others, as the travelers had already departed.

The new information is a message from Abū l-ʿAlā's father, a gentle reproach for Halevi's failing to give instructions regarding some business that the father was supposed to transact on Halevi's behalf. In the absence of instructions, Abū l-ʿAlā is holding off purchasing certain merchandise. The word meaning "provisions" has been interpreted as meaning passage on a ship; Halevi, according to this interpretation, was supposed to instruct the father as to whether to buy him passage to the east (Palestine) or to the west (back to Spain), giving rise to speculation that Halevi had not yet decided whether to continue his pilgrimage or to return home. But this interpretation of the Arabic word is unsupported.[29] Whatever the business he was entrusted with on Halevi's behalf, Abū l-ʿAlā's father stands ready to travel to Cairo to meet with Halevi to get his instructions, if Halevi has not decided to return to Alexandria. This could mean that as late as March, Halevi was still hesitating about whether to attempt to reach Palestine overland or to return to Alexandria and continue his pilgrimage by ship.

By "substitute myself for this letter," Abū l-ʿAlā means that he would have liked to have come to Fustat to attend Halevi in person instead of writing. His saying that he might make the trip during the week of Passover implies that the letter was written around the end of February or early March, when the festival, which began on March 25, was neither imminent nor very far in the future. Abū l-ʿAlā's saying that he does not care about the "kind of worldly things" that concern others means that he does not mind shutting down his business for the entire week of the holiday. Work was prohibited during the first two and last two days of the eight-day festival, as well as on the Sabbath, which fell that year on one of the four intermediate days; there was no strict prohibition against working on the three remaining days, but it was considered meritorious to refrain. Abū l-ʿAlā is saying that he is not so driven by desire for profits that he cannot shut down his business in order to spend the festival in Cairo.

The letter's second subject is the even more sensitive matter of the publicity given Halevi's poems by someone who had compiled and circulated the panegyrics and the lighthearted poems that Halevi had written him and that person's own poems written in reply. This person, mentioned not by name but by title alone, was none other than Halevi's chief Alexandrian host, Aaron Ibn al-ʿAmmānī, for most of Halevi's poems referred to in this letter are known to have been written to him: the poem about the pool and the fountain is the memorable panegyric quoted in the preceding chapter, of which Ibn al-ʿAmmānī could justly have been proud. The poem about chickens has likewise been mentioned, as has the poem that Halevi sent Ibn al-ʿAmmānī on Hanukkah. The poem written in a dream also has been plausibly identified.[30] As for Ibn al-ʿAmmānī's replies, these were probably contrafactions, poems written in the same meter and rhyme as the originals. The *dīwāns* of the great medieval Hebrew poets contain many such pairs of poems exchanged by the poets and other grandees.

There would have been nothing intrinsically wrong with Ibn al-ʿAmmānī's circulating the panegyric, for the social function of panegyric was not merely to flatter its recipient in privacy but to enhance his social status in the community. As for the poetic epigrams on frivolous topics, Jewish grandees in al-Andalus regularly amused themselves in their leisure by competing in this genre. The practice must not yet have been common among Halevi's Egyptian counterparts, since Abū l-ʿAlā says that Halevi's epigrams were particularly displeasing to those who were not used to that sort of writing.[31] In that case, Ibn al-ʿAmmānī must have been delighted to show off the new fashion to his friends and to display his own skill at it, not realizing that doing so afforded those who resented Halevi a weapon with which to attack him.

For the poems circulated by Ibn al-ʿAmmānī reinforced another complaint about Halevi: the resentment against his apparent exclusivity, which had caused tension almost from the moment that he set foot in Egypt. Today, it is hard to judge whether this complaint was justified. Halevi did insist on limiting the homes that he would visit. Perhaps he did so out of a sense of his own dignity that would not permit him to mix with any but the most exalted community leaders; nothing we know of him through the extant writings suggests this kind of snobbery, but the Jewish grandees of al-Andalus were capable of behaving loftily. Or perhaps he may have kept to himself on account of his age and frailty.

But it is probably best to take Halevi at his word as set forth in his letter to Ḥalfon quoted in chapter 4: he had turned pilgrim because he wanted to live out his old age in a sober frame of mind, not to dissipate his latter days in entertainment and social events. Yet there were people in Egypt whom he really did want to visit, and whose invitation it would have been churlish to refuse; and he was, to some extent, dependent on the hospitality of others. Being a sociable person, he easily slipped back into the kind of behavior that had always come naturally to him. On the whole, he tried to avoid such situations.

In Alexandria, those who resented his refusing their invitations found it easy to attack him for continuing to write frivolous poetry. We need not assume that these people had any objections to poetry in itself; they were merely repaying Halevi for his apparent exclusivity by calling him a hypocrite. Panegyric was not bad in itself, but panegyric in the mouth of someone who claimed that he was above paying homage to men seemed hypocritical; we have seen Halevi's own reservations on the subject. Epigrams on everyday objects were not bad in themselves, but they seemed frivolous in the mouth of a pilgrim, a *ṭālib ḥajj*, as he is called in the letter, using the Islamic term. Erotic poetry seemed particularly hypocritical in a supposedly holy man. All these cavils were only excuses for the real complaint: that Halevi visited one and not the other.

Ibn al-ʿAmmānī was probably a conventionally pious man of the type Halevi was fleeing Spain to escape, an admirable man who led an exemplary life as a rabbi and communal official but who saw nothing wrong with giving himself a little publicity by circulating Halevi's poems. By doing so, he showed himself insensitive to Halevi's position as one who no longer wanted to be thought of as a glib wordsmith, and he showed himself insensitive to the members of his community whose invitations Halevi had turned down. Particularly thoughtless was Ibn al-ʿAmmānī's circulating the poem "Unhappy Are My Thoughts This Hanukkah" (which we encountered at the end of chapter 4) because of its last lines:

Swear by your friendship, friend, swear by
the Hasmonean priest and by his sons,
to keep your friends in mind while you're away
and keep them ever in your heart, so wise.
Remember, lions are not lambs,
or roses the same as thorn-bush cuttings!

In these lines, Halevi unambiguously disparaged others. These lines of verse handed Halevi's detractors something specific to be insulted about.

Abū l-ʿAlā's irritation in the letter from which we learn about this contretemps is expressed as if directed primarily at Ibn al-ʿAmmānī; but perhaps we may read between the lines some reproach to Halevi, too, for trusting Ibn al-ʿAmmānī to use the poems with discretion, and perhaps even for Halevi's exclusive policy of visiting only a chosen few, this being the true source of the problem.[32] But we latter-day admirers of Halevi are in debt to Ibn al-ʿAmmānī, for it is probably due to his self-advertising that so many of Halevi's Alexandrian poems have been preserved. No doubt the first compiler of Halevi's *dīwān* worked from small compilations made by Ibn al-ʿAmmānī and other recipients of Halevi's poems.

We do not know exactly when Halevi left Cairo; it is reasonable to assume that he remained with Ḥalfon through the Passover festival. He returned to Alexandria accompanied only by Abū l-Rabīʿ, for Isaac Ibn Ezra stayed behind.

Halevi parted from Cairo and from Ḥalfon with a formal epistle, which is lost, and a poetic complement. It is based on the notion, already mentioned, that the Nile is one of the four rivers of paradise:[33]

Two were born in Egypt's Eden,
Ḥalfon one; the Nile the other.
When we parted they conspired
to smooth my path and light my way.
With Ḥalfon and the Nile for leaven,
Egypt lacks no luxury.

6

Alexandria Again

On May 8, 1141, six weeks after Passover and five days before Shavuot, Halevi boarded a ship in the harbor of Alexandria and began the wait for a westerly wind that would carry him on the last leg of his journey to Palestine.

In the days immediately prior to his embarkation, Halevi found himself once more in the center of a disturbance, this one rather more serious than the imbroglio about the collection of his poems. We learn about this episode from two meaty letters written by Abū Naṣr on May 11, after Halevi had embarked but before his ship sailed. Abū Naṣr reports that on that day, a traveler arrived from al-Andalus carrying four letters from Almería: two for Halevi, one for Ḥalfon, and one for a certain Master Isaac in Fustat. Abū Naṣr brought the two letters for Halevi—which are now lost—to him on the ship. He forwarded the other two letters to Ḥalfon, with instructions to forward Master Isaac's letter on to him. To each of these two letters, Abū Naṣr attached a cover letter. These two cover letters have survived and are full of information about Halevi's activities during his last days in Egypt. Here is the account from Abū Naṣr's letter to Ḥalfon:[1]

> A mail carrier arrived from Almería today, and I went to him and found that he had with him two letters for our Master Judah and a letter for Master Isaac and a letter for your honorable self. I gave him some money and took them

> and brought our Master Judah his letters, and I am enclosing with this letter the one for your honorable self and the letter for Master Isaac. Would you be so kind as to forward them to him, after singling him out on my behalf with the best and most effusive greetings, and let him know how I long and yearn for him and how sorry I am to be missing the opportunity of seeing him. . . .
>
> Another matter: no one has ever had to undergo what happened to our Master Judah on account of that dog, Ibn al-Baṣrī the apostate. This is how it happened. The apostate made a complaint to the head of the secret service saying, "There is a Jewish man here with whom my brother sent thirty dinars for me. This man is going to Palestine. He told me that he would not turn the money over to me unless I go to Palestine with him so that he can return me to Judaism; but I am a believing Muslim." The head of the secret service summoned Halevi. But when he saw him—the judge came with Halevi and told the head of the secret service who Halevi was and how important he was—he said, "Go to the religious court." Then Ibn al-Baṣrī denounced Halevi to the emir, who summoned him, and when he saw him, he, too, said, "Go to the religious court." So they brought him to the *qāḍī*, and Ibn al-Baṣrī demanded his thirty dinars. Master Judah denied that he had the money, so he had to swear an oath. There was hubbub and commotion about it in the streets, and if Master Judah were not an important man and well known in the town, the Muslims would have eaten him alive, but he had stature, so the Muslims nearly killed the apostate. Then Master Judah took the oath and so was acquitted. We refused to compromise by paying him a small sum because we were afraid that the Muslims would then suspect Master Judah.

It would appear that, while in Cairo, Halevi had been entrusted with a large sum of money to convey to one Ibn al-Baṣrī in Alexandria by the latter's brother and that Halevi, either on his own initiative or at the brother's request, tried to use the money to induce the apostate to return to Judaism. This would have been a dangerous ploy, for the reversion of a Muslim convert to Judaism was a capital offense in the law of Islam, as was suborning such reversion.

Religious affiliation was not a matter of private conscience, for it involved the very definition of a person's legal status. Nor could it be kept secret in the close-knit world of the medieval city, where it was hard to keep anything a secret, and where the practice of religion involved visible public acts, such as attendance at religious services as well as smaller-scale acts of allegiance, such as the way one referred to others (note the epithet "that dog," which Abū Naṣr prefixes to the name of the apostate Ibn al-Baṣrī). The decision to convert to Judaism or Christianity or to convert back from Islam to one's original religion ordinarily meant self-imposed exile, for one could only convert by going to a place where one was not known. Halevi's impending voyage to the Land of Israel would have provided an excellent opportunity for making the attempt to bring the apostate back to Judaism.

But Halevi was taking some risk in making this attempt, perhaps even courting martyrdom. He must have calculated that the apostate might denounce him, and once brought into court and confronted with having the money in his possession, Halevi would have been in very serious trouble. How Halevi prepared for this eventuality, we shall shortly see.

From Abū Naṣr's parallel account of the incident in his letter to Master Isaac, we learn that the money was given to Halevi in the form of a bill of exchange, an instrument often used to transfer large sums. This was an instruction to a businessman in another town or country to pay the bearer a certain sum of money against the writer's account (usually consisting of goods belonging to the writer held by the addressee on consignment).

As we shall see, Abū Naṣr was incensed at the Cairene brother's bad judgment. But there would have been no intrinsic harm in merely sending a bill of exchange with Halevi, so Abū Naṣr's anger must have been about the scheme to get the brother to return to Judaism. This suggests that it was the Cairene brother who took the initiative in trying to get Ibn al-Baṣrī to return to Judaism. Meeting Halevi in Cairo and learning that he was bound for Palestine, he must have conceived the plan of offering his brother a large sum of money on condition that he go with Halevi and revert to Judaism in the Holy Land, hoping that money and the persuasive powers of a dignitary and religious model of Halevi's stature would do the trick. It seems less likely that the idea of using the money to induce Ibn al-Baṣrī to return to Judaism was Halevi's own, for if the Cairene brother had not put any conditions on his delivering the bill of exchange, Halevi, by imposing a condition of his own, would have been acting irresponsibly toward him; yet Abū Naṣr expresses no irritation or anger with Halevi, but only with the apostate and his brother.

In any event, Ibn al-Baṣrī evidently had no interest in returning to Judaism. He told the chief of the secret service that he was a "believing Muslim," a convert of conviction, not opportunism, and he countered Halevi's ploy by denouncing him to the authorities. It would be surprising if Halevi had not considered the possibility that the apostate would make this move. Even if the idea originated with the apostate's brother, Halevi's willingness to take the risk suggests a kind of pious recklessness or perhaps confidence in the rabbinic maxim that someone on a mission to do a pious act is protected from harm by divine providence.

It is testimony to the commitment to social order and legal procedures of Muslim state institutions in this period that even in this case of a serious religious offense by a *dhimmī*, the chief of the secret service did not deal with the matter arbitrarily but advised Ibn al-Baṣrī to take his case for adjudication under religious law by the *qāḍī*. The danger for *dhimmī*s came from the emotions of the crowd, as attested here by the mention of the hubbub and commotion in the street during the legal proceedings. It is another interesting reflection on *dhimmī* status that Ibn al-Baṣrī tried to circumvent the legal system's penchant for due process by bringing his complaint first to the secret service, then to the emir; he may have foreseen that the *qāḍī* would insist on following strict legal procedures that might afford Halevi a means of escape. But both refused to make a peremptory decision and insisted that the case be dealt with in accordance with legal procedures.

Once in court, Halevi simply denied the entire story. Since the case came down to his word against that of Ibn al-Baṣrī, he was required to take an oath, a procedure that was regarded as probative by both Islamic and Jewish law; Halevi established his veracity by swearing that he did not have the money after all. But this turns out to have been true only in the technical sense, for, as Abū Naṣr goes on to relate:

> Two days later, the apostate summoned Sulayman ben Joseph, Halevi's traveling companion, to the *qāḍī* and demanded the thirty dinars of him and the *qāḍī* required him to swear, but he could not, because he actually had some of the apostate's money in his possession. But the people got them to compromise for a sum of money and he got clear of him.

Sulayman ben Joseph is the man we have been referring to as Abū l-Rabīʿ Ibn Gabbai, Halevi's remaining traveling companion. It turns out that, anticipating that he would be required to swear that he did not have the money, Halevi entrusted it to his companion, a common but shabby ruse that permitted him to take the oath. It is an interesting reflection on the status of *dhimmī*s that the Muslim court regarded the Jew's oath as probative; and interesting about the limits of religious behavior that Halevi and his friend Abū l-Rabīʿ were willing to subvert the legal system on religious grounds and willing to lie to save their skins but were not willing to swear falsely.[2]

Abū Naṣr concludes this version of his account by laying some of the blame for the incident at Ḥalfon's door:

> I am actually surprised at your honor. You know the man's bad character and how he behaves with people in Damietta and else-

> where. Yet when people of little sense come and cause trouble for strangers because of this piece of trash, you don't put a stop to it, and the result is all this hullabaloo. May God grant no good reward to whoever was the cause.

Abū Naṣr is complaining that Ḥalfon, as Halevi's protector in Cairo, could have prevented this trouble, since he knew the Cairene brother to be a man of bad character and little sense, based on his behavior in Damietta.

Abū Naṣr is even more indignant against the Cairene brother in his other letter on the subject, the one he addressed to Master Isaac. Surprisingly, in this version, Abū Naṣr does not identify the man in Cairo as Ibn al-Baṣrī's brother but refers to him using neutral terms equivalent to "someone" in English.

> Can there be in the whole world anyone madder than a person who would impose this kind of meddling[3] on a foreigner? And he has done things like this before in Damietta and elsewhere! The right thing for him to do would be to hide this piece of trash with himself and not send him bills of exchange with such people as these. But the person who did this [i.e., the apostate?] can only be full of spite and hatred to a fearful degree, for I swear that every Jew in Alexandria was outraged by what he did, and the Muslims were very upset by the harsh way he treated Halevi, so much so that the Muslims nearly killed the apostate.
>
> I serve your Excellency by sending my best and most perfect greetings, and the sheikh Abū l-Najm and the sheikh Abū Mūsā both serve you with lavish greetings, as do the brethren, your servants all. "God is sufficient for me, and He is the best to be trusted."
>
> 3 Ramadan[4]

Thus the incident of the apostate was resolved and Halevi continued his preparations for the journey eastward. At last, on May 8, 1141, he boarded a ship bound for Palestine.[5] The sailing, however, was delayed, for the wind was blowing favorably only for the westbound ships, as we learn from another passage in Abū Naṣr's letter to Master Isaac just quoted:

> As for other matters, the ships of al-Andalus, al-Mahdiyya, Tripoli, Sicily, and Byzantium left and found a good wind; only the ship of the ruler of al-Mahdiyya remains[6] and has not moved yet. As for our master, Judah Halevi, may God keep him, he has embarked and has spent four days but the wind has not been favorable. May God inscribe his welfare.

This passage, the source of our information about the date of Halevi's embarkation, also provides a lively picture of the activity in the harbor of Alexandria, at the beginning of the shipping season of 1141. All the ships mentioned must have been waiting in the harbor throughout the winter; the ships from the west and the north had begun their return trips with a good east wind, while the one ship bound for the east had to wait.

One of these westbound ships was undoubtedly the one that carried Abū l-Rabīʿ Ibn Gabbai back to the Muslim West, and it was probably during Halevi's long wait on board that he bade farewell to this faithful companion. An echo of their parting is preserved in a short poem that concludes with a poignant exclamation:

This day, my eyes are red and worn with yearning,
weeping tears cascading as I moan,
tears burning with the pain that burns my heart,
each tear a coal that glows in a hailstone.
To part from Isaac yesterday seemed easy,
although my heart was skipping beats with fear
but now, it nearly stops, since Solomon
has left, and left me solitary here.
No friends or brethren will I see again—
he was the last of all my friends from Spain.[7]

The "coal that glows in a hailstone" is a reference to the miraculous and terrible hail that God brought down on the Egyptians at the time of the Exodus, "hail with fire burning inside the hail."[8] The image serves the poet well to describe the combined pain of loss (represented by flames) and anxiety for the future (represented by cold) that Halevi must have felt as he embraced the last countryman of his that he would ever see. Since Abū l-Rabīʿ seems to have been responsible for Halevi's arrangements and provisions,[9] Halevi was now left to his own devices; after parting from Abū l-Rabīʿ, he must truly have felt that he had thrown himself on the protection of God alone.

The two letters that Abū Naṣr brought to Halevi on shipboard are not extant, but we happen to know that one of them was from someone back in al-Andalus named Judah Ibn Ezra. This person, who is called "the youth" in our source, was certainly a relative of Isaac Ibn Ezra, Halevi's companion, and of Abraham Ibn Ezra, Isaac's father and Halevi's townsman.[10] The letter contained the information that the young Judah was planning to travel to the East—for what purpose, we do not know. Halevi must have been very excited at the news, for he immediately made arrangements to provide the young Judah with funds and left instructions that upon arrival in Alexandria, he should proceed immediately to join him in Palestine without making a side trip to Cairo. What these arrangements were, we shall soon learn.

Abū Naṣr's two letters also provide a glimpse of Halevi on shipboard in the harbor of Alexandria. In the letter to Ḥalfon, after telling the story of the apostate, Abū Naṣr sends greetings to various acquaintances in Cairo and goes on to describe some business transactions, one of which concerned Halevi:

> I sold the Jerba cloth for twenty-five and three-quarters dirhams and the one Jalón cloth[11] for five and a half. Master Judah took the other and offered me its price. I said to him, "It already belongs to someone," and he said, "You absolutely have to take the price!" But I didn't do it.

Like Halevi's letter written soon after his arrival in Egypt in which he began by speaking of his desire to retreat from the world and concluded by referring to business affairs, so this letter shows that Halevi continued to transact business right down to the days immediately preceding the consummation of his pilgrimage. The verbal exchange between Abū Naṣr and Halevi is not entirely clear because of its vernacular character. Probably by saying, "It already belongs to someone," Abū Naṣr meant, "It already belongs to you," meaning that he was giving the Jalón cloth to Halevi as a gift. Halevi tried to insist on paying for it, but Abū Naṣr prevailed. The same letter concludes with information about the status of Halevi's ship.

> As for Master Judah, if you come down after the festival you will not find him, for he is on the ship. If the wind would shift to the west this minute, he would sail. May God inscribe his welfare. I wish your honor pleasure in this coming festival. May God the highest grant you many good and delightful years. Next year in Jerusalem! May he have the fortune to behold the splendor of God and to visit His sanctuary, to see the rebuilding of the Ariel[12] and the ingathering of the Jewish people.
>
> I beg your honor to inform me that this letter has arrived so that I can be certain about it. Also forward the letter to the great elder Abū Isḥāq the Representative quickly, if you please. "God is sufficient for me, and He is the best to be trusted."
>
> 3 Sivan

"The festival" referred to here is the two-day holiday of Shavuot, which fell that year on Wednesday, May 14, and Thursday, May 15. It is one of the three pilgrim festivals, which the ancient Israelites observed by offering sacrifices in Jerusalem. Abū Naṣr's wish that Ḥalfon live to see the rebuilding of Jerusalem and the reinstituting of the sacrificial rites is the kind of holiday greeting often found in personal letters. We may imagine that Halevi, as he watched the port of Alexandria recede, reflected with satisfaction that the last leg of his own pilgrimage was thus linked with the ancient pilgrimage that he had often celebrated in his liturgical poetry.

Ibn al-ʿAmmānī must have come on board during these days to visit Halevi, and each visit would have been a farewell. In a little poem that Halevi probably wrote for him at this time, he playfully thanks the eastern wind for delaying his departure from his friend, thus giving voice, up to the very last minute, to the ambivalence that had accompanied him throughout the journey.[13]

Calm down, raging sea! Permit
a schoolboy to approach and kiss his teacher's face,
his master, Rabbi Aaron. The sap has not
dried up from his tribe's stock.
He teaches freely, never tells his mouth, "Be still!"
Bestows his gifts, and never tells his hand, "Enough!"
Today I thank the eastern wind. But in a day or two
I'll curse the western wind,
for I am sick like someone stung by scorpions,
and it will put behind me Gilead's healing balm.
Who would trade the leafy shade
for heat and freezing cold and scorching winds?
But I can give up the master's cooling shade
to reach the shade the Master's house affords.

On Tuesday, May 13, the eve of the festival, the faithful Abū Naṣr paid his farewell visit to Halevi, bringing him letters and transacting business. He must have intended this visit to be a quick one; after six days of waiting and several visits, there can have been little left to say, and the eve of the festival would have been a short workday on which Abū Naṣr would expect to return home early. Halevi gave Abū Naṣr a letter for Samuel ben Ḥanania in reply to one brought to him by Abū Naṣr on an earlier visit. Halevi had occupied some of his waiting time by writing an elaborate epistle in reply, probably glad to have a literary chore to occupy him. The Nagid's epistle has not survived, and the extant part of Halevi's reply is only a fragment that has come down to us not in Halevi's hand but in a copy made by the Nagid's chancery, with a heading in Arabic:[14]

. . . to our master the Nagid Samuel (may his name be established forever!), when he was on a ship . . . [Alexan]dria.

May God bless you. . . . Given all this, and seeing that there is no man of your rank, with what gift can I greet you but a poem . . . by Judah Halevi

> *your servant and son . . . who declares to his master that his dear epistle and his splendid composition*[15] *have arrived, silencing the storm and calming the waves of the sea and . . . ; the depth became quiet and longing was renewed.*

The storm and surge of the sea to which Halevi refers at the end could well have been suggested by Halevi's being on a ship, but they do not have to be interpreted literally;[16] they are probably simply metaphors for Halevi's anxiety at the prospect of venturing out again onto the ocean and a formal expression of sorrow at parting forever from the Nagid.

That the final meeting between Halevi and Abū Naṣr occurred on Tuesday is a reasonable inference: even if Abū Naṣr did not visit Halevi on the ship every day, he would have made a special effort to visit him to wish him well on the eve of the festival, and it is most unlikely, on religious grounds, that he would have visited Halevi on the ship on the festival itself. Thus, on Tuesday, May 13, Halevi had his last glimpse of Abū Naṣr, and on Wednesday, the first day of Shavuot, Halevi's ship finally sailed. This information derives from a note (which has become tattered over the centuries) that Abū Naṣr dashed off the following Monday, May 19, to Ḥalfon:[17]

> . . . about that which I do not have to repeat.
>
> I have written these two lines to inform you that Master Judah Halevi (may he be remembered for thousandfold peace) sailed on Wednesday, the first day of the festival of Shavuot. He handed me a letter that he had written in haste to our lord the Nagid. Please be so good as to forward it to him. May God inscribe his welfare and unite us with him. God knows—and His knowledge suffices Him—the . . . that entered my heart. . . . The ships for the west have departed and [the wind has] turned. . . .
>
> . . . serve your honor. "God is sufficient for me, and He is the best to be trusted."
>
> 11 Sivan, written at night in haste, with apologies. . . .

It may seem jarring to read that Halevi, a pious man and a pilgrim, set sail on a festival day, when travel is prohibited. Abū Naṣr reports the fact with no apology or comment because in a community that actually lived by religious law, everyone knew that, though it was prohibited to embark or disembark on the Sabbath or a festival, a person who was already on the ship before the holy day might sail with an easy conscience. By the time that the setting sun marked the onset of the festival, Halevi had already been on board for nearly a week.

Did Halevi fulfill his dream of reaching the Land of Israel, dying there, and mingling his body with its soil? There is no concrete evidence one way or another. But the journey from Alexandria to Acre or Ashkelon, Palestine's main ports, ordinarily took only about ten days,[18] and since Halevi died in midsummer, as we shall see, there is no reason to doubt that he made the voyage successfully. If he did arrive, he must have sent word to his loyal friend Ḥalfon, and since so many letters to Ḥalfon have been preserved, perhaps someday we will be lucky enough to find one from Halevi confirming his arrival in Palestine.

Benjamin of Tudela, who visited the Holy Land sometime between 1169 and 1171, thirty years after Halevi's death, says that among the graves of famous men he was shown in the vicinity of Tiberias was the grave of Judah Halevi. But his account is not conclusive, for there is reason to think that he actually meant to refer not to the grave of Judah Halevi but to that of the ancient rabbi Jonathan ben Levi.[19]

Halevi undoubtedly reached Palestine, visited the holy sites in Jerusalem and Hebron—although Jews were not permitted to live in Jerusalem, they were permitted to visit the shrines as pilgrims—and died soon thereafter. He was elderly, had gone through considerable strain, and had set himself down in a place where living conditions were less settled and comfortable than they had been in Egypt, and where he had no friends like Ibn al-ʿAmmānī and Ḥalfon to care for him.

It has often been observed that people whose bodies have nearly given out manage to stay alive until reaching a milestone, such as a birthday, an anniversary, a holiday, the wedding of a child, or the birth of a grandchild. Perhaps Halevi held out until the Ninth of Av, the summer fast day commemorating the destruction of Jerusalem, when, in post-destruction times, Jews had customarily made pilgrimage to the Mount of Olives. In any case, it is easy to imagine Halevi expiring once he had fulfilled the demanding vow about which he had written so movingly. We should not be disturbed by the absence of documentation; it is a miracle that we possess the documentation that we do, and any letters that Halevi may have written from Palestine could easily have gone astray before reaching the geniza.

More than eight hundred years later, Halevi's poems still carry to our ears his hopes and anxieties, his certainties and ambivalences, his love of this temporal world, and his longing for contact with the divine world. But the last extant word bearing on his pilgrimage written by a contemporary of his is a mundane piece of business related in a letter by the faithful agent Abū Naṣr ben Abraham to Ḥalfon Halevi. The letter was written in November 1141, several months after Halevi's death.[20]

> In the Name of the Merciful One:
>
> If I were attempt to describe to your Excellency, my high and noble lord and master, how I long and yearn for him, how I incline toward him, and how I sorrow for not being able to see him, I would be wordy, writing too much and saying too little. May God grant that we be speedily united, God willing. The reason my letters have been so long in reaching you is that I was occupied with preparations for a journey, and when they were completed, I fell ill, I and every human soul in my house. But all is now well, thank God, and I hope that with God's grace all will turn out well.

Abū Naṣr takes up several business arrangements not of interest to us, and goes on to recall the day in the preceding May, when the four letters we have already discussed, including two for Halevi, arrived from Almería. The pious formula that Abū Naṣr employs after mentioning Halevi's name is history's first word to us that Halevi is already dead:

> As for the turban and the gown that you referred to as belonging to our Master Judah Halevi (the memory of the righteous is a blessing), what you were told is wrong. The truth of the matter is this: when the letters arrived with the post from al-Andalus, I brought them to the ship. Among them was a letter from Judah Ibn Ezra in which he stated that he had no intention of remaining and that he had made up his mind to come. Halevi gave me a turban and said, "If Judah arrives this year, give it to him to sell and use the money to join me." He also wrote him a note, which is in my possession, saying that he should not go up to Cairo and not go against [his] advice. Then Halevi said to me, "If Judah does not arrive this year, keep the turban and gown with you until you receive instructions from me to sell them and to buy some things that I may want with the proceeds." How could I have entrusted it to the sheikh Abū l-Maʿālī? It is in my house, under the care of the sheikh Abū Najm al-Ḥamawī. If the young man arrives, he can take it; otherwise, it will stay there until someone who has a right to it claims it. That is the true story of what happened.

Abū Naṣr's letter affords us a last glimpse of Halevi as he made final arrangements with his Egyptian friends on the ship in the harbor of Alexandria on Sunday, May 11, 1141, three days before sailing. We can easily imagine his delight on learning that young Judah, another member of the Ibn Ezra family, had decided to come east,[21] though we cannot tell from the letter whether young Judah was intending to go to Palestine or only as far as Egypt. In any case, Halevi immediately took steps to help young Judah join him in Palestine, removing a turban and a gown from his merchandise and giving it to Abū Naṣr in trust for the young man. (That a turban and a gown are treated as objects of value is no surprise, for wealth often took the form of expensive fabrics.) Why did Halevi leave instructions for Judah not to go to Cairo? Perhaps he was afraid that Judah would be diverted from completing his journey, as Halevi nearly had been; or perhaps he was eager to have a relative with him as soon as possible.

Abū Naṣr goes on to discuss other items of business. In passing, he observes that three great men, including Halevi, had died within a recent five-month period.[22] From this statement and from what is known about the other two men named, it can be deduced that Halevi died between June 8 and August 5, making it just about certain that he lived long enough to reach his destination. But Abū Naṣr does not linger. He concludes with a complaint about his health, a frequent theme in his letters, and with his customary pious formula:[23]

> God only knows how I have managed to write this couple of lines. If I would get a little stronger, I wouldn't stay in town another moment. But God is sufficient for me, and He is the best to be trusted. 11 Kislev.

Thus, a harried businessman, not in the best of health, ends a letter about secular affairs with a pious formula shared by Jews and Muslims, answering his own anxieties with a religious sentiment that cancels out all worldly anxieties. He uses the formula in a conventionally pious way, for though he professes to affirm that God is the best One to be entrusted with one's needs, his letter, like most of his extant letters, betrays the day-to-day worldly concerns of a class of people who devoted most of their thoughts to business and their material welfare. The irony is that he is writing about Judah Halevi, a man who saw the hollowness of such pious formulas and who attempted to put them into practice; who accepted their challenge, put his worldly concerns behind him, and, placing his trust in God, plunged into the heart of the sea.

Part III

The Pilgrim Speaks

7

An Epistle

We now have an overall picture of Halevi's religious outlook and its development, and we have followed the story of his pilgrimage. It is time to think about Halevi's motive in deciding that the pilgrimage was the appropriate way to spend his declining years.

Several themes emerging from the poems that we have read are relevant to this decision. The unsettled conditions of his time may have caused Halevi to despair of any solution to the problem of Jewish political status in exile and may have made him sympathetic to messianic thinking; they may even have impelled him to take the matter of Jewish exile into his own hands by going to Palestine at all costs—alone, if necessary. Some readers of Halevi's works have even proposed that his journey was itself a messianic venture, a summons to the Jewish people to leave their exile and thereby force the coming of the messianic age. Other readers have emphasized the element of social critique in Halevi's writing: his expressions of distaste for the worldliness and acculturation of the Jewish elite of al-Andalus; and his longing for a purer, more authentic, variety of Judaism than he could find in his homeland. These themes are all present in his writing, and undoubtedly there were elements of all of them in Halevi's thinking during the years in which he considered the plan.

But no merely negative cause seems adequate to explain the pilgrimage. Halevi's pilgrimage poetry does not deal with the sufferings and exile of the Jewish people (except in the Ode to Jerusalem, which deals with their dispersal). It is devoid of messianic material.

Halevi could have made his social critique in other ways: by writing a book of religious exhortation like that of Baḥya Ibn Paquda; by retreating from public life and devoting himself to rabbinic scholarship (as he had fantasized doing in his epistle to Rabbi Ḥabīb of al-Mahdiyya and as would have been natural for a rabbinic Jew of traditionalist bent); or by simply fleeing inward, as Baḥya recommended, living in the world but maintaining an inner distance from worldly affairs.[1] If we allow ourselves to be guided by the poetry that we have read and by the pilgrimage poetry that we are soon to read, we are led surely to Halevi's personal piety and individual religious vision as the chief motivation for his pilgrimage.[2]

In all Halevi's extant writings, there is only one passage in his own voice in which he offers to explain the pilgrimage. It occurs in the Hebrew epistle that he sent to Samuel ben Ḥanania from Alexandria prior to their meeting in Cairo in early 1141. In chapter 4, we read the parts of this epistle that were relevant to the pilgrimage narrative; now we turn to the part omitted there, Halevi's explanation of his pilgrimage:[3]

> *And now, permit my tongue to speak confidentially to my lord about the thoughts that drove me out of my homeland. After giving thanks and making confession to Him who granted me favors and answered me amply, I dedicated to Him my heart's praises and my mind's gratitude, while . . . vows . . . the lower soul in its calculations, the spirit in its . . . and the higher soul in its delights. All these came together . . . to trap the truth in a narrow confine from which there is no escape right or left, no room for escape.*

The small lacunae in the manuscript are an annoyance, but they do not prevent us from following Halevi's train of thought. He has found the certainty that he sought; the soul's three parts, functioning in harmony after a lifetime of confusion, have trapped it, as he says, so that it cannot escape.[4] He sees clearly the futility of philosophical speculation:

> *And the philosophy of the Greeks, so praised, is merely crazed; it claims to shed light but only yields blight. One of its spokesmen says this and the other says that: one praises pleasure—the lute and the flute—while the other says, "Better to go to the house of mourning," while a third says, "Both pleasure and sorrow are hollow." Disagreement rules; doubt and darkness dominate. There is no one to settle an argument, no one to make a clear statement or proclaim an answer.*

Elsewhere, Halevi disparages philosophy on account of the disagreements among its practitioners on matters of metaphysics and cosmology; here, he disparages it on the grounds of their disagreements about ethics, touching on hedonism, asceticism, and cynicism.[5] Philosophy, he goes on to say in the next passage, is a limited and uncertain tool, but the Torah provides truth, guaranteed as it is by a reliable chain of tradition going back to the exodus from Egypt and the revelation at Sinai. Philosophers had long spoken of reason as a lamp that guides man to eternal truth; by calling the Torah "the pure lamp," Halevi signals the replacing of the philosopher's lamp of reason with the divine lamp of revelation.[6] He goes on to explain his pilgrimage in the light of some absolute truths known from revelation:

> *But then came the pure lamp, the Torah, and opened men's eyes and ears, confounding their opinions and spoiling their thoughts, and said, Upside-down! You give counsel according to your own interest. My thoughts and my ways are not yours; there is no wisdom, no insight, no counsel in the face of God's. Not every living creature is a human being, not every human being is an Israelite, not every Israelite is a priest, and not every priest is Moses or Aaron; not every land is Canaan, not all of Canaan is the gates of heaven, and not all the gates of heaven are Jerusalem. Not all days are festivals, not all festivals are the Sabbath, not all Sabbaths are the Day of Atonement. Not all service of God is sacrifice, not all sacrifices are whole offerings, not all whole offerings are offered in the inner chamber. But there are holy men in the Holy Land. . . . Therefore there is no adding or taking away: the laws are righteous ones, authenticated by tradition, not to be transgressed or doubted. The evidence—the wonders and miracles seen by the eyes, heard by the ears in the wilderness and in Egypt, a sign and a testimony for past and present. So I said, "I have come, I have heard, and I believe. I shall not question or test the Lord."*[7]

God, in Halevi's view, has created a world of hierarchies. Among living creatures, man is superior to animals, Israelites to ordinary men, priests to ordinary Israelites, Moses and Aaron to ordinary priests. Among lands, Palestine (called here by its biblical name Canaan) is superior to all other lands, the places where prophecy occurred are superior to the other places in Palestine, and Jerusalem is superior to the other places where prophecy occurred. Likewise, there is a hierarchy of times, with the Day of Atonement superior to all other times; and a hierarchy of liturgical rites, with the whole offerings sacrificed in the inner precincts of the Temple at its apex.

The superiority of Israelites consists in their possessing a particular trait, a divine quality that enables them alone to receive prophecy. The hierarchies of species, place, time, and ritual represent four dimensions of contact with the divine, four vectors pointing toward access to God at the intersection of a divinely chosen site and a divinely ordained ritual performed by a divinely chosen caste at a divinely appointed time. The ultimate religious experience is therefore unattainable, for Jerusalem lies in ruins, the priests and Levites scattered, and the sancta of Israel buried beneath the Temple's rubble.[8] As long as Israel is unredeemed, our attempts to come near to God are merely substitute measures, expressions of our good intentions. Yet there is value in the longing itself.

> *Seeing that all Israel bows toward the House of God, my heart yearned for my father's house and my soul longed for the Holy Mountain—to prostrate myself to it nearby, among the priests, where the ark lies buried, and to say to the Lord: "Rise and have mercy on Zion! For Your servants take pleasure in her stones and cherish her soil." My love was stirred . . . lest my face be one of those turned aside from God at the sound of the call: "For who will have mercy on you, Jerusalem? Who will mourn you? Who will turn aside to ask about your welfare? There is none to care for her!"*
>
> *If you desire to get me my desire,*
> *send me to my master; let me go.*
> *For nowhere will my foot find rest*
> *until I make my home inside His home.*
> *Do not detain me from the journey,*
> *lest disaster overtake me. All I ask*
> *is shelter underneath God's wings,*
> *a grave among my fathers' graves.*

What is lost is not just Israel's sovereignty, control over her own destiny, or her pride; the loss that Halevi mourns is access to God, expressed here as sorrow for the ruin of the land, on which alone God's presence can be truly encountered. This passage is the full flowering of the anxiety adumbrated in "Where Can I Find You, Lord?" (poem 2). Halevi yearned for the presence of the divine but never felt assured of the possibility of achieving that presence until he focused on prophecy, which seemed to be authenticated by reliable tradition. But that realization led to another frustration, for the means to achieve prophecy prescribed by God Himself were not at hand.

Yet, though the conditions could not be fulfilled, Halevi felt driven to do as much as humanly possible. Others might be content with their conventional religious lives and their rabbinically sanctioned substitute rituals; but Halevi, in his longing for the thing itself, had to follow those four vectors as far as he could, as far as the ruins of Jerusalem, where he, a Levite, could abide in God's land—the land of the Temple, the land of prophecy—the land that is full of gates to heaven, as he often says[9]—awaiting his opportunity to serve God in the Temple. And if that opportunity should not arise in his lifetime, if the coming of the Messiah were to be further delayed, at least he would be there, his body mingled with the soil of revelation, ready to be among the first on the day of resurrection, when man would see God eye to eye.[10]

The soil of the Land of Israel, in which Halevi hoped to be buried, came to play an enormous role in Halevi's religious and poetic imagination. He found expression for his devotion to it in Ps. 102:14–15:

> You will arise and have mercy on Zion,
> for it is time to favor her; the appointed time has come.
> For Your servants take pleasure in her stones
> and cherish her soil.[11]

These words expressed his own passionate longing for restoration: not of the fortunes of the Jewish people, not of the Jews' status in the eyes of the nations of the world and their own, not for their release from exile—though those would undoubtedly result if the prayer were granted—but for restoration of the Land of Israel itself, with the rebuilding of the Temple, the resumption of sacrificial worship, and the reinstatement of prophecy. Above all, the redemption would restore the divine presence to the land, would bring Israel face-to-face again with God. The power of prophecy, somehow buried in anticipation of the destruction of Jerusalem together with the ark of the covenant, the Temple candelabrum, the sacred fire, and the golden cherubim, would emerge with them to the light of day.[12]

The masses of the Jewish people, their communal leaders, and their rabbis might plead for the people's salvation from exile, their religious vindication, and their national sovereignty; but who cared about the land, bereft of the *Shekhina,* the presence of God? And, for that matter, who cared about the *Shekhina* itself, in exile from its land? Halevi turned his attention away from self-interested prayer for the redemption of the folk, and toward prayer for the redemption of the land.

The reason that Ps. 102:14–15 was so important to Halevi was its emphasis on the land itself, its evocation of the stones and the soil. Ever seeking the most concrete possible expression of religious experience, Halevi directed his piety toward the land in its irreducibly physical aspect; and like many a worldly lover, he came to be obsessed with his beloved's humblest features.

Halevi evokes this verse often in the poems that we will be reading and, most prominently, in the Kuzari, where it serves as the text for a brief and touching concluding homily.[13] The rabbi ends the dialogue by announcing his intention to depart for Palestine. Unhappy to lose his company, the king attempts to dissuade him, arguing that since the *Shekhina* is absent from the land, and since God's presence can be found anywhere by a person who is moved by intense religious devotion and sincere longing for God, it should not matter where the rabbi resides. In response, the rabbi makes two points: in a nod toward technical ritual observance, he reminds the king that certain commandments can only be performed in Palestine, so there is a specialized sense in which religious life cannot be complete anywhere else; and the rabbi makes the broader point that "the heart is not purified and the intention is not completely devoted to God except in the place of which it is certain that it is dedicated to God." This is the point that Halevi spelled out in more detail in his epistle to Samuel ben Ḥanania when he said that the *Shekhina* makes its presence felt only at the conjunction of the person, the land, the time, and the ritual. No amount of mere inner devotion can substitute for the specificity of the place. Intentions are not as pleasing to God as actions; only when it is truly impossible to perform the commandment is God satisfied with good intentions, as when prayers are offered in lieu of the sacrifices that are no longer possible in the absence of the Temple.

Clearly, the argument is moving in the direction of stating that a man who merely longs for God, but does not physically remove himself to God's land, cannot experience God's presence to the fullest, for this is what the rabbi needs to say in order to justify his decision to the king, and it is clearly what he had in view when he began his speech. But at the last minute, his discourse swerves away from the individual and toward the national. The rabbi says that whoever inspires his fellow Jew to love the land chosen by God helps to bring about the messianic era and will be rewarded for his good deed, citing as a prooftext Ps. 102:14–15 and explaining it as follows: "Jerusalem will not be rebuilt until all Israel desires it with perfect desire, to the point that they long for its very stones and soil."

The king is now satisfied; he praises the rabbi and offers his help—but does not offer to accompany him. Nor has the rabbi any parting reproaches for the king for staying in his own land. The king, now a full-fledged and committed convert to Judaism, will carry on his life of political leadership and conventional religious probity in the land of the Khazars, a course good enough for a man of ordinary religious constitution, the best that can be expected from the Jewish people. The rabbi, as an individual, has higher religious aspirations, makes greater demands of himself. Through his action, he sets an example of love of Zion, a love that, if it were more deeply rooted and more widespread among the Jews, might have redemptive power. But the rabbi's departure for the Land of Israel is not a declaration of the messianic era or a summons for other Jews to follow. Like Halevi himself, the rabbi goes a solitary way. The swerve that his discourse takes near the end is merely a quiet parting rebuke to a nation that is content with its exile. In it, we hear the voice of a visionary who, while driving himself to fulfill his own vision, is reconciled to men of average heart and their more limited vision.

Halevi strikes the same tone earlier in the Kuzari, when the rabbi and the king discuss the question of settling in the Land of Israel in more detail. Having established the qualities of the Jewish people that make them suitable to be the people of prophecy, the rabbi expatiates on the qualities of the land that suit it to be the place of prophecy. His evidence ranges from biblical laws and narratives through astronomical and meteorological data to a digest of Talmudic regulations and folklore; it is actually a brief but thorough discourse on what the Khazar king calls the *faḍāʾil* (excellent qualities) of the Land of Israel (Kuzari 2:15). This Arabic term is the name of a literary genre consisting of books lauding a particular place. Muslims had written such books on Mecca, Medina, and other places since the late ninth century, and on Jerusalem, since the early eleventh; chapters of this type were incorporated into larger books even earlier.[14] Some of the points made in this excursus will come up in the poems to be read in the ensuing chapters. What interests us now is the king's reaction to the rabbi's disquisition.

The king exclaims on the Jews' hypocrisy: believing that the Land of Israel has such virtues and constantly praying to be restored to it, they make no effort to actually go there and settle it. In one of the most memorable passages in the book, the rabbi confesses that his people are indeed to blame. God was ready to restore the Jewish kingdom in the sixth century BCE, at the time of Ezra, had the leaders been willing to leave Babylon and return. "If we were ready to meet the Lord of our fathers with pure intention, He would help us as He helped our ancestors in Egypt." Likewise, if the desire were sincere and sufficiently powerful, the redemption would come today, as it came to the Jews in Egypt. But the people are not worthy. Genetically predisposed to be prophets, they have degenerated to the level of ordinary people, absorbed in their day-to-day affairs, routinely pious, and comfortable in exile; and God punishes them by leaving them to be merely what they are.

With that, the subject is dropped. Halevi has no expectation that the salvation is at hand or that it will come from human initiative. This passage was clearly a reproach to Halevi's contemporaries—perhaps for not taking more seriously the various messianic movements of his time—but it is no more a call for a mass movement to Zion than is the rabbi's solitary departure at the Kuzari's end. If we are to read Halevi's pilgrimage in the light of the Kuzari, all we can say is that it was the act of a man who had given up on the masses and the leaders of his people and on the idea of an imminent redemption altogether, but who believed that there were steps that a person could take who wanted to come as close as possible to the divine presence. He would do God's will the best he could, even at the cost of giving up his comfortable religious life.

This reading of the rabbi's intentions at the end of the Kuzari, so contrary to the meaning attached to them by readers who see Halevi's pilgrimage as a messianic venture, is confirmed by the elegiac ending of this section of Halevi's epistle to Samuel ben Ḥanania and the touching little poem that rounds it off. After quoting the passage from Psalms, which speaks of the people at large taking pleasure in her stones and cherishing her soil, he lapses immediately into the first-person singular. The people have not lived up to the verse. He alone is loyal. His words become a pastiche of biblical phrases signifying that the people have abandoned the land and do not concern themselves with it.[15] The phrase "at the sound of the call" is pregnant. In its source, the call is that of the angels proclaiming God's holiness and summoning Isaiah to take up his duties as a prophet. Halevi seems to imagine a similar call, telescoped into this brief sequence of biblical phrases, addressed to mankind—a divine lament on Jerusalem, abandoned by her people, and a summons to her scattered people to come to care for her. He dreads being rejected by God for having neglected to answer that call.

It summons him not to assemble the Jewish people to the Land of Israel or to proclaim the advent of the messianic era but to go to God's house, there to find rest, there to live and there to die. Not messianism, but solitary devotion, is the constant theme of the poems that we are about to read.

8

In Imagination

The poems presented in this chapter resemble the dream poems of chapter 3 in their visionary quality. Though barely mentioning Halevi's pilgrimage, they give the impression that the poet has brooded so much on the Land of Israel that he almost imagines himself there. But these poems do not represent themselves as products of revelation, as do the poems of chapter 3, but as products of meditation. Thus, the address to the site of Moses' grave in "Hail, Mount Avarím!" (poem 13) is in the voice of a speaker who has meditated so intensely on the great man buried there that he imagines himself standing before the grave.

The drive toward the Land of Israel is motivated partly by Halevi's belief that religious fulfillment is only possible through particularly Jewish forms of holiness. Thus, the historical fate of the Jewish people and of its land is immensely important to Halevi's system, as we have seen. Yet the reality that the land is in ruins and the Temple destroyed is merely background information in "O Lovely Hill, World's Joy" (poem 14) and "My Heart in the East" (poem 15), for the focus in these poems is on the poet's yearning. In the great Ode to Jerusalem (poem 16), the reality of the land's ruined state is far more pronounced; indeed, mourning for the land plays such a large role in the poem that the poem has often been described as a lament. Yet even in the Ode, the poet keeps his own feelings, aspirations, and vision in the center of the reader's attention and subordinates the state of the land to these. Given a balanced reading, the Ode seems to be at least as much about Halevi's pilgrimage as it is about the land itself.

13

שָׁלוֹם לְךָ, הַר הָעֲבָרִים!
שָׁלוֹם לְךָ מִכָּל עֲבָרִים!
בָּךְ נֶאֱסַף מִבְחַר אֱנוֹשׁ,
וַיְהִי בְךָ מִבְחַר קְבָרִים.
אִם לֹא יְדַעְתָּהוּ, שְׁאַל
יַם-סוּף, אֲשֶׁר נִגְזַר גְּזָרִים.
וּשְׁאַל סְנֶה, וּשְׁאַל לְהַר
סִינַי, יְשִׁיבוּךָ אֲמָרִים.
הַנֶּאֱמָן עַל מַלְאֲכוּת
הָאֵל, וְהוּא לֹא אִישׁ דְּבָרִים.
אִם הָאֱלֹהִים עוֹזְרִי,
עָלַי לְשַׁחֲרֵךְ נְדָרִים.

The speaker stands in imagination at the foot of Mount Avarím, also known as Mount Nebo,[1] the site of Moses' grave, and salutes the mountain in terms that reflect his meditation on Moses' career. The salute takes the form of a pun on the mountain's name (*'avarim*), to which greetings come "from all sides" (*'avarayikh*), as if the speaker is addressing the mountain in the name of the entire exiled Jewish people. This sweeping style of salutation was familiar to Halevi's readers from the letters written by the heads of the academies to Jewish communities, which often begin as if addressed to the Jewish people at large, though the actual addressee was only a particular community; Halevi adopts it again in his Ode to Jerusalem (poem 16).[2]

Medieval Jews, like Muslims and Christians, frequented saints' tombs and considered such visits to be meritorious religious acts. The purported graves of Ezra, Daniel, and Ezekiel in Iraq were visited by Muslims as well as Jews. Benjamin of Tudela, who traveled through the Middle East only thirty years after Halevi, systematically lists the graves of religious figures that were venerated by the pious, and Judah al-Ḥarizi, an Andalusi Jew who traveled about the Middle East between 1215 and 1225, describes his visits to the tombs of Ezra and Ezekiel. Some of these sites also had a regular annual pilgrimage. Such a place was Dammuh, just south of Cairo. In local lore, the place was associated with Moses; some scholars theorize that the occasion for the pilgrimage was the commemoration of Moses' death on 7 Adar (i.e., about three weeks before the beginning of spring). But Moses' grave

13

Hail, Mount Avarím!
The world salutes the place
where mankind's best
was gathered to his kin,
and somewhere on your slope he lies,
buried in the best of graves.

Don't you know him?
Ask the sea who split it, ask the Bush or Sinai—
they will tell you in plain words:
he was faithful to God's message,
he was not a man of speeches.
I have vowed that, if God help me,
I shall come to pay you homage.

in the Transjordan could not be the object of pilgrimage, since the Bible says that no one knew the exact site where Moses was buried (Deut. 34:6).

There was no need to name Moses, for Halevi's readers knew their Bible well and could easily identify him by the name of his burial place. The epithet "the best [*mivḥar;* literally, "chosen" or "choicest"] of all mankind" also names Moses, whom the Jewish tradition regards as the greatest of the prophets, the only one to see God face-to-face.[3] The special place reserved for Moses in Halevi's system is also indicated in "Can a Body Be a Room" (poem 20), where Halevi names Mount Avarím and Sinai in the same breath, as if considering them equivalent in sanctity.

The apostrophe to Mount Avarím is formulated as a riddle. Who is the man buried here? Hint follows hint: Who was it who split the Red Sea? Who spoke to God in the Bush? Who stood on Sinai? It is as if Mount Avarím, though infused with the sanctity of the "best of men," needs to be guided to self-awareness. Halevi's strategy of instructing Moses' own grave as to the identity of its inhabitant through a series of questions permits him to present the reader with a select list not of Moses' attributes but of his actions.

Central to Halevi's religious mentality is the specificity of place and of action. We have repeatedly seen him yearning for God in terms of place, and we now see him speaking of piety in terms of action. He underscores the point through contrast when, at the climax of his list of Moses' attributes, he describes Moses as not being a man of words. Moses, of course, was the purported author of some of the most eloquent speeches in the Bible, but this phrase echoes his own self-characterization in the biblical story of his election to lead the people out of bondage.[4] Moses only meant to say that he was unworthy for this task, being a man of clumsy speech. Halevi turns this negative attribute into a positive one by saying that Moses was not *merely* a man of words, not a man of theological argumentation and philosophical speculation (the Hebrew word *devarim* used here can serve as the equivalent of the Arabic word *kalām,* which bears both significations) but a man of miraculous deeds. Moses did not need to speculate or rationalize, for he had seen God face-to-face, learned God's will by visions, and performed specific actions at God's behest. He was thus the very model of Halevi's own religious aspiration.

The devaluation of philosophical discourse to the status of mere talk that, though it might point in the direction of the truth, could not produce true reli-

(*Commentary continues on the next page*)

14

יְפֵה נוֹף, מְשׂוֹשׂ תֵּבֵל, קִרְיָה לְמֶלֶךְ רָב!
לָךְ נִכְסְפָה נַפְשִׁי מִפַּאֲתֵי מַעְרָב.
הֲמוֹן רַחֲמַי נִכְמָר כִּי אֶזְכְּרָה קֶדֶם
כְּבוֹדֵךְ אֲשֶׁר גָּלָה וְנָוֵךְ אֲשֶׁר חָרָב.
וּמִי יִתְּנֵנִי עַל כַּנְפֵי נְשָׁרִים עַד
אֲרַוֶּה בְדִמְעָתִי עֲפָרֵךְ וְיִתְעָרָב!
דְּרַשְׁתִּיךְ וְאִם מַלְכֵּךְ אֵין בָּךְ, וְאִם בִּמְקוֹם
צֳרִי גִלְעָדֵךְ נָחָשׁ שָׂרָף וְגַם עַקְרָב.
הֲלֹא אֶת אֲבָנַיִךְ אֲחֹנֵן וְאֶשָּׁקֵם,
וְטַעַם רְגָבַיִךְ לְפִי מִדְּבַשׁ יֶעְרָב.

gious conviction was one of the main themes of the Kuzari. For Halevi, true conviction can arise only from the direct experience of revelation or from the record of revelation in the Jewish tradition. The starting point of Halevi's religious theory is the revelation at Sinai, with Moses at its center.

If the poem was written when Halevi was already in Egypt, it may mean that he had begun to wonder why he had allowed his journey to become so protracted and, as some moderns wonder, whether the delay cast doubt on his sincerity. He must have looked with admiration at Moses, who actually accomplished what he set out to do, freeing his people and leading them—even after a forty-year delay—to their destination. Advanced in years at the time of his pilgrimage, Halevi may also have contemplated the example of Moses with dismay, fearing that he, too, might die before reaching the Holy Land.

14

O lovely hill, world's joy, the Great King's home!
My heart is yearning for you
from the wide world's western edge.
My heart goes out to you
when I think of times gone by,
your glory gone away,
your Temple now a ruin.
If only I could perch on eagle's wings and come
to wet your soil and knead it with my tears!
For though your king is gone, and though for balm
you now have serpents, snakes, and scorpions,
yet I would seek you out and fondle, kiss your stones,
and taste the honey in your holy clods.

Like much of medieval Hebrew poetry, this poem depends heavily for its effect on echoes of the Bible. The auditor is expected to recognize the allusions and bring to his hearing of the poem the original emotional environment of the biblical text.

Halevi begins by addressing Jerusalem in the words of Psalm 48, itself one of the Bible's great hymns to Jerusalem. The Jerusalem of the psalmist's imagination was a city to be proud of: a great and smiling city on a hill with imposing walls and towers; the fortress of a great king; a place that, once having seen it, you would talk about until your dying day. That city, the object of Halevi's longing, exists only in memory.

The speaker wishes for the wings of an eagle that would carry him to the ruined remains of that glorious city. The reader would have thought first of the complaint of the psalmist in Ps. 55:7, who wishes for the wings of a dove that could carry him off to a place of refuge from his enemies. He would also think of the bird in Ps. 84:4 that finds her home in the Temple. Also in the background are biblical verses that depict God as carrying Israel through the desert on eagle's wings,[5] an association that in this context would add the element of divine protection during the journey.

Halevi wishes for eagle's wings so that he can moisten the soil of the Holy Land with his tears. These tears could be tears of sorrow for the ruin of the Temple, the city, and the Holy Land, but Halevi could have lamented the ruin of the Holy Land from anywhere in the world—even, most conveniently, from his own homeland, as Jews customarily did in their prayers. He did not need to

(Commentary continues on the next page)

15

לִבִּי בְמִזְרָח וְאָנֹכִי בְּסוֹף מַעֲרָב.
אֵיךְ אֶטְעֲמָה אֵת אֲשֶׁר אֹכַל וְאֵיךְ יֶעֱרָב?
אֵיכָה אֲשַׁלֵּם נְדָרַי וֶאֱסָרַי, בְּעוֹד
צִיּוֹן בְּחֶבֶל אֱדוֹם וַאְנִי בְּכֶבֶל עֲרָב?
יֵקַל בְּעֵינַי עֲזוֹב כָּל טוּב סְפָרַד, כְּמוֹ
יֵקַר בְּעֵינַי רְאוֹת עַפְרוֹת דְּבִיר נֶחֱרָב.

go to the Land of Israel, even in imagination, to shed them. Rather, these tears are tears of pure emotion. They are also the means by which the speaker imagines consummating his longed-for union with the land, for, being fluid, they can interpenetrate the soil as the solid body cannot. In this striking and original verse, Halevi has fully realized the potential of Ps. 102:14–15, so often on his lips: "For Your servants take pleasure in her stones and cherish her soil." Just as he brooded on the redemption and on the Temple service so intensely that he dreamed of them, so must he have brooded on this verse so intensely that its image became concretized in his poetry as he wished it to be in his life.

Yet with a final biblical allusion, Halevi pushes the thought of the stones and soil of the Holy Land even a step further, to touch on another theme of his pilgrimage. The picture of the poet fondling the stones may seem grotesque, and the taste of honey in the clods edges perilously close to a cliché. But to a reader of the Bible, the word "clod" rings with the specificity of Job 21:33, which says of a man who dies happy: "The clods of the valley shall be sweet to him." For the biblically informed reader, the taste of the soil's clods is not a hackneyed metaphor for kissing the soil but a way of speaking of a person who dies happy. In "O Lord, All My Desire Is Plain to Thee" (poem 1), Halevi said that if he could please God only for a moment, he would be ready to die. In our poem, that generalized religious aspiration has been fulfilled in a very specific way: by the speaker's dying in the Land of Israel and mingling his body with its soil. The verse is also a reminder that Halevi went to the Land of Israel not primarily to live there, but to die there.

15

My heart in the East, and I in the West,
as far in the West as west can be!
How can I enjoy my food?
What flavor can it have for me?
How can I fulfill my vows
or do the things I've sworn to do,
while Zion is in Christian hands
and I am trapped in Arab lands?
Easily I could leave behind
this Spain and all her luxuries!—
As easy to leave as dear the sight
of the Temple's rubble would be to me.

This is not the first we have heard of vows. In Halevi's song of Neoplatonic aspiration "My Soul Is Yearning" (poem 3), he spoke of his soul's vow to seek wisdom, and in his apostrophe to Moses' burial place, "Hail, Mount Avarím!" (poem 13), he spoke of a vow to visit the spot. But the unfulfillable vows in "My Heart in the East" are unspecified. Halevi is not speaking of a vow to go to Palestine, for the poem states that he is prevented from fulfilling the vow by Arab and Christian domination. Yet their domination did not prevent anyone from traveling to Palestine, for, as we have seen, the Mediterranean was constantly being crisscrossed by Jewish travelers in this period, and there were Jewish settlements in Palestine throughout the period of the Crusades. Therefore, the vow must be one that cannot be fulfilled while Christians and Muslims dominate the world, that is, in this premessianic period.

The vow must therefore be a metonymy for the complete religious life that Halevi dreamed of. The train of thought seems to be that since there is no way to live a complete religious life as long as Israel is unredeemed, the speaker has little appetite for life anywhere. Convinced of the inadequacy of conventional religious life and feeling betrayed by philosophy, Halevi sought a solution in the service of God and proximity to the *Shekhina,* which, he believed, was possible only on the soil of revelation. But the messianic route to religious fulfillment seemed to be blocked, as the Christian and Muslim domination showed no signs of ending in his lifetime. The spirit needs to be in the Holy Land, but the body is trapped at the other end of the earth.

Though this uncomfortable split has been created by the unredeemed state of Israel, the lament is not in the voice of the nation but in the voice of the individual speaker. The division of this speaker's self into a heart in the East and a body in the West casts its rhetorical shadow over the entire poem, which is largely composed of balanced antithetical clauses. The perfectly balanced hemistich of the last verse—a superb example of the rhetorical style characteristic of the Arabic poetry of the age—yields a calculation in favor of abandoning al-Andalus for Palestine, but the balancing also suggests a stasis that is at odds with the calculation. There is no forward motion in this poem, for all its pairs are in equipoise: East and West, Zion and Christians, al-Andalus and Arabs, the wealth of al-Andalus and the ruins of the Temple.

This conflict is expressed by another outstanding feature of this poem's form: its play on the Hebrew root *ʿ-r-v*. This root of many meanings appears in the words "west," "sweet," and "Arabs" at the end of three of the poem's six hemistichs; we are clearly intended to ponder the intersection of these significations. "West" in Arabic refers not only to the direction west but to the westernmost territories of the Islamic domain, that is, Spain and northwest Africa. In his youth in Christian Spain, Halevi had referred to himself as a child of the "East" who yearned for the refined life and high culture of this sweet Arabic "West." He is now considering replacing this rich West with a ruined land in the East. The word for "ruin," from the root *ḥ-r-b,* picks up the sound of the thrice-repeated, nearly identical root *ʿ-r-b*. In its negative content, it contrasts with the three near-homophones. By picking up their sound, it casts some of its negativity back on them, telling us that the apparently flourishing West is the real ruin. Yet, by picking up their sound, it also casts some of their opulence on the ruined East. Thus, the play of sounds reinforces the poem's prevailing sense of balance and indecision.

The poem seems to mark a turn in Halevi's inner life: the moment when he definitively stopped pinning his hopes on a speedy messianic return to the East and replaced this hope with a private dream of his individual return. Perhaps this poem captures the moment of Halevi's realization that such religious fulfillment as is possible is entirely in his hands. But the poem offers no summons to action and no resolution. The inclination has been forcefully expressed, but no decision has been made.

16

צִיּוֹן! הֲלֹא תִשְׁאֲלִי לִשְׁלוֹם אֲסִירַיִךְ
 דּוֹרְשֵׁי שְׁלוֹמֵךְ, וְהֵם יֶתֶר עֲדָרָיִךְ?
מִיָּם וּמִזְרָח וּמִצָּפוֹן וְתֵימָן שְׁלוֹם
 רָחוֹק וְקָרוֹב שְׂאִי מִכֹּל עֲבָרָיִךְ,
וּשְׁלוֹם אֲסִיר תַּאֲוָה נוֹתֵן דְּמָעָיו כְּטַל
 חֶרְמוֹן, וְנִכְסָף לְרִדְתָּם עַל הֲרָרָיִךְ.
לִבְכּוֹת עֱנוּתֵךְ אֲנִי תַנִּים, וְעֵת אֶחֱלֹם
 שִׁיבַת שְׁבוּתֵךְ, אֲנִי כִנּוֹר לְשִׁירָיִךְ.
לִבִּי לְבֵית אֵל וְלִפְנִיאֵל מְאֹד יֶהֱמֶה,
 וּלְמַחֲנַיִם וְכָל פִּגְעֵי טְהוֹרָיִךְ.
שָׁם הַשְּׁכִינָה שְׁכֵנָה לָךְ, וְהַיּוֹצְרֵךְ
 פָּתַח לְמוּל שַׁעֲרֵי שַׁחַק שְׁעָרָיִךְ,
וּכְבוֹד אֲדֹנָי לְבַד הָיָה מְאוֹרֵךְ, וְאֵין
 שֶׁמֶשׁ וְסַהַר וְכוֹכָבִים מְאִירָיִךְ.
אֶבְחַר לְנַפְשִׁי לְהִשְׁתַּפֵּךְ בְּמָקוֹם אֲשֶׁר
 רוּחַ אֱלֹהִים שְׁפוּכָה עַל בְּחִירָיִךְ.
אַתְּ בֵּית מְלוּכָה, וְאַתְּ כִּסֵּא אֲדֹנָי, וְאִם
 יָשְׁבוּ עֲבָדִים עֲלֵי כִסְאוֹת גְּבִירָיִךְ.
מִי יִתְּנֵנִי מְשׁוֹטֵט בַּמְּקוֹמוֹת אֲשֶׁר
 נִגְלוּ אֱלֹהִים לְחוֹזַיִךְ וְצִירָיִךְ!
מִי יַעֲשֶׂה לִּי כְנָפַיִם וְאַרְחִיק נְדֹד,
 אָנִיד לְבִתְרֵי לְבָבִי בֵּין בְּתָרָיִךְ.
אֶפֹּל לְאַפַּי עֲלֵי אַרְצֵךְ, וְאֶרְצֶה אֲבָ-
 נַיִךְ מְאֹד, וַאֲחוֹנֵן אֶת עֲפָרָיִךְ,
אַף כִּי בְעָמְדִי עֲלֵי קִבְרוֹת אֲבוֹתַי, וְאֶשְׁ-
 תּוֹמֵם בְּחֶבְרוֹן עֲלֵי מִבְחַר קְבָרָיִךְ.
אֶעְבֹּר בְּיַעְרֵךְ וְכַרְמִלֵּךְ, וְאֶעְמֹד בְּגִלְ-
 עָדֵךְ וְאֶשְׁתּוֹמְמָה אֶל הַר עֲבָרָיִךְ--

16

Jerusalem! Have you no greeting
for your captive hearts, your last remaining flocks,
who send you messages of love?
Here are greetings for you from west and east,
from north and south, from near and far, from every side—
greetings also from a certain man,
a captive of your love,
who pours his tears like dew on Mount Hermon,
and longs to shed them on your slopes.
My voice is like a jackal's when I mourn your suffering,
but when I dream of how your exiles will return,
I turn into a lyre.
My heart is aching for Beth-el, Peníel, Maḥanayim,
every place where saints met messengers from God;
where the *Shekhina* is your neighbor;
where your Maker made your gates
facing the gates of heaven;
where the Glory of the Lord serves you for light,
not merely luminescent bodies—
sun and moon and stars.
You are the house of kings, the throne of David's God,
though slaves are sitting on your nobles' thrones.
I wish my soul could overflow
where once the holy spirit poured out
over your elect. I wish that I could wander
where the Lord appeared to visionaries, prophets;
wish that I had wings
to fly away to you—so far!—
and place the pieces of my broken heart
among your jagged mountains,
throw my face down to your ground,
fondle your gravel and caress your soil.
Even more would I delight
to stand beside the tombs
of ancestors and patriarchs,
and gaze at your choice graves;
to cross your fields and forests,
stand at Gilead, gaze at Avarím—

הַר הָעֲבָרִים וְהֹר הָהָר אֲשֶׁר שָׁם שְׁנֵי
אוֹרִים גְּדוֹלִים מְאִירַיִךְ וּמוֹרַיִךְ.
חַיֵּי נְשָׁמוֹת אֲוִיר אַרְצֵךְ, וּמִמָּר-דְּרוֹר
אַבְקַת עֲפָרֵךְ, וְנֹפֶת צוּף נְהָרַיִךְ.
יִנְעַם לְנַפְשִׁי הֲלֹךְ עָרֹם וְיָחֵף עֲלֵי
חָרְבוֹת שְׁמָמָה אֲשֶׁר הָיוּ דְבִירַיִךְ,
בִּמְקוֹם אֲרוֹנֵךְ אֲשֶׁר נִגְנַז וּבִמְקוֹם כְּרוּ-
בַיִךְ אֲשֶׁר שָׁכְנוּ חַדְרֵי חֲדָרַיִךְ.
אָגֹז וְאַשְׁלִיךְ פְּאֵר נִזְרִי וְאֶקֹּב זְמָן
חִלֵּל בְּאֶרֶץ טְמֵאָה אֶת נְזִירַיִךְ.
אֵיךְ יֶעֱרַב לִי אֲכֹל וּשְׁתוֹת בְּעֵת אֶחֱזֶה
כִּי יִסְחֲבוּ הַכְּלָבִים אֶת כְּפִירַיִךְ?
אוֹ אֵיךְ מְאוֹר יוֹם יְהִי מָתוֹק לְעֵינַי בְּעוֹד
אֶרְאֶה בְּפִי עוֹרְבִים פִּגְרֵי נְשָׁרַיִךְ?
כּוֹס הַיְגוֹנִים, לְאַט! הַרְפִּי מְעַט! כִּי כְבָר
מָלְאוּ כְסָלַי וְנַפְשִׁי מַמְּרוֹרַיִךְ.
עֵת אֶזְכְּרָה אָהֳלָה אֶשְׁתֶּה חֲמָתֵךְ, וְאֶזְ-
כֹּר אָהֳלִיבָה וְאֶמְצֶה אֶת שְׁמָרַיִךְ.
צִיּוֹן כְּלִילַת יֳפִי! אַהֲבָה וְחֵן תִּקְשְׁרִי
מֵאָז, וּבָךְ נִקְשְׁרוּ נַפְשׁוֹת חֲבֵרַיִךְ.
הֵם הַשְּׂמֵחִים לְשַׁלְוָתֵךְ וְהַכּוֹאֲבִים
עַל שׁוֹמְמוּתֵךְ וּבוֹכִים עַל שְׁבָרַיִךְ.
מִבּוֹר שְׁבִי שׁוֹאֲפִים נֶגְדֵּךְ וּמִשְׁתַּחֲוִים
אִישׁ מִמְּקוֹמוֹ אֱלֵי נֹכַח שְׁעָרַיִךְ
עֶדְרֵי הֲמוֹנֵךְ אֲשֶׁר גָּלוּ וְהִתְפַּזְּרוּ
מֵהַר לְגִבְעָה וְלֹא שָׁכְחוּ גְּדֵרַיִךְ,
הַמַּחֲזִיקִים בְּשׁוּלַיִךְ וּמִתְאַמְּצִים
לַעְלוֹת וְלֶאְחֹז בְּסַנְסִנֵּי תְמָרַיִךְ.

Hor and Avarím—where lie two luminaries,
men who brought you light and taught you wisdom.
Your air—the breath of life!
Flowing myrrh, the dust that rises from your soil!
Your rivers, molten honeycomb!
What joy my soul would have if I could walk
naked, barefoot, on the ruins,
on the rubble that your Temple has become,
where once your covenant-tabernacle was,
now hidden,
site of your two cherubim
that once resided in your inner chamber.
I'd shear and throw away my splendid locks,
and curse the fate that has defiled your Nazirites
in an unclean land.
What pleasure can I get from food and drink
when I have to see the dogs dragging
your lions with their teeth?
How can my eyes enjoy the daylight
when I see your eagle's corpses
in the mouths of crows?
Gently, cup of sorrow! Let me be!
Long enough have my guts been filled with gall.
To contemplate the fate of Ohola
is to gulp your poisoned brew;
to think of Oholiva's fate—
to suck the dregs.
Jerusalem! O perfect beauty!
You bind your hair in love and grace
as your true friends have bound their souls to you—
your friends, whose joy is your tranquility,
who ache at your destruction, weep for your disasters,
yearn for you from their captivity,
bow, wherever they may be, toward your gates—
your flocks, your exiled throngs,
scattered from hill to hill,
who still recall your folds,
who hold onto your hem,
who stretch themselves to rise
and grasp the branches of your palms.

שִׁנְעָר וּפַתְרוֹס הֲיַעַרְכוּךְ בְּגָדְלָם? וְאִם
הֶבְלָם יְדַמּוּ לְתֻמַּיִךְ וְאוּרָיִךְ?
אֶל-מִי יְדַמּוּ מְשִׁיחַיִךְ? וְאֶל-מִי נְבִי-
אַיִךְ? וְאֶל-מִי לְוִיַּיִךְ וְשָׁרַיִךְ?
יִשְׁנֶה וְיַחֲלֹף כְּלִיל כָּל-מַמְלְכוֹת הָאֱלִיל;
חָסְנֵךְ לְעוֹלָם, לְדוֹר וָדוֹר נְזָרַיִךְ.
אִוֵּךְ לְמוֹשָׁב אֱלֹהַיִךְ, וְאַשְׁרֵי אֱנוֹשׁ
יִבְחַר יְקָרֵב וְיִשְׁכֹּן בַּחֲצֵרַיִךְ!
אַשְׁרֵי מְחַכֶּה וְיַגִּיעַ וְיִרְאֶה עֲלוֹת
אוֹרֵךְ, וְיִבָּקְעוּ עָלָיו שְׁחָרַיִךְ,
לִרְאוֹת בְּטוֹבַת בְּחִירַיִךְ וְלַעְלֹז בְּשִׂמְ-
חָתֵךְ בְּשׁוּבֵךְ אֱלֵי קַדְמַת נְעוּרָיִךְ.

Halevi's Ode to Jerusalem is his most famous poem and one of the most famous Hebrew poems of the entire Middle Ages. It has even found its way into the liturgy among the laments for Jerusalem that make up the service for the fast day of the Ninth of Av, commemorating the destruction of the Temple.[6] Yet this poem, which has been recited by millions, can only be fully appreciated if it is read in the context of Halevi's individual religious development. And to read this rich and complicated masterpiece as a mere lament would be simplistic, for it does not portray a land that is dead, like the ruined campsites of Arabic love poetry, but one that is merely dormant.

Indeed, the Ode to Jerusalem has much in common with early Arabic odes with their customary erotic preludes. Such odes, whatever their subject, commonly begin with a speaker lamenting the ruins of a campsite where he and his beloved used to meet, addressing the ruins, complaining of their silence, and lamenting his bygone youth. Often, he names the place and other nearby places and describes the desert landscape. Eventually, a transition verse marks the introduction of the Ode's main theme.

Likewise, our speaker begins by apostrophizing Jerusalem, complains about her failure to return his greeting, laments the vanished past, and names several sites associated with that past. Like Arabic love poetry, the Ode to Jerusalem is

Babylon and Egypt at their height—
what were they to you?
How could their superstitions be a match
for the Urim and Tumim that were yours alone?
Did they have God-anointed kings,
or prophets, Levites singing in their temples?
The crown of all the ungodly kingdoms
is doomed to tarnish and to pass away;
your greatness will endure, your crown is everlasting.
God chose to dwell in you,
and happy is the man He chooses to bring near
to make his home within your courts;
who waits and lives to see your rising sun,
the new dawn breaking over you;
who lives to see your chosen ones in bliss,
rejoicing in your joy,
to see you once again as once you were
when you were young.

---

as much about the lover's sorrow at his separation from the beloved and his sensitivity to the experience of love as it is about the beloved and her beauty. And as the Arabic ode is ordinarily divided into two clear parts, the Ode to Jerusalem is segmented by the renewal of the apostrophe to Jerusalem ("Jerusalem! O perfect beauty!," v. 24).[7]

The renewed apostrophe also announces a readjustment of the speaker's role. In the opening apostrophe, he had appeared as the spokesman of Jerusalem's "captives" who "seek her welfare," the "remnant of her flock." He then shifts attention to himself, speaking—though still in the third person—first as a member of the whole set of Jerusalem's admirers, then as her chief mourner (v. 3), and from verse 4 through verse 23, he speaks openly for himself in the first person. In this long passage, all the descriptions of Jerusalem's greatness and ruin are framed by the speaker's personal response to her plight, and all the expressions of longing are framed as the speaker's personal emotions. But with the apostrophe in verse 24, the speaker resumes his initial role as spokesman for Jerusalem's admirers and true friends and retains it until the end. He also reverts to motifs of the opening verses, calling Jerusalem's admirers a flock in verse 27, as in verse 1; he speaks of them as scattered and longing for Jerusalem from all the corners of the world in verse 27, as in verse 2; and he refers to their captivity in verse 26, as in verse 3. It is as if, having made a false start in verse 3, he refreshes his purchase on the poem by means of these reprises in order to restart it.

Who are the principals on whose behalf he now speaks? That the poem came to be included in the liturgy shows that later readers took them to be the Jewish people as a whole. Indeed, Halevi's language seems inclusive at first, but a closer examination shows that he speaks here for a narrower circle within the Jewish people, the small group of the uniquely committed, those few "captives" (v. 1) whose spirit is bound up with the fate of Jerusalem. These are the chosen, who, at the poem's end, are to be brought near to God's courts, there to behold the dawning of the messianic era and the city's restoration. The eschatological language at the end of the poem recalls the visions of Daniel; like his visions, they are meant to bring comfort to the people as a whole but are so worded as to apply to the truly faithful among them. The speaker is the spokesman of a small coterie. As in love poetry the lover is unique in his devotion, so the faithful few represented by Halevi are alone among the many, and so scattered that for most of the poem's first part, he can let them slip his mind.

The poem's first part centers on an extended imaginary tour of the Holy Land, beginning with "I wish my soul could overflow," for which verses 1–7, describing the poet's mourning and naming specific sites for which he longs, serve as preparation. The three places named in verse 5 were not picked merely for nostalgia's sake, as in early Arabic love poetry. They establish the reason for the land's hold on the poet, being places where, in the biblical account, the patriarch Jacob encountered angels: Beth-el, where he saw angels ascending and descending the ladder to heaven; Peníel, where he wrestled with an angel; and Maḥanayim, where he encountered a troop of angels on his return to the Land of Israel after his exile to Padan-Aram. Further, all the encounters with angels alluded to by these three place names occur at liminal moments, when Jacob is either just leaving or just entering the Land of Israel. Halevi is using the nostalgic convention of love poetry to establish the essential quality of the Land of Israel that is the focus of his ode: it is the place where God shows Himself. The place names anticipate the visionary journey that occupies the center of the poem's first part.

The past experience of prophecy, exemplified by Jacob's experiences, leads to the assertion that even in its ruined state, the Land of Israel stands opposite the gates of heaven and is illumined by divine light.[8] This absolute and eternal quality of the Land of Israel outweighs any personal or even national historical association with that land or any other. Brooding on this property of the land throws the poet into the visionary mode, as we have seen happen in other poems; and in this mode he embarks, beginning with verse 10, on a tour of the holy sites. Borne from home through the air to the Land of Israel, as on bird's wings—how often that image appears in Halevi's poetry!—he is deposited on the ground in verse 12, where he fondles the stones and soil in accordance with his talismanic verse, Ps. 102:14–15.

From this posture of mourning and adoration, the poet rises and wanders, now on foot, to the patriarchs' graves in Hebron, and then, by way of forest and field, to the Gilead and to the Transjordan.[9] The ground beneath the pilgrim's feet gradually rises until it brings him to the grave of Moses, on Mount Avarím, and the grave of Aaron, on Mount Hor. From this elevation, his gaze continues briefly upward to contemplate the air (v. 15a), then turns down to the soil (v. 15b) and continues downward until it rests on the sacred relics—the Holy Ark, the golden cherubim—once hidden in the innermost precincts of the Temple, now buried beneath its ruins (v. 18).

The end of the visionary journey finds the poet angry at all that has been lost: divine revelation in the only place where revelation is possible; and the splendor of the Israelite kingdom. He reaches the place of his aspirations too miserable to enjoy the ordinary pleasures of life: food, drink, and light. His mixed feelings of celebration and anger are expressed by his professed readiness to "throw off his splendid locks," for this is a gesture of double valence. On the one hand, it signifies mourning. On the other, it suggests the fulfillment of a Nazirite vow in which one vows not to cut the hair or drink wine for a certain period. In his compact way, Halevi portrays himself experiencing both the satisfaction of one who has achieved his goal and the sorrow of one who experiences great loss. The sorrow modulates quickly into anger, and the anger generates the outburst in verses 22 and 23, in which the poet's "cup of sorrows" turns into a cup of poison as he contemplates the fate of the two sisters, Ohola and Oholiva. It is a strange passage that deserves special attention.

Halevi's contemporaries would have recognized in the sisters the allegory of two harlots (Ezekiel 23) representing the two kingdoms of ancient Israel—Judah, the southern kingdom, and Israel, the northern kingdom—into which the united kingdom of David and Solomon was divided ca. 920 BCE. The kingdoms' futile attempts, in the eighth and seventh centuries BCE, to strengthen themselves through alliances with the greater empires that threatened each other and them are depicted as the lusts of a lewd woman, and the empires as her lovers. The chapter in Ezekiel is marked by the obsessively sexual language of a prophet who seems half-mad with rage and so carried away by his sexual rhetoric that he seems to forget that the depraved women are merely allegorical stand-ins for political entities. Ohola, the northern kingdom, he rages, has already been destroyed by her lovers (as indeed the northern kingdom of Israel was destroyed by the Assyrians in 722 BCE). Likewise, he threatens, Oholiva will be destroyed by her lovers, the Assyrians and Babylonians. The climax of his tirade is addressed to Oholiva: "Thus says the Lord, God: The cup of your sister, deep and wide, you shall drink and become an object of laughter and derision—holding so much! You will be filled with drunken sorrow—the cup of desolation and horror—the cup of Samaria, your sister—you will drink it, suck it, grind it, and tear off your own breasts; for I have spoken."

The reference to Ezekiel 23 deepens considerably the theme of the poet's loss of appetite that was touched on lightly, even wittily, in "My Heart in the East" (poem 15). The motif of that poem—"what flavor does food have for me?"—is intensified here into "food and drink are bitter for me" (v. 20). This bitter taste had first appeared in the bitter cup (v. 22), a common metaphor for suffering. The bitter cup, in turn, is identified as the cup of Ohola and Oholiva, representing God's rage. With this last transformation, a bit of Ezekiel's obsessiveness rubs off on our poem, and what began as a nostalgic love poem climaxes in a passionate outburst of anger with a hint of erotic perversion.

But the author quickly diverts the accusation away from Zion and toward himself, for he alone drinks the cup of sorrow and sucks its lees. It is as if in recalling Ohola and Oholiva, he takes upon himself the accusation of faithlessness originally directed against the land. In this roundabout way, we encounter for the first time an undertone of guilt that figures occasionally in Halevi's pilgrimage poems; perhaps it is the poet's way of confessing his earlier neglect of the Land of Israel. But the storm is immediately over; the sorrow, anger, and guilt of the preceding section give way to a mood of tranquility and certainty.

Verse 24 wipes the emotional slate clean and restarts the poem with the renewed apostrophe of Jerusalem. She who a moment earlier had been portrayed as a degenerate harlot again wears a crown of beauty and grace. As at the beginning, the speaker mentions her devoted friends, again describes them as being bound (earlier by hope, now by love), as striving from all directions toward her, and as flocks. But the poet no longer singles himself out. He will not make another first-person appearance in the poem.

While the Ode's first part was about Jerusalem in reference to the speaker, the second part is about Jerusalem in reference to this select group, of which he is a member. With his fellows, he takes satisfaction in the certainty that Jerusalem will be vindicated against its seemingly victorious competitors, for she has the superior claim to temporal and religious supremacy. He reviews these claims, ending with the biblical theme that Jerusalem is the place that God has chosen. This theme of the chosen city brings the poet back to the chosen people—not the Jewish people, as in the familiar cliché,[10] but Jerusalem's special friends, those whom God has chosen because they have chosen Jerusalem. Halevi effects this parallelism of people and place by bringing together the biblical phrase "the place that God has chosen" (Deut. 12:5 and many other passages) with the verse from Psalms: "Happy is he whom You choose to bring near, to dwell in Your courts, to fill himself with bounty of Your house, the holiness of Your chamber" (Ps. 65:5). In the psalm, the pilgrim is described as blessed by virtue of having come into the presence of God; in the Ode, the person who has come into the presence of God in Jerusalem is described as having come there by virtue of being one of God's chosen. This theme is powerfully reinforced by the poem's close, which brings in another biblical verse about the chosen: "Happy is he who waits and reaches the days."[11] This visionary passage from Daniel speaks of the chosen few who will survive the sufferings of the present and live to see the messianic redemption.

By juxtaposing these two biblical verses, Halevi seems to be explaining his own intentions and making a statement about his own envisioned pilgrimage: "Happy is the man whom God has chosen to come to the Temple, there to await the messianic redemption." Does this mean that the redemption is imminent? Not if we take the biblical quotation seriously, for Daniel, in the immediately preceding passage, had given only teasing hints about the duration of the exile, conundrums that famously defied authoritative interpretation. Nor does Halevi, any more than Daniel, say that by going to settle in the Land of Israel, the chosen ones help to bring about the redemption. At the end of this poem, Halevi envisions going to Jerusalem and awaiting God's pleasure. If the redemption does not occur until long after the pilgrim's death, he will be the happier knowing that he is awaiting it there among the elect.

The poem implies the pilgrimage, but without a clarion announcement that the pilgrimage is imminent or that a practical decision to make it has even been taken; in fact, its central part is devoted to a merely imaginary pilgrimage. The author is master of a visionary power that makes the Holy Land a reality to him without his setting foot on it. It has dawned upon him that those who share his clear vision are few. The Ode to Jerusalem owes at least some of its poignancy to its oblique expression of the poet's discovery of just how alone he is, even among his few fellows, as it is always poignant when one realizes belatedly that the givens of one's inner life are not shared by others.

9

Argumentation

Several of Halevi's pilgrimage poems deal with objections that were raised to his pilgrimage by some who did not share his vision; but the person Halevi had to work the hardest to convince was undoubtedly himself. He could not have taken his decision lightly; he may indeed have lingered over it for years, as is generally assumed, despite our utter inability to determine when he first began contemplating it. Friends and family must also have tried to dissuade him, knowing that they would never see him again. Most people must have had trouble accepting the force of convictions that made this course right for him.

The poems in this chapter all involve an element of argument and persuasion. In "Still Chasing Fun at Fifty" (poem 17), the discussion is completely inward, with Halevi challenging himself about his way of life and offering himself a vision of the pilgrimage as a better way. In "Your Words Are Scented" (poem 18) and "Praise to Egypt!" (poem 19), the poet responds to interlocutors who have attempted to dissuade him from his pilgrimage. In "Can a Body Be a Room" (poem 20), the arguments with such friends about the pilgrimage are mentioned in passing, but the real debate is inward, and it is nearly over; the poet knows his course from the beginning of the poem but writes for his own assurance, reviewing the mental steps that have led him to his decision. By the end, any doubts that the poet may have had have been resolved, and the journey has actually begun, at least in imagination.

We do not know who the friends were who tried to dissuade Halevi from his journey; such discussions are mentioned only three times in all of Halevi's enormous corpus of poetry (poems 18, 19, and 20), and in only one (poem 18) is the discussion worded as if directed at another person. Undoubtedly, the real debate was inside Halevi's mind, and the inner debate is represented as if it were an argument with another person, a literary technique akin to the dialogue.

Readers who stress the rejection of Judeo-Arabic culture implicit in Halevi's pilgrimage tend to read the poems of argumentation as evidence that Halevi's departure was a cause of resentment, controversy, and scandal. That seems to me to be an exaggeration. Undoubtedly, Halevi's pilgrimage did imply his rejection of a Jewish elite culture that he had come to see as denatured and worldly; perhaps he did have to explain himself again and again. But we should not lose sight of the fact that in every extant writing in which Halevi's name is mentioned—and most of these writings date from after he left Spain—it is wreathed in titles of respect and admiration. His pilgrimage and the poems in which he explained it to others and to himself imply a rejection of his community's values, but there is no evidence that they offended anyone or that Halevi was reviled for them. Halevi's pilgrimage seems to have been understood as an extreme gesture—even an unnecessary one—but it must have been within the range of intelligible religious behavior or he would not have continued to receive the accolades and support documented by the letters that we have read in part II.

The argument in the four poems assigned to this chapter concerns two aspects of religiosity: the private and the public. The private theme is the position of a man who has come to think of his life in the community as servitude to man, who wants to devote the remainder of his life to the service of God, and the drastic challenge presented by the particular solution that he is contemplating. The public theme is the essential role of the Land of Israel in Jewish spiritual life and the continued religious viability of the land, despite its no longer being the home of the Jewish people and despite its devastation. The private theme predominates in poems 17 and 20, and the public theme predominates in poems 18 and 19. Poem 20 also engages the public theme in passing, but it is mostly concerned with the resolution of the inner tensions caused by the disparity between the poet's actual state and his religious ideals.

17

הֲתִרְדֹּף נַעֲרוּת אַחַר חֲמִשִּׁים,
וְיָמֶיךָ לְהִתְעוֹפֵף חֲמֻשִׁים?
וְתִבְרַח מֵעֲבֹדַת הָאֱלֹהִים,
וְתִכְסֹף אֶל עֲבֹדַת הָאֲנָשִׁים?
וְתִדְרֹשׁ אֶת פְּנֵי רַבִּים, וְתִטֹּשׁ
פְּנֵי אֶחָד לְכָל חֵפֶץ דְּרוּשִׁים?
וְתֵעָצֵל לְהִצְטַיֵּד לְדַרְכָּךְ,
וְתִמְכֹּר חֶלְקְךָ בִּנְזִיד עֲדָשִׁים?
הֲלֹא אָמְרָה לְךָ עוֹד נַפְשְׁךָ "הוֹן!"
וְתַאֲוָתָהּ תְּבַכֵּר לָחֳדָשִׁים?
נְטֵה מֵעַל עֲצָתָהּ אֶל עֲצַת אֵל,
וְסוּר מֵעַל חֲמֵשֶׁת הָרְגָשִׁים,
וְהִתְרַצֵּה לְיוֹצֶרְךָ בְּיֶתֶר
יְמוֹתֶיךָ אֲשֶׁר אָצִים וְחָשִׁים.
וְאַל תִּדְרֹשׁ בְּלֵב וָלֵב רְצוֹנוֹ,
וְאַל תֵּלֵךְ לְךָ לִקְרַאת נְחָשִׁים.
הֱיֵה לַעֲשׂוֹת רְצוֹנוֹ עַז כְּנָמֵר,
וְקַל כִּצְבִי, וְגִבּוֹר כַּלְּיָשִׁים.
וְאַל יִמּוֹט בְּלֵב יַמִּים לְבָבְךָ,
וְהָרִים תֶּחֱזֶה מָטִים וּמָשִׁים,
וּמַלָּחִים יְדֵיהֶם כַּמְּלָחִים,
וְחַכְמֵי הַחֲרָשִׁים מַחֲרִישִׁים--
שְׂמֵחִים הוֹלְכִים נֹכַח פְּנֵיהֶם,
וְשָׁבִים אֶל אֲחוֹרֵיהֶם וּבוֹשִׁים--
וְאוֹקְיָנוֹס לְפָנֶיךָ לְמָנוֹס,
וְאֵין מִבְרָח לְךָ כִּי אִם יְקוּשִׁים,
וְיָמוּטוּ וְיָנוּטוּ קְלָעִים,
וְיָנוּעוּ וְיָזוּעוּ קְרָשִׁים,
וְיַד רוּחַ מְצַחֶקֶת בְּמַיִם
כְּנוֹשְׂאֵי הָעֳמָרִים בַּרְּיָשִׁים,
וּפַעַם תַּעֲשֶׂה מֵהֶם גְּרָנוֹת,
וּפַעַם תַּעֲשֶׂה מֵהֶם גְּדִישִׁים--
בְּעֵת הִתְגַּבְּרָם דָּמוּ אֲרָיוֹת,
וְעֵת הֵחָלְשָׁם דָּמוּ נְחָשִׁים--

17

Still chasing fun at fifty, like a boy!—
and yet your time could run out any day.
You flee God's service,
have no better aspiration
than to be a slave to men.
You seek the favor of the many, turn away
from One who has it in Him
to answer every man's desire,
if they would only ask.
You won't be bothered gathering provisions for your journey,
but lightly trade the banquet of eternity
for lentil stew.
When will your appetite say, "Enough"?
When will your lust
stop growing back her maidenhead every month?
Turn from her advice to God's,
abandon those five senses.
Make peace with your Creator
while your remaining days are speeding by.
Do not expect halfhearted deeds will please Him,
or go to serpent-oracles to learn your fate.
To do His will, be tiger-fierce, gazelle-fleet, lion-mighty.
And do not lose heart in the heart of the sea,
when mountains seem to be sliding, shifting,
when sailors' hands are limp as rags
and skillful seamen silent, helpless
(they were jaunty sailing forward;
cross now, thrust backward).
You've nowhere but the ocean to escape to,
the trap of doom your only refuge.
The sails are tilting, slipping,
boards shift and tremble.
The wind toys with the water
like harvesters bringing sheaves to threshing,
pats the water flat as a threshing floor,
then heaps it up like mounds of grain.
The waves surge up like lions leaping,
then recede in foam that coils like serpents.

וְרִאשׁוֹנִים דִּלְקוּם אַחֲרוֹנִים,
כִּצְפְעוֹנִים וְאֵין לָהֶם לְחָשִׁים,
וְצִי אַדִּיר כְּקָט יִפֹּל בְּאַדִּיר,
וְהַתֹּרֶן וְהַנֵּס נֶחֱלָשִׁים,
וְהַתֵּבָה וְקִנֶּיהָ נְבֻכִים,
כְּתַחְתִּים שְׁנִים כַּשְּׁלִשִׁים,
וּמוֹשְׁכֵי הַחֲבָלִים בַּחֲבָלִים,
וְנָשִׁים וַאֲנָשִׁים נֶאֱנָשִׁים,
וְרוּחַ חֻבְּלָה מֵחוֹבְלֵיהֶם,
וְקָצוּ הַגְּוִיּוֹת בַּנְּפָשִׁים,
וְאֵין יִתְרוֹן לְחֹזֶק הַתְּרָנִים,
וְאֵין חֶמְדָּה לְתַחְבּוּלַת יְשִׁישִׁים,
וְנֶחְשְׁבוּ לְקַשׁ תָּרְנֵי אֲרָזִים,
וְנֶהֶפְכוּ לְקָנִים הַבְּרוֹשִׁים,
וְנֵטֶל חוֹל בְּגַב הַיָּם כְּתֶבֶן,
וּבַרְזִלֵּי אֲדָנִים כַּחֲשָׁשִׁים.
וְעַם יִתְפַּלְּלוּ כָּל אִישׁ לְקָדְשׁוֹ,
וְאַתְּ פּוֹנֶה לְקֹדֶשׁ הַקֳּדָשִׁים.
וְתִזְכֹּר מִפְלְאוֹת יַם סוּף וְיַרְדֵּן,
אֲשֶׁר עַל כָּל לְבָבוֹת הֵם חֲרוּשִׁים.
תְּשַׁבֵּחַ לְמַשְׁבִּיחַ שְׁאוֹן יָם
בְּעֵת שֶׁיִּגְרְשׁוּ מֵימָיו רְפָשִׁים.
וְתִזְכֹּר לוֹ זְכוּת לִבּוֹת טְמֵאִים,
וְיִזְכֹּר לָךְ זְכוּת אָבוֹת קְדֹשִׁים.
יְחַדֵּשׁ נוֹרְאוֹתָיו כִּי תְחַדֵּשׁ
לְפָנָיו שִׁיר מְחוֹל מַחְלִים וּמוּשִׁים,
וְיָשִׁיב הַנְּשָׁמוֹת לַפְּגָרִים,
וְיִחְיוּ הָעֲצָמִים הַיְבֵשִׁים.
וְרֶגַע יִשְׁתְּקוּ גַּלִּים, וְיִדְמוּ
עֲדָרִים עַל פְּנֵי אֶרֶץ נְטוּשִׁים.
וְהַלַּיִל, כְּבוֹא שֶׁמֶשׁ בְּמַעְלוֹת
צְבָא מָרוֹם--וְעָלָיו שַׂר חֲמִשִּׁים--
כְּכוּשִׁית מִשְׁבְּצוֹת זָהָב לְבוּשָׁהּ,
וְכִתְכֵלֶת בְּמִלּוּאַת גְּבִישִׁים.
וְכוֹכָבִים בְּלֵב הַיָּם נְבוּכִים
כְּגֵרִים מִמְּעוֹנֵיהֶם גְּרוּשִׁים,

Waves succeed those waves and chase them—
vipers that no charmer can control.
Here comes a mighty blow! The mighty ship might founder!
Mast and pole are shivered.
The decks, all three,
and all their chambers are in chaos.
Rope-men are in terror,
passengers (not only women) are collapsing.
Sailors' spirits fail, and people faint.
The strength of masts and skills of men mean nothing,
when cedar masts behave like chaff,
and cypress turns to reeds,
when ballast hits the sea like straw,
and iron bars like stubble.
Each man is praying to whatever he holds holy,
but you are facing God's own Holy Temple,
remembering the Sea of Reeds, the Jordan—
miracles engraved on every heart—
and praising Him who smoothes the sea
when it churns up scum.
You beg that He may purify your heart.
He will spare you for the sake of holy ancestors,
renew His miracles as you renew
the Levites' dance and song to Him.
He will restore the souls to bodies,
put back life in desiccated bones.
At once, the waves are calm;
they seem like flocks of sheep
scattered on a meadow.
The sun is setting and the stars are rising,
with the moon as captain, watching over them.
The night is like a Moorish woman dancing,
wearing an embroidered cloth with eyes,
cloth of sky-blue set with crystals.
Lost in the heart of the sea, the stars
dart and wander, like men compelled
to leave their homes as exiles;

וְכִדְמוּתָם בְּצַלְמָם יַעֲשׂוּ אוֹר
בְּלֵב הַיָּם כְּלֶהָבוֹת וְאִשִּׁים.
פְּנֵי מַיִם וְשָׁמַיִם עֲדָיִים
עֲלֵי לַיִל, מְטֹהָרִים לְטוּשִׁים.
וְיָם דּוֹמֶה לְרָקִיעַ בְּעֵינוֹ;
שְׁנֵיהֶם אָז שְׁנֵי יַמִּים חֲבוּשִׁים,
וּבֵינוֹתָם לְבָבִי יָם שְׁלִישִׁי
בְּשׁוֹא גַלֵּי שְׁבָחַי הַחֲדָשִׁים.

The argument of this poem is between the poet and his own self. It begins with a conventional reproach to himself for his own worldly behavior and with advice to devote himself instead to God's will. The remainder of the poem takes advantage of Halevi's powers as visionary poet to imagine what it would be like to actually do so. The speaker formulates a thought-experiment, conjuring up a storm at sea and imagining what its inward effect on him would be. How would it feel to put one's self completely in God's hands? Has the poet really made trust in God the Archimedean point of his religious life? Throughout the admonition and the imaginary test, the poet addresses himself using the second person. Only once the trial has been weathered, in the last line, does he speak in his own name.

The destination is hardly identified. We who know Halevi's biography know from the first that he is headed for the Land of Israel, but by keeping its identity in reserve for a full twenty-six verses, the poet creates a meaningful silence, signifying that not the destination but the voyage itself is his theme.

Though the poem turns out to be one of Halevi's masterpieces, it begins unpromisingly enough, with a versified sermon in the style of *zuhd* poetry. Halevi was not the first or the last Hebrew poet to write in this particularly stylized vein. Like many such poems in Arabic, this one begins by mentioning the age of the imaginary addressee,[1] reflecting the general idea that it is normal and right that people undergo a shift in outlook as they age; youth is for pleasure, age for contemplation of death and preparation for judgment. It is not only foolish, but undignified for a person who has reached the second part of his life to behave as if he were in the first.

Halevi takes this theme of late-life repentance in his own direction. He does speak of the need to give up worldly pleasures, but he is less concerned with crushing the soul and its appetites than with the sincere service to God. He reproaches himself not so much for having devoted his early life to possessions, food, and erotic activity, as for serving men and seeking their favor instead of

they make little lights in their own image,
little flames and flares in the heart of the sea,
pairs of ornaments on sky and water
to adorn the night.
Sea and sky, so like in color, seem to merge,
while in between
my heart makes yet another sea,
as my new songs and praises upward surge.

God's. He calls the religious life practiced by a person so engaged "seeking His favor with two hearts." In the rabbinic tradition, the expression "two hearts" suggests the two inclinations—one for good and the other for evil—traditionally believed to reside within man. But in the mouth of a poet, it suggests insincerity or, at best, confusion. The poem will attempt to turn insincerity to sincerity, confusion to clarity, by fusing the two hearts into one.

But first that heart must be tested. Will it prove "tiger-fierce, gazelle-fleet, lion-mighty" in God's service? The only way to find out is to plunge it into a crucible where it can be assayed—the heart of the sea. Nor is there any grace period: the moment that the poet's imagination enters the ship, it is already pounded by a storm. Sound effects in verse 14 (*veyamuṭu veyanuṭu qela'im / veyanu'u veyazu'u qerashim*) imitate the howling of the wind in the sails, which are soon thrown onto the deck as the masts collapse. Able sailors are helpless; the ship lists, and the waves turn into a surreal landscape inhabited by lions, snakes, and vipers. As in a nightmare, no human action seems to have any effect. All that is left is prayer.

But not for Halevi. Like Jonah, he is the only passenger who is not desperately praying to his God. The parallelism in the Hebrew in verse 26 ("Each man is praying to whatever he holds holy") is antithetical, enforcing a contrast between Halevi and the other passengers: they pray to whatever they call holy, but he is merely facing the Holy of Holies. He takes no action and need take no action, for the ship, by virtue of its eastward course, is facing God's Temple, which, even in its ruined state, retains its power to mediate between man and God. Facing the Temple, Halevi observes but does not share in the panic that surrounds him. His mind is full, not with fear but with memories of the evidence of God's power, compared to which the storm seems puny. He recalls how God split the Red Sea and the Jordan, and he praises the God Who has the power to allay the storm if He chooses. God can again perform miracles as He did in the past, just as Halevi can compose hymns to Him in the spirit of his ancestors, the Levites, who once sang hymns, the Psalms, in that very Temple. As a reenactment of the ancient Temple rites, are not Halevi's hymns themselves a testimony that the dead can live again?

At the mention of Halevi's hymns, the storm subsides as abruptly as it had begun upon his boarding the ship. Not petition but praise, uttered at the brink of disaster by a trusting, adoring heart, turns the scene from impending destruction to salvation and resurrection. The restoration of the passengers and crew (described in the language of the revival of Ezekiel's dry bones), who lay fainting on the deck throughout Halevi's meditation, quietly foreshadows the still-greater restoration anticipated for the world's future: life for mankind's dead and sovereignty for Israel, the politically dead. But these thoughts are transient; attention shifts again to the sea, now calm as evening comes on. The trial is over.

The poem ends with lines that are among the most moving that Halevi would ever write. As the sun sets, the moon rises, and the sky darkens, what catches the speaker's attention is the sparkling of the moonlight on the now-billowing ocean surface. Halevi describes this in a series of images that unite the night sky with the ocean. The ocean becomes a dancing woman wearing jewels that

(*Commentary continues on the next page*)

18

דְּבָרֶיךָ בְּמוֹר עוֹבֵר רְקוּחִים
וּמִצּוּר הַרְרֵי הַמּוֹר לְקוּחִים,
וְלָךְ וּלְבֵית אֲבוֹתֶיךָ חֲמוּדוֹת
אֲשֶׁר יִלְאוּ לְהַשִּׂיגָם שְׁבָחִים.
פְּגַשְׁתַּנִי בְּמִדְבָּרִים עֲרֵבִים
בְּתוֹכָם אוֹרְבִים נוֹשְׂאֵי שְׁלָחִים--
דְּבָרִים אָרְבוּ תוֹכָם דְּבוֹרִים,
וְתוֹךְ יַעְרַת דְּבַשׁ קוֹצִים כְּסוּחִים,
וְאִם כִּי לֹא שְׁלוֹם שָׁלֵם יְבַקֵּשׁ
בְּעוֹדָהּ מָלְאָה עִוְרִים וּפִסְחִים,
לְמַעַן בֵּית אֱלֹהֵינוּ נְבַקֵּשׁ
שְׁלוֹמָהּ, אוֹ בְּעַד רֵעִים וְאַחִים.
וְאִם כֵּן-הוּא כְּדִבְרֵיכֶם, רְאוּ חֵטְא
עֲלֵי כָל כּוֹרְעִים נֶגְדָּהּ וְשׁוֹחִים,
וְחֵטְא הוֹרִים שְׁכָנוּהָ כְּגֵרִים
וְקָנוּ שָׁם לְמֵתֵיהֶם צְרִיחִים,

shimmer as her body moves. The sparkles on the waves are stars in the ocean's depths whose instability calls to mind strangers wandering in confusion from their homes (like the pilgrim who observes them from the deck) and flashing flames. The sparkling water and the sparkling sky are gems. Sea and sky merge in a dark mass dotted with glittering, shimmering flecks.

It is the poet's heart, the source of his song, that unifies the heights and the depths. As his moral faculty, the heart began the poem divided against itself; cast into the assaying crucible of the sea, it has been not only tested but melted down and re-fused and has emerged from its ordeal in harmony with itself. As the seat of his imaginative faculty, it observes the reciprocal relationship of sky and sea and makes a song in celebration of their—and its own—harmony after conflict. In this state of grace, the poet fills the space between the heart of the sea and the heart of the sky with the song of his own heart, and for the first time in the poem, introduces himself—yet only through a single pronoun—explicitly into the poem.[2]

In this poem, as in several others we have read, Halevi identifies his poetry with the songs of his ancestors, the Levites. We have also heard him say several times that he was dedicating his poetry to God.[3] Perhaps he hoped that his coming into physical proximity with God would elevate his work from a poetic skill to a divinely inspired Levitical act, like the book of Psalms.

18

Your words are scented with perfume of myrrh—
words quarried, as it were, from great myrrh-mountains—
and you and all your people have such qualities
that praise exhausts itself in praising you.
Now you come to meet me in a wilderness—
a wilderness of honeyed words,
where warriors lurk with swords—
words concealing bees,
honeycomb studded with thorns.
Is Zion really no concern of ours
because the blind and halt inhabit it?
Surely we should care for what is left
of the House of God, for friends and kin still there.
If you are right, then it must be a sin
to bow toward it or to reverence it.
If you are right, our ancestors were sinners,
when they went there to live as strangers,
bought caves there for graves.

וְתֹהוּ מַעֲשֵׂה אָבוֹת חֲנוּטִים
וּפִגְרֵיהֶם אֱלֵי אַרְצָהּ שְׁלוּחִים--
וְהָיוּ בַעֲבוּרָהּ נֶאֱנָחִים,
וְהָאָרֶץ מְלֵאָה נֶאֱלָחִים--
וְלָרִיק מִזְבְּחוֹת אָבוֹת בְּנוּיִים,
וְלַשָּׁוְא קָרְבוּ שָׁם הַזְּבָחִים.
הֲטוֹב שֶׁיִּהְיוּ מֵתִים זְכוּרִים
וְהָאָרוֹן וְהַלּוּחוֹת שְׁכוּחִים?
נְשַׁחֵר אֶת מְקוֹם שַׁחַת וְרִמָּה,
וְנִטֹּשׁ אֶת מְקוֹר חַיֵּי נְצָחִים?
הֲלָנוּ נַחֲלָה רַק מִקְדְּשֵׁי אֵל?--
וְאֵיךְ נִהְיֶה לְהַר קָדְשׁוֹ שְׁכֵחִים?
הֲיֵשׁ לָנוּ בְּמִזְרָח אוֹ בְּמַעְרָב
מְקוֹם תִּקְוָה נְהִי עָלָיו בְּטוּחִים,
אֲבָל אֶרֶץ אֲשֶׁר מָלְאָה שְׁעָרִים
לְנֶגְדָּם שַׁעֲרֵי שַׁחַק פְּתוּחִים?--
כְּהַר סִינַי וְהַכַּרְמֶל וּבֵית אֵל
וּבָתֵּי הַנְּבִיאִים הַשְּׁלוּחִים,
וְכִסְאוֹת כֹּהֲנֵי כִסֵּא אֲדֹנָי
וְכִסְאוֹת הַמְּלָכִים הַמְּשׁוּחִים.
וְלָנוּ גַּם לְבָנֵינוּ יְעָדָהּ,
וְאִם צִיִּים שְׁכָנוּהָ וְאֹחִים.
הֲלֹא כֵן נִתְּנָה קֶדֶם לְאָבוֹת,
וְכֻלָּהּ נַחֲלַת קוֹצִים וְחֹחִים,
וְהֵם מִתְהַלְּכִים אָרְכָּהּ וְרָחְבָּהּ
כְּמִתְהַלֵּךְ בְּפַרְדֵּס בֵּין צְמָחִים,
וְהֵם גֵּרִים וְתוֹשָׁבִים, וְדוֹרְשִׁים
מְקוֹם קֶבֶר וּמָלוֹן שָׁם כְּאוֹרְחִים,
וְשָׁם הִתְהַלְּכוּ לִפְנֵי אֲדֹנָי
וְלָמְדוּ הַשְּׁבִילִים הַנְּכֹחִים.
וְאָמְרוּ כִּי רְפָאִים שָׁם יְקוּמוּן
וְיֵצְאוּ שׁוֹכְנִים תַּחַת בְּרִיחִים,
וְכִי שָׁם תַּעֲלֹזְנָה הַגְּוִיּוֹת,
וְתָשֹׁבְנָה נְפָשׁוֹת לַמְּנוּחִים.
רְאֵה נָא גַּם רְאֵה דוֹדִי וְהָבֵן,
וְסוּר מִמּוֹקְשִׁים צִנִּים וּפַחִים,
וְאַל תַּשִּׁיאֲךָ חָכְמַת יְוָנִית
אֲשֶׁר אֵין לָהּ פְּרִי כִּי אִם פְּרָחִים.
וּפִרְיָהּ כִּי אֲדָמָה לֹא רְקוּעָה,

In vain they had themselves embalmed,
and had their bodies sent there to be buried,
sighed for it when it was occupied
by idol-worshipers; in vain
they built their altars, offered sacrifice.
What sense is there in honoring our dead,
when we neglect the tablets and the ark?
What sense in visiting the place of graves and worms,
when we neglect the sources of eternal life?
Are synagogues our only sanctuaries?
How can we forget the holy mountain?
Can we have hope or certainty in East or West
or anywhere but in the one land full of gates
that face the open gates of heaven?—
places like Carmel, Beth-el, and Sinai,
once the homes of prophets, messengers from God,
the place where thrones were set
for priests who served God's throne,
as well as thrones for our anointed kings?
He promised it to us,
though only owls and jackals haunt it now.
What was in that place but thorns and thistles
when God bestowed it on our fathers long ago?—
And yet they paced its length and breadth
like people strolling in a flower garden,
lived in it as strangers, transients,
each night seeking somewhere to put down their heads,
always on the lookout for some plot
where, dead, they might be buried.
There they learned to walk before the Lord,
adopted ways of righteousness.
They said that there the dead will rise,
that those who lie beneath the barriers will emerge,
that there the bodies will rejoice again,
and souls return to those who lie at rest.
Look here, friend, use your judgment, think it over,
save yourself from mental traps;
above all, don't let Greek philosophy seduce you;
it may have flowers, but it never will bear fruit.
Or if it does, it only comes to this:

וְכִי לֹא אָהֳלֵי שַׂחַק מְתוּחִים,
וְאֵין רֵאשִׁית לְכָל מַעֲשֵׂה בְרֵאשִׁית,
וְאֵין אַחֲרִית לְחִדּוּשׁ הַיְרָחִים.
שְׁמַע דִּבְרֵי נְבוֹנֶיהָ נְבוּכִים,
בְּנוּיִים עַל יְסוֹד תֹּהוּ וְטִחִים,
וְתָשׁוּב לְךָ בְּלֵב רֵיקָם וְנָעוּר
וּפֶה מָלֵא בְּרֹב שִׂיגִים וְשִׂיחִים.
וְלָמָּה זֶה אֲבַקֵּשׁ לִי אֳרָחוֹת
עֲקַלְקַלּוֹת וְאֶעֱזֹב אֵם אֳרָחִים?

In “Still Chasing Fun at Fifty” (poem 17), we overheard the poet as he argued with himself. In “Your Words Are Scented,” we listen in as he argues with a friend, whether real or imaginary. We never hear the friend’s voice, but we can infer the points that he has been making from the speaker’s reply, which takes the discussion into a direction that the friend probably never expected.

The Arabic headings to this poem in the medieval copies by which it has been preserved tell us that Halevi wrote this poem in response to someone who tried to dissuade him from the pilgrimage. That may be true, but the poem does not mention the pilgrimage. After the complimentary preamble, the speaker argues: “Is Zion really no concern of ours / because the blind and halt inhabit it?” The friend, therefore, must have claimed that Jerusalem no longer deserves to be an object of our veneration because it is occupied by Gentiles. Now this is self-evidently a straw-man position, for surely the friend was not advocating that the prayers be changed to eliminate the countless references to Jerusalem and the Holy Land or that the Jews stop facing Jerusalem in prayer. The friend cannot have been saying that the Holy Land is no longer holy. He must have been trying to moderate Halevi’s obsessive concern with the land by arguing that its holiness is in suspension as long as the Temple is in ruins, the land occupied by non-Jews, and Jerusalem without a Jewish community.

The Arabic heading in the medieval copy says that Halevi responded by praising the land. It is true that Halevi’s words include praise of the land, but his praise is not a comprehensive list of the excellent qualities (*faḍā’il*) of the Land of Israel.[4] The praise is focused on a very specific group of themes, and it modulates to a subject that at first seems unrelated: Halevi’s famous denunciation of philosophy.

Only by studying the specific points raised by Halevi in praise of the land will we understand why this poem ends as it does. His first point is that the

the world was not created;
and no one stretched the heavens like a tent;
in the beginning there was no Creation;
the moon will wax and wane forever.
Just hear the incoherence of their doctrines,
constructed out of chaos and pretension;
they only leave a hollow in your heart,
and nothing in your mouth but syllogisms.
Why should I go following such twisting trails,
abandoning the mother of all highways?

---

patriarchs came to the land, built altars in it, bought graves there, and had their embalmed corpses sent there for burial, even though it was inhabited by pagan Canaanites. His second point is that if, in our own country, we visit the graves of our dead, all the more should we pay reverence to the place that contains the graves of Israel's most sacred objects and that is the source of eternal life. Both points emphasize the sanctity of what is buried beneath the soil of the Holy Land: Israel's patriarchs, who communicated with God, and the sacred implements of Israel's communication with God.

Having juxtaposed the graves in al-Andalus with the graves in the Land of Israel, Halevi goes on to juxtapose the synagogues in al-Andalus with the Temple in the Land of Israel—or rather, since the Temple is destroyed, the mountain on which the Temple stood. This mention of the Temple Mount shifts our attention, which had been focused downward (on the ground and on things beneath the ground), to the heights; likewise, the mention of the gates of Jerusalem turns our attention to the gates of heaven, which they face. Among such gates, Halevi names Mount Sinai (which he considered part of Palestine), Mount Carmel (scene of Elijah's confrontation with the priests of Baal, where divine fire descended to earth),[5] and Beth-el, where Jacob had his vision of the ladder, and which Jacob dubbed "The Gate of Heaven."[6]

These shifting images are united by the theme of death and burial. The antagonist depicted the Land of Israel as nothing more than a huge charnel house; Halevi's point is that the remains buried there are not merely the remains of people but vestiges of revelation, for the land was once the land of revelation and will be so again. The land is also the place of resurrection, where those touched by God in their earthly life will eventually revive to eternal life and experience His presence as Israel did of old. Having made these points in the abstract, Halevi concretizes them beginning in verse 20 of the Hebrew text by pointing to the lives of the patriarchs, who lived in the Land of Israel even when its other inhabitants were idolaters, and who received their prophecies there, sought to be buried there, and proclaimed it to be the place of resurrection.

The speaker interrupts the flow of his argument in verse 26 and renews his address to the friend. Like the renewed apostrophe in the Ode to Jerusalem, this apostrophe segments the poem—in this case, marking the beginning of the famous tirade against Greek philosophy. From Halevi's other writings, we learn not to take this rant as denying the validity of philosophical thinking or of the utility of its intellectual procedures; it is not philosophy per se that offends Halevi but its pretensions to authority in the areas dealt with more effectively by religion.[7] Let us examine first Halevi's complaint against philosophy, and afterward we shall see how it relates to the first part of the poem.

Halevi begins with a metaphor that he made famous: Greek philosophy is a tree that bears flowers but no fruit—attractive but sterile. Greek philosophy was indeed attractive to people of Halevi's circle. It had the intrinsic attractions of a comprehensive intellectual system embracing the sciences as well as metaphysics and carrying all the prestige of antiquity. On the social plane, it had the attraction of providing entrée—via medicine, astronomy, mathematics—into prestigious and remunerative professions in which Jews could take part alongside Muslims and Christians. Halevi had personally enjoyed both attractions of philosophy in the earlier part of his life. But two features of Greek philosophy offend him. One is the Aristotelian tenet that the cosmos has existed and will endure eternally, denying that the world was created, as told in the Bible. The other is the fact that pure reason leads different thinkers to take different positions, resulting in endless argumentation and the failure to produce definite solutions to the important problems.

Halevi did not need to write a poem in order to make these points; both are covered more than adequately in the Kuzari. Nor are they tacked on arbitrarily to the praise of the Land of Israel. The poem's two parts in reality treat a single theme.

Philosophy provides no certainty; being a dialectical process, it is a crooked path to the truth, infinitely inferior to the direct path provided by God's word. But even if philosophy could demonstrate absolutely the truth of the Aristotelian system, it would not nourish or delight. The fruit that we seek is not certainty in the abstract but the certainty of particular, desirable beliefs of a kind that only revelation can provide.

Halevi tells us one such desirable belief in the first part of the poem. There, the themes were revelation, death, and resurrection, and they are what we should look for in the poem's second part. The fruit we crave is some degree of contact with God while we are living and assurance that our lives are not over when we die. These assurances Halevi found in the Land of Israel, as the place where God reveals His will and intentions to prophets and as the place that Halevi particularly identified with the resurrection of human bodies in the World to Come. Aristotelianism tears these assurances out of our hands, with its doctrines of an unchanging cosmos driven mechanically by a prime mover, of a world with no creator, no divine will, and, at best, a disembodied hope for man.

No wonder that philosophers' wisdom leaves you hungering. Not only is their chatter inconclusive, but such conclusions as they profess to reach provide no nourishment. Halevi says that they leave your mouth full of *sigim vesiḥim,* an alliterative phrase derived from 1 Kings 18:27, where Elijah mocks the worshipers of Baal. Its first word was understood by medieval lexicographers to mean "preoccupation."[8] The second, by a poetically useful coincidence, means both "speech" and "bushes." "Speech" fits the overt theme of the passage, and "bushes" fits the metaphor that Halevi is exploring. It suggests that philosophical discourse fills one's mouth not with delicious fruit but with dry twigs, neither sweet nor nourishing.

This image of dry twigs in the mouth brings us back to the beginning of the poem, where the poet characterized the interlocutor's speech as honeycomb concealing thorns. We have had ample opportunity to familiarize ourselves with the constant stream of flattery and praise customary in Halevi's world; we have also read of Halevi's desire to escape that world. The opening of this poem alludes to its verbal style, in which insincerity and treachery were customarily buried beneath a blanket of rhetoric. The poem thus uses the image of non-nourishing food at its beginning and at its end: first, to characterize courtly rhetoric; and then, to characterize philosophical speech. This envelope structure enables the poet to pillory both the high status of courtly life, here mocked for its empty flattery; and the vogue of philosophy, here lampooned for its sterile argumentation. The two are united by their common fault of denatured speech.

Before leaving this poem, it is well to clear up the meaning of the lines "Can we have hope or certainty in East or West / or anywhere but in the one land full of gates / that face the open gates of heaven?" (v. 15).[9] To readers who approach all of Halevi's poetry from the perspective of Jewish exile, the security that Halevi is speaking of is political and social. The assumption is that the interlocutor had pointed out to Halevi that the Land of Israel is not in Jewish hands and is therefore no less safe than al-Andalus, and Halevi replies that no place is really safe for the Jews. Our analysis of the poem has shown it to be a well-integrated exploration of a completely different set of interrelated problems; the political interpretation of verse 15 would make it the only passage in the poem to deal with the problem of exile, an isolated theme brought in without preparation and without relevance for the poem as a whole.

But beyond the objection on the grounds of literary coherence, the political interpretation seems contradicted by the exceptive clause that it introduces, which, literally translated, reads: “Have we a place of hope in which we can be secure except a land that is full of gates, toward which the gates of heaven are open?” This clause makes clear that the security of which Halevi is speaking is not security from attack but certainty of religious convictions, certainty that prayer is heard, certainty that the promises of the prophets will come true. The verse encapsulates Halevi’s making the Land of Israel the fulcrum of his religious conviction, as enunciated in his epistle to Samuel ben Ḥanania discussed in chapter 7.[10]

19

לְמִצְרַיִם עֲלֵי כָל עִיר תְּהִלָּה
אֲשֶׁר הָיָה דְבַר אֵל שָׁם תְּחִלָּה.
וְשָׁמָּה נִטְּעָה גֶּפֶן בְּחוּרָה,
וְהָיוּ אַשְׁכְּלֹתֶיהָ סְגֻלָּה.
וְשָׁם נוֹלְדוּ שְׁלוּחֵי אֵל, וְהָיוּ
שְׁלוּחֵי אֵל כְּבֵין חָתָן וְכַלָּה.
וְשָׁם יָרַד כְּבוֹד הָאֵל וְהָלַךְ
בְּעַמּוּד אֵשׁ וַעֲנָן וַחֲתֻלָּה.
וְשָׁמָּה נַעֲשָׂה קָרְבַּן אֲדֹנָי,
וְנִתַּן דַּם בְּרִית וַיְהִי גְאֻלָּה.
וְשָׁמָּה מַעֲמַד מֹשֶׁה לְהַעְתִּיר,
וְאֵין מַעֲמָד כְּמוֹ זֶה לַתְּפִלָּה.
וְיִשְׂרָאֵל לְמִצְרַיִם וְאַשּׁוּר
שְׁלִישִׁיָּה, וּבֵינוֹתָם מְסִלָּה.
וּמִזְבֵּחַ לְאֵל הָיָה בְתוֹכָהּ
לְרוֹמֵם אֶת שְׁמוֹ עַל כָּל תְּהִלָּה,
וְהָאֹתוֹת וְהַמּוֹפְתִים וְהַשֵּׁם
אֲשֶׁר עוֹלָם בְּהוֹד זִכְרוֹ מְמֻלָּא;
וְגַם מִנַּהֲרֵי עֵדֶן נְהָרָהּ,
וְטוּב אַרְצָהּ בְּגַן עֵדֶן מְסֻלָּא.

19

Praise to Egypt!
Great above all other lands,
for there God first addressed His people;
where He planted His most treasured vine,
a vine that yielded clusters with the finest fruit;
birthplace of the messengers of God,
emissaries as between a bride and groom;
where God came down to earth,
walked in fire, upright like a pillar,
in a cloud enveloping;
where sacrifice was made, blood sprinkled—
a covenant of redemption;
where Moses stood in prayer, beseeching—
and what a prayer that was!
Israel, Egypt, Babylonia—
three equal nations,
connected by a highway!
In its midst, an altar built for God,
to elevate His Name above all praise.
Miracles were there, and wonders, and the Name
whose glory fills the earth.
Its river one of four
flowing from God's own garden;
bountiful as paradise.

חֲקַרְנוּהָ וְכֵן הִיא, אַךְ לְבָבִי
יְמָאֵן לַמְרַפִּים עַל נְקַלָּה.
וְאֵדַע כִּי שְׁכִינָה נָטְתָה שָׁם
כְּאוֹרֵחַ לְצֵל אַלּוֹן וְאֵלָה;
וְעִם שָׁלֵם וְצִיּוֹן הִיא כְאֶזְרָח,
וְשָׁם תּוֹרָה וְשָׁמָּה הַגְּדֻלָּה--
מְקוֹם הַדִּין, מְקוֹם הָרַחֲמִים שָׁם,
וְשָׁם יְחַל אֱנוֹשׁ לִשְׂכַר פְּעֻלָּה;
וְהַר נִקְרָא לְאֵל הַר נַחֲלָתוֹ,
וְהִפְרִישׁוֹ לְהַקְדִּישׁוֹ כְּחַלָּה.
וְיוֹרֵד מִקְּדֻשָּׁתָהּ לְבָבֶל
וּמִצְרַיִם כְּמוֹעֵל בָּהּ מְעִילָה.
אֲבָל אִישׁ יַעֲלֶה מִכָּל אֲרָצוֹת
לְצִיּוֹן, מַעֲלָה הִיא לוֹ מְעֻלָּה.
וְלָמָּה יִלְעֲגוּ עָלַי מְלִיצִים?
וְלָמָּה אֶהֱיֶה לָהֶם לְמִלָּה,
אֲשֶׁר אִם הֵם בְּדָת אֵל מַאֲמִינִים
אֲדִינֵמוֹ בְתוֹרַת הַקְּהִלָּה;
וְאִם לֹא יַאֲמִינוּ, הֵן מְחִיצָה,
וְאֵין בֵּינִי וּבֵינֵיהֶם מְחִלָּה.

Halevi's arguments did not end when he left Spain, for in Egypt he found a community very much like the one he had left. There, too, he found himself having to explain and justify his pilgrimage. Now, however, he was on weaker ground, for Egypt played a central role in the sacred history of the Jewish people and in the history of prophecy.

In the Kuzari, Halevi had insisted that prophecy could occur only in the Land of Israel. He therefore had to explain the anomaly that several of Israel's prophets prophesied elsewhere, including Moses, the greatest of all the prophets, who never lived in the Land of Israel and who received his prophecies in Egypt. Halevi did his best to explain this outstanding exception and other lesser exceptions, partly by extending the geographical boundaries of the Land of Israel to the Red Sea—thus including Sinai—and partly by pointing out that such prophecies as occurred outside this greater Land of Israel had as their subject the Jewish people's relation to the land and thus were not a serious infringement of his rule.[11]

All this is true, we've studied it,
and yet my heart rejects facile dissuasion.
God may have turned aside there, the way a traveler
stops to rest beneath an oak or terebinth,
but His real roots are in Jerusalem,
where majesty and Torah come together,
judgment joins with mercy,
and labors of a lifetime are rewarded.
The hill is there, too, that He called
"the Mount of His Inheritance,"
separated, sanctified by Him
as a housewife sets aside a portion of her dough,
to offer to the priests.
Whoever leaves its sanctity
for Babylonia or Egypt has abused it;
but he who leaves his land and goes to Zion
lays claim to highest virtue.
Why then do the glib so mock me?
Why am I the topic of their gossip?
If they believe in God's religion,
I will judge them by our people's laws.
If they do not—a barrier between us,
a barrier that never can be crossed.

This poem is a response to the arguments of Egyptian friends who wanted to divert Halevi from his plan to settle in the Land of Israel, claiming that Egypt had sufficient religious merit that he could stay there while remaining true to his principles.[12] The points in favor of Egypt were: Egypt was the place where God first revealed Himself to the Jewish people as a whole, where the descendants of Jacob actually became a nation, and where God intervened actively in Jewish history by liberating the Jews from Egyptian bondage. (In the Kuzari, Halevi made this event the foundation of his religious system, more fundamental to it than the Creation itself.) The liberation of Israel was also the model of the future redemption and the basis of hope for Israel's vindication in the messianic age. Halevi's statement in the poem that Egypt is "great above all other lands" is a clear echo of his own words in Kuzari 2:22.[13]

In this poem, Halevi concedes these points. He even concedes the popular notion that the Nile is one of the four rivers of paradise.[14] But he insists on three points that establish an insuperable difference between the lands: (1) God may have visited Egypt, as a traveler spends a night in an inn, but His home is the Land of Israel; (2) the Land of Israel, not Egypt, is the place where Israel received the Torah (according to the view that Sinai is in Palestine) and enjoyed sovereignty; and (3) the Land of Israel is the site of the resurrection and final judgment.

The poem is divided into two exactly even parts: verses 1 through 10 rehearse the arguments in favor of Egypt, and verses 11 through 20 refute them and state the poet's point of view. (The turn is signaled by the introduction of the first-person pronoun, rendering a judgment on the points made in the first part.) The refutation, truth to tell, is not very strongly written. It makes its three points one by one in unadorned language and alludes briefly to some of the rabbinic traditions that give legal status to the superiority of the Land of Israel. Halevi seems to be rushing through the argument, and the state of the Hebrew text is not completely satisfactory.[15]

Perhaps the weakness of the poem's end is due to Halevi's eagerness to express his anger at having to engage in this argument at all. For the poem ends on an uncharacteristically angry note, with Halevi threatening to see his interlocutors punished under religious law or to shun them altogether. The reader

(*Commentary continues on the next page*)

20

הֲיוּכְלוּ פְגָרִים   הֱיוֹתָם חֲדָרִים
לְלִבּוֹת קְשׁוּרִים   בְּכַנְפֵי נְשָׁרִים
לְאִישׁ קָץ בְּחַיָּיו   וְכָל מַאֲוַיָּיו
לְגוֹלֵל לְחָיָיו   בְּמִבְחַר עֲפָרִים.
וּפָחַד וְחָרֵד   וְדִמְעוֹ בְּמוֹרָד
לְהַשְׁלִיךְ סְפָרַד   וְלָתוּר עֲבָרִים,
וְלִרְכֹּב אֳנִיּוֹת   וְלִדְרֹךְ בְּצִיּוֹת

wonders why the response of this ordinarily genial poet is so immoderate. Perhaps the word *melitsim* (v. 18), which he uses to refer to his interlocutors (here translated "the glib") is the clue. The word is susceptible to several interpretations. It occurs once in the book of Psalms, meaning "scoffer." Job uses it to refer to his querulous friends. The usual meaning is "spokesman," and it was commonly used in medieval Hebrew for speakers of eloquent language and poets.[16] All these meanings could be relevant; taken together, they suggest that Halevi is responding to a poem or an epistle that criticized or mocked him.

In the Judeo-Arabic cultural world, it was natural to express criticism in the form of a poem, even a lampooning poem if the author wanted not merely to raise the topic for discussion but to cause pain or to damage someone's reputation. If Halevi received a poem satirizing him for his plan to leave Egypt and continue his pilgrimage, he would indeed have been hurt, and that would explain his tone. But while it is easy to imagine friends trying to dissuade Halevi from going on to Palestine on the grounds that Egypt is sacred enough, it is hard to imagine them mocking him on those grounds or trying to hurt him. Perhaps the dissuasion was meant good-naturedly, but he had become short-tempered at having to explain himself or at being attacked with weapons that he himself had provided in the Kuzari.

20

Can a body
be a room
to hold a heart
attached to eagle's wings,
when a man
detests his life,
only wants
to roll his cheeks
in the earth's
best soil;
trembles with holy fear,
always weeping;
wants to
abandon Spain
wander far,
sail ships
cross fens,

מְעוֹנוֹת אֲרָיוֹת וְהַרְרֵי נְמֵרִים;
וְגָעַר בְּדוֹדִים וּבָחַר נְדוֹדִים,
וְנָטַשׁ חֲדָרִים וְשָׁכַן חֲרֵרִים.
וּמָצְאוּ בְעֵינָיו זְאֵבֵי יְעָרִים
כְּחֵן הַבְּתוּלוֹת בְּעֵינֵי נְעָרִים.
וְחָשַׁב יְעֵנִים לְשָׁרִים וְנוֹגְנִים,
וְשַׁאֲגַת כְּפִירִים שְׁרִיקוֹת עֲדָרִים.
וְשָׂם שַׁעֲשׁוּעָיו בְּמוֹקְדֵי צְלָעָיו
וּפַלְגֵי דְמָעָיו כְּפַלְגֵי יְאֹרִים.
וַיַּעַל גְּבָעוֹת וְיֵרֵד בְּקָעוֹת
לְהָקִים שְׁבוּעוֹת וְשַׁלֵּם נְדָרִים.
וַיִּסַּע וַיִּצְעַן וַיַּעְבֹר בְּצֹעַן
לְאֶרֶץ כְּנַעַן לְמִבְחַר הֲרָרִים,
וְתוֹכְחוֹת מְרִיבָיו חֲלִיפוֹת סְבִיבָיו
וְיִשְׁמַע וְיַחֲרִישׁ כְּלֹא אִישׁ דְּבָרִים.
וְכַמָּה יְרִיבֵם, וְכַמָּה יְשִׁיבֵם,
וּמַה יַּעֲצִיבֵם, וְהֵמָּה שְׁכוּרִים?
וְאֵיךְ אִשְּׁרוּהוּ בְּעַבְדוּת מְלָכִים
אֲשֶׁר הִיא בְעֵינָיו עֲבוֹדַת אֲשֵׁרִים?
הֲטוֹב כִּי יְאֻשַּׁר אֱנוֹשׁ תָּם וְיָשָׁר
כְּצִפּוֹר מְקֻשָּׁר בְּיַד הַצְּעִירִים?--
בְּעַבְדוּת פְּלִשְׁתִּים וְהַגְּרִים וְחִתִּים
וְלִבּוֹ מְפַתִּים אֱלֹהִים אֲחֵרִים,

lions' lairs, tiger-mountains;
fights with friends,
decides to leave;
abandons home,
dwells in deserts;
finds he likes
forest's wolves
more than youths like pretty girls;
takes ostriches for singers,
lions' roars for shepherds' whistles;
loves the heat
that burns within him,
needs no
fresh rivers
with his own streaming eyes;
heads up hills,
down valleys
true to his oaths and vows,
travels, journeys,
crosses Egypt
toward Canaan,
to the mountain—
to that very best of mountains?
Reproachers surround him
taking turns, arguing;
he listens, says nothing,
like a man who can't find words.
Why fight them? Why argue
when it only makes them madder?
They must be drinking
to think that he's a big success
for catering to kings
(which is just idolatry).
Do you congratulate a man—
a good man, an honest man—
for being tied up like a bird,
a live toy for boys to play with?—
for slaving for Philistines,
Hagrites, and Hittites,
who are only out to win him

לְבַקֵּשׁ רְצוֹנָם   וְלַעֲזֹב רְצוֹן אֵל
וְלִבְגֹּד בְּיוֹצֵר   וְלַעֲבֹד יְצוּרִים?
פְּנֵי הַשְּׁחָרִים   בְּעֵינָיו שְׁחֹרִים,
וְכוֹס מַמְתַּקִּים   בְּפִיו מַמְרוֹרִים--
מִיְּגָע וְעָמֵל   וְלָחוּץ וְאֻמְלָל
וְנִכְסָף לְכַרְמֶל   וְקִרְיַת יְעָרִים,
לְבַקֵּשׁ סְלִיחוֹת   בְּקִבְרֵי מְנוּחוֹת
לְאָרוֹן וְלוּחוֹת   אֲשֶׁר שָׁם קְבוּרִים.
אֲצַפֶּה לְעָבְרָם,   וְאֶעְטֹף בְּקִבְרָם,
וְעֵינַי לְשִׁבְרָם   יְפִיצוּן נְהָרִים.
וְכָל רַעְיוֹנַי   חֲרֵדִים לְסִינַי,
וְלִבִּי וְעֵינַי   לְהַר הָעֲבָרִים.
וְאֵיךְ לֹא אֲבַכֶּה   וְדֶמַע אֲפַכֶּה
וּמִשָּׁם אֲחַכֶּה   תְּחִיַּת פְּגָרִים?
וְשָׁם הַכְּרוּבִים   וְלוּחוֹת כְּתוּבִים
בְּעַד הָרְגָבִים   וּבִמְקוֹם סְתָרִים,
מְקוֹם הַפְּלָאוֹת   וְעֵין הַנְּבוּאוֹת
וּבִכְבוֹד צְבָאוֹת   פְּנֵיהֶם מְאִירִים.
עֲפָרוֹ אֲחֹנֵן,   וְאֶצְלוֹ אֲקוֹנֵן,
וְעָלָיו אֲקוֹנֵן   כְּעַל הַקְּבָרִים.
וְסוֹף מַחְשְׁבוֹתַי   הֱיוֹת מִשְׁכְּבוֹתַי
בְּקִבְרוֹת אֲבוֹתַי   וּבִרְשׁוּת טְהוֹרִים.

over to their own gods,
get him to serve them,
give up serving God,
betray the Creator by serving His creatures?
Morning light is dark to him,
wine is bitter on his tongue.
Weary, exhausted,
battered and sorrowing,
he dreams of Carmel,
and Qiryat Yeʿarim,
dreams of doing penance
at the graves, at the place
where lies the ark
where God's two tablets
lie beneath the ground.
I see myself passing there,
melting at their sepulcher,
pouring eye-rivers over their ruin.
No room in my mind
for anything but Sinai;
this heart, these eyes
see Mount Avarím already.
What is there for me to do
but mourn them, throb tears,
wait for the dead to rise
where the golden cherubim
where the tablets of the law
lie in a secret place
hidden in the holy soil—
place of wonders, home of prophets,
where God's splendor
lights up every face?
There, I want to make my nest,
caress the soil, mourn the land
as if it were a huge grave.
All that I want is
to rest till the end of days
alongside the patriarchs,
those pure saints.

עֲלִי הַסְּפִינָה,   וְדֹרְשֵׁי מְדִינָה
אֲשֶׁר לַשְּׁכִינָה   בְּתוֹכָהּ חֲדָרִים!
וְחוּשִׁי בְּעוּפֵךְ,   וְיַד אֵל תְּנִיפֵךְ,
וְקִשְׁרִי כְּנָפֵךְ   בְּכַנְפֵי שְׁחָרִים--
לְנָדִים וְנָעִים   בְּרוּחַ קְלָעִים
וְלִבּוֹת קְרוּעִים   לְאֶלֶף גְּזָרִים.
וְיָרֵא אֲנִי מֵ-   עֲוֹנוֹת נְעוּרִים
אֲשֶׁר הֵם בְּסִפְרֵי   אֱלֹהַי סְפוּרִים,
וְאַף כִּי עֲוֹנוֹת   יְמֵי הַזְּקוּנוֹת
חֲלִיפוֹת וּמִתְחַ-   דְּשׁוֹת לַבְּקָרִים.
וְאֵין לִי תְשׁוּבָה   בְּעַד הַמְּשׁוּבָה,
וְאָנָא אֲנִי בָא   בְּבֵין הַמְּצָרִים?
אֲסַכֵּן בְּעַצְמִי   וְאֶשְׁכַּח אֲשָׁמִי
וְנַפְשִׁי וְדָמִי   בְּיַד חֵטְא מְסוּרִים,
אֲבָל יֵשׁ בְּטֹחַ   בְּמַרְבֶּה סְלֹחַ
וְחַיִל וְכֹחַ   לְמוֹצִיא אֲסִירִים.
וְאִם דָּן וְנִפְרַע   וְיוֹסִיף וְיִגְרַע,
עֲלֵי טוֹב וְעַל רָע   שְׁפָטָיו יְשָׁרִים.

So up, ship!
forward drive
to where the *Shekhina* lies
in her secret rooms.
Swiftly fly,
fluttered by
God's hand,
sails tied
to dawn's wings,
for the sake of wanderers,
fugitives,
carried by
sails, winds,
hearts shredded,
hearts ripped,
crumbled in a thousand bits.
I tremble for my early sins,
all recorded in God's book,
and even more for recent sins,
sins of my old age,
new sins every day.
No way
to repent my waywardness—
what to do in this distress?
I put my life in my two hands,
and my soul and my blood
(all now thralls to sin),
put sin behind me,
throw myself in perfect trust
on One who forgives much,
One with power, One with might,
One who sets the bondsman free.
Let Him judge or chastise
with harshness or leniency;
whatever the outcome,
righteous is His decree.

This magnificent work is a summa of the themes and images of Halevi's pilgrimage. Its peculiar rhythm, its careful design, and its passionate concluding confession give it a claim to being Halevi's supreme literary treatment of the subject.

Arguments with peers occupy only three verses of the poem (vv. 11–13), so that the formal conceit of argumentation does not control the poem's structure, as it did the two preceding poems. But the defensive style of the opening serves an important function nevertheless, for it implies that the speaker's mind is still engaged in an argument, though his decision has been taken. If the pilgrim can imagine the argument, already silenced in real life, continuing internally, he must still be trying to assure himself of the rightness of his course.

All the other poems in this book, like most Hebrew poetry written in quantitative meter, are built up out of long monorhymed lines composed of two segments of equal or nearly equal length (called hemistichs), with the rhyme at the end of the second hemistich. Such poems were experienced at a leisurely pace; the reciter would patiently build tension as he worked his way up to the end of the first hemistich, and then relax the tension as he worked his way down to the rhyme syllable. This poem, though monorhymed, uses a less common pattern: it has an internal rhyme scheme that divides each line into four short segments, most of them consisting of only two words apiece—three segments rhyming with one another, and the fourth bearing the rhyme of the poem as a whole. The poet exploits the essentially kinetic effect of this meter mostly to mirror his own unsettled mental state. Yet, thanks to his customary technical virtuosity, Halevi manages to exploit it in the course of the poem, to express other, less anxious moods.

Like the Ode to Jerusalem (poem 16), this poem is divided into two parts by apostrophe and by the resumption of imagery adumbrated in the opening lines. Here, the apostrophe is the address to the ship, and the resumed imagery is that of birds' flight. The break corresponds to a shift away from the inner meditation that dominates the poem: after brooding for twenty-six verses, the speaker turns to the ship and addresses it as a bird, urging it to take flight to the Holy Land; he then lapses back into the inner meditation that carries the poem to its end. This division corresponds with the shifting presence of the speaker. At the poem's beginning, he is but vaguely seen, but he emerges into clarity as he comes to describe what it is that he yearns for. The poem's turn occurs at a moment when he has arrived at the most concrete definition of his desire, and therefore at the clearest identification of his own self. The apostrophe concluded, the poet lapses back into the meditative voice, in which he finally lays out his motives.

The speaker at the beginning of the poem goes out of his way not to identify himself. He begins with a question about "bodies"; in verse 2, this body becomes a person and, in verse 3, a particular person—presumably himself—with a particular plan in mind. As in the opening of the Ode to Jerusalem, the speaker comes into focus only gradually; but in this poem, the first-person voice is withheld for twenty verses so that the speaker long remains strangely disembodied. As verse after verse goes by, we learn a great deal about the frustrations of this third-person figure; yet, though he is none other than the speaker himself, he almost seems to be a bit of a stranger until, in verse 20, he at last emerges into the first person. The distancing technique employed in the first nineteen verses permits Halevi to represent the self-conscious feeling that we often have when undergoing momentous changes, observing the events that befall us as if they were happening to someone else and saying, in our prosaic manner, "Can this be happening to me?"

It is the naming of his goal that permits the speaker to become fully present to us. The first part of the poem dealt mostly with the negative part of his enterprise—his dissatisfaction with his life and his desire to flee (we remember reading about it in Halevi's epistle to Rabbi Ḥabīb). In verse 18, he begins to speak about the Land of Israel, hitherto mentioned only in passing (v. 10)—identifying it as his goal, describing his longing for it, and naming two particular places in it. Only now that we learn what he is escaping to, does he stand before us as a distinct person who speaks in the first person (v. 22).

Having taken shape, this distinct person can control his own destiny. He is no longer caged in his body, as in the opening line, and no longer is it only his heart that is tied to eagle's wings. Fully realized, he can board the ship and bid her unfurl her wings and carry him bodily to the place where he longs to be. He had begun by imagining his heart caged in his body but tied to eagle's wings, that is, divided against himself and blocked from a solution; now he imagines himself as an integrated whole on a ship tied to the wings of dawn that soars with him to the Land of Israel—division resolved, blockage cleared.

The reader cannot miss the Neoplatonic background of the image of hearts trapped in bodies at the beginning of this poem—for that is the soul's predicament in all Neoplatonic literature—nor will the reader fail to see the irony of the poet's finding resolution in imagining his body soaring as on ship's wings at the poem's turn. By using imagery of flight to describe his yearning for a material solution to his heart's dislocation, Halevi announces his complete overthrow of Neoplatonic religious values. God is not to be sought in the (abstract) One, nor is religious fulfillment to be achieved by the ascent of the individual soul and its merging with the world-soul. God is available to the man of flesh and blood who will seek Him in the soil and stones of the place where He reveals Himself to man and where the body of each individual man will be resurrected to behold Him. As early as the opening lines, the imagery brings the reader's sight down from the eagle's wings to the soil of the Land of Israel. There, the heart's motion, though on eagle's wings, is downward; here, the body's motion is upward, as Halevi strives for a corporeal solution to the problem of religious experience.

What is he leaving? The speaker mentions in a cursory way his friends, luxuries, and pleasures, but he dwells mostly on his busy life of service to kings and courtiers. This is the real trap that he yearns to escape—humbling himself to men and praising them, compromising his own dignity and his religious commitments. He even hints that he has been under pressure to apostatize.[17] Any such pressure need not have been overt; the temptation was inherent in the position of a Jew in society and in an ambitious person's drive to fit smoothly into a world that offered opportunities for advancement. Others had succumbed. Altogether, serving human masters seems like serving idols.

Almost worse than the service itself are the friends who reproach him for complaining about it. To them, he seems lucky to be so close to the powerful, but to himself, he seems merely a toy for kings to play with—a pet bird tied to a child's hand, as he says. (Note that this is the poem's third bound bird, coming between the image of the heart tied to eagle's wings at the beginning and the ship-bird tied to the dawn near the end.) To Halevi, his worldly success is slavery.

What does he seek? He touches quickly on forgiveness and rest and his desire to lament the destruction of the land; but it is soil and graves that occupy most of his attention in verses 18 through 26. He is drawn especially to the burial place of the prophets and the fragments of Israel's sancta: the tablets of the law, the ark of the covenant, the golden cherubim that once stood on the ark and upon which God revealed Himself—all buried beneath the soil of the Land of Israel. At the climax of this Land of Israel passage, Halevi again quotes his talisman, Ps. 102:14–15, and expresses his wish to be buried in that same soil cherished and longed for by God's servants, there to await the resurrection of the dead. (In this brush with eschatology, there is no mention of the redemption of Israel, as there is not in any of the pilgrimage poems.)

The poem is suffused with elegiac language. Early on, we hear about the speaker's fears and weeping (v. 3), his bitterness (v. 17), his misery (v. 18), and his desire for forgiveness (v. 19). His vision of the emotional state that he will experience, once having arrived in the land, is dominated by a desire to lament (vv. 20, 22, and 25). It is thus completely different from the Ode to Jerusalem, where, though the speaker does anticipate sorrow and even anger at the sight of the ruins, he mostly looks forward to a state of religious bliss. What is all this sorrow about? The destruction of the land, though alluded to several times, does not seem to be chiefly what is on his mind. We do not find out until we cross the barrier of verse 28.

The speaker's apostrophe of the ship in verse 28 and the image of the ship-bird's flight to freedom in the ensuing verses provide a burst of positive energy that contrasts with everything that came before. Its call makes us realize retroactively how oppressed we felt by the speaker's gloom and unsettled state while reading the first twenty-seven verses. But now that he has identified himself by clarifying his goal, we feel that we ourselves are breathing the salt air, feeling the breeze, and cheering the ship as it ties its sails to the rising sun and surges effortlessly upward and eastward. Even the poem's peculiar rhythm, so effective earlier in mimicking the speaker's unsettled state, now seems perfectly suited to express the jauntiness of a man who has been released from bonds and of the ship on which he is now free to seek his goal.

But the poet is not finished with himself and his sorrow. Free to set sail, he is free to speak of his motivation. Other passengers may sorrow at what they are leaving behind, but he sorrows only for one thing: sin. He divides his sins into two chronological categories: sins of youth, a familiar expression, denoting the pursuit of pleasure associated with the young, the kind of religious misbehavior that older people wink at; and sins of old age, committed in full rational consciousness and despite awareness of approaching death and final reckoning. Here is Halevi's clearest statement that the voyage includes an element of expiation. There does not have to be a scandal or a dark secret behind this passage. Expiation is needed for a life led with too easy a religious conscience, a life based on the compromises that all well-adjusted people make. In the light of the prospect of death and the final reckoning, in the light of the demands of the true service of God, the life of courtiers, businessmen, pillars of the community, even of rabbis and teachers of religious law, yes, even the life of the authors of deathless liturgical poetry who live among men and for the regard of men and whose religious thought is governed by mere human reason—all this is a life of sin, and it calls for extreme measures of atonement.[18]

Halevi concludes the poem by laying out the means of expiation that he has chosen: he will put his life in God's hands through the perilous voyage. The voyage is the emblem of his *tawakkul,* demonstrating that he trusts in God (v. 34) rather than any human agency to carry him through what remains of his life. By making trust in God the Archimedean point of his religious life, he turns from being a slave to men into a slave to God. The poem ends on a serene note dominated by acceptance of God's will.

An Islamic tradition illuminates the last part of the poem: "This world is a deep ocean in which many have drowned. If you are able to make faith in

God your ship, obedience to Him your cargo, and trust in Him [*tawakkul*] your sails, you may come through in safety."[19] It almost seems as if the end of Halevi's poem was conceived in order to concretize this beautiful extended metaphor.

By the end of this poem, the speaker has gone from thought to action by mentally plunging himself into the ocean. At the decisive moment, he has touched on the danger of his act. This theme, and other reservations, will preoccupy Halevi in the poems in which he describes his feelings on shipboard, to which we now turn.

10

The Voyage

The poems in this chapter chronicle Halevi's voyage—not the external motion from west to east but the internal journey of the pilgrim's heart, with the external events serving merely its occasion. They represent a range of moods unified by a common voice and style, and, though not designed by the poet as a cycle, they fall naturally into a coherent sequence.

The poet's absorption in his own emotional and religious state is so complete that he hardly refers to his destination, the Land of Israel, or to the large external themes that motivated his pilgrimage, such as the history and destiny of the Jewish people or the special character of the Land of Israel. That his destination is the Holy Land, that the land is the node where God and the world interact, and that it has a special connection with the Jewish people are all taken for granted. The focus is nearly entirely on the pilgrim's inner experience.

It is pleasant to speculate on whether the individual poems in this group were written soon after the poet left his home or late in the voyage; during a storm; while in port awaiting a change of wind; or on some other identifiable occasion. Scholars have indulged in such speculation, but it runs against the grain of the poems, and the results are unconvincing, as a moment's reflection will reveal. Absent external evidence, it is impossible to determine whether a particular poem describing a storm was written after a storm (emotion contemplated in tranquility), in anticipation of one (the poet as visionary), or during a storm (the one time that a poem probably was not written!). As a craftsman of words, heir to a literary tradition, and possessor of a cultivated imagination, Halevi was surely capable of writing about a storm that he was experiencing in imagination or in memory. As in all medieval Hebrew poetry, descriptive passages are not portraits of reality from life but rather ingenious manipulations of the language and the literary tradition. The storms and calms undergone by Halevi's ship happened in real life, but his writing about them is a manifestation of the literary tradition.

Poetry is always written for an audience; when the poet appears to be speaking to himself, it is a carefully crafted illusion. But it is harder to imagine the audience for the poems of this group than it is for most medieval Hebrew poems. Our poems do not have an obvious public function, nor are they stylized reworkings of traditional themes of individual piety. They are an exploration of individual piety to which the poet is spurred not by abstract meditation, as in the famous and beautiful short liturgical poems of Ibn Gabirol, but by a specific autobiographical experience. They therefore represent a major step in the development for the poetry of individual piety in Hebrew.

The poems in this group do not belong to any standard genre. One begins in the style of a message home. Others read more like private meditations. Some are formulated as prayers, or at least begin in the style of prayer. Of these, only "God's Will Rules Heaven's Heights" (poem 30), the last in our group, may

(*Commentary continues on the next page*)

21

יוֹם נִכְסְפָה נַפְשִׁי לְבֵית הַוַּעַד,
וַיֹּאחֲזֵנִי לַנְּדוּדִים רַעַד,
סִבֵּב גְּדָל-עֵצָה עֲלִילוֹת לַנְּדֹד,
וָאֶמְצְאָה לִשְׁמוֹ בְּלִבִּי סַעַד.
עַל כֵּן אֲנִי מִשְׁתַּחֲוֶה אֵלָיו בְּכָל
מַסָּע, וְאוֹדֶנּוּ עֲלֵי כָל צַעַד.

actually have been written in order to be used as a prayer in public worship. The Hebrew poets of al-Andalus, including Halevi, pioneered the composition of poems intended for use in the liturgy that spoke in the voice of an individual worshiper in meditation or addressing God intimately, poems that blur the lines between public and private prayer.[1] Such poems give the auditor the sensation of listening in on a private meditation, the feeling conveyed by the poems presented in this chapter.

The theme most pervasive in these poems is the poet's doubts and fears, an almost unparalleled confession of self-doubt and ambivalence in a literature dominated by absolute statements, universal judgments, and strong personal affirmations. Even as Halevi assures himself that his decision was right, that the goal is worth the losses and the risks, he seems to be asking himself whether he did the right thing, whether he did not give up too much, and whether he will survive the journey. But throughout the poems runs an unmistakable undercurrent of religious thought, centering on themes that we have learned to see as central to Halevi's religious makeup: the service of God, trust in God, and the matching of one's will with the will of God. Halevi seems to see his voyage with its terrors and dangers as a self-imposed challenge to his commitment to *tawakkul* and a religious ordeal through which that commitment is tested. It is astounding to note that, through all the dangers and terrors, he never prays to be saved.

21

I longed to reach the House of Destiny,
but fear of travel shook me with dismay.
Then God provided opportunity;
His Name within my heart lent me its aid.
And so I bow to Him at every stage,
give thanks for every step along the way.

This epigram places the pilgrim at the very beginning of the journey, when the impulse to defer or cancel the whole venture has been overcome and the first step has been taken. External factors may have been partly responsible for the delay. Perhaps, too, there was a deeper impediment arising from the equilibrium of desire to act, on the one hand, and a commitment to passivity as a principled religious posture, on the other. But in his conscious mind, he identifies the real impediment as fear. He feels that it took divine intervention to clear his way.[2]

That fear was allayed by the Name of God inside his heart. The poet does not mean merely that he takes comfort in the thought of divine providence and assistance, that fallback of the religiously complacent. He is thinking of the actual name of God. He imagines himself as an inert clay figure animated by the power of the divine name implanted in his heart by God like an amulet. This is not the only place where Halevi concretizes the Name of God; in another poem, he describes it as an object of adoration, as a partner, a lamp, and a support. He sometimes uses the Name of God to represent God's immanence—in his typical way, finding a concrete way to think of the abstract.[3]

(*Commentary continues on the next page*)

22

הֱצִיקַתְנִי תְשׁוּקָתִי לְאֵל חַי
לְשַׁחֵר אֶת מְקוֹם כִּסְאוֹת מְשִׁיחַי
עֲדֵי כִּי לֹא נְטָשַׁתְנִי לְנַשֵּׁק
בְּנֵי בֵיתִי וְאֶת רֵעַי וְאַחַי.
וְלֹא אֶבְכֶּה עֲלֵי פַרְדֵּס נְטַעְתִּיו
וְהִשְׁקִיתִיו, וְהִצְלִיחוּ צְמָחַי.
וְלֹא אֶזְכֹּר יְהוּדָה וַעֲזַרְאֵל,
שְׁנֵי פִרְחֵי יְקָר מִבְחַר פְּרָחַי,
וְאֶת יִצְחָק אֲשֶׁר כַּבֵּן חֲשַׁבְתִּיו--
יְבוּל שִׁמְשִׁי וְטוּב גֶּרֶשׁ יְרָחַי.
וְכִמְעַט אֶשְׁכְּחָה בֵית הַתְּפִלָּה
אֲשֶׁר הָיוּ בְמִדְרָשָׁיו מְנוּחַי,
וְאֶשְׁכַּח תַּעֲנוּגֵי שַׁבְּתוֹתַי
וְהַדְרַת מוֹעֲדַי וּכְבוֹד פְּסָחַי.
וְאֶתֵּן אֶת כְּבוֹדִי לַאֲחֵרִים
וְאֶעְזֹב לַפְּסִילִים אֶת שְׁבָחַי.
הֲמִירוֹתִי בְּצֵל שִׂיחִים חֲדָרַי,
וּבִמְשׂוּכַת סְבַךְ חֹסֶן בְּרִיחַי.

The pilgrim's goal is the *beit hava'ad,* here translated as the House of Destiny. There is some precedent for this term being used to refer to the Temple or to Jerusalem,[4] but it is rare enough to have puzzled Halevi's commentators. The basic meaning of *va'ad* is "appointment," or "meeting"; *beit hava'ad* ordinarily means a meeting place for scholars. To a native Arabic speaker, the word would naturally recall its paired Arabic cognates: *wa'd* (promise) and *wa'īd* (threat), which in Islamic religious language refer to the divine promise of reward and punishment in the afterlife. An Arabic speaker might also connect the Hebrew word's connotation of assembly with the Qur'anic image of the resurrected being assembled for judgment at the end of time, the fearful *yawm al-nashr,* the Day of Assembly. My translation attempts to convey some of these portentous overtones. For Halevi, the site of the Temple is not merely a holy place like other holy places, not even a holy place that is holier than other holy places. It is a case by itself, the place opposite the gates of heaven, the place where the resurrected dead will gather, as he often says.[5]

22

So pressed by longing for the living God,
to greet the seat of my people's kings,
I never stopped to kiss my wife,
my children, friends, or kin.

I never weep for the orchard I planted,
the garden I watered, my plants that bloomed;
I never think of Azarel and Judah,
my two precious flowers, the best of my blossoms,
or Isaac, the boy whom I counted a son
(he thrived in my sun, my moon made him flourish).

I'll soon be forgetting the house where I worshiped,
where sacred books were once my refreshment;
the pleasure of Sabbaths, the splendor of festivals,
Passover's dignity, all are forgotten.
I now turn my dignities over to others;
let idols enjoy the praises once mine!

For chambers I have the shade of scrub bushes,
and thickets of thorns for palace gates.

וְנַפְשִׁי שָׂבְעָה רָאשֵׁי בְשָׂמִים,
וְרֵיחַ נַעֲצוּץ שַׂמְתִּי רְקָחַי.
וְחָדַלְתִּי הֲלוֹךְ עַל כַּף וְעַל אַף,
וְנָתַתִּי בְּלֵב יַמִּים אֳרָחַי
עֲדֵי אֶמְצָא הֲדוֹם רַגְלֵי אֱלֹהַי,
וְשָׁמָּה אֶשְׁפְּכָה נַפְשִׁי וְשִׂיחַי.
וְאֶסְתּוֹפֵף בְּהַר קָדְשׁוֹ, וְאַקְבִּיל
לְפִתְחֵי שַׁעֲרֵי שַׁחַק פְּתָחַי.
וְאַפְרִיחַ בְּמֵי יַרְדֵּן נְרָדַי,
וְאַשְׁלִיחַ בְּשִׁלֹחַ שְׁלָחַי.
אֲדֹנָי לִי! וְאֵיךְ אִירָא וְאֶפְחַד
וּמַלְאַךְ רַחֲמָיו נוֹשֵׂא שְׁלָחַי?
אֲהַלֵּל אֶת שְׁמוֹ מִדֵּי חֲיוֹתִי,
וְאוֹדֶנּוּ עֲדֵי נֵצַח נְצָחַי.

The poet begins by speaking of his "longing for the living God," but the medieval copyist who recorded the poem perceptively prefaced it with the words, "He said, longing for his family and homeland." Indeed, as much as the poem looks forward to ending the wandering at the "place where God's own feet find rest," it looks backward at what has been left behind. The quest is the result of desire, love, or lust—all possible translations of the word here rendered "longing." On account of this longing for the "living God"—not a God Who is merely a product of logical demonstrations but a God Who can be experienced—he has left his family, friends, comfortable home, community, and dignities, and thrown himself into uncertainties.[6]

The moment in which the speaker places his meditation is soon after the departure, when the farewells are recent and the destination still far off. We readers do not believe for a moment that Halevi did not kiss his family goodbye; but we can easily imagine that, once alone on the ship, he passed days and weeks reliving the farewells. In retrospect, they seemed quickly over, for what parting embrace could be long enough when the parting is forever?

The poet recalls his family generally, and three young people in particular—two youths he had cultivated and a third who was like a son to him. (There is no way of knowing whether they were grandchildren, protégés, or disciples.[7] With sadness, he recalls his synagogue—Halevi would have been one of its dignitaries—the religious studies that he pursued there, and the Sabbaths and festivals

My taste for the best in perfumes and incense
is satisfied now with the fragrance of brambles.

I am finished, now and forever, with creeping
on palm and face in the presence of men.
I am making my way through the heart of the sea
to the place where God's own feet find rest,
there to pour out my soul and my sorrow.

His holy mountain will be my doorsill,
my gate will face the gates of heaven.
I will strew the Jordan river with saffron,
put out my shoots on the stream of Shiloah.

What should I fear? God is with me,
His love is the angel that carries my weapons.
As long as I live I will sing His praise—
till the end of time, till the end of my days.

---

that he celebrated there. With rue, he thinks of the dignities he enjoyed and the praises to which he was accustomed. Those dignities he now leaves to others; his praises, to idols. A prolific composer and frequent recipient of panegyric poetry, he knew well how little those courtesies were worth in a culture in which poets were hired to sing the praises of rulers and dignitaries. We ourselves have seen the overblown language of panegyric in poems, epistles, and even ordinary letters, and have encountered Halevi's compunctions about them. Now, he declares that he is done with that, both as giver and as recipient. As he puts it, he bequeaths his praises to idols, and he gives up walking on hands and on face—an Arabism signifying subservience—before other men

Walking on hands and on face in service to men may be servile, but it is secure, for the hands and face are at least in contact with terra firma. Halevi has replaced this secure, servile life with the insecure passage on the ocean. If to be servile is to be on solid ground, to be spiritually free is to be in the place of instability and danger. Nor is the ocean, the place of passage, the only unstable place, for in the latter part of the poem, the Land of Israel itself is portrayed as an aquatic medium—a place of the spirit, yes, but also a place of fluidity and instability.

This characterization of the Land of Israel was prepared for at the poem's beginning, where images derived from the vegetable kingdom first appear in the second verse, furnishing a motif that shapes the entire poem. The home that the speaker has abandoned is a garden or an orchard (an image conventionally used for al-Andalus as a whole),[8] and the speaker's young protégés were his flowers. The passage to his destination—in reality, an ocean—is described figuratively as a desert; it is, after all, only a passage, with no intrinsic value. The speaker's destination is a place where he expects to replant himself. But the anticipated field is a surprisingly liquid one, for he imagines himself strewing the Jordan with saffron and putting out shoots on the brook of Shiloah (Jerusalem's main water source in antiquity). Halevi makes sure that we notice this fluidity by cramming the verse in which it is mentioned with sound effects—a***sh***lia***ḥ*** be***sh***iloa***ḥ*** ***sh***ela***ḥ***ai—and through the use of a pair of rhyming verbs that call attention to themselves by their double meanings: *afriaḥ* and *ashliaḥ*. Both have an obvious meaning related to planting—"to make bloom" and "to put forth shoots"—but they could also mean "to make fly" and "to let loose." The choice of verbs makes us reflect on the medium in which Halevi plans to plant himself. The Land of Israel may be blessed, but it is a place where what one means to plant might well be scattered, dissipated, flushed away.

It is unlikely that Halevi is troubled by anything as mundane as the politically unsettled state of the Land of Israel in the period of the Crusades. What

(*Commentary continues on the next page*)

23

קִרְאוּ עֲלֵי בָנוֹת וּמִשְׁפָּחוֹת
שָׁלוֹם, וְעַל אַחִים וְעַל אָחוֹת
מֵאֵת אֲסִיר תִּקְוָה אֲשֶׁר נִקְנָה
לַיָּם וְשָׂם רוּחוֹ בְּיַד רוּחוֹת.
דָּחוּי בְּיַד מַעְרָב לְיַד מִזְרָח
(זֶה יַעֲבֹר לַנְחוֹת וְזֶה לִדְחוֹת).
בֵּינוֹ וּבֵין מָוֶת כְּפֶשַׂע, אַךְ
בֵּינוֹ וּבֵינָיו מַעֲבֵה לוּחוֹת.
קָבוּר בְּחַיָּיו בַּאֲרוֹן עֵץ, לֹא
קַרְקַע וְלֹא אַרְבַּע אֲבָל פָּחוֹת.
יוֹשֵׁב וְאֵין לַעְמֹד עֲלֵי רַגְלָיו,
שׁוֹכֵב וְאֵין רַגְלָיו מְשֻׁלָּחוֹת.
חוֹלֶה וְיָרֵא מִפְּנֵי גוֹיִם,
גַּם מִפְּנֵי לִסְטִים וּמֵרוּחוֹת.
חוֹבֵל וּמַלָּח, כָּל בְּנֵי פִרְחָח,
הֵם הַסְּגָנִים שָׁם וְהַפַּחוֹת.

troubles him is the prospect of a more subjective insecurity. Will the Land of Israel become a spiritual home to him to replace the material one that he has left? (Perhaps he is still thinking of the objection of his interlocutor in "Your Words Are Scented" [poem 18], that the land has lost its sanctity.) Will he prove to be the man of faith he thought he was, able to live alone with God? Can he live up to his image of himself? Too late to turn back now; all he can do is to rebuke himself for his fear and turn to the praise of God.

It is hard to escape the impression that in writing his poem, Halevi was consciously thinking of Psalm 84 and, in part, adapting it to his specific condition. Like our poem, the psalm begins with the speaker's expression of longing for the living God, mentions the weary journey, and ends by contrasting the sense of divine protection in the House of God (in words quoted by Halevi in v. 13 of our poem) with an ordinary life lived among the wicked. The psalm ends with the words "Happy is he who trusts You," words that must have rung with particular significance to Halevi, given the centrality of this theme in his religious poetry. Contrasted with the elegant but self-satisfied voice of the speaker in the psalm, Halevi's voice in this poem conveys a very human and touching note of uncertainty.

23

Hail, my daughters! Hail, my family!
Sisters, brothers, kinsmen, hail to all!
Greetings from a prisoner of hope,
who sold himself to the sea and put
his spirit in the power of the winds.
Shoved by the west wind eastward, then shoved back
by the east wind to the west, advanced, repelled.
Just a step between himself and death—
just the thickness of a board.
Interred alive in a wooden box,
a place too small even to call a space.
No room to stand, and lying down, no room
to stretch his feet; no choice but sit.
Seasick, afraid of Gentiles, panicky
because of pirate ships and hurricanes.
A place of salts and rope-men, riffraff all—
such scum are lords and masters of this place.
A sage's fame means nothing here,

לֹא לַחֲכָמִים שֵׁם וְגַם לֹא חֵן
    לַיּוֹדְעִים רַק יוֹדְעִים לְשַׁחוֹת!
יִתְעַצְּבוּ רֶגַע לְזֹאת פָּנַי,
    אַךְ יַעֲלֹז הַלֵּב וְהַטֻּחוֹת
עַד אֶשְׁפְּכָה נַפְשִׁי בְּחֵיק הָאֵל
    נֹכַח מְקוֹם אָרוֹן וּמִזְבָּחוֹת.
אֶגְמֹל לְאֵל גּוֹמֵל לְחַיָּבִים
    טוֹבוֹת בְּטוּב שִׁירוֹת וְתִשְׁבָּחוֹת.

The poet's meditation begins again with thoughts of his family, this time in the form of an imaginary letter home. We would love to know more about the family that Halevi left behind. His not mentioning a wife does not mean that he did not have one, for it was not normal to mention one's wife in a public document. His not mentioning a son might reasonably be the basis for conjecture that he did not have one, or that any son he may have had was no longer alive. His mentioning daughters, in the plural, is suggestive, but it seems to contradict the suggestion in "Anxious or Secure, My Soul Is Yours" (poem 25) that he had only one daughter. Perhaps the entire list of relatives is merely generic.

Halevi cannot greet his people in person because he is a prisoner of the winds, which, like human jailers, restrict his motions and cause him torments. But the winds are only material jailers; his real prison is hope. The typically Halevian expression "prisoner of hope," originating in the Bible,[9] is used here to express compactly the positive and negative valences of Halevi's situation. "Prisoner" suggests that he is in bondage, for once having chosen his course, he became a passenger, a prisoner. (How free was he to refuse this imprisonment, anyway, when the hope itself was a compulsion, a call he had no choice but to answer?) But the bondage is a desirable one, because the slave of God is truly free, as Halevi said in his famous epigram,[10] and that freedom is his hope.

The theme of bondage is represented by motifs of passivity and constriction. Pushed and pulled by the winds, the poet can do nothing to help himself but await the outcome. The space in which he waits is both physically and emotionally uncomfortable: physically, because it is not big enough for his body; emotionally, because the walls that separate him from the deadly waters are thin,

and nothing that you've learned has any use
unless you've learned to swim!

These thoughts throw shadows on my face,
but only briefly, for my core,
my inner self, is joyous. Soon
I will be pouring out my heart
to God, where once the ark and altar stood.
There I will repay Him, giving thanks
as due to Him from me, imperfect man,
and offering Him my best: my song and praise.

---

and the space they define is as narrow as a grave. In fact, they are smaller than the Jewish legal tradition considers to be the minimal size of a grave—smaller even than the space that the Jewish tradition considers the minimal extension of a legal "self."[11] He is not even a person.

But, as bondage to hope signifies a paradoxical religious freedom, so the constrictions of the ship signal a paradoxical elevation of the speaker's religious state. Having elected to be a slave of God, having adopted *tawakkul* as his religious posture, he finds himself as a result of these decisions in a constricted cabin feeling like a corpse in a grave—a concretization of the Muslim pietists' simile comparing the man who truly trusts in God to a corpse in the hands of the washer.[12]

Our genial poet immediately relieves this gloomy image with a wry description of his predicament—unable to stretch his legs out, seasick, fearful not only of the winds but of the people in charge: the crude sailors, men with strength and skill but no culture or respect for the cultured. Whatever freedom of action is available on a ship is available only to these practical men, who do not hesitate to remind the scholarly passenger that the only knowledge that really matters on a ship is knowing how to swim.

Halevi's tone is light, but the dangers were real; the pirates he mentions here and in "Anxious or Secure, My Soul Is Yours" (poem 25) are the captains of enemy ships who might seize any ship that they could and sell the passengers as slaves in some foreign land. It was known that Jewish communities would put up good money to ransom Jewish victims of this practice—the going rate was thirty-three and one-third dinars—and Halevi himself had been one of a group of leaders who organized a collection to redeem a Jewish woman captive some years earlier.[13]

Halevi can keep his tone light; he must keep it light in order to convince himself and us readers that he is confident of reaching his destination. As he had opened the poem with thoughts of his security-ensuring institution back home—his family—he ends it with thoughts of the secure environment awaiting him: the synagogue at his destination. There, he imagines himself reciting the benediction prescribed by tradition for persons who have crossed the desert, risen from a sickbed, been released from prison, or, as the Talmud puts it, "come up" from the ocean.[14] The Hebrew wording of the poem's last line alludes to this benediction, but Halevi seems to contemplate fulfilling the obligation by reciting his own poetry.

24

זֶה רוּחֲךָ צַד מַעֲרָב רָקוּחַ--
הַנֵּרְדְּ בִּכְנָפָיו וְהַתַּפּוּחַ.
מֵאוֹצְרוֹת הָרוֹכְלִים מוֹצָאֲךָ,
כִּי אֵינְךָ מֵאוֹצְרוֹת הָרוּחַ.
כַּנְפֵי דְרוֹר תָּנִיף, וְתִקְרָא לוֹ דְּרוֹר,
וּכְמָר-דְּרוֹר מִן הַצְּרוֹר לָקוּחַ.
מַה נִּכְסְפוּ לָךְ עַם אֲשֶׁר בִּגְלָלְךָ
רָכְבוּ בְּגַב הַיָּם עֲלֵי גַב לוּחַ!
אַל נָא תְּרַפֶּה יָדְךָ מִן הָאֳנִי
כִּי יַחֲנֶה הַיּוֹם וְכִי יָפוּחַ,
וּרְקַע תְּהוֹם, וּקְרַע לְבַב יַמִּים, וְגַע
אֶל הַרְרֵי קֹדֶשׁ, וְשָׁם תָּנוּחַ.
וּגְעַר בְּקָדִים הַמְסָעֵר יָם עֲדֵי
יָשִׂים לְבַב הַיָּם כְּסִיר נָפוּחַ.
מַה יַּעֲשֶׂה אָסוּר בְּיַד הַצּוּר אֲשֶׁר
פַּעַם יְהִי עָצוּר וְעֵת שָׁלוּחַ?
אַךְ סוֹד שְׁאֵלָתִי בְּיַד מָרוֹם, וְהוּא
יוֹצֵר מְרוֹם הָרִים וּבוֹרֵא רוּחַ.

24

This wind of yours is a perfumed wind, O West,
with saffron in its wings and apple scent,
as if it came from the perfumer's chest,
not from the chest of the winds.

The wings of swallows flutter to your breath.
You set them free,
like myrrh-tears, from a bundle poured.
And how we long for you,
we who ride a board on the back of the sea!

Never release your grip from the ship
when the day makes its camp, when the day blows away.
Flatten the deep, rip the heart
of the seas, hit the holy mountains
and there take your rest,
wind of the west!
Shout down the east wind when it makes
the ocean break and creates
a seething pot in the heart of the sea.

What can a man, God's captive, achieve,
who is sometimes shut in and sometimes let free?
All my desire I entrust to Him,
Who shaped the mountains, Who made the wind,
Who knows man's heart and its mysteries.

It has been conjectured that this poem was written during Halevi's wait on shipboard in the harbor of Alexandria for the wind to shift so that he could complete his voyage, but it seems to be less about the weather than about the writer's mental state as he contemplated the voyage. It could just as well have been written in Spain or Alexandria, in anticipation of the voyage.[15] But even if written earlier, it could well have come to Halevi's mind as the ship left the port of Alexandria behind and as he took up a place at its bow to await his first glimpse of the Holy Land.

The western wind that blows the poet toward the Holy Land resembles the zephyr in Western literature, the breeze that wafts over the *locus amoenus* and brings to the poet the scent of his beloved. In Arabic literature, this role is normally played by the east wind, which Halevi portrays as seeking to frustrate his forward motion toward Palestine.[16] Heir to a precious literary tradition in both Arabic and Hebrew of garden poetry and love poetry, Halevi begins by praising the western breeze in the language of that tradition. But though he praises it, he will not be seduced by it; he begs it to shed its gentleness and turn violent so as to overcome the contrary force of the east wind and bring him to the Holy Land.

The conflict of eastern and western winds is not merely external and geographical; it is inward and literary. The eastern wind, the nostalgic breeze of Arabic literature, would return Halevi to his homeland, to the life that he is attempting to shed; he has to fight it by summoning the western wind. But the western wind, which has the power to sweep him to his destination, is redolent with personal memories of home, keeping them alive and preventing him from accomplishing the inner task of freeing himself from family, community, and culture. He must turn it into something unfamiliar, threatening, and dangerous—into a storm wind that can purge him of home so that he can accomplish his mission.

This Halevi accomplishes with a bravura concentration of sound effects that there is no hope of imitating in translation. Each line of the poem ends with the syllable *-aḥ,* a kind of audible breeze that accompanies the poem from beginning to end.[17] To this recurring sigh, there is a counterpoint in verse 3, which the poet builds around the sound *-ror,* using a triple pun on the word *dror* (meaning 1. "swallow," 2. "freedom," or 3. "pure" or "flowing" when associated with the word for myrrh, as it is here) and throwing in the rhyming word *ṣeror,* "bundle," for good measure. Halevi whips the west wind into violence in lines 6 and 7 with a hard series of gutturals (*urqaʿ . . . uqraʿ . . . vegaʿ . . . qodesh . . . ugʿar*), which were pronounced clearly by medieval Hebrew readers, though they are elided in most systems of Hebrew pronunciation current today. In the last part of verse 7, the gutturals are replaced by a series of sibilants that seems to imitate the hissing of the ocean's foam as the wave's violence relaxes. Thus the poem's shifting music turns the breeze into a storm that then subsides and reverts to breeze.

The image of the swallow, so heavily underscored by the sound effects just mentioned, is packed with associations. We have already seen how enamored Halevi was of bird imagery.[18] The swallow here comes from a passage in Psalms (already referred to several times), where it serves the psalmist as an example for his own longing to visit the Temple: "Even the bird finds a home, even the swallow her nest, for she places her fledglings on Your altar, O Lord of Hosts, my king and God" (Ps. 84:4). He is thinking of the myriad birds that were sacrificed on the altar (they were the animals most commonly offered by individuals) and imagines them as gladly laying down on it their lives and those of their children for God's sake. The image of the birds being sacrificed on the altar expressed for Halevi the notion that his pilgrimage would be a kind of martyrdom, a theme that has come up before and that we shall encounter again.[19]

The series of imperatives addressed to the wind tells us about Halevi's religious stance. Whereas in other poems Halevi expresses terror at the thought of storms at sea, in this poem he begs for a storm and bids the wind rage harder in order to thrust him forward. His violent, alliterative language sounds like a charm intended to conjure violent weather with violent words. He longs for strong winds not only to propel him to his destination but as a manifestation of God's power, to which he can abandon himself. Whereas earlier, Halevi had written in some agitation about being a prisoner on board the ship, now he portrays himself as enthusiastically embracing his submission to God's power and revels in describing himself as a passive object pushed now eastward, now westward, now blocked, and now pushed forward. God knows the poet's physical destination and may or may not permit him to fulfill it; but his spiritual goal—the mystery of his heart, the inner meaning of this journey—is, in a sense, fulfilled as soon as Halevi truly feels himself to be passive in God's hands. He thus begs not for the Land of Israel but for the storm that will carry him there.

25

לְךָ נַפְשִׁי, בְּטוּחָה אוֹ חֲרֵדָה;
לְךָ מִשְׁתַּחֲוָה תָּמִיד וּמוֹדָה.
בְּךָ אֶשְׂמַח בְּיוֹם אָנַע וְאָנוּד,
וְלָךְ אוֹדֶה בְּכָל נִיעָה וְנִידָה,
וּבִפְרֹשׂ הַסְּפִינָה לַעֲבֹר בִּי
כְּנָפַיִם כְּכַנְפֵי הַחֲסִידָה,
וְעֵת תֶּהֱֹם תְּהוֹם תַּחְתַּי וְתִנְהֹם
כְּאִלּוּ מִקְּרָבַי הִיא לְמֵדָה,
וְתַרְתִּיחַ כְּסִיר אֶת הַמְּצוּלָה,
וְיָם תָּשִׂים כְּמֶרְקָחָה יְקוּדָה,
וְצִים כִּתִּים בְּבוֹאָם יַם פְּלִשְׁתִּים,
וְהַחִתִּים נְחִתִּים בַּמְּצוּדָה,
וְהַחַיּוֹת בְּהָדְפָם לָאֳנִיּוֹת,
וְתַנִּינִים מְצַפִּים לַסְּעוּדָה,
וְעֵת צָרָה כְּמַבְכִּירָה, וּבָנִים
עֲדֵי מַשְׁבֵּר, וְאֵין כֹּחַ לְלֵדָה,
וְאִלּוּ אֶחֱסַר מַאֲכָל וּמִשְׁתֶּה,
נְעִים שִׁמְךָ בְּפִי אָשִׁים לְצֵידָה.
וְלֹא אֶדְאַג עֲלֵי קִנְיָן וּבִנְיָן,
וְלֹא עַל הוֹן וְלֹא עַל כָּל אֲבֵדָה,
עֲדֵי כִּי אֶטְּשָׁה יוֹצֵאת חֲלָצַי--
אֲחוֹת נַפְשִׁי, וְהִיא לִי רַק יְחִידָה--
וְאֶשְׁכַּח אֶת בְּנָהּ, פֶּלַח כְּבֵדִי,
וְאֵין לִי בִּלְעֲדֵי זִכְרוֹ לְחִידָה--
פְּרִי מֵעַי וְיֶלֶד שַׁעֲשׁוּעַי--
וְאֵיךְ יִשְׁכַּח יְהוּדָה אֶת יְהוּדָה?
וְנָקַל זֹאת לְנֶגֶד אַהֲבָתְךָ
עֲדֵי אָבוֹא שְׁעָרֶיךָ בְּתוֹדָה.
וְאָגוּר שָׁם, וְאֶחְשֹׁב אֶת לְבָבִי
עֲלֵי מִזְבַּחֲךָ עוֹלָה עֲקוּדָה.
וְאֶתֵּן אֶת קְבוּרָתִי בְּאַרְצָךְ,
לְמַעַן תִּהְיֶה לִי שָׁם לְעֵדָה.

25

Anxious or secure, my soul is Yours,
submissively and gratefully.
I roam, I wander, filled with joy in You
and thanking You in all my wanderings.
And when this ship unfurls its falcon-wings
and carries me away;
and when beneath, the Deep shrieks, howls,
storms like my bowels,
potboils the abyss and turns the sea to stew;
when Christian ships slip into the Berber sea,
and pirates descend to set their trap,
when ocean monsters pound against the ship,
and dragons are looking forward to a meal,
when you scream for fright like a woman in labor,
in labor with her first, when it first breaks through,
when she screams until she has no strength to scream . . .

If I lacked food and drink,
the taste of Your Name in my mouth
would be enough.
I care for nothing that I've bought or built,
for any property I've owned or lost,
not even for my daughter, my own flesh,
the sister of my soul, my soul itself!
Not even for her son, slice of my heart;
I've nothing but his name
with which to conjure wispy images of him,
fruit of my body, child of my delight—
can Judah put his Judah out of mind?

These hardships will be nothing to Your love,
when, singing songs of thanks, I reach Your gates.
There I will live, there I will lay my heart
upon Your altar as an offering;
there I will die, and there my tomb will bear
eternal witness to this wandering.

The theme of security and anxiety adumbrated in poems 22 and 23 is again on the poet's mind at the opening of this poem, which opens with fear, moves on to loss, and ends with the consolatory vision of the goal. Concentrated sound effects in verses 4 and 5 of the Hebrew mimic the terrors of the ocean's rolling and roaring, and in verse 6, they focus the attention on the fear of being taken captive. The ocean monsters of verse 7 may sound to us like mere folklore, but ships were small, rickety things in Halevi's time, susceptible to foundering on impact with anything, even a large marine creature; tales of encounters with such "monsters" were commonly told.[20]

The traveler's terror climaxes in verse 8, with the screams of a woman giving birth. He is calmed by the Name of God, inscribed in his heart, as in "I Longed to Reach the House of Destiny" (poem 21), and which now, in his mouth, serves as an amulet. Fear vanishes, to be replaced by the ache of loss, here focused on his daughter and grandson. This is the only definite reference in any of Halevi's works to particular members of his own family. In poem 22, he named some people left behind without telling us what their connection to him was, and in poem 23 he mentioned some categories of relations left behind. To give up worldly things, even the people who make up a person's world, is no sacrifice compared with the satisfaction of achieving God's favor. But when he speaks of his daughter and grandson here, he is not merely speaking of what he has given up. Something additional is at stake here, as we can perceive if we concentrate not just on what is said but in the manner of its being said.

At the climax of the description of the speaker's panic, he invokes the screams of a woman in childbirth, and two expressions keep the thought of childbirth alive even after the anguish for the sake of which it was invoked subsides. Halevi refers to his daughter in Hebrew as "she who emerged from my loins" and calls his grandson "the fruit of my entrails." Loins and entrails may both be used to denote the male role in generation, but the overall effect of these two expressions coming on top of the image of birth pains is to connect the speaker, rather, with the mother's role, feminizing the speaker. This feminization is reinforced when the speaker calls his daughter "the sister of my soul," for the word "soul" is feminine in Hebrew, making us imagine the poet and his daughter as a pair of coeval girls. He then emphasizes the identity of the daughter with himself by calling her his "only one" at the end of verse 11, a word that was commonly used by medieval Hebrew poets to mean the soul (and so translated here).[21]

Thanks to some poetic magic, the concatenation of all these words of feminine import turns the poet into a childbearing woman, the fruit of whose womb is the boy Judah. Halevi is writing about his struggle to give birth to a new Judah—a new spiritual self who will replace the gradually vanishing memory of the flesh-and-blood grandson, symbol of his own former self and life. Reaching the Land of Israel, he will be dying spiritually in order to be spiritually reborn as a sacrificial animal bound upon God's altar. The word used for "bound" puts the Hebrew reader in mind of the binding of Isaac. The reader might have anticipated that this theme was on its way, because the term "only one," used earlier to mean "soul," recalls God's command to Abraham: "Take your son, your only one, the one you love, Isaac, and offer him up as a sacrifice."[22] The allusion is not at all far-fetched for readers steeped in the rabbinic literary tradition, for this use of the term "only one" in the story of Abraham and Isaac was the basis of a familiar midrash.

Halevi thus envisions himself giving birth in the Holy Land to a new self, which in turn becomes his own only beloved son, in order to bind this self on the altar and die in the love of God. In addition to its connotation of self-sacrifice, even martyrdom, the image of the poet bound on the altar is a way of representing his placing himself in God's hands, a Jewish variant of the corpse-in-the-hands-of-the-washer motif and an even more telling one than the picture of the poet in his grave-cabin in "Hail, My Daughters!" (poem 23). Nor is this the only place in his oeuvre where Halevi uses the binding of Isaac to signify *tawakkul*.[23] Halevi thus sees himself as giving up not only all worldly possessions but all worldly activity. His death in the Land of Israel is to be a spiritual martyrdom, as implied in the word "testimony," the last word of the poem (in the Hebrew): not the martyrdom of national suffering, with its promise of national redemption, but martyrdom to the love of God.

For the Jewish religious tradition, the binding of Isaac is a hallmark of the covenant, the basis of Israel's collective claim to a particular relationship with God; in this sense, it has been a constant theme of preaching and liturgy throughout the ages. Halevi has turned it into a symbol for his own private sacrifice and his religious aspirations, an outstandingly daring personal appropriation of the national theme.

26

אֹמַר בְּלֵב יַמִּים לְלֵב רַגָּז,
חָרֵד מְאֹד כִּי נָשְׂאוּ דָּכְיָם:
אִם תַּאֲמֵן בָּאֵל אֲשֶׁר עָשָׂה
הַיָּם וְעַד נֵצַח שְׁמוֹ קַיָּם,
אַל יַחֲרִידְךָ יָם בְּשׂוֹא גַלָּיו,
כִּי עִמְּךָ הַשָּׂם גְּבוּל לַיָּם.

26

Trapped in the heart of the sea,
I say to my terrified heart
as it beholds in fear
the terrible toss of the waves,
"If you will trust in God,
the God Who created the sea,
the God Whose Name will endure
till the end of time and beyond—
have no fear of the sea
when its breakers surge toward the sky;
the God Who created the shore
to contain them is at your side."

The heart of the sea is the laboratory in which the poet tests his own heart. Does it truly trust in God? The verb translated in this context as "trust" in other contexts means "to believe"; to the Hebrew-speaking mind, the concepts overlap, as to some extent they also do in English. This same verb is the one used by the narrator of Exodus to describe the Israelites at the Red Sea, when he says, "And they believed in God and in Moses, His servant."[24]

But by alluding to this verse, Halevi has raised the stakes of faith. In the story of the Exodus, the Israelites cross the Red Sea, observe the Egyptians being drowned in the attempt to pursue them, and, as a result, "they believed in God and Moses, His servant," that is, as a result of being saved, they realized that God and Moses were trustworthy. Halevi challenges himself to reverse the order, saying to himself, "If you trust in God, you will not be frightened by the sea." He is to trust God not after experiencing His miraculous help, but in anticipation of it.

Judged by a strict standard, trust is the natural outcome of faith, as is commonly pointed out by Muslim pietist writers. The Qur'an itself makes trust a kind of test of faith when it says, "Trust in God, if you are believers" (Qur'an 5:26). Halevi makes his journey into a similar test, saying to himself, "If you really believe in the God you have been professing and on Whose account you have come this way, you would trust Him enough to face the storm with calm." But the poet is only human, as we shall see in the opening of the next poem.[25]

27

אֶצְעַק בְּלֵב נָמֵס וּפִיק בִּרְכַּיִם
לָאֵל, וְחַלְחָלָה בְּכָל מָתְנַיִם,
יוֹם תּוֹפְשֵׂי מָשׁוֹט תְּמֵהִים לַתְּהוֹם,
גַּם חוֹבְלִים לֹא יִמְצְאוּ יָדַיִם.
אֵיךְ לֹא אֱהִי כֵן, וַאֲנִי עַל גַּב אֳנִי
תָּלוּי בְּבֵין מַיִם וּבֵין שָׁמַיִם?
אָחוֹג וְאָנוּעַ, וְנָקֵל זֹאת עֲדֵי
אָחֹג בְּתוֹכֵכִי יְרוּשָׁלַיִם.

27

I shout to God
when my heart turns to slush,
when my knees give way,
when my gut is tight with fear,
when oarsmen gape,
when rope-men lose their grip.
How else could I be?
Just look at me—
suspended—
on a boat, between the wave and water,
I whirl and wander like a drunk.
But what matter?
In a while
I will whirl
more drunk than now,
among your streets,
Jerusalem.

The terrors of the ocean voyage are a test of the speaker's trust in God, as in "Still Chasing Fun at Fifty" (poem 17). The speaker's dismay at the helplessness of the ship's crew echoes an Arabic sermon on *tawakkul* with which Halevi could well have been familiar.[26]

The poet feels himself to be suspended as the ship is tossed by the waves—not only between sky and water or between life and death, but between the profane and the sacred as he makes his way from home to the Holy Land. In the last verse, he describes himself as "whirling and wandering," a phrase used in the Bible to describe a storm-tossed ship, which it compares to a drunken man (Ps. 107:27). The translation here makes explicit the image of the drunk, which medieval readers would have supplied automatically from their memory of that verse. The expression "to whirl like a drunk" does not have the negative connotations in medieval Hebrew that it might have in English, for in Hebrew, lovers often compare themselves to drunks; that is the medieval way of describing the sensation of being lost in sensation—what we call ecstasy.[27]

The Hebrew word translated "whirling" (*aḥog*) is the same as the word for "celebrating a festival." The connection is not as far-fetched as it seems, for the root meaning of the Hebrew word is "to go around"; it can denote the wild whirling of a drunk or of a storm-tossed ship as well as the circumambulation of the altar, a feature of ancient sacrificial rites. It is cognate with the root of the Arabic word for pilgrimage, *ḥajj*, and pilgrim, *ḥajjī*.

It is a common experience that on rejoining terra firma after being in motion for a long time—on a boat, a train, a roller coaster—one retains the feeling of being in motion even to the point of unsteadiness. The verb *aḥog* used here permits Halevi to imagine himself walking around Jerusalem in this physical condition of unsteadiness and, at the same time, in religious ecstasy because of being in contact with the holy soil and the holy sites. The verb also enables him to connect his spiritual state with the verb's liturgical meaning, to perform the pilgrimage.

28

אֱלֹהַי, אַל תְּשַׁבֵּר מִשְׁבְּרֵי יָם,
וְאַל תֹּאמַר לְצוּלַת יָם "חֱרָבִי"
עֲדֵי אוֹדֶה חֲסָדֶיךָ, וְאוֹדֶה
לְגַלֵּי יָם וְרוּחַ מַעֲרָבִי.
יְקָרֵבוּ מְקוֹם עֹל אַהֲבָתְךָ,
וּמֵעָלַי יְסִירוּן עֹל עֲרָבִי.
וְאֵיךְ לֹא יִתְּמוּ לִי מִשְׁאֲלוֹתַי?--
וּבְךָ אֶבְטַח, וְאַתָּה הוּא עֲרָבִי.

28

My God, I beg You not to break the breakers
or turn to dust the waters of the sea,
until the day when I will offer thanks
to the ocean waves, the western wind, and You.
They drive me to the place of Your love's yoke,
and from the Arab yoke they set me free.
How can the wish I beg not be fulfilled,
when You I trust, You are my surety?

The poet prays not that God save him from the storm but that He keep the ocean rolling until he reaches his destiny.[28] The poem is a bravura elaboration on three of the numerous meanings of the Hebrew root *ʿ-r-v*, which occurs at the end of the last three verses: "west," "Arab," and "guarantor." A fourth meaning—"sweet"—does not occur in this poem but does not fail to occur to the Hebrew reader. Here, the poet has achieved and briefly holds on to the religious equanimity to which he challenged himself in "Trapped in the Heart of the Sea" (poem 26).[29]

The ancient Rabbis used the metaphor "accepting the yoke of the kingdom of heaven" to express the Jewish national ideal of being servants to God. Halevi replaces this metaphor with the more paradoxical "yoke of Your love" to say that love of God is a joyous servitude, as contrasted with servitude to worldly things. Those worldly things are verbally represented in this poem by "Arabs." This term is used here not to denote a political entity but a spiritual condition, for by going to Palestine the poet was not freeing himself from political subjugation. He was well aware that Palestine was under the control of others.[30]

29

הֲבָא מַבּוּל וְשָׁם תֵּבֵל חֲרֵבָה?
וְאֵין לִרְאוֹת פְּנֵי אֶרֶץ חֲרֵבָה.
וְאֵין אָדָם וְאֵין חַיָּה וְאֵין עוֹף--
הֲסָף הַכֹּל וְשָׁכְנוּ מַעֲצֵבָה?
וּבִרְאוֹת הָר וְשׁוּחָה, לִי מְנוּחָה,
וְאֶרֶץ הָעֲרָבָה לִי עֲרֵבָה;
וְאַשְׁגִּיחַ לְכָל עֵבֶר, וְאֵין כֹּל
אֲבָל מַיִם וְשָׁמַיִם וְתֵבָה,
וְלִוְיָתָן בְּהַרְתִּיחוֹ מְצוּלָה--
וְאֶחְשֹׁב כִּי תְהוֹם יַחְשֹׁב לְשֵׂיבָה.
וְלֵב הַיָּם יְכַחֵשׁ בָּאֳנִיָּה,
כְּאִלּוּ הִיא בְּיַד הַיָּם גְּנֵבָה.
וְיָם יִזְעַף, וְנַפְשִׁי תַעֲלֹז כִּי
אֱלֵי מִקְדַּשׁ אֱלֹהֶיהָ קְרֵבָה.

29

Is this the Flood, and has the world been drowned?
You can't see land, or beast, or bird, or man.
Are they all finished, lying in the pit of sorrow?
If only I could only see a mountain,
or dry, pitted ground,
even a desert, that would do me good;
but as I look around me, all I see
is endless ocean, endless sky
and a helpless boat!
Leviathan whips the deep so white
I think I see an old man's hair
beneath the waves.
The sea pretends it hasn't seen our ship,
keeps us hidden in its heart like stolen goods.
Rage away, sea! My heart is glad
for each toss nearer to God's sanctuary.

Not the terror of the storm, but the anxiety caused by a calm, unbroken sea extending to the horizon dominates this poem. The sheer emptiness of the landscape mirrors the pilgrim's loneliness, and the lack of motion fills him with futility. He imagines that this water is no ocean but the Flood—that he is the last surviving man and that all Creation has been reduced to water, sky, and ship. And the ship, measured against the sky and the sea, is so small; it seems to vanish in the troughs between the swells, as if the sea were a robber making off with booty.

The image of the old man under the water started out as a comparison of foam to white hair in the book of Job 41:24. I hope that I am not superimposing my own imagination on that of the poet, but I cannot escape the feeling that to Halevi, the appearance of foam on the ocean's surface suggested an actual old man—himself—under the water, another measure of his anxiety on a calm day at sea.

30

יוֹעֵץ וּמֵקִים   בִּמְרוֹם שְׁחָקִים,
וְעַל יָם רְחוֹקִים   צִדְקוֹ סָרָח;
לֹא לְאִישׁ דַּרְכּוֹ,   וְאִם אֵין כְּמַלְכּוֹ,
שֶׁקֶר נִסְכּוֹ   וְלָרִיק יִטְרָח.
עוֹלֶה מִבּוֹר   יוֹם, רָץ לַעֲבֹר
יָם, וְשָׂשׂ כְּגִבּוֹר   לָרוּץ אֹרַח--
חֶטְאוֹ עִקֵּשׁ,   דַּרְכּוֹ בְּמוֹקֵשׁ,
וּמַעֲרָב בִּקֵּשׁ   וְהִנֵּה מִזְרָח.
יָדַע כִּי לֹא   בְכֹחוֹ וְשִׂכְלוֹ
יַעֲמִיד דִּגְלוֹ   וְיִסַּע וְיֶאֱרָח.
אָז שָׁב וְהוֹדָה   בְּנֶפֶשׁ חֲרֵדָה,
וּמֵרֹב עֲבוֹדָה   קוֹל מַר יִצְרָח:
אָנָא אֵלֵךְ   מֵרוּחֶךָ?
וְאָנָא מִפָּ-   נֶיךָ אֶבְרָח?

הָמוּ גַלִּים   בְּרוּץ גַּלְגַּלִּים,
וְעָבִים וְקַלִּים   עַל פְּנֵי הַיָּם.
קָדְרוּ שָׁמָיו   וְיֶחֶמְרוּ מֵימָיו,
וְעָלוּ תְהוֹמָיו   וְנָשְׂאוּ דָכְיָם.
וְסִיר יַרְתִּיחַ   וְקוֹל יַצְרִיחַ,
וְאֵין מַשְׁבִּיחַ   לַהֲמוֹן קָשְׁיָם.
וְרָפוּ חֲזָקִים   וְנֶחְלְקוּ אֲפִיקִים--
חֶצְיָם עֲמֻקִּים   וְהָרִים חֶצְיָם.
וְהָאֳנִי חוֹלָה   יוֹרְדָה וְעוֹלָה,
וְעַיִן תּוֹלָה   לְחוֹבְלִים: אַיָּם?
וְלִבִּי מַחְשֶׁה,   אֲקַוֶּה לְמַמְשֶׁה
כְּעַל יַד מֹשֶׁה   אַהֲרֹן וּמִרְיָם.
אֶקְרָא אֲדֹנָי,   וְאִירָא עֲוֹנָי,
פֶּן תַּחֲנוּנַי   יִהְיוּ טֹרַח.

וְיָם מִתְרוֹצֵץ,   וְקָדִים יְפוֹצֵץ
אֲרָזִים, וְיָפֵץ   רוּחַ קִצְפָּיו.
שָׁחָה קַרְנָם   וְנִבְהַל סַרְנָם
וְנִלְאָה תָרְנָם   לְפְרֹשׂ כְּנָפָיו.
יִרְתַּח בְּלִי אֵשׁ,   וְלֵב מִתְיָאֵשׁ
בְּעֵת הִתְבָּאֵשׁ   בְּמָשׁוֹט מְנִיפָיו.

30

God's will rules heaven's heights;
His justice rules the farthest seas.
Man cannot choose his path;
his thoughts are wasted, labor vain.
He hauls himself up from the pit of Time
dashes headlong, crosses oceans—
but sin twists his path to traps.
Heads west, finds east instead;
sees that neither strength nor mind
can set mast firm to sail, sojourn
as he has chosen. Comes back
shaken, worn, weary; cries,
bitterly conceding:
    "Where shall I go from Your spirit?
    Where shall I flee from Your presence?"

Waves rage, spheres spinning,
thick clouds, thin clouds cover ocean,
black sky, roiling waters,
depths rise, lift crushers,
sea a boiling pot, shrieking,
hard surge—who can smooth it?
Breakers fall, split in channels,
valleys, mountains, mountains, valleys.
Ship writhes upward, downward;
Sailors drop ropes, vanish.
I hold my breath, hope for a savior,
one like Moses,
Aaron, Miriam,
who could draw us from the water.
    I cry to God, but know I'm sinful,
    fear my prayers annoy Him.

Ocean rushes, crushes, east
wind splits cedars, gale
spits foam. Prow downward,
boards groan, mast fails
stretched sails. Sea boils
though no fire. Heart despairs
at worthless oarsmen, helpless mates,

דַּלִּים מוֹשְׁלָיו   וְנִרְפִּים סוֹבְלָיו
וּבוֹעֲרִים חוֹבְלָיו   וְעִוְרִים צוֹפָיו.
וְהָאֳנִי כְּשִׁכּוֹר   יִתְעַתַּע וְיִהְכֹּר,
בְּלִי הוֹן יִמְכֹּר   שׁוֹכְנֵי כְתֵפָיו.
וְזֶה לִוְיָתָן   בְּעַד יָם אֵיתָן
יַקְדִּישׁ כְּחָתָן   לְמִשְׁתֶּה אֲסוּפָיו.
וְיַד אוֹקְיָנוֹס   תְּאֱהַב לִכְנוֹס,
וְאָבַד מָנוֹס   וְאֶפֶס מִבְרָח.

דַּלּוּ עֵינַי   נֶגְדְּךָ, אֲדֹנָי,
וְאֶת תַּחֲנוּנַי   שַׁי אָשִׁיבָה.
אֶחֱרַד לְעִתַּי,   וְאֶרְגַּז תַּחְתַּי,
וְקוֹל בֶּן אֲמִתַּי   לְךָ אַקְרִיבָה.
בְּזָכְרִי יַם סוּף   אֲשֶׁר לֹא יָסוּף,
עָרֵב וְכָסוּף   שִׁיר אֵיטִיבָה.
וְנוֹרְאוֹת יַרְדֵּן   בָּם אֶתְעַדֵּן,
וּכְמוֹ בְעֵדֶן   לֵב אַרְחִיבָה
לְמַמְתִּיק מָרָה   וְהוֹפֵךְ לְעֶזְרָה
יוֹם אַף וְעֶבְרָה   וְיוֹם מֵי מְרִיבָה.
וְהָעֵינַיִם   לְאֵל שָׁמַיִם
נוֹתֵן בְּמַיִם   עַזִּים נְתִיבָה.
חֹם אַדְמָתוֹ   מֵחֲמָתוֹ,
וּמִנִּשְׁמָתוֹ   יִתֶּן-קָרַח.

הֵשִׁיב חֲמָתוֹ   מִבֶּן אֲמָתוֹ,
וְאֶת נִשְׁמָתוֹ   מִשְּׁאוֹל פָּדָה.
וְרָצוּ מְרוֹמוֹת   לַעֲשׂוֹת שְׁלוֹמוֹת
בֵּין הַתְּהוֹמוֹת,   וְאֵין קוֹל חֲרָדָה.
וּמֵימֵי קִנְאָה   הָפַךְ לְחֶמְאָה,
וְסָרָה יִרְאָה   וְנָסָה קְפָדָה,
וְשָׁמְעוּ עֲגוּמִים   לְמַלְאַךְ רַחֲמִים
מִן הַמְּרוֹמִים   קוֹל הַצְּעָדָה.
כָּכָה יְבַשֵּׂר   עִם קֵץ בְּמַאֲסָר,
וְיַד צָר וּמוּסָר   עָלָיו כָּבְדָה.
וְסֹעֲרָה עֲנִיָּה   דָּמְתָה אֳנִיָּה
תִּשְׁמַע שְׁנִיָּה   מִזְמוֹר לְתוֹדָה:
צְאִי בַּת אֱמוּנַי   מֵאֹפֶל עֲנָנַי,
כִּי כְבוֹד אֲדֹנָי   עָלַיִךְ זָרָח!

lazy porters, brutish rope-men,
blind lookouts. Drunken ocean
toys, mocks, trades folk for no price.
Kraken deep in endless ocean
summons fellow-beasts to feast.
    The ocean gladly gathers all.
    No place for a man to flee, no refuge!

I lift my eyes to You, O Lord,
send You my gift of prayer.
I fear my end, and in my anguish,
offer Jonah's prayer to You.
The thought of how You split
the Jordan is a comfort now,
and thinking how You split the Red Sea—
deathless miracle—makes me sing,
make songs I hope may please You,
You Who sweetened Marah's waters,
and Meribah in the desert,
You Who turn a day of terror,
horror into victory.
My eyes look up to God, Who smoothes
a path amid the raging waters,
    Who coddles, warms the earth with sun;
    or breathes the ice at will.

He turned His anger from His servant,
saved him from the horror.
Graciously, the stars made peace
among the angry waters.
Terror ceased, fear fled; foam
subsided, turned to butter.
Men in anguish caught the sound
of kindly angels marching by.
So may tidings reach a people
who have had enough of bondage
and the heavy hand upon them.
May that people, wretched, storm-tossed—
like our ship—hear words of comfort:
    "Leave the clouds, my faithful daughter!
    See God's splendor shining on you!"

This poem is quite different in form from the others on its theme. It has some features of a liturgical poem—strophic pattern, acrostic, last line containing a biblical verse that could link it to a specific site in the liturgy—but the point of view in the middle three stanzas is distinctly personal. The poem's short lines and insistent internal rhymes lend it a certain breathlessness, which I attempted to imitate in the translation by adopting a choppy phrasing and loose syntax in the poem's more descriptive parts.

The medieval copyist who preserved the poem was of the opinion that it is a liturgical poem, for he labeled it *me'ora,* a poem designed to be recited in the synagogue in the morning service to introduce the benediction that thanks God for creating the luminaries.[31] True to the genre, it ends with a quotation from Isaiah that employs an image of light in anticipation of Israel's redemption. But three of the five strophes describe a storm at sea from the point of view of someone who speaks about it in the first person, and most of the last strophe is about the calm that followed the storm. Though the poet exploits this movement from storm to calm as a hopeful anticipation of the redemption of Israel after its long experience of exile and persecution, this messianic theme makes its appearance only as the poem is about to end; the strongest impression left by the poem is one of personal experience.

The storm scene is prepared for by a meditation on God's control of all things, summarized compactly in the poem's first two words, *yo'ets umeiqim*—literally, "[God] decides and fulfills"—and reinforced by a maxim paraphrased from Jeremiah, "Man's path is not his to choose."[32] Effort, even in a holy cause, is of little worth, because only God knows what is best, and only God can unfailingly make a plan take effect. The biblical quotation was often used by medieval Jews when describing a personal disaster or reversal.[33] Halevi applies it to his own situation when he says that a man who tries to go west sometimes finds that he has actually gone east. An acute awareness that our fate is out of our hands leads to trust in God, the only true actor, a theme of which we have seen in many variations in this book. It appears again in the biblical quotation that caps the strophe, "Where shall I go from Your spirit?" (Ps. 139:7), its meaning modified by its new setting in Halevi's poem. In the book of Psalms, these words express the speaker's conviction of God's omnipresence and benign providence, but in our poem, they express resignation in the face of a powerful awareness of man's lack of control over his own destiny.

The second and third strophes evoke the storm at sea and its terrors. The poem's rapid, nervous movement, arising from the constant internal rhyming that subdivides each line into four small segments, mimics the ship's instability and the poet's disquiet. What is the pilgrim doing as the ship rises and sinks, as sailors struggle to stabilize it, as the sharks grin in anticipation of a feast? He is holding his breath and hoping for a miracle, too conscious of his sinful nature to dare to pray.

Here is yet another example of the contained quality of Halevi's religiosity. There is no making of a case for salvation—no prayers for help, no reminders of ancestral and personal merit, no calling in of divine promises, as we find in the prayers inserted into the war poems of Samuel the Nagid. Nor is there even a call for divine grace, as is common in the liturgy. Instead of words, there is a physical posture—eyes lifted up to God—that the poet mentions twice. In this posture, the speaker does not pray but recalls past events, all miracles that had to do with water: Jonah in the belly of the fish, Israel at the Red Sea, Joshua at the Jordan, Moses at the bitter lake and at the rock. He recalls these as an offering to God, as he says—and as a comfort to himself, as he does not need to say.

And so, without a word of petitionary prayer, the storm subsides and the pilgrim is saved, as God's will turns the raging foam to butter. The sound—not the voice, and certainly not his sight—of the angel arriving, hovering over the passengers and lifting them out of danger, is perceived by the despairing wretches on the ship. Nothing they or the poet could have done would have been effective, for only God has the power to act. Given this reality, the only appropriate stance for the pious is hopeful trust, an attitude that Halevi commends to the Jewish people at large as the poem reaches its liturgical conclusion.

Epilogue

More than four hundred years later, the Italian Jewish Renaissance scholar Gedalia Ibn Yaḥya, in his chronology of Jewish history entitled *The Chain of Tradition,* told the story of Halevi's death that would become a canonical part of the Jewish tradition:[1]

> It is written in the *Book of Genealogies* that Master Judah Halevi was fifty years old when he went to the Land of Israel, as can be seen from his poems. I have a tradition from a certain elder that when Halevi reached the gates of Jerusalem, he tore his clothes and walked with his knees[2] on the ground to fulfill the scripture: "For Your servants take pleasure in her stones and cherish her soil" [Ps. 102:15]. He was reciting the lament he had composed, "Jerusalem! Have you no greeting," when an Arab, observing his fervor, was overcome with religious zeal against him. He bore down on him with his horse, trampled him, and killed him.

This story is full of problems and improbabilities. At the time of Halevi's arrival in Jerusalem, if he did indeed arrive there, there were no Muslims in Jerusalem—at least none living openly as Muslims, as the crusaders had closed the city to both them and the Jews upon capturing it in 1099.[3] None of the letters exchanged by Halevi's friends after his death alludes to his meeting such a dramatic end. Ibn Yaḥya offers as his source for the story of Halevi's martyrdom no authoritative witness, no chain of tradition, but only a personal communication by a mysterious unnamed elder; this vagueness suggests that we are dealing with a folk tradition rather than with history. Indeed, his accounts of several of Halevi's contemporaries include fanciful tales of a folkloric nature.

But even if Halevi died a natural death after reaching the Holy Land, it is not altogether surprising that he should have been spoken of as a saint and that a legend about his death something like this one should have emerged. Besides his general reputation for piety and the unusual story of his pilgrimage, the poems that he wrote about his pilgrimage and about his broader religious life created a specific image of him for future generations. These poems circulated already in his lifetime among the business and intellectual elite of the Mediterranean world and continued to be copied, read, and used liturgically long thereafter. It was probably out of the poems, as much as out of the pilgrimage itself, that the legend of Halevi's death as a martyr to the Land of Israel emerged.

Every detail of Ibn Yaḥya's account—even his mistakes—is related to some aspect of Halevi's poetry. Ibn Yaḥya himself says that he derived the statement that Halevi was fifty at the time of his pilgrimage from one of his poems—obviously, "Still Chasing Fun at Fifty" (poem 17). His portrayal of Halevi dying at the very threshold of the fulfillment of his vow, within sight of a Holy Land that remains just beyond his reach, lends his death some of the pathos of the death of Moses, spoken of in "Hail, Mount Avarím!" (poem 13) and in the Ode to Jerusalem (poem 16). The posture in which Ibn Yaḥya says that Halevi died suggests a religious spirit of submission that is characteristic of his religious poetry, a spirit that among medieval Hebrew poets he made distinctively his own. And perhaps it would not be too far-fetched to connect the brevity of Halevi's moment of fulfillment, as depicted in the folktale, with his poignant wish that we encountered in the first poem to be read and analyzed in this book: to please You just one moment, then die.[4]

Above all, it is Ibn Yaḥya's depiction of Halevi dying with his face crushed into the stones and the soil of the Land of Israel that points to the spiritual, if not the historical, authenticity of his account. Ibn Yaḥya himself calls attention to the literary character of the death that he is assigning Halevi by putting Ps. 102:14–15 into Halevi's mouth at the supreme moment of his life. Halevi did not select this verse for such a prominent place in the Kuzari and in the Ode to Jerusalem merely because it expresses love for the Land of Israel. The verse was important to him because it speaks of the Land of Israel in its most concrete aspect: its actual stones and soil. The land was not only Israel's ancient home, not only the place that could scientifically be proved to have the most salubrious and agreeable climate and geography: it was where God had revealed Himself to man in the past, where the bones of patriarchs and prophets still lay buried alongside the remains of the Temple's sacred objects and the smashed fragments of the tablets of the law, where the dead would first enjoy the resurrection, rise from the soil and themselves become the recipients of revelation. The ground itself was suffused with God's presence, and Halevi was determined to bury himself in it, to mingle his body with the sacred presence, and be as united with God as is possible until the day of which the prophets said: "For they will behold, eye to eye, when the Lord returns to Zion.[5]

Halevi's Ode to Jerusalem embodies his most moving statement of longing to dwell in the presence of God in the Land of Israel. By Ibn Yaḥya's time, it had become part of the liturgy for the Ninth of Av, the fast day commemorating the destruction of the Temple, and it is still recited on that day by the pious. It received the tribute of being imitated by later poets, creating a genre of poetry on Zion, many examples of which are found in the liturgy.[6] Ibn Yaḥya's picture of Halevi dying with this sacred text on his lips would naturally remind the educated Jewish reader of the second-century Rabbi Akiba, the archetypal martyr, who is said to have died with the profession of God's unity on his lips. Ibn Yaḥya's story makes the love of Zion into an article of faith and makes Halevi into a martyr.

The Ode to Jerusalem and the other references to the soil of the Land of Israel in Halevi's poems combine to show how focused Halevi was on dying there. Halevi's obsession with this theme, beginning with dying in God's favor in "O Lord, All My Desire Is Plain to Thee" in the first poem of this book and ending with the pilgrimage poems, must have created an atmosphere of martyrdom about him. But this kind of martyrdom is different from the martyrdom of Rabbi Akiba, the model of martyrdom in the face of persecution. This is a Middle Eastern martyrdom, a religious reflex of the Arabic theme of the martyr of love. The martyrdom that Halevi longed for was the death of the lover who wanders, half-mad with longing, about the places where he had encountered his beloved and at last lays his head down on the ground and expires. The stones and clods of the Land of Israel were for Halevi the lap of his beloved. Perhaps this Arabic tradition even underlies Halevi's fantasy tour of the Land of Israel in the Ode to Jerusalem.

Perhaps the Ode to Jerusalem itself, already widely familiar through the liturgy, was enough to generate the story. Whoever invented it—whether an anonymous old man or Ibn Yaḥya himself—was no longer in touch with the literary tradition that lay behind Halevi's poetry and religious imagination. To him, martyrdom meant confronting the enemies of Israel and dying by their sword. The story that emerged was almost true to Halevi's intentions—except in its crude realization.

In October 1141, Nathan ben Samuel, the secretary of Samuel ben Ḥanania, the Nagid of Egypt, wrote a letter in Hebrew to Abraham ben Mazhir, a distinguished religious scholar in Damascus. Incidentally to other subjects that were his real purpose for writing, he includes the following statement:

> I assume your Excellency is aware of the matter of Master Judah Halevi, that righteous and saintly man (the memory of the saintly is a blessing) about whom the true prophets prophesied truly, "The eye has never seen" [Isa. 64:3]. He was a knight of piety and Torah. . . . His righteousness is attested by his words . . . that sing like birds . . . to eternal rest . . . in the garden of the Lord.[7]

Nathan seems to have gone on to speak of Halevi for a few more lines; unfortunately, the manuscript, already somewhat broken, becomes virtually illegible just at this point. But what we have already read contains important information. Nathan assumes that the addressee already knows that Halevi is dead. The expression "the matter" could be a euphemism for "the death of," but it could also hint at something special about Halevi's death. What is particularly interesting is that Nathan alters the pious formula customarily used when mentioning a dead person; instead of the usual "the memory of the righteous is a blessing," a biblical quotation,[8] he says, "the memory of the saintly [*qadosh*] is a blessing." This alteration heightens the degree of respect for Halevi far above that generally accorded an ordinary worthy. The Hebrew word *qadosh* was sometimes used as a term of special respect in introducing a living person's name—we have encountered it in documents quoted in this book—but when referring to the dead, it was often used to mean "martyr." Nathan's extraordinary claim that Halevi's advent was predicted by the prophets heightens the intensity yet again. He caps the tribute by quoting a passage from Isaiah, as if to say merely that no one has ever seen Halevi's like, but the quotation was fraught with eschatological overtones, as the verse was traditionally understood to be about the vision of God that is the anticipated reward of the righteous in paradise. We have already discussed Halevi's use of this verse in eschatological poetry and its connection with his yearning for visual experience of God.[9] By quoting it here, Nathan is attributing to Halevi that ultimate spiritual fulfillment. Nor is Nathan the only contemporary to refer to Halevi in such lofty terms; in a letter written a little less than a year after Halevi's departure from Alexandria, our old friend Amram ben Isaac speaks of the poems of lament that he and one of his friends composed in memory of "Judah Halevi, the righteous and saintly man."[10] Halevi's contemporaries thus confirm that his pilgrimage was understood as a supreme act of self-consuming personal piety. It has been the contention of this book that that is exactly what he intended.

Notes

INTRODUCTION

1. The most important scholarly accounts of Halevi's life and intellectual career are: Kaufmann, "Jehuda Halewi"; Schirmann, "Ḥayei yehuda haleivi"; idem, "Hashlamot leḥayei yehuda haleivi"; idem, *Toledot hashira haʿivrit bisfarad hamuslimit*, 421–80; Baron, "Yehudah Halevi"; Goitein, *Mediterranean Society*, 5:448–68; and Brann, "Judah Halevi."

2. For a thorough account of the Cairo geniza, see Reif, *A Jewish Archive from Old Cairo;* of the Arabic geniza documents pertaining to Halevi, see Goitein, *Mediterranean Society*, 1:1–28. All the relevant documents bearing on Halevi are published in their original languages and with Hebrew translation, in Gil and Fleischer, *Yehuda haleivi uvenei ḥugo;* since Gil and Fleischer provide full bibliography, enabling the interested reader to track down the original publications of the documents, this information will not be repeated in these notes.

3. This last point is made forcefully by Komem in his seminal article "Bein shira linvuʾa: ʿIyunim beshirei yehuda haleivi."

CHAPTER I

1. On ambivalence to Golden Age culture on the part of its greatest exponents, see Scheindlin, "Moses Ibn Ezra on the Legitimacy of Poetry"; and, at length, Brann, *Compunctious Poet*, particularly the chapter on Halevi (84–118).

2. For a short but comprehensive account of medieval Judeo-Arabic culture, see Scheindlin, "Merchants and Intellectuals, Rabbis and Poets: Judeo-Arabic Culture in the Golden Age of Islam"; for the Jews of al-Andalus, see Ashtor, *Jews of Moslem Spain*. For an introduction to Hebrew

Golden Age poetry, see Scheindlin, *Wine, Women, and Death: Medieval Hebrew Poetry on the Good Life,* and idem, *The Gazelle: Medieval Hebrew Poetry on God, Israel, and the Soul.* For essays on the literary culture of Muslims, Jews, and Christians in the period and on some representative figures, including Halevi, see Menocal, Scheindlin, and Sells, eds., *Literature of Al-Andalus.*

3. The evidence for the place is about evenly balanced, but the fact that Halevi constantly referred to himself as Castilian and as having come from Christian territory tips the scales slightly in favor of Toledo.

His birth date is usually given as about ten years earlier, with some scholars pushing it back as far as 1070. These early dates are computed on the basis of three assumptions: that Halevi met Moses Ibn Ezra in Granada as a youth; that at the time of their meeting, he was already old enough to make a stunning impression in poetic improvisation; and that Moses Ibn Ezra left Granada soon after the Almoravid takeover of the city in 1090. But we have no idea how long thereafter Moses Ibn Ezra stayed in Granada; all we do know is that his brothers left him behind when they departed, in 1091, and that he departed at some undetermined time later. As far as we know, the youthful Halevi could have met him in Granada at any time in the 1190s.

My reasoning in placing Halevi's birth ca. 1085 is as follows. His "Still Chasing Fun at Fifty" (poem 17), in which he says that he is over fifty years old, appears from its contents to have been written in imminent anticipation of his pilgrimage, which began in 1140. Halevi was therefore probably between fifty and sixty at the time of the pilgrimage, so he was probably born between 1080 and 1090. This range can be further narrowed to the first part of the decade by the two panegyrics (not, in this case, intimate poems but formal ones intended for formal public recitation) that Halevi wrote in honor of the accession of Joseph Ibn Megas to the leadership of the academy of Lucena in 1103 (Brody, *Dīwān,* 1:141–42 [poem 95] and 1:173–74 [poem 114]), for it seems reasonable to assume that the author of such poems was past his earliest youth; if Halevi was in his late teens when he wrote the poems, he was born in the mid-eighties. Of course, if many years passed after he wrote "Still Chasing Fun at Fifty" before he embarked on his pilgrimage, he could have been born that many years earlier, but we have no way of knowing. I do not consider it relevant to Halevi's birth date that he wrote a poem celebrating the circumcision of a grandson of Isaac ben Barukh Ibn al-Baliya (Brody, *Dīwān,* 1:120 [poem 84]), who died in 1094, because the terms in which Ibn al-Baliya is mentioned in the poem suggest that he was already dead (pointed out by Rapoport, as quoted in Kaufmann, "Jehuda Halewi," 140). As conjectural as my calculations are, they seem more solidly grounded than those based on the unknown date of Moses Ibn Ezra's departure from Granada.

4. That he was in North Africa at least once is attested by his younger associate Solomon Ibn Parḥon, *Maḥberet heʿarukh,* 2:4b column 1. Halevi may have visited Egypt before his pilgrimage, as a letter dated 1130 from a writer in Spain to Ḥalfon ben Nethaniel, the Egyptian Jewish businessman who will occupy a large place in this account, congratulates Ḥalfon on Halevi's arrival or proposed arrival; see Gil

and Fleischer, *Yehuda haleivi,* 327–31 (doc. 20). But we do not know where Ḥalfon was when this letter was sent to him; he could have been in his home in Cairo, but as a man who traveled widely, he could have been anywhere else, including North Africa (but probably not Spain), when this letter was written. Gil and Fleischer assume that Ḥalfon was in Egypt and make this assumption the basis of the theory that Halevi attempted to make the pilgrimage as early as 1130. But that Halevi met Ḥalfon as early as 1130 is unlikely because in 1141 Halevi implied in a letter that he had known Ḥalfon personally for only two years; see below, 114. And if he did travel to Egypt in 1130, there is no evidence that it was for any purpose other than business.

5. Abraham Ibn Daud (c. 1110–80), whose *Sefer haqabala* is particularly concerned with the history of the rabbinate in al-Andalus, lists Halevi—whom he merely names—among the poets, not among the rabbis; see G. D. Cohen, *The Book of Tradition (Sefer ha-Qabbalah) by Abraham Ibn Daud,* 72–73 (Hebrew section). In the many letters written to Halevi or mentioning him, he is called *rabi* (master) and *rabeinu* (our master), which were merely titles of respect in his time, but never *ḥaver,* the ordinary title for a rabbi in Halevi's world (incidentally, this is the title used for the rabbi of the Kuzari). He is called *harav* (rabbi) by the nameless petitioner from Burgos mentioned at the end of this paragraph, but never by writers who knew him or belonged to his circle.

Halevi's epistle to Rabbi Ḥabīb of al-Mahdiyya, quoted below, depicts him as an intermediary to Ibn Megas. The epistle he composed on behalf of Ibn Megas is the one addressed to the sages of Narbonne (Brody, *Dīwān,* 1:217–18, epistle 4). Yet when Halevi lived in Toledo, he himself needed help in getting Ibn Megas's attention, as attested by his letter to Ḥalfon in Gil and Fleischer, *Yehuda haleivi,* 314–15 (doc. 15). The letters about ransoming the captive woman have partly been published in English in Goitein, *Mediterranean Society,* 5:462–64; the originals are in Gil and Fleischer, *Yehuda haleivi,* 314–15 (doc. 15); 319–21 (doc. 17); and 322–23 (doc. 18); the attribution of this last document to Halevi has been questioned.

6. "Body and soul" would seem to be an appropriate English equivalent to the Arabic phrase "sentence and meaning" used in the letter, which appears in Gil and Fleischer, *Yehuda haleivi,* 327–31 (doc. 20). Goitein's translation is "quintessence and embodiment" (*Mediterranean Society,* 5:448 and elsewhere); Gil and Fleischer's (ibid., 330) is *tamṣit umashmaʿut* ("essence and meaning"). Neither translation recognizes the grammatical terminology underlying this unusual metaphor. The nearest expression to it that I have been able to find is a line from the tenth-century Arabic poet al-Mutanabbī, who praises the object of a panegyric by saying that without him the rest of mankind would be "like speech without meaning"; see al-Mutanabbī, *Al-ʿarf al-ṭayyib fī sharḥ dīwān abī l-ṭayyib,* 595.

The author of the letter from the would-be visitor, which appears in Gil and Fleischer, ibid., 445–49 (doc. 45), was not from Badajos, as maintained by those who have dealt with it until now, but from Burgos, as the manuscript clearly says Burgushi, not Badakhosi. In any case, a person from Badajos was not called a Badakhosi in the Arabic of the period, but a Batalyawsi. In addition, the writer identifies himself as a Castilian; yet Badajos was still al-Andalus in Halevi's lifetime.

Contrary to the opinion of Goitein, followed by Gil and Fleischer, that this document is a typical begging letter, it does not contain any of the characteristic features analyzed by Mark R. Cohen's study of nearly five hundred such letters in his *Poverty and Charity in the Jewish Community of Medieval Egypt.*

7. For Halevi's relations with other poets and intellectuals, see Schirmann, "Ḥayei yehuda haleivi"; for such connections in his early years, see Brenner, *Judah Halevi and His Circle of Hebrew Poets in Granada.*

8. Ratzhaby, "Igeret meirabi yehuda haleivi lerabi ḥabīb." The epistle does not say that Halevi was still a student at the time of writing, as asserted by Gil and Fleischer in *Yehuda haleivi,* 177; rather, it makes the impression that Halevi was already a senior dignitary. "Among the columns" is an expression that the Babylonian Talmud uses several times in its Aramaic form (e.g., Berakhot 8a) as a designation of the *beit midrash,* the study hall. In the Islamic world, lectures were typically held in mosques, with the teacher sitting by or reclining against a pillar, and Halevi's phrase may reflect a similar practice among the Jews.

9. Brody, *Dīwān,* 1:219–22 (epistle 5) and 224–25 (epistle 7), at 224. The two fragments are parts of a single epistle, as was recognized by Brody. Kalkol and Darda were two ancient sages named in 1 Kings 5:11 as being inferior in wisdom to Solomon, implying that they were very wise indeed. The concluding quotation is from Jer. 51:9.

10. Brody, *Dīwān,* 2:319–20.

11. Ibid., 2:300 (poem 83).

12. The definition of the Hebrew word *zeman* (time) presupposed here was adopted by the Golden Age poets from its Arabic cognate *zamān,* which has a long history in Arabic poetry. In pre-Islamic poetry, it is the nearly personified figure of ineluctable fate; in later Islamic poetry, especially of the moralizing kind, it was often used simply to mean "temporal things." Yosef Tobi, in his *Qeruv udeḥiyya,* 215–16, reads the epigram as a satire against those who "believe in fate and predestination." For a more accurate formulation, see Elizur, "Vehayamim metsuvim me'eloa," esp. the discussion on 42–43; and Tsur, *ʿIyunim bashira haʿivrit biymei habeinayim,* 34–36.

The paradox that, in some cases, only the slave is truly free is also found in Arabic love poetry, in the line by Abū Bakr Ibn Ammār: "Do not seek power in love; in the law of love, slaves are the free men" (in al-Marrākushī, *Al-Muʿjib fī talkhīs akhbār al-maghrib,* 78).

13. A typical biblical usage is: "For Israel are slaves to me; they are my slaves, whom I brought out of the land of Egypt; I am the Lord" (Lev. 25:55). On voluntary servitude, rabbinic tradition (e.g., Babylonian Talmud, Qidushin 22b) puts into God's mouth the words: "The ear that heard My voice at Sinai saying, 'For Israel are slaves to Me' and sought a human master deserves to be bored with an awl," explaining the rule in Exod. 21:2–6 that a slave who chooses permanent servitude is to have his ear bored; pointed out by Schirmann, *Hashira haʿivrit,* 1:521.

14. Halevi, of course, was not the first Hebrew poet to describe a pious individual as a slave of God, but this image occurs only sporadically in the work of earlier poets; its frequency in Halevi is additional support for my argument for defining Halevi as the spokesman of a passive type of piety, as contrasted with Ibn

Gabirol; see Scheindlin, "Contrasting Religious Experience in the Liturgical Poems of Ibn Gabirol and Judah Halevi," where the conclusion emerges from a comparison of the metrical religious poetry of the two. Within the semantic field of slavery, Ibn Gabirol's four-line poem beginning "The sun like a bridegroom" (Jarden, *Shirei haqodesh lerabi shelomo ibn gabirol,* 2:466 [poem 141]; Schirmann, *Hashira ha'ivrit,* 1:252 [poem 105], v. 4) provides an instructive contrast: "Since the day that he joined Your service, he has come to rule; likewise, any slave who glorifies his master is himself glorified." The glorious servitude to God envisioned by Ibn Gabirol could not be further from the abject servitude envisioned by Halevi.

The use in Hebrew prose of the word *'oved* in the sense of a pious person apparently begins with the medieval translators of Arabic into Hebrew; see Judah Ibn Tibbon's translation of Halevi's Kuzari 3:1.

15. Brody, *Dīwān,* 3:228–29 (poem 126, lines 1–5; 23–27). "Own": the word means both "bought" and "created," and both meanings are relevant; "bought" belongs to the theme of servitude in the preceding line, while "created" belongs to the theme of man's transparency before God in the following line (based on Ps. 139:13). The two meanings overlap again in the last lines, where "buy me again" could equally be translated as "create me again," i.e., make me a new man through forgiveness. The word "again" in the penultimate line is borrowed from the language of national redemption, which is sometimes (as in Isa. 11:11 and in the liturgy) called a second redemption vis-à-vis the first, the exodus from Egypt. Applied to the individual soul, it refers to the hope of the soul's restoration to its divine source after death. See Scheindlin, "Redemption of the Soul in Golden Age Religious Poetry."

16. As used here, Hebrew *hineini* is equivalent to the Arabic ritual cry to God *labbayka;* but no Muslim writer would put this word into the mouth of God.

17. Brody, *Dīwān,* 2:268. Because the three verses begin successively with the first three letters of the poet's name, it has been conjectured that the poem originally had five verses and that two verses have been lost.

18. See Scheindlin, *Gazelle,* 41–49; and idem, "Redemption of the Soul."

19. Jarden, *Shirei haqodesh lerabi yehuda haleivi,* 3:854 (poem 374). "Form and matter," literally, "their foundation and their mystery"; this rhyming pair (*yesod/sod*) is associated with the poetry of Solomon Ibn Gabirol, and I have translated them as his usage is generally understood; see Ibn Gabirol's "The Kingly Crown" (*Keter malkhut*), in Schirmann, *Hashira ha'ivrit,* 1:257, line 7, and the commentary on 258; Tanenbaum, *Contemplative Soul,* 66–67. For reservations, see the commentary by Gluck, in *Solomon Ibn Gabirol.*

20. Brody, *Dīwān,* 3:203–4 (poem 113), lines 10–14. The phrase "days in prayer and nights in fasting," a common one in Islamic piety (many sources cited by Ratzhaby in "Yesodot she'ulim befiyutei yehuda haleivi," 170), was used also in Baḥya Ibn Paquda, *Al-hidāya ilā farā'iḍ al-qulūb,* ed. Kāfiḥ, 314. There is an unusually concrete evocation of a prayer vigil in Halevi's poem "My Thoughts Arouse Me," Brody, *Dīwān,* 3:182–83 (poem 99).

21. Baḥya Ibn Paquda, *The Book of Direction to the Duties of the Heart,* trans.

Mansoor, 402–25. The work is read as a critique of the Jewish courtier class by Safran in "Baḥya Ibn Paquda's Attitude Toward the Courtier Class."

22. For a study of the Islamic inspiration behind Baḥya's work, see Goldreich, "Possible Arabic Sources for the Distinction between 'Duties of the Heart' and 'Duties of the Limbs,'" and Lobel, *A Sufi-Jewish Dialogue*. For Sufi themes in Halevi's Kuzari, see Lobel, *Between Mysticism and Philosophy*.

23. The relevant verses are Qur'an, 3:122; 5:11; 9:51; 12:67; 14:11, 12; 39:38; 58:10; 64:13. The term *al-Mutawakkil* was taken as a regnal name by an Abbasid caliph; it also appears as the name of an Andalusi Jew, for which see below, n. 26. The Arabic slogan became notorious in the West when the in-flight recorder of EgyptAir flight 990, which crashed on October 31, 1999, revealed that it was uttered eleven times by the copilot, Gamil al-Batouti, during the airplane's descent, suggesting to many that he had intentionally caused the crash.

24. Qur'an 65:3.

25. The fullest treatment of the subject in Western academic literature is Reinert, *Die Lehre vom Tawakkul in der klassischen Sufik*. A good sketch is found in Vajda, *La Théologie ascétique de Baḥya ibn Paquda*, 60–67, which is based largely on Abū Ṭālib al-Makkī, *Qūt al-qulūb*. This last, a moderate Sufi text of the tenth century (dated 996), is one of the classics of Islamic religious literature. Al-Ghazzālī also included an important chapter on the subject in his *Iḥyā ʿulūm al-dīn*, 4:238–86.

26. Examples from Jewish letters are quoted below, 101, 145, 147, 149, 152; for Islamic examples, see Diem, *Arabische Privatbriefe des 9. bis 15. Jahrhunderts: Textband*, 24, and elsewhere. Yequtiel Ibn Ḥassan, a Jewish courtier in Saragossa and the patron of Solomon Ibn Gabirol, was called al-Mutawakkil in Arabic; see Schirmann, *Toledot*, 273.

27. This passivity comes out very strongly when Halevi's religious verse is compared with that of Solomon Ibn Gabirol, as pointed out briefly in my discussion of this poem in Scheindlin, *Gazelle*, 130–35, and at length in idem, "Contrasting Religious Experience."

28. Brody, *Dīwān*, 3:116 (poem 58). Discussed in Scheindlin, *Gazelle*, 214–17, where the theme of *tawakkul* is also touched on, 114–19.

29. Cf. "I cannot even speak but by Your leave" at the end of the poem quoted above, 20.

30. Reinert, *Die Lehre*, 94, 96; Nicholson, *Mystics of Islam*, 41–42.

31. Brody, *Dīwān*, 4:262 (poem 336). Cited by Mirsky, *Meḥovot halevavot leshirat halevavot*, 184. The heading is quoted from MS Oxford 1971. The heading in MS Schocken 37 also uses typically Islamic terminology: "By him [Halevi], about trust in God, the great and exalted [*al-tawakkul ʿalā l-lāhi ʿazza wa-jalla*]." The poem appears a second time in MS Oxford 1971 with the heading *ʿose shalom*, indicating that the copyist considered it a liturgical poem to be recited as part of the nineteenth benediction of the Amida.

32. Brody, *Dīwān*, 2:248 (poem 27). The Arabic heading in MS Oxford 1970 is *wa-lahu fī l-zuhd ayḍan* ("About withdrawal from the world, he also said") and in MS Oxford 1971 is *wa-qāla mutazahhidan* ("He said, in an ascetic vein"), using *zuhd* (asceticism), another term of Islamic piety that is the subject of an entire chapter

(chapter 9) of Baḥya's *Hidāya*. "The graves of lust" is a translation of the suggestive place name Qivrot Hata'ava, in Num. 11:34. The allusion is apposite, because, according to the biblical story, the place was named for an episode during the Israelites' wandering in the desert when their lust for meat caused them to abandon their trust in God's sustenance.

On the address to the soul in Arabic and Hebrew poetry, see Scheindlin, "Ibn Gabirol's Religious Poetry and Sufi Poetry."

33. The word's root is cognate with the root of the Hebrew *teshuva* ("repentance").

34. Abū l-ʿAtāhiya, *Dīwān*, ed. Faysal, 44 (poem 38). Other examples on 22 (poem 18), 30 (poem 23), and elsewhere in the *dīwān*.

35. The Hebrew maxim is in Avot 2:10. For further discussion of the *tokhaḥa* and other Hebrew *zuhd* poetry, see Scheindlin, *Wine, Women, and Death*, 135–41; and idem, "Old Age in Hebrew and Arabic *Zuhd* Poetry."

36. Abū Ishāq al-Ilbīrī (Granada, eleventh century), quoted in Scheindlin, "Old Age," 93. For an example of such comments at age sixty, see Ibn Khāfāja (Valencia province, 1058–1139), *Dīwān*, ed. Ghāzī, 64–65. For age seventy, al-Maqqarī, *Nafḥ al-Ṭīb min ghuṣn al-andalus al-raṭīb*, ed. I. ʿAbbās, 3:296. For age eighty, al-Maqqarī, ibid., 4:316.

37. E.g., Ibn Qudāma, *Kitāb al-tawwābīn*.

38. An outstanding example is Ibn Mar Saul's famous poem "O God, Do Not Judge Me in Accordance with My Sin," still used in the Sephardic liturgy. With all the similarities between Jewish and the Islamic *zuhd* poetry, there remain significant differences; see Scheindlin, "Old Age."

39. On Moses Ibn Ezra, see Scheindlin, "Old Age," 100–101, including a partial translation of the poem; my translation of the entire poem, with notes, appeared as "The Lamp Within." His Arabic treatise on poetry is *Kitāb al-Muḥāḍara wa l-mudhākara*, ed. Halkin; his relevant remarks are on 90.

40. We can discount the hypothesis that it was fear of assassination or some other political motive that impelled al-Ghazzālī to his change of life, a theme of some prominence in Ghazzālī studies; for a summary, see McCarthy, *Al-Ghazali: Deliverance from Error*, 26–37. Even if these suggestions turn out to be true, what is important for our purposes is al-Ghazzālī's own explanation of his behavior, which was circulated worldwide in his *Deliverer from Error* and was accepted at face value by his readers. Laoust, *La Politique de Gazali*, 90–105, combines the testimony of al-Ghazzālī's autobiographical *Al-Munqidh min al-ḍalāl* with the religious message of his *Iḥyā ʿulūm al-dīn* to yield a convincing study of al-Ghazzālī's inner motivations.

41. Al-Ghazzālī's works were widely disseminated and controversial in twelfth-century Spain; see Fierro, "La Religion," 483–85. On al-Ghazzālī's works in the geniza, see Fenton, *Treatise of Pool*, 5 and n. 14; and Goitein, "A Jewish Addict to Sufism," 38 nn. 5–6. There even exists a manuscript of al-Ghazzālī's works whose title page contains a note (in Arabic but written in Hebrew script) that reads: "Abū Ḥāmid al-Ghazzālī, may the memory of the righteous be a blessing" (MS Escorial 631). The application to Ghazzālī of the Jewish formula typically used after naming a

dead rabbi or other religious authority shows to what extent this exemplary Muslim figure became naturalized in Jewish piety. (A photograph of this remarkable page accompanies the article on al-Ghazzālī in the *Encyclopaedia Judaica.*)

42. In all the scholarly discussion of the extent of al-Ghazzālī's influence on Halevi, the obvious parallel between al-Ghazzālī's and Halevi's personal acts of *tawba* has been pointed out, as far as I am aware, only by Itzhaki in her " 'Hetsiqatni teshuqati' liyhuda haleivi."

43. This schematization comes from McCarthy, *Al-Ghazali,* 15, 26.

44. That some of Halevi's poetry is a reaction to the work of Ibn Gabirol is one of the claims of my article "Contrasting Religious Experience." I hope to develop this theme on a larger scale in a future publication.

45. On Jewish Neoplatonism, see Colette Sirat, *A History of Jewish Philosophy in the Middle Ages* (Cambridge: Cambridge University Press, 1990), 57–112.

46. Tanenbaum, *Contemplative Soul,* a whole book devoted to Neoplatonism in the Hebrew poetry of this period, includes thorough analyses of many poems; chapter 8 deals in detail with a *tokhaḥa* by Halevi. Neoplatonic motifs in other genres of Hebrew liturgical poetry of Halevi's age are discussed, with many examples, in Scheindlin, *Gazelle,* chapter 2. On the adaptability of Neoplatonism to Judaism and Islam, see Hughes, *Texture of the Divine,* 41.

47. For a full and authoritative study by a historian of the status of the Jews in medieval Islam, see M. R. Cohen, *Under Crescent and Cross.*

48. See the sources cited above in n. 15, and Tanenbaum, *Contemplative Soul,* index, s.v. redemption, national vs. individual.

49. See Scheindlin, "Contrasting Religious Experience," 141–62.

50. Examples: Brody, *Dīwān,* 3:35 (poem 17); 3:257 (poem 138).

51. Ibid., 4:212 (poem 105); but the attribution does not seem to be firm. "The mountain of God" is Sinai. "The land of my footstool and throne" is the Land of Israel.

52. From "Can a Body Be a Room" (poem 20).

53. The element of expiation comes up in Kuzari 5:23 and in Halevi's epistle to Nathan ben Samuel, in Brody, *Dīwān,* 1:214–16 (epistle 3), partly translated below, 127–28. For more on expiation, see below, 213 and especially n. 18.

54. The source of this phrase is Eccles. 3:11.

55. Anonymous maxim in Ibn ʿAbd Rabbihi, *Al-ʿIqd al-farīd,* 3:135. Baḥya, *Hidāya,* 319 (and in his poetic meditation appended to the *Hidāya,* 434–41), and Maimonides (*Mishne tora,* Teshuva 2:1) also urge not postponing repentance until old age. That men become pious in their old age is a commonplace of Arabic and Hebrew literature. For more sources, see Scheindlin, "Old Age."

56. This expression echoes that of the prayer of the early Muslim mystic Dhū l-Nūn al-Miṣrī: "My wish is that once before I die I might know Him for an instant," quoted by Schimmel, *Gärten der Erkentniss,* 28. Halevi's prayer even goes a step further, for Dhū l-Nūn's statement reads like a wish for a gift from God to the worshiper. In this poem, to please God is to make a gift to God—the gift of the will. A similarly passionate expression may be found in Halevi's "Toward the Fountain of True Life" (poem 10).

57. For Islamic and Jewish sources, see Stern and Altmann, *Isaac Israeli,* 201–2;

Pagis, *Shirei levi ibn al-tabban,* 173–74; and Levin, "Haberiḥa min haʿolam el haʾelohim."

58. The echo of the Kuzari is noted by Diana Lobel, in *Between Mysticism and Philosophy,* 147–48. The poem actually inverts the problem of the king of the Khazars. The king has the right intentions but is performing the wrong actions, as he is informed in his dream; but the speaker in the poem is presumably leading a correct external life; his problem is how to achieve the correct inner state.

The interpretation of our poem advocated above is strengthened by comparing it with a similar one that was undoubtedly Halevi's model: "Eloah al tedineini kemaʾli," by Ibn Mar Saul, in Schirmann, *Hashira haʿivrit,* 1:50–52, for which, see my "Islamic Motifs."

59. Such paradoxes are commonplaces of Islamic pietistic writing. See Qushayri, *Risāla,* ed. Maḥmūd and Sharīf, 2:424; and Reinert, *Die Lehre,* 134, 137. (For a fuller discussion of the theme of *tawakkul* in Halevi's poetry, see Scheindlin, "*Tawakkul* in the Poetry of Judah Halevi.")

60. Massignon, "Essay on the Origins of the Technical Language of Islamic Mysticism," 134.

61. The Qur'anic words occur at 5:119–122; 9:100–101; 58:22; 98:8; cf. also 9:72. The former interpretation is in Makkī, *Qūt al-qulūb* (Cairo, 1351/1932), 3:56, quoted by Reinert, *Die Lehre,* 104; the latter is in Qushayri, *Risāla,* 2:423.

62. The problem of the conflict between the idea of prayer and the principle of *tawakkul* was taken up by Muslim thinkers; see Reinert, *Die Lehre,* 109–13; and Schimmel, *Mystical Dimensions of Islam,* 156, 161.

63. My translation of *tsidqatekha* in v. 21 as "Your grace" is dictated by the context; this usage, not found in the Bible and not clearly attested in ordinary rabbinic Hebrew, occurs occasionally in liturgical texts; examples may be found in Goldschmidt, *Maḥzor layamim hanoraʾim,* 2:24, 35, 57.

64. In chapter 3, we shall see that at a later stage, Halevi indeed spoke of seeing God literally.

65. For a classic evocation of this image, see Moses Ibn Ezra, "The Lamp Within."

66. Scheindlin, *Gazelle,* 185.

67. The pantheistic reading described is best represented by Heinemann, who draws on Goethe's *Faust* and various Christian mystics of the Middle Ages. David Kaufmann was more sensitive to the poem's uncertainties. I believe that my interpretation is supported by his "Torat haʾelahut shel rabi baḥya ibn paquda," 68, where he discusses the Arabic maxim "My God, where can I find You, but where can I not find You," translated and incorporated by Halevi as the leading strophe of our poem.

68. The ultimate source is Plotinus, *Enneads* III.8.10; V.2.1; VI.7.12. The image of the fountain has left its trace in the title of Ibn Gabirol's metaphysical treatise *The Fountain of Life.*

69. For an extended study of this complex of ideas, see Altmann, "The Delphic Maxim in Medieval Islam and Judaism."

70. Most solemnly in his poem "I Am the Man," in Brody and Schirmann, *Shelomo ibn gabirol,* 116–17 (poem 93).

71. In Kuzari 2:20, Halevi points out that Christians and Muslims make pilgrimage to Jerusalem, yet Israel is barred from doing so because of her exile.

72. Reiner, "ʿAliya vaʿaliya leregel, 1099–1517," 23. One wonders whether the historical memory of the Sukkot pilgrimage is the basis for the recitation of the poem on the eighth day of that festival in various Sephardic rites and in the Yemeni rite.

73. Perhaps we have here a case of the practice of repentant poets rewriting their secular poems as religious ones. See below, chapter 2, n. 13.

CHAPTER 2

1. The classic study of Halevi's understanding of the political realities of his time is Baer, "Hamatsav hapoliṭi shel yehudei sefarad bedoro shel rabi yehuda haleivi"; see also his *History of the Jews in Christian Spain,* 1:67–77. Baer's focus is on Christian Spain; his treatment of the state of the Jews in al-Andalus under the Almoravids is sketchy by contrast. Baer did not attempt to explain Halevi's pilgrimage, but his description of the state of.the Jews underlies such authoritative presentations of Halevi's pilgrimage as that of Schirmann in his posthumous *Toledot hashira haʿivrit bisfarad hamuslimit,* which, oddly, for a work of literary history, foregrounds political considerations.

2. Brody, *Dīwān,* 4:131–33 (poem 58, lines 7–10), quoted by Baer, "Hamatsav," 6–7, and others. The same sentiment is expressed in "Philistines Gather" in Brody, *Dīwān,* 4:134 (poem 59), lines 11–14; and in "Seraphs of Fire," ibid., 4:205–6 (poem 99), lines 9–11.

3. Brody, *Dīwān,* 4:230 (poem 119), trans. and commented on in Scheindlin, *Gazelle,* 52–57.

4. Brody, *Dīwān,* 4:3 (poem 1).

5. Ibid., 2:272 (poem 51). I have taken a liberty with the poem's opening, which, translated literally, is "lazy one!" My version makes explicit that the poem is addressed to Halevi's own self.

6. The view of Halevi's pilgrimage as a social and cultural critique of his elite class is found, in nucleus, in Baer's "Hamatsav" and was brilliantly developed by G. D. Cohen in his *Book of Tradition,* 295–302. The following summary expands on Cohen's presentation.

7. Kraemer, *Humanism in the Renaissance of Islam,* 57–60. A good statement of the leveling effect of philosophy on the three religions is in Rahman, *Prophecy in Islam,* 40.

8. On the corrosive effect of philosophical relativism on ties to religion, see Stroumsa, "On Jewish Intellectuals Who Converted in the Early Middle Ages," 196. See also the discussion of "Your Words Are Scented" (poem 18).

9. Kuzari 2:69–80.

10. The text of his tiny treatise on metrics has never been published in its original form. The Arabic portions were published by Schirmann, "Hameshorerim benei doram shel moshe ibn ʿezra viyhuda haleivi." The Hebrew verses that it contains were published by Brody, *Die schönen Versmasse.* A complete version, but with the Arabic portions

translated into Hebrew, was published by Tova Rosen as an appendix to her "Hamahalakh hasṭrofi beshirat yehuda haleivi—poeṭiqa alternaṭivit?" Brody—who first called attention to the treatise, identified its author, and published the Hebrew verses that it contains—entitled his publication "The Beautiful Meters," showing that Halevi's critique of quantitative metrics did not distract him from the treatise's purpose: not to discredit the use of quantitative metrics in Hebrew but to demonstrate that they can be beautiful. The thorough study of the treatise in Brann, *Compunctious Poet,* 96–106, stresses the undeniable ambivalence in Halevi's treatment of the subject.

The tempting but indemonstrable suggestion that Halevi experimented with nonquantitative meters in his secular poetry in fulfillment of his vow to stop using quantitative meters was made by Rosen in the article cited earlier in this note.

11. Solomon Ibn Parḥon, *Maḥberet heʿarukh,* 1:4b–5a. Although Solomon refers to Halevi and others as "my masters," it seems unlikely that he was Halevi's disciple in any formal sense, as was perceptively noted by Solomon Rapoport by S. G. Stern in his edition of *Maḥberet heʿarukh,* 1:xviii, note *. Doubts about the vow were expressed by Baron in his "Yehudah Halevi: An Answer to an Historic Challenge," 256, and more recent literature has followed his lead in taking the claim with a grain of salt; for example, Schirmann, *Toledot,* 445; and Brann, *Compunctious Poet,* 89–90.

12. And for other reasons elaborated in Goldziher, *Muslim Studies,* 1:144; and Bonebakker, "Prejudice Against Poetry in Early Islam."

13. The first four examples and others are found in Bonebakker, "Prejudice," 89; Kraemer, *Humanism in the Renaissance of Islam,* 218–19; and Brann, *Compunctious Poet,* 22. The Andalusi is Bakkār al-Marwānī (b. 1048/49), whose delightful story is told by al-Maqqarī, *Nafḥ al-ṭīb min ghuṣn al-andalus al-raṭīb,* 3:334–40. Another famous Andalusi who gave up poetry was Ibn Khafāja, as he reports in his *Dīwān,* 10, though his motives are not clear. The famous Andalusi poet and anthologist Ibn ʿAbd Rabbihi (860–940) wrote poems of atonement (calling them *mumaḥḥisāt*); see Ibn ʿAbd Rabbihi, *Dīwān,* ed. al-Dāya, 71. Ibn Sanā al-Mulk (1155–1211) describes poems of atonement (calling them *takfīr* poems); see Stern, *Hispano-Arabic Strophic Poetry,* 81–82.

14. The same could be said of Moses Ibn Ezra's supposed renunciation of poetry in his *Muḥāḍara,* 90, mentioned above in chapter 1, n. 39.

15. Such as the movement of Moses Darʿi in the mid-1120s or the calculation of Abraham bar Ḥiyya, suggesting that the messianic era might begin as early as 1136. Other movements and calculations are listed in Silver, *A History of Messianic Speculation in Israel,* 58–74. Gerson D. Cohen, *Book of Tradition,* 288, sums them up by saying, "At no time in the history of the Jews after the second century was there such a concentration of messianic speculation . . . as there was in Andalus in the eleventh and twelfth centuries."

16. Brody, *Dīwān,* 4:7–8 (poem 4, lines 1–4). Ḥamat and Yanoḥa are places in the Land of Israel, the former mentioned in Josh. 19:35 and the latter in Josh. 16:6–7. Ḥamat is identified in the rabbinic tradition with Tiberias. Samuel the Nagid, too, uses obscure place names as synecdoche for the Land of Israel, in Jarden, *Dīwān shemuel hanagid,* 35 (poem 9). Perhaps Halevi was consciously echoing the Nagid's

poem. Dinaburg (later Dinur) provides an ingenious suggestion as to why Halevi did so in "ʿAliyato shel rabi yehuda haleivi leʾerets yisraʾeil vehatesisa hameshiḥit beyamav," 8 n. 7.

17. The foundational article for this interpretation of Halevi and his pilgrimage is Dinaburg, "ʿAliyato."

18. Jarden, *Shirat haqodesh lerabi shelomo ibn gabirol,* 2:463 (poem 137).

19. Ibid., 2:480 (poem 155). Ḥabor and Ḥalaḥ are among the places to which the Assyrians exiled the ten northern tribes in 722 BCE (2 Kings 17:6).

20. Ibid., 2:323 (poem 95).

21. Nearly all the examples of the messianic call motif cited by Dinaburg as evidence for his thesis that Halevi was summoning the Jews to return to the Land of Israel are vitiated by the holistic approach advocated here, and some of the poems that he cites actually turn into counterexamples, such as the one in Brody, *Dīwān,* 4:248 (poem 127, cited by Dinaburg for some reason from the edition of the *dīwān* by Luzzatto, *Dīwān rabi yehuda haleivi,* 12b), and Brody, *Dīwān,* 3:18–19 (poem 12). Of the twenty-six passages quoted by Dinaburg, only two appear to support his case: one is "Distant Dove, Sing Your Song Well" (poem 6); the other is "O You Who Sleep" (Brody, *Dīwān,* 3:67 [poem 34]), trans. and discussed in Scheindlin, *Gazelle,* 84–89. But whether the latter poem actually supports Dinaburg's thesis depends on which of the two interpretations offered there is adopted.

22. Lines 9–12, not quoted by Dinaburg.

23. Brody, *Dīwān,* 3:18 (poem 12), inexplicably cited by Dinaburg as evidence for his thesis; cited in the preceding note as a counterexample. Baer, "Hamatsav," 23, applied this passage to Halevi's disappointment with the political optimism of his contemporaries, but it seems more natural to apply it to failed messianic expectations. Moses Darʿi and his movement are described respectfully by Maimonides in *Igeret teiman,* 100–102.

24. This interpretation of Halevi's development was adumbrated by Luzzatto, *Dīwān,* 2b, in his headnote to "Distant Dove, Sing Your Song Well" (poem 6). Similarly, Komem, in "Bein shira linvuʾa," 685, builds his interpretation of Halevi's spiritual biography upon Halevi's presumed disappointment in his own messianic prediction embodied in "You Dozed and Fell Asleep" (poem 11). I would not like to base any far-reaching theory on the evidence of this poem alone; but Halevi's realization that his hope of redemption for the year 1130 had not been fulfilled could have been one disappointment among many that led to his break with active messianism.

Gerson D. Cohen, in his seminal paper "Messianic Postures of Ashkenazim and Sephardim (Prior to Sabbethai Zevi)," interpreted Halevi's pilgrimage as a break with what he understood as the activist messianic tradition of Sephardic Jews. While his typology of Ashkenazic and Sephardic messianism appears today to be in need of refinement, his interpretation of Halevi's pilgrimage is undoubtedly correct. As he puts it, "the Kuzari suggested no date for the Messiah. . . . The Almighty would act in His good time; man's task was but to try to earn His mercy. Judah ha-Levi's departure for Palestine was an act in that direction and nothing more" (283).

25. Babylonian Talmud, Berakhot 55b.

26. Brody, *Dīwān*, 2:20 (poem 19). The last line, literally, is "Let me interpret your dream."

27. Dinaburg, "ʿAliyato," 168, quotes lines 9–10 and 15–16, oblivious to their quietism, as if they support his thesis.

28. See especially the discussion of "This Wind of Yours" (poem 24).

29. At least five of Halevi's poems—the present poem, three others listed in the index of Brody, *Dīwān*, and one in Jarden, *Shirei haqodesh*, 3:864 (poem 381)—begin with phrases taken from the words of the heading of Psalm 56, and many of his poems include references to it. The interpretation of the psalm's heading derives from the ancient Aramaic translation of the psalm. I have explored some of Halevi's usages of bird imagery in Scheindlin, "The Song of the Silent Dove: The Pilgrimage of Judah Halevi," in *Bringing the Hidden to Light*. See also the discussion of "This Wind of Yours" (poem 24).

30. "Why this complaint" represents Hebrew words whose literal meaning is "why do you quarrel?" Dinaburg, "ʿAliyato," 169, adopted the alternate manuscript reading *tashivi*, which he explained in n. 7 as "to invalidate" and interpreted as meaning, "why do you refuse to answer the call to go to the Land of Israel?" I find this interpretation philologically far-fetched; but to be fair to him, I cannot say that I have ever seen the verb *lariv* used of the dove's complaint.

31. For a fuller discussion of the theme in love poetry, both Arabic and Hebrew, see Scheindlin, *Gazelle*, 79–83.

32. Noted by the thirteenth-century copyist of MS Oxford 1971, Joshua Halevi, and pointed out by Levin, "Biqashti eit sheʾahava nafshi," 118.

33. The Sufi, Ibn al-ʿArīf, lived in Almería, where Halevi had good connections. For his use of the poem, see his *Maḥāsin al-majālis*, 50, 91, and my discussion in Scheindlin, "Ibn Gabirol's Religious Poetry and Sufi Poetry."

34. Schirmann, *Hashira haʿivrit*, 1:429, says that this poem shows the state of Halevi's thinking before the Kuzari, since its way of thinking is not reflected there at all. It seems to me that Halevi's poem is quite in the spirit of the rabbi's remark in the Kuzari (1:115) that Israel ought to accept her humiliation in the spirit of subjugation to God's will.

CHAPTER 3

1. Brody, *Dīwān*, 3:220 (poem 122, lines 25–36).

2. The favorable interpretation is not arbitrary; it is made possible by the dreamer's application of the image of the mountain to the figure representing sin. A famous Talmudic passage says that at the time of the last judgment, the saved, observing the collapse of the forces of evil, will exclaim at what a great mountain they managed to overcome in life (Babylonian Talmud, Suka 52a).

Another encounter with one's own sins in a dream and the quest for an interpreter occurs in a poem by Halevi published by Fleischer, "Ḥomarim veʿiyunim liqrat mahadura ʿatidit shel shirei rabi yehuda haleivi," 116. In the poem at Brody,

Dīwān, 3:182–83 (poem 99), Halevi imagines an angel at his bedside waking him to a night vigil.

3. Jewish: Babylonian Talmud, Berakhot 57b. Philosophical: Israeli, "Book on the Elements," with a discussion of the antecedents in Islamic and Greek philosophy.

4. Kuzari 3:5. See Silman, *Philosopher and Prophet*, 246 and n. 36.

5. From "My Meditations on Your Name," Brody, *Dīwān*, 3:65, trans. and interpreted in Scheindlin, *Gazelle*, 164–69, and in Wolfson, *Through a Speculum*, 174. The allusion to Moses is via the quotation of Exod. 34:6 at the end of this selection.

6. Brody, *Dīwān*, 3:3 (poem 1), undoubtedly, to judge from its last verse, a *reshut* for Nishmat, which began the public part of the services of Sabbaths and festivals.

7. Ibid., 3:230 (poem 128, vv. 16–19). This important poem is discussed at length by Heinemann, "Hafilosof vehameshorer," 163–68, whose reading *tekhunato* instead of Brody's *tevunato* in v. 17 I have adopted. The word I have translated "unbounded" is interpreted as "indefinable" by Heinemann. For the mirrors, see Lev. Rabba 1:14, commenting on Ezek. 43:3.

8. Lines 4 and 5 of the poem just quoted.

9. Silman, *Philosopher and Prophet*, 183–215; Wolfson, *Through a Speculum*, 163–73. Wolfson's important discussion of the vision of the divine in Halevi, emphasizing Halevi's continuity with *merkava* mysticism, is supported by his many quotations from Halevi's poetry, 173–81. Lobel, *Between Mysticism and Philosophy*, 89–145, provides a thorough discussion of the vocabulary of witnessing God's presence in the Kuzari and in Islamic mystical and philosophical writings.

10. Brody, *Dīwān*, 3:122–23 (poem 64), lines 6–12. Like poem 2, it is an *ofan*, designed for the *qedusha* preceding the *Shema* in the morning service.

11. Jarden, *Shirei haqodesh*, 3:889 (poem 393), lines 8–10. The attribution of the poem to Halevi was apparently rejected by Schirmann; for his reason, see Davidson, *Otsar hashira vehapiyut*, 4:343 (no. 2206). But the counterarguments by Shimon Bernstein, in "Shelosha shirim bilti yeduʿim shel rabi yehuda haleivi," seem reasonably convincing.

12. Brody, *Dīwān*, 3:7–8 (poem 6), lines 10–13.

13. Ibid., 4:179–80 (poem 79), lines 18–20. Similar sentiments are found in Brody, *Dīwān*, 4:194 (poem 91), and Jarden, *Shirei haqodesh*, 3:855 (poem 375).

14. The phrase "other than You" is connected with the faculty of sight in Isa. 64:3: "No eye *other than Yours* has seen what He will do for those who wait for Him." The rabbinic tradition (Babylonian Talmud, Sanhedrin 99a and elsewhere) applies the verse to the World to Come, as if it means that no one but God can imagine what the rewards of the righteous in the World to Come will be like. Halevi is taking it to mean that the eye cannot see God, but it can infer things about Him by contemplating something else, i.e., His acts.

15. Brody, *Dīwān*, 3:6–7 (poem 5), lines 4–6.

16. Altmann, "The Delphic Maxim in Medieval Islam and Judaism."

17. The wording is that of Wolfson, *Through a Speculum*, 164, based on Wolfson's analysis of the relevant passages in the Kuzari.

18. Brody, *Dīwān,* 3:3–4 (poem 2, v. 3).

19. Ibid., 3:286–93 (poem 145, lines 39–42).

20. Ibid., 3:304 (poem 152, lines 1, 5–6, 13–14).

21. Ibid., 3:153 (poem 84, lines 5–7).

22. As demonstrated amply by Elliot Wolfson in the pages cited in the preceding notes. See also Hughes, *Texture of the Divine,* a study of three medieval texts dealing with the divine vision, two by Muslims and one by a Jew.

23. Lobel, *Between Mysticism and Philosophy.*

24. Wolfson, *Through a Speculum,* 172 n. 178.

25. Kuzari 4:17; discussed by Lobel, *Between Mysticism and Philosophy,* esp. 90–91, and already noted by Kaufmann, *Jehuda Halewi,* 114.

26. Brody, *Dīwān,* 3:74–75 (poem 37, v. 5). For good notes on this important but neglected poem, see Hazan, *Torat hashir bapiyuṭ hasefaradi,* 263–64.

27. The image is all the stronger for echoing a powerful moment in the story of Jacob and his sons, Gen. 43:9.

28. Isa. 22:1.

29. Oblivious to the poem's liturgical function, Jarden actually placed it among the pilgrimage poems in his edition.

30. Notably in "So Pressed by Longing" (poem 22) below.

31. Genesis Rabba 55:2; ed. J. Theodor and Ch. Albeck, 2nd ed., 1:592.

32. For more on the connection between this poem and the traditions of love poetry, see Scheindlin, *Gazelle,* 200–201.

33. This, at least, is the interpretation of Abraham Ibn Ezra, Halevi's famous contemporary.

34. The numerical value of *titots* is 890, which, omitting the thousands, as is customary when using Hebrew letters to indicate dates, indicates the year 4890. Persons who are accustomed to using the Hebrew calendar never fail to notice such coincidences.

35. Gerson D. Cohen points out in his "Messianic Postures," 279, that the Hebrew word *titots,* meaning "you will overturn" (with its numerical value), was one of several Hebrew words that had long figured in messianic calculations. For more bibliography on this subject, see Scheindlin, *Gazelle,* 252 n. 3.

This poem does not have to be taken as evidence that 1130 was a turning point in Halevi's life, as is often said in the scholarly literature, certainly not as evidence that Halevi began planning his pilgrimage as a result of the dream. All that the poem proves is that Halevi was capable of being caught up in the messianic enthusiasm characteristic of his age. Baron wisely advises caution in assessing this poem's due historical weight; see the remark in his "Yehudah Halevi: An Answer to an Historic Challenge," 270 n. 56. Gil and Fleischer (*Yehuda haleivi,* 188–89) connect the date of the poem with their conjecture that Halevi intended to go to Egypt in 1130; but the journey in 1130 is only weakly attested; see above, chapter 1, n. 4, and below, chapter 4, n. 28.

36. For another, complementary explanation of the shift to Aramaic, see Komem, "Bein shira linvu'a: ʿIyunim beshirei yehuda haleivi," 685.

37. True, the biblical passage (Num. 12:8) speaks of dreams, like *ḥidot,* as a lower degree of revelation than Moses' direct vision (*mar'e*), but we must not read Halevi's poem casuistically. For the purposes of this poem, and by contrast with *ḥida,* the intense visual quality of the dream is tantamount to the Bible's *mar'e.* And even the biblical passage says that dreams are a kind of revelation.

CHAPTER 4

1. Gil and Fleischer, *Yehuda haleivi,* 421–26 (doc. 40). A reminder to the reader: throughout chapters 4, 5, and 6, texts translated from Arabic are in Roman type, and texts translated from Hebrew are in italics.

2. The poem is found in Brody, *Shirei haḥol: Moshe ibn ezra,* 1:384, poem 64.

3. His father, Abraham Ibn Ezra (1089–1164), was a famous poet, scientific scholar, and the author of a series of Bible commentaries widely studied to this day, a contemporary and townsman of Halevi's, who reports on conversations with Halevi in his commentaries. Isaac Ibn Ezra, Halevi's traveling companion, was also a poet and scientific scholar. Goitein conjectured that he was Halevi's son-in-law. The conjecture hinges on the Arabic word *ʿammuhum,* used in a letter addressed to Isaac to describe Halevi's relationship to Isaac's family (Gil and Fleischer, *Yehuda haleivi,* 332–37 [doc. 21]). The meaning "father-in-law" is not given for the word *ʿamm* by any reference book that I have managed to consult. It means "paternal uncle" and is used as a term of respect for any elder. It can be applied to a father-in-law—or anyone else deserving a respectful term of address or reference—but the pronoun "their" attached to the word in the letter makes "father-in-law" a most unlikely referent, for Halevi could not have been the father-in-law of Isaac's whole family. Goitein himself seems to have changed his mind about the matter, as reported by Menahem Schmelzer, *Isaac ben Abraham Ibn Ezra: Poems* (Hebrew), 14 n. 50; but his original opinion has been perpetuated in the secondary literature and has become the basis of further fanciful conjectures. See below, chapter 6, n. 21, and chapter 10, n. 7. Medieval reports, beginning with Gedalia Ibn Yaḥya and often repeated, that Abraham Ibn Ezra himself was Halevi's son-in-law are merely folklore.

4. Gil and Fleischer, *Yehuda haleivi,* 430–34 (doc. 42). The identification of the author is a plausible conjecture of Goitein, "Mikhtav el rabeinu yehuda haleivi ʿal asifat shirav," 349.

5. Goitein points out that this was accepted social behavior.

6. Brody, *Dīwān,* 3:227 (poem 125). For the diffusion of this poem in Near Eastern rites, see Davidson, *Otsar hashira vehapiyut,* 2:404, no. 3162.

7. From "So Pressed by Longing" (poem 22).

8. Isaac Alfasi, *Halakhot,* Megila 14a, quoted in Maimonides, *Mishne Tora,* Laws of Prayer 11:4.

9. Gil and Fleischer, *Yehuda haleivi,* 427–29 (doc. 41). In translating this letter and others, I have moved the address, ordinarily written on the document's verso, to the beginning so that it will resemble the salutation in our epistolary style.

10. Presumably, devoted to taking care of Halevi, as in the preceding passage.

11. Brody, *Dīwān*, 2:262 (poem 36).

12. Num. 17:23.

13. Brody, *Dīwān*, 2:257–58 (poem 32).

14. Miriam Frenkel, in "Qehilat yehudei aleksandria batqufa hafaṭimit uvatqufa ha'ayubit," 1:126–27, denies him the title of judge because surviving documents of the Alexandrian court to which he was a signatory never refer to him as judge or *ḥaver*. But it is hard to believe that Halevi would so regularly both address and refer to Ibn al-ʿAmmānī by these titles if Ibn al-ʿAmmānī were not entitled to them, and I am not convinced by Frenkel's attempts to resolve the conflict. The silence of court documents does not amount to a refutation of Halevi's explicit testimony.

15. Brody, *Dīwān*, 2:258–60 (poem 33, vv. 1–10).

16. Gil and Fleischer, *Yehuda haleivi*, 324–26 (doc. 19); trans. also by Goitein, *Mediterranean Society*, 5:465. The original letter, presumably in Halevi's own hand, is reproduced as the frontispiece of this book. The letter contains no indication of date, place of writing, or address of the recipient, nor do its contents provide any clear chronological guidance, so all proposals for placing it in the story are completely conjectural. It is generally placed in al-Andalus, soon before Halevi's departure for Egypt, because it mentions Halevi's desire to go east; but the expression would be equally appropriate if the letter had been written in Alexandria.

17. The verse is by Halevi, from a poem published in Stern, "Arabic Poems by Spanish-Hebrew Poets," 262–63. It becomes intelligible in light of a pair of related rabbinic maxims, "A man's feet are his guarantors: they carry him to the place where he is wanted" and "To the place I love, thither my feet carry me" (Babylonian Talmud, Suka 53a). The poet means that though his feet cannot bring him to his friend, his love makes a link between them.

18. Brody, *Dīwān*, 1:23–24 (poem 17, v. 15).

19. Ibid., 2:183 (poem 21). I assume that the two additional lines reported by Brody that occur in the version of this poem used in the Sephardic liturgy are spurious and that they were added in order to adapt the poem to the liturgy. They do not appear in the manuscript tradition of the *Dīwān*. Moreover, the statement that the speaker longs for Jerusalem as the soul longs for the body can have been composed only by someone who was deaf to the conception of body and soul that was current in the writings of Halevi and his contemporaries.

20. Many scholars have suggested that Halevi intended from the first to travel to Palestine via the Sinai. This notion would seem to be ruled out by Halevi's own account of his journey in his epistle to Samuel ben Ḥanania (to be discussed later in this chapter and again in chapter 7), where he explains that he intended to pass through Alexandria directly to Palestine but that he was detained by Ibn al-ʿAmmānī; only when he received an epistle from the Nagid, he says, did he resolve to postpone his pilgrimage in order to come to Cairo. It is entirely possible that when he decided to go to Cairo, he conceived the idea of traveling on to Palestine by the overland route.

That Halevi did not originally intend to go to Cairo would gain support also from his protestation in document 19 (Gil and Fleischer, *Yehuda haleivi*, 325) that he has no intention but to go east as soon as possible—if my assumption that document 19 was written in Alexandria could be substantiated. But this is just as much an assumption as is the opinion that it was written in Spain. It would also gain support from my interpretation of the line "Canaan is my destination, but Cairo is his residence" (quoted in the preceding paragraph but one in the text), if there were any way of knowing for certain that the poem was written in Alexandria when Ḥalfon was in Cairo.

The idea that Halevi might have embarked on his pilgrimage intending to travel overland from Cairo rests on: (1) A passage from Halevi's "Can a Body Be a Room" (poem 20), probably written in al-Andalus, in which he envisions himself traversing deserts as well as oceans. It should go without saying that this is figurative language depicting not a specific itinerary but a journey through liminal space. (2) The Arabic heading to the poem quoted below, 121–22, supposedly mentioning Halevi's return from the road, which has been explained as referring to a failed attempt by Halevi to set out for Palestine from Cairo via the Sinai; but as pointed out below in chapter 5, n. 8, it is impossible to determine whether the pronoun in the heading refers to Halevi or to Ḥalfon. The poem was probably written not in Egypt but in Spain, on internal grounds; and there is no special reason to trust the heading, since we do not know who wrote it or when and whether he had documentary information or was just extrapolating from his interpretation of the poem. (3) The notion that there was a preferred pilgrimage route for Jews leading through the Sinai. The refutation of this fanciful idea would take too long for an endnote; suffice it to say that it is essentially an extrapolation from documents that do not lend themselves to this interpretation.

21. Mann, *The Jews in Egypt and in Palestine under the Fatimid Caliphs,* 1:228–29, citing Wüstenfeld, *Geschichte der Fatimiden-Chalifen,* 80–81.

22. Brody, *Dīwān,* 1:211–14 (epistle 2), contains only part of the epistle. With the subsequent discovery of other fragments, nearly the entire epistle is now extant. See Abramson, "Mikhtav rav yehuda haleivi ʿal ʿaliyato leʾerets yisraʾeil," and the additional fragment in Yahalom, "ʿAliyato shel rabi yehuda haleivi leʾerets yisraʾeil." Since Abramson's article was written before Goitein's publication of the letters by and about Halevi, some of his assumptions have to be updated.

23. The elevation of Jehoiachin by Evil-Merodach, the king of Babylonia, is recorded in 2 Kings 25:27–30 and Jer. 52:31–34. The Hebrew word *nagid* (= leader) is particularly associated with David, and therefore with the entire Judean royal house, in the prophetic writings. See Franklin, "Cultivating Roots."

24. Saladin's provisions for pilgrims are praised by Ibn Jubayr, the Muslim traveler mentioned earlier; see his *Travels,* 55, trans. Francis E. Peters, in idem, *The Hajj,* 110. On the exploitation of pilgrimage as a strategy to obtain charity, see M. R. Cohen, *Poverty and Charity in the Jewish Community of Medieval Egypt,* 80.

25. I.e., he is continually exerting himself for the visitors' comfort.

26. Shiloah is a proverbially gentle stream in Judea; the passage is based on Isa. 8:6 and 8:8.

27. Obscure phrase from Gen. 20:17, apparently used here to mean "protector."

28. The phrase seems to obviate the theory that Halevi traveled to Egypt in 1130,

derived from document 20 by Gil and Fleischer, *Yehuda haleivi* (see above, chapter 1, n. 4, and chapter 3, n. 35). It could be harmonized with the theory by interpreting it to mean that Ḥalfon became Halevi's benefactor two years previously, but that they had met much earlier, but this interpretation seems forced.

29. Note the similar expression in the Arabic letter quoted on 120.

30. Gen. 26:20, where the key words mean "contention" and "contended." Halevi cites the same verse from Genesis with the same distortion of its meaning in his epistle to Ḥabīb of al-Mahdawi, quoted above, 16.

31. Brody, *Dīwān*, 1:144–48 (poem 97, vv. 27–38). On the identification of the Nile with Pishon, see Golb, "Topography of the Jews of Medieval Egypt."

32. Gil and Fleischer, *Yehuda haleivi*, 439–44 (doc. 44).

33. On expressions of anxiety about travel on the Nile, see Goitein, *Mediterranean Society*, 1:296–301, including reference to another letter between the brothers in a similar vein.

34. Brody, *Dīwān*, 1:116 (poem 80). The poem has been interpreted by meaning that Halevi was the one who had gone away and that he was already in Cairo. But the wording of vv. 2 and 4 and the heading in MS Oxford 1970 lend themselves better to the interpretation given here.

35. The meaning of this line is unclear. My translation takes the verb as meaning "to dance" and interprets it as a metaphor for joy. The verb could also mean "occurred" and the line translated "The days of Sukkot fell with you," i.e., fell when I was in your home; but this requires a slight forcing of the language, especially since the subject seems to be "thoughts," rather than "days." A different line of interpretation takes the verb as meaning "to be sick." The line would then imply that Halevi and Ibn al-ʿAmmānī had not been together on Sukkot; Sukkot was metaphorically sickly, but Hanukkah is dead (Gil and Fleischer, *Yehuda haleivi*, 214). This interpretation seems less likely to me in view of the antithesis in the next verse.

CHAPTER 5

1. The epigraph for this chapter is from Brody, *Dīwān*, 2:183–84 (poem 22).

2. Gil and Fleischer, *Yehuda haleivi*, 450–57 (doc. 46, undated).

3. Remember the similar expression in the portion of Halevi's Hebrew epistle to Samuel ben Ḥanania quoted in chapter 3.

4. I.e., his wife, but decorum prevented him from using the word. See the discussion of "So Pressed by Longing" (poem 22) for what may be a similar reticence on Halevi's part.

5. A translation appears in Weinberger, *Twilight of a Golden Age*, 107–12, where the poem is attributed to Abraham Ibn Ezra.

6. Brody, *Dīwān*, 1:40 (poem 30).

7. *Mekhilta derabi yishmaʿel*, ed. Horovitz and Rabin, 81, commenting on Exod. 13:21.

8. Brody, *Dīwān*, 1:73–74 (poem 55). The main argument in favor of the poem's having been written in Spain is that the striking pair of images in the first full stanza—the sundial going backward and the Nile washing the mountains of Spain—

taken together with the reference to Ḥalfon's help in the second stanza gives the impression that Halevi is expressing gratitude to Ḥalfon, in Spain, for offering to help him accomplish his pilgrimage. (An analogous image of the waters of one place washing the land of another occurs in Brody, *Dīwān,* 1:2 [poem 2, v. 5], providing some support for my interpretation.) There is no strong internal argument in favor of its having been written in Egypt. The headings attached to the poem in the manuscripts, insofar as they have been reported in academic articles, provide no sure foothold. They say that the poem was written when someone unexpectedly returned from a trip, but their use of pronouns is so ambiguous that it is impossible to know whether it was Halevi or Ḥalfon who returned; they also do not specify the trip's destination. Readers who take the vague pronouns as referring to Halevi say that the poem was written when Halevi returned from a failed attempt to reach Palestine (which is neither in the heading nor in the poem). Some of these readers make the additional assumption that the failed attempt was to reach Palestine overland from Cairo, while others insist that it was to reach Palestine from Spain. We have no reason to assume that the trip so casually mentioned was anything as momentous as Halevi's journey to Palestine.

9. Zech. 8:19.

10. Brody, *Dīwān,* 2:180 (poem 18).

11. Ibid., 2:182 (poem 20).

12. The connotations of Time were discussed above, 124 and 256 n. 12.

13. Nathan ben Samuel, the secretary of Samuel ben Ḥanania, is well known to geniza scholars. For information about his activities, see Ben-Sasson, "Hamivne, hamegamot, vehatokhen shel ḥibur rav natan habavli," 166–67.

14. Brody, *Dīwān,* 1:112–15 (poem 78, vv. 1–12 and 24–34).

15. Ibid., 1:214–16 (epistle 3, lines 27–68).

16. Cherethites and Pelethites in the Bible were the bodyguards of David, and Benaiah ben Jehoiada was their chief (2 Sam. 20:23); Ethan the Ezrahite was a legendary wise man (1 Kings 5:11).

17. Lit., "He was a Levite and he sojourned there," Judg. 17:1; the significance of this allusion is discussed below.

18. Brody, *Dīwān,* 1:207–10 (epistle 1, lines 9–15; 40–97, with trivial omissions).

19. A witty appropriation of Jer. 2:18; Jeremiah, of course, does not name Cairo, since he wrote more than twelve hundred years before the city existed. But Arabic-speaking Jews like Halevi often used the Hebrew word *mitsrayim,* which in the Bible means "Egypt," to refer to Cairo, because the city is called Miṣr in Arabic (as well as al-Qāhira, from which we get Cairo).

20. An expression from the Babylonian Talmud, Berakhot 5b, meaning "wealth."

21. Davidic language from Ps. 132:18.

22. A play on a familiar rabbinic maxim: "Holy things may be traded upward, not downward" (Babylonian Talmud, Berakhot 28a and elsewhere).

23. Based on a slight emendation proposed by Brody in his commentary.

24. Some manuscripts read *aron* ("box" or "ark") instead of *toren* ("mast"). I prefer *toren* because it yields a more regular rhyme, and because it is unlikely that Halevi meant to say that the ark of the covenant or the ark of Noah were made of

pine, since the Bible orders different woods for their construction. The repeated rhetorical pattern "Not every *x* is a *y*" in this passage recalls a passage in the epistle to Samuel ben Ḥanania, below, 157.

25. Quotation from the Mishna, Menaḥot 4:4, but given a completely different meaning: The Nagid is compared to the golden altar in the Temple, and Aaron Ibn al-ʿAmmānī is compared to the incense that made it functional when offered on it; the meaning is that the Nagid cannot function without Ibn al-ʿAmmānī's help.

26. Brody, *Dīwān,* 1:99–102 (poem 70).

27. Gil and Fleischer, *Yehuda haleivi,* 462–66 (doc. 48).

28. Goitein read the word as "razors," but the reading of Gil and Fleischer seems more likely.

29. This interpretation was offered by Goitein on first publishing the letter in his article "Mikhtav el rabeinu yehuda haleivi ʿal asifat shirav." Gil and Fleischer (*Yehuda haleivi,* 223–24) also think that Abū l-ʿAlā's letter refers to buying passage on a ship, but they interpret the words "east or west" to mean that Halevi had not yet decided whether to travel to Palestine by sea or overland; they justify this interpretation by pointing out that "east or west" is a vague expression that could mean "of any kind at all." But the Arabic word *jihāz* does not ever seem to have meant "voyage" (*haflaga*), as translated by Goitein, or "journey" (*masaʿ*), as translated by Gil and Fleischer. The attested meanings are "merchandise," "provision," "equipment," or "bridal trousseau." While this book was in the press, Professor Joshua Blau's long-awaited *Milon leṭeksṭim ʿarviyim-yehudim* (Jerusalem: Hebrew Language Academy, 2006) appeared. In the entry *jihāz* (100), the meaning "preparations for sailing" is included among other definitions, but the only source cited is Goitein's edition and interpretation of this letter, so the meaning proposed by Goitein remains unattested.

When Abū l-ʿAlā says in the next line that he awaits word "regarding the journey," that could refer to Halevi's trip to Palestine, but it could refer to many things besides doubt as to whether Halevi was still planning to go there; it could just as well be a question of when, to which port, or whether by land or by sea.

30. The poem describing the fountain and pool was quoted above in chapter 4 as "I know a man." The poems on chickens and Hanukkah are Brody, *Dīwān,* 1:196–97 (poem 134), which Halevi sent to Ibn al-ʿAmmānī's son Abū l-Faḍā'il Mevorakh; and ibid., 1:116 (poem 80), quoted at the end of the last section as "Unhappy are my thoughts this Hanukkah." The poem written in a dream, Gil and Fleischer propose, could be Brody, *Dīwān,* 1:175–76 (poem 117). Goitein, "Mikhtav," 343 n. 2, implies that Halevi's poem of consolation to an Egyptian friend on the death of his concubine could also have been cited as an example of a poem on a frivolous subject; but the tone of the poem is not at all jocund and suggests, rather, that the death of a concubine was indeed a death to be taken seriously.

31. The phrase in the letter could also mean "for one who had not seen other poems of Halevi's" and therefore did not realize that he was a very serious person.

32. For a similar view, see Katz, *Benot hashir hanavot,* 80–82.

33. Brody, *Dīwān,* 1:106 (poem 73). The heading in the medieval manuscripts says that it accompanied an epistle.

CHAPTER 6

1. Gil and Fleischer, *Yehuda haleivi,* 470–75 (doc. 50).

2. The second letter, addressed to Master Isaac, in Gil and Fleischer, *Yehuda haleivi,* 476–81 (doc. 51), has substantially the same account as the first:

> Another matter: Someone meddled [on the translation, see n. 3 below] with Master Judah and sent with him a bill of exchange for the apostate Ibn al-Baṣrī. On account of him, he [i.e., Halevi] underwent things that enraged everyone in Alexandria against him [i.e., Ibn al-Baṣrī]. He tried first to get help from the head of the secret service by saying to him, "There is a Jew here with whom my brother sent thirty dinars and he has not turned them over to me. I am a believing Muslim, yet he says to me, 'Travel with me to Palestine so that I can return you to being a Jew.'" The messengers of the secret police went after Halevi and [weari]ed him and when he arrived, [the head of the secret police] knew that that it would be [held] against him, so he said, "This case between you and him is one for the law." Ibn al-Baṣrī returned on the next day and presented himself to the emir, who summoned Halevi, then said, "Go to the court of law." So Ibn al-Baṣrī dragged him to the *qāḍī* and sued him for the thirty dinars and Master Judah was required to take an oath. There was a hubbub against him and if Master Judah were not well known in the town, trouble would have been inevitable. He took the oath and a settlement was written up between them, and Ibn al-Baṣrī started shouting in the streets, "This head of the Jews, their leader, swore a false oath to me!" Afterward, Abū l-Rabīʿ, Master Judah's companion, was summoned to the *qāḍī* and required to take the oath. But he could not swear, because he had a little in his possession, so they made a settlement for a few dirhams and wrote it up.

3. The Arabic word is *tafaḍḍul,* the verbal noun of *tafaḍḍala* used at the beginning of the account translated above in n. 2. This form of the root (fifth conjugation) ordinarily means "to do a favor" and the like, and it is so translated by Gil and Fleischer. But as that meaning seems inappropriate here (unless intended sarcastically), I have translated it as if it were a denominative from *fuḍūlī,* meaning an officious, meddling, or interfering person, though the dictionaries do not give this meaning for the verb.

4. Through a slip of the pen, the writer wrote the name of the Islamic, instead of the Hebrew, month. Goitein deals with this minor confusion in "Haʾim higiaʿ rabi yehuda haleivi el ḥof erets yisraʾeil?," 246.

5. Gil and Fleischer, *Yehuda haleivi,* 480 n. 16, infer that he embarked on May 7; but I think Abū Naṣr would have counted the day he was writing on as one of the four days, so Halevi was probably on the ship on May 8, 9, 10, and 11.

6. Reading the three consonants as *ybq* (= to remain), with Goitein, though it really does look more like the unintelligible *yfq,* as transcribed by Gil and Fleischer.

7. Brody, *Dīwān,* 1:13 (poem 11).

8. Exod. 9:24.

9. Inferred from the poem in Brody, *Dīwān,* 1:67–68 (poem 50), by Goitein, "Mikhtav," 345.

10. For attempts to identify him more exactly, see n. 21 below.

11. Goitein, "Haparasha haʾaḥarona beḥayei rabeinu yehuda haleivi," 21–47 (where the document was first published), conjectures at p. 41 that *shalunya* is a cloth made in a Spanish town that he calls (using Hebrew characters) "Shalon," presumably Jalón; he says that it is near Saragossa and that it was famous for its fabrics. But I can find no such place mentioned in the source cited by Goitein.

12. I.e., the Temple; the epithet comes from Isa. 29:1.

13. Brody, *Dīwān,* 1:10 (poem 8). Goitein, in "Haparasha haʾaḥarona," 28, thinks that the poem was written on Halevi's arrival in Alexandria; Schirmann (*Letoledot,* 1:307), on returning from an unknown trip eastward; Yahalom ("Dīwān and Odyssey," 42 n. 64), while on the ship in Alexandria waiting to sail for Palestine.

14. Scheiber, "Igeret lo yeduʿa miyhuda haleivi lishmuʾeil hanagid, negid mitsrayim," with an important interpretive contribution by Goitein, "Leʾigarto haḥadasha shel rabeinu yehuda haleivi zqʾl." That the epistle, of which only a fragment remains, was written on the ship in Alexandria is far from certain. The Arabic heading is broken at the beginning of the lines, so that all that can be read is ". . . for resurrection to our master and Nagid Samuel, may his name be established forever, when he was on the ship. . . . dria." Goitein asserts that the opening word is part of the eulogy for the dead and that the opening originally read, "By Judah Halevi, may his memory be for blessing and resurrection," though there does not appear to be nearly enough room for all those words. Scheiber and Goitein agree that the broken word ending with the letters "dria" was Alexandria. But Scheiber proposes to read "to Alexandria," and Goitein proposes "in Alexandria." There is no basis for a decision, and neither scholar considers that it could just as well have been "from Alexandria." In reading "to Alexandria," Scheiber assumes that the author of the letter was on a ship approaching Alexandria from the Mediterranean (and was therefore written in 1140) and does not consider that it could equally have been written while Halevi was approaching Alexandria on the Nile after meeting with the Nagid. Goitein was influenced in his interpretation by the metaphor of storm and waves in line 10, which made him think of the ship in harbor unable to sail, as stated in Gil and Fleischer, *Yehuda haleivi,* 470–75 (doc. 50); Goitein also connected both passages with "This Wind of Yours" (poem 24). But the document says explicitly that Halevi was detained not by a storm but by a contrary wind, and the poem could have been written at any time.

15. Not necessarily a *maqāma,* as assumed by Scheiber; more likely a poem, because the practice was to attach a poem to an epistle. The Hebrew word *maḥberet* did not yet exclusively mean a *maqāma,* as it later would; since it literally means "something put together," like *ḥibur,* it could be used as a calque of the Arabic word *ta'līf* (a composition), as in Abraham Ibn Daud's *Sefer haqabala;* see G. D. Cohen,

Book of Tradition, 59 of the Hebrew section; or of *naẓi,* a common word for poetry that literally means "stringing together."

16. As do Scheiber and Goitein in their articles mentioned above in n. 14.

17. Gil and Fleischer, *Yehuda haleivi,* 482–83 (doc. 52).

18. Goitein, "Haʾim higiaʿ rabi yehuda haleivi el ḥof erets yisraʾeil?," 245–50.

19. The reason for preferring the printed editions' reading "Jonathan ben Levi" over the manuscripts' reading "Judah Halevi" in Benjamin's account is that all the other graves near Tiberias mentioned by him are of first- and second-century rabbis, not of medieval figures. Ordinarily, there would be a presumption that the manuscript readings are to be preferred over those of the printed edition; accordingly in his note, Adler accepted the identification of Halevi's grave as certain and proving that Halevi reached Palestine; see Benjamin of Tudela, *Travels,* ed. Adler, 29 n. 1; his opinion is accepted by Elḥanan Reiner in his "ʿAliya vaʿaliya leregel, 1099–1517," 31. Thanks to Professor Reiner for calling my attention to these sources. The tradition that Halevi is buried somewhere in the Land of Israel is affirmed by other traditions cited by Reiner, 31 n. 20. But to confirm our suspicions, Isaac ben Joseph, an Aragonese kabbalist who visited Tiberias in 1334, also reports on graves of tannaim there, including Jonathan ben Levi and of two medieval figures—Maimonides and Rabbi Zemah Gaon—but not Halevi's; nor does Halevi's grave figure in the thorough inventory of graves of important ancient and medieval Jewish figures in the travelogue by an unnamed disciple of Naḥmanides dating from about 1306 to 1312; see Simḥa Assaf, "Toṣeʾot erets yisraʾeil," 74–90, esp. 84. Other distinguished Andalusi sages were fancifully said to have been buried in Palestine; a few examples are given in Kaufmann, "Jehuda Halewi," 150. Thus, doubt lingers.

20. Gil and Fleischer, *Yehuda haleivi,* 491–94 (doc. 54).

21. Goitein, *Mediterranean Society,* 2:592 n. 17, identifies him as a brother of Isaac Ibn Ezra, a guess as good as any other. It is also conceivable that he was a son or grandson of one of Moses Ibn Ezra's brothers, as suggested by Dinur, *Yisraʾeil bagola,* vol. 3, part 3, 448 n. 37. Sarah Katz, working on the assumption that Isaac Ibn Ezra was Halevi's son-in-law, suggested that young Judah was Halevi's grandson, presumably Halevi's namesake mentioned in "So Pressed by Longing" (poem 22). This suggestion was adopted by Fleischer in his "Rabi yehuda haleivi," 270–73, necessitating an elaborate disquisition on the ages of the various characters in their n. 127. Fleischer spun this identification into a family drama according to which Halevi was angry that Judah was coming because he had long before conceived and dictated to his family a plan for Judah and his mother to follow him only after he was settled in Palestine. This fantasy has no textual foundation whatever. Furthermore, as we have seen, the notion that Isaac Ibn Ezra was married to Halevi's daughter can confidently be rejected; see above, chapter 4, n. 3.

22. What Abū Naṣr says is, "He said that Master Joseph ben al-Shāmi died in Nisan and Joseph Ibn Megash in Sivan; see how these three excellent men died within five months." It was reasonably assumed by Goitein, who first published the document, that the third unnamed person is Halevi and that he must have died in Tammuz or Av.

23. Remember the discussion of it in chapter 1, above, 23.

CHAPTER 7

1. Baḥya Ibn Paquda, *Al-hidāya ilā farā'iḍ al-qulūb,* 392.

2. The astute early study of Kaufmann, "Jehuda Halewi," provides the fullest account of this type. Franz Rosenzweig, in his commentary on the poems, was also thoroughly attuned to themes of personal piety in Halevi's pilgrimage; see his *Jehuda Halevi: Zweiundneunzig Hymnen und Gedichte Deutsch.* Fleischer absolutely denies that internal religious motives played any role in Halevi's pilgrimage; see his "Tamtsit artseinu umashma'utah," in which he characterizes Halevi's journey as "essentially political, not religious" and calls Halevi "not a pilgrim but an *oleh,*" a perversely modernizing reading that flies in the face of Halevi's own words.

3. For sources, see above, chapter 4, n. 22.

4. That the soul has three parts or faculties is standard medieval theory, going back to Plato. These three were associated with the Hebrew synonyms used here: *nefesh* (vegetative soul); *ruaḥ* (animal soul); and *neshama* (rational soul).

5. "Your Words Are Scented" (poem 18); Kuzari 1:13 and 4:25, near the end.

6. See, for example, Abraham Ibn Ezra's commentary on Prov. 20:27. The expression "pure lamp" is found in Exod. 31:8 and elsewhere.

7. "I have heard, and I believe" recalls the familiar Arabic expression of obedience to a superior, *sam'an watā'atan* ("to hear is to obey"), but more to the point, it recalls a similar expression in Halevi's important anti-philosophical poem "O You Whose Name Is Yah," Brody, *Dīwān,* 3:230 (poem 128).

8. According to the rabbinic tradition, the sacred objects of the Tabernacle and the Temple were buried for safekeeping in anticipation of the destruction of the Temple in 586 BCE; for versions of and sources for this legend, see Ginzberg, *Legends of the Jews,* 1:573, 643, and esp. 645.

9. In the Ode to Jerusalem (poem 16); the gates of Zion and the gates of heaven figure prominently in poems 19, 20, 26, and in the story told in the epilogue. They are also mentioned in the Kuzari (2:14, 23). The expression originates in the story of Jacob's ladder (Gen. 28:10–22), according to which Jacob named the site of the vision Beth-el and called it "the gate of heaven." Rabbinic exegesis associated the place with the site of the Temple. But Halevi extended the image to all the places where prophets received revelations, i.e., the entire Land of Israel and associated regions. Perhaps the prominence of these spiritual gates in his imagination has something to do with the fact that the gates of Jerusalem were objects of veneration for Jewish pilgrims, as shown by a geniza text noted by Mann, *Texts and Studies,* 1:458, which preserves prayers to be recited in their presence; the text was published by Lea Goldenfeld in the newspaper *Ha'arets,* May 18, 1972. See also J. Braslavi (Braslavsky), "Madrikh yerushalayim min hageniza haqahirit"; and Halevi's poem in Brody, *Dīwān,* 3:86–87 (poem 45).

10. Isa. 52:8, quoted by the rabbi in connection with his journey to the Land of Israel in Kuzari 5:23: "The visible *Shekhina* appears only to a prophet or a community acceptable to God in the special place; that is what is expected because of His saying: For they will see eye to eye when God returns to Zion," and as we say in our prayers: "May our eyes behold You returning to Your home, to Zion."

That preferential treatment will be accorded those buried in the Land of Israel at the time of resurrection is mentioned in many rabbinic sources such as Babylonian Talmud, Ketubot 111b and Genesis Rabba 96:5, ed. Theodor and Albeck, 2:857 and 3:1198. I have not found any clear statement in the ancient Jewish tradition that the Land of Israel is the exclusive site of the resurrection of the dead, as seems to be implied in "Your Words Are Scented" (poem 18), where this doctrine is attributed to the patriarchs. In the Kuzari, Halevi twice puts into the mouth of the king the statement that this is the belief of Christians. There are many sources in both Judaism and Islam for the Land of Israel as the site of the last judgment. Islamic tradition, too, accords priority in resurrection to those buried near the Temple Mount or on the Mount of Olives: see Hirschberg, "The Sources of Moslem Traditions Concerning Jerusalem," 344.

11. Bible translations misleadingly render the Hebrew word *ʿafar* in this verse and elsewhere in the Bible as "dust," but in premodern Hebrew, it means "earth," or "soil," as in "for you are earth, and to earth you will return" (Gen. 3:19). Halevi's interpretation plays on the similarity of the verbs used in the petition and the justification, *laḥon* and *leḥonein*. These verbs, from the same root, cover a range of meanings, including "to show favor," "spare," "be gracious," and "pity." God is asked to restore Jerusalem because her servants care deeply for her. We can see how the nuances of the verse's verbs were understood in Halevi's time by means of Saadia's Arabic translation-paraphrase: "I ask you, O Lord, to take charge of Zion in Your mercy, for it is time to have pity on her, the time has come; and Your servants are satisfied even with its stones and have pity on its soil out of reverence." In his commentary, he adds: "When the people formerly were in the Holy Land, they took it lightly and sinned in it, but now that it is a ruin they seek it and revere its soil; all the more [would they if it were] rebuilt." From *Tehilim ʿim targum ufeirush hagaʾon rabeinu saʿadya ben yoseif al-fayyumi*, ed. Kāfiḥ, 223.

12. It is tempting to believe that this variant of the legend of the things buried before the destruction that will reappear at the redemption, found in *Midrash Tanḥuma*, ed. Buber, *Behaʿalotekha* 16, f. 25b, was known to Halevi and influenced his thinking. It may be a coincidence, but the expression "the pure lamp," commented on a few paragraphs back, occurs in the same passage in the *Tanḥuma*.

13. It has already come up twice, in the poem "Detour Me through Cairo," quoted above, 110; and in "Sweet Singers, Bring Your Lyres to Lovelies," quoted above, 132–34. See also the discussions of poems 14, 16, 20, and the Epilogue. The Kuzari's concluding section begins in 5:22.

14. Kuzari 2:9–24. On the *faḍāʾil* of Jerusalem in Arabic literature, see Sivan, "The Beginnings of the *Faḍāʾil al-Quds* Literature."

15. In rapid succession, from Isa. 6:4; Jer. 15:5; and Isa. 51:18.

CHAPTER 8

1. Deut. 32:49.

2. See, for example, the letter published in Mann, *The Jews in Egypt and in Palestine under the Fatimid Caliphs*, 2:189–91.

3. Deut. 34:10.

4. Exod. 4:11.

5. Ps. 84:4; Exod. 19:4; Deut. 32:11. For more on bird imagery in Halevi's poetry, see the discussion of "Distant Dove, Sing Your Song Well" (poem 6) and "This Wind of Yours" (poem 24).

6. Yosef Yahalom, in his "ʿAliyato shel rabi yehuda haleivi leʾerets yisraʾeil," 38, offers the inviting suggestion that it was adopted by Ashkenazic Jews resident in Acre at the time of Halevi's arrival in Palestine.

7. The segmentation in the Ode to Jerusalem is, however, not effected by the kind of transition-verse (*takhalluṣ*) typical of the *qaṣīda*. On the formal level, the Ode to Jerusalem has much in common with Halevi's unusually long and notably personal love poem in Brody, *Dīwān,* 2:7 (poem 4).

8. The prominence of the gates of Jerusalem in Halevi's imagination and the tradition behind it was pointed out above, 159, and chapter 7, n. 9.

9. *Karmel* in v. 14 refers not to Mount Carmel, the site of Elijah's confrontation with the priests of Baal, but means "agricultural land," as in Isa. 29:17 and 32:15. Contrast the usage in "Your Words Are Scented" (poem 18).

10. Expressions connoting "chosen" occur vastly more frequently in the Bible with reference to Jerusalem than in connection with the Jewish people.

11. Dan. 12:12.

CHAPTER 9

1. On *zuhd* poetry, see above, 25–26. Halevi wrote a penitential meditation in which he mentions being forty; see Brody, *Dīwān,* 4:138–57 (poem 62, line 29).

2. On the heart as the seat of the imaginative faculty in Halevi, see Wolfson, *Through a Speculum,* 181–87.

3. The former in "O God, the Joy of Being near You" (poem 12); the latter, in the poems and epistles to Nathan and Samuel ben Ḥanania.

4. See above, 161.

5. Coming in the context of other sites at which God revealed Himself to prophets, *karmel* in this poem should be taken as a place name; contrast the more general usage in the Ode to Jerusalem (poem 16, v. 14).

6. On the motif of gates, see above, chapter 7, n. 9.

7. This point emerges from a balanced reading of the Kuzari. See, for example, Kogan, "Al-Ghazali and Halevi on Philosophy and the Philosophers."

8. It is so explained by Ibn Janāḥ and David Qimḥi in their eleventh- and twelfth-century Hebrew-Arabic dictionaries.

9. Lit., "Have we in East or West a place of hope on which we can be secure except. . . ."

10. Neither Samuel David Luzzatto—in his *Betulat bat yehuda,* 56 n. 1, or his *Dīwān rabi yehuda haleivi,* 42—nor Brody, *Dīwān,* 2:119–20 (commentary section), explained this verse in political terms. The political interpretation appears in Baer, "Hamatsav," 23, and it figures prominently in the touching historical tale "Hanishʾar betoleda," by Asher Barash.

11. Kuzari 2:13–14. Halevi justifies his conception of the extent of the Holy Land by citing Exod. 23:31 and Deut. 1:19.

12. This poem is often said to be a response to a person or persons who criticized Halevi for going to Fustat instead of going directly to Palestine. This interpretation goes back to the Arabic headings in several of the medieval *dīwāns*, but it is not borne out by an independent reading of the poem that gives due attention to the poem's structure or sufficient weight to the turn in v. 11. The headings in medieval copies of Halevi's poems are no more authoritative than any other secondary literature, since they often reflect not an independent tradition about a poem's background and meaning but the copyist's own, sometimes faulty, interpretation of the text. Modern readers who were not led astray by the headings of this poem include Graetz, *Geschichte der Juden,* 6:139; Brody (in the heading that he composed for the poem in his edition); and Brann, "Intertextual Irony," 372. Of the medieval manuscript headings that have been published, one got it right: see Ratzhaby, "Miluʾim likhtovot ʿarviyot leshirei yehuda haleivi," 153–55, item 53.

13. In the Arabic edition by Baneth and Ben-Shammai, 56. The similarity in wording to the medieval translation by Judah Ibn Tibbon is particularly striking.

14. This opinion, though rejected by Halevi's friend Abraham Ibn Ezra in his commentary on Gen. 2:10–11, was generally accepted by medieval Jews.

15. The translation of verse 16 of the Hebrew text is based on the emendation proposed by Ehrlich and quoted by Brody in his notes. In v. 17, the translation follows the reading of a Saint Petersburg manuscript cited by Yosef Yahalom, in his forthcoming article "Maʿagalot erets yisraʾeil"; my thanks to Professor Yahalom for permitting me to read a draft of the article.

16. "Scoffer," in verbal form, is found in Ps. 119:51; "friend" in Job 16:2; "spokesman" in Job 33:23; "eloquent," as in the noun *melitsa,* Prov. 1:6 and in accordance with the most common meaning of the word in medieval Hebrew; see Eliezer Ben-Yehuda, *Milon halashon haʿivrit,* 4:3040b and 3041b.

17. The references cited by Kaufmann, "Jehuda Halewi," 129 n. 2, make a plausible case that Halevi was subject to pressure to convert, as was undoubtedly routine in Muslim and Christian courts alike. As Baron put it in his "Yehudah Halevi," 252: "The close social and intellectual intercourse with [the Jews'] Moorish neighbors had produced assimilatory trends which threatened to submerge the identity of large portions of peninsular Jewry."

18. The Kuzari (5:23) mentions the quest for expiation, but this motive is only one among several—and not the primary one—that the rabbi gives for making his journey. Halevi mentions his regret for the sins of his youth in (oblique) connection with his pilgrimage also in his epistle to Nathan ben Samuel above, 128. Based on the passage of the Kuzari and the poem under discussion, Kaufmann, "Jehuda Halewi," 130–31 and 149–50, emphasizes Halevi's guilt as his primary motive for the pilgrimage and attributes this guilt to Halevi's regrets about the earlier stage in his life when he, like so many others, had fallen into religious doubt and gone astray after foreign thought. Ephraim Hazan, in his *Torat hashir bapiyut hasefarad,* 296, rightly criticizes Kaufmann for citing as evidence passages from Halevi's liturgical

poems, with their conventional expressions of public sentiments. But the connection between the pilgrimage and expiation is confirmed by the personal poems and documents cited above. The guilt was present, but I would relate it to Halevi's regret for his whole earlier, more worldly, way of life—with philosophy as only one aspect of that worldliness.

19. Quoted by Ibn Abī Dunyā, in *Kitāb al-tawakkul ʿalā l-lāh,* 43; for another use of the image of ships and sailing in preaching on *tawakkul,* see below, chapter 10, n. 26.

CHAPTER 10

1. "Where Can I Find You, Lord?" (poem 2) is a good example.

2. The verb used here to describe God's act has a rich religious history, both in its Hebrew form *sibeiv* and its Arabic form *sabbaba,* as do the cognate nouns *siba* in Hebrew and *sabab* in Arabic. As a philosophical term, the noun means "cause" and can be used of God in the sense that He is the First Cause, the source of the motion of the universe. As a religious term, it is used to refer to the mundane causes to which people attribute the things that befall them; in the religious discourse of Islam, one who practices *tawakkul* attributes his fortune, whether good or bad, to no intermediate cause but to God.

3. The poem is "With All My Heart," in Brody, *Dīwān,* 2:221 (poem 10); Scheindlin, *Gazelle,* 130–35. The Name of God is often, in Halevi's poetry, "a hypostatic entity . . . inscribed within the soul," as formulated by Wolfson, *Through a Speculum,* 183–85, where this and other examples are adduced. Wolfson's point is that in so concretizing God's Name, Halevi is continuing a tradition of *merkava* mysticism. That may be so; but the concretizing of the abstract is also characteristic both of Halevi's poetics and of his life story.

4. Dov Jarden, in his commentary to this poem (*Shirei haqodesh lerabi yehuda haleivi,* 4:936), cites two passages in Halevi's poetry, both of an eschatological nature, and one passage from the Talmud in support of this usage.

5. For references to the gates of heaven in Halevi, see above, chapter 7, n. 9. For the special status of the Land of Israel with respect to resurrection, see above, chapter 7, n. 10.

6. The phrase rendered "my wife, my children" is the vague *benei beiti,* literally, "members of my household." I have included "wife" in the translation because the Hebrew phrase is the sort of expression regularly used for wife in a culture that considered it rude to mention one's wife by name or even to use the word. Documented circumlocutions include Hebrew *baʿalei habayit* and Arabic *ahl al-bayt,* both temptingly similar to the expression used in the poem. The Arabic phrase *man ʿindī* ("the one with me") in the document quoted above, 120, is another example of this reticence. But the expression could well have been intended in the more general sense.

7. I cannot accept Gil and Fleischer's assumptions that: (1) the Isaac mentioned in this poem is necessarily Isaac Ibn Ezra (since Isaac was one of the most common

Hebrew names used in this period); (2) Isaac Ibn Ezra was Halevi's son-in-law (refuted above, chapter 4, n. 3); (3) Halevi attempted to make the pilgrimage twice, once in 1130 and again in 1140 (even if he did go to Egypt in 1130, there is no reason to assume that he went for the same reason as in 1140); and (4) Halevi would not have written two poems dealing with similar content on the same occasion. I therefore see their discussion as unnecessarily confusing the issue.

8. Scheindlin, *Wine, Women, and Death,* 3–4; for a full study of garden imagery in this period in both Hebrew and Arabic, see Decter, *Iberian Jewish Literature.*

9. Zech. 9:12. Notice how the national valence of the expression as used in Zechariah has been replaced in the poem by the personal.

10. See above, 17–18.

11. Literally translated, v. 5 reads: "Buried alive in a wooden box (or coffin), neither / land nor four but less." The Talmudically educated reader immediately recognizes the number four in connection with land as referring to the minimal sizes of a grave or of a person's legal extension; see *Entsiqlopedya talmudit,* ed. Meir Bar-Ilan, 2:156–59. The verse translation "a place too small even to call a space" is an attempt to cram this concept into ten intelligible syllables.

12. The concept and the image were discussed above, 24.

13. Goitein, *Mediterranean Society,* 5:462. The date of the incident has recently come into question.

14. Babylonian Talmud, Berakhot 54b.

15. Goitein, *Mediterranean Society,* 5:461, connects this poem and "My God, I Beg You Not to Break" (poem 28) with the geniza fragment published in Gil and Fleischer, *Yehuda haleivi,* doc. 51, and translated above, 145, describing Halevi's wait in the harbor of Alexandria for the wind to shift to the west. Goitein thinks that "This Wind of Yours" (poem 24) was written during the waiting period, and "I Shout to God" (poem 27) on the last day, when the wind was already shifting, and that both poems were given to Abū Naṣr b. Abraham along with the letter for Samuel ben Ḥanania, and in that way they entered the *dīwān* that was collected in Egypt. It seems to be poor historical methodology to assume that a poem written during a storm must have been written during the one storm that the historian happens to know about, and poor literary criticism to assume that a poet must have written about a situation at the moment of experiencing it, rather than while contemplating it in tranquility, in Wordsworth's phrase.

16. Stetkevych, *Zephyrs of Najd,* 114–34.

17. For this very technique using the same rhyme, in a Hispano-Arabic poem that Halevi could have known, see al-Sawisi, *Malik ishbīliya al-shāʿir al-muʿtamid ibn ʿabbād,* 164 (poem 67).

18. See the discussion of "Distant Dove, Sing Your Song Well" (poem 6) and, among the pilgrimage poems, "Can a Body Be a Room" (poem 20).

19. Moses Ibn Gikatilla, as quoted by Abraham Ibn Ezra in his commentary on Psalms, gave the verse a Neoplatonic twist as expressing the soul's yearning to be united with its divine source. Abraham Ibn Ezra, perhaps surprisingly, rejected Ibn Gikatilla's philosophical interpretation of the verse, which was probably inspired by Avicenna's *Recital of the Bird;* see Corbin, *Avicenna and the Visionary Recital,* 186–92.

Halevi was undoubtedly as familiar as his friend Abraham Ibn Ezra with Islamic writings of this type, in which the bird symbolizes the soul returning to its divine source, but he was obviously no longer thinking in Neoplatonic terms by the time that he wrote this poem. See also Tobi, *Proximity and Distance,* 89–90.

20. There is even a Hebrew poem on the subject, by Samuel the Nagid; see Jarden, *Dīwān shemuel hanagid,* 261–66 (poem 108).

21. This usage originated in Ps. 22:21 and 35:17. It is explained by Abraham Ibn Ezra in his commentary to Ps. 22:22 as meaning "separate," i.e., separated from the world-soul while temporarily in the human body; Saadia explains it as meaning "unique," i.e., not comparable to anything terrestrial or celestial; see his *Book of Beliefs and Opinions,* trans. Rosenblatt, 244.

22. Gen. 22:2.

23. Cf. "Stop, My Heart," Brody, *Dīwān,* 2:218 (poem 8, v. 14).

24. Exod. 14:31, which actually describes the Israelites' state after emerging from the Red Sea.

25. The relationship between faith and trust is discussed in Reinert, *Die Lehre,* 13–16; indifference to danger as a hallmark of *tawakkul,* ibid., 162–70.

26. It is found in *Rasā'il ikhwan al-ṣafā',* 4:70–71. For another image of ships in connection with *tawakkul,* see above, chapter 9, n. 19.

27. But this poem should not be connected with the drunken and whirling piety of Sufi poetry, which originated only later, as far as I can determine.

28. The second half of the first verse is an exact quotation from a poem by Ibn Gabirol in Brody and Schirmann, *Shelomo ibn gabirol,* 11 (poem 17, v. 1b), where it is used metaphorically to ask that an uncomfortable situation be allowed to continue.

29. "My Heart in the East" (poem 15) also plays with the same root in its various meanings.

30. Yahalom, "Dīwān and Odyssey," 41–42. I think that Yahalom takes the text too literally when he says that the line about being freed from the Arab yoke implies that the poem cannot have been written on the way from Spain to Alexandria.

31. I.e., to be inserted before the words "Blessed are You, God, Creator of the luminaries." In the current Ashkenazi liturgy, the benediction is preceded by a different biblical verse (Ps. 136:7), but the one used by Halevi in this poem (Isa. 60:1) is found in this position in some texts of the old Palestinian rite; see Elbogen, *Jewish Liturgy,* 19.

32. The verb *y'ts* means "to give" or "to take counsel," hence "to decide," as in Isa. 14:24–27. The source of the maxim is Jer. 10:23.

33. For the use of the Hebrew maxim in geniza documents, see Goitein, *Mediterranean Society,* 5:245 and 329.

EPILOGUE

1. Ibn Yaḥya, *Shalshelet haqabala,* 91–92. This is apparently the earliest occurrence of the story. Its lack of historicity was observed already by Luzzatto, *Betulat bat yehuda,* 25–26.

2. Text says "ankles," obviously a mistake on the part of Ibn Yaḥya.

3. The prohibition was later relaxed, as is evident from the account of a pilgrim (perhaps Maimonides, who was in Palestine in 1165) and other sources cited by Reiner, "ʿAliya vaʿaliya leregel, 1099–1517," 34–36.

4. Poem 1, v. 2.

5. Isa. 52:8, quoted by the Kuzari's rabbi at 5:23, the opening of his final remarks to the king.

6. There is an impressive list of medieval imitations in Goldschmidt, *Seder haqinot letishʿa beʾav,* 14, and 14 n. 40. Another example, perhaps, is the anonymous poem in Carmi, *Penguin Book of Hebrew Verse,* 368, beginning "Come with us, you of the smitten cheeks," which has the same meter as our poem and echoes its phrasing. See also Einbinder, *Beautiful Death,* 70–99.

7. Gil and Fleischer, *Yehuda haleivi,* 484–90 (doc. 53).

8. Prov. 10:7.

9. Above, chapter 3, n. 14.

10. Gil and Fleischer, *Yehuda haleivi,* 495–600 (doc. 55).

Poem Sources

POEM 1

Brody, *Dīwān*, 3:266–68 (poem 141). For a more detailed thematic study of this poem, see Scheindlin, "Islamic Motifs in a Poem by Judah Halevi"; for a detailed structural study, see Tsur, *ʿIyunim bashira haʿivrit biymei habeinayim*, 83–99.

POEM 2

Brody, *Dīwān*, 3:150–51 (poem 82). This poem was the subject of a valuable discussion by Heinemann, "Hafilosof vehameshorer," 168–76 (1945); 176–91 (reprint). Heinemann's reading, though full of wisdom, is very much that of a historian of philosophy. As the ensuing discussion will make clear, I believe that giving due attention to the poem's rhetorical character results in a view of the poem as less self-assured, less comforting than Heinemann makes it out to be.

POEM 3

Brody, *Dīwān*, 2:306–7 (poem 89).

POEM 4

Brody, *Dīwān*, 3:144 (poem 76). A version of the poem with a different last verse is provided by Yahalom, "ʿAliyato shel rabi yehuda haleivi le'erets yisra'eil," 43. Yahalom also compares this poem with poem 3 but reaches a different conclusion. For another liturgical poem presupposing a similar situation and using similar wording, see "The Daughter Who Went out to Meet You," in Brody, *Dīwān*, 4:228 (poem 117).

POEM 5

Brody, *Dīwān*, 3:171–72 (poem 92). The third place name in the second strophe is Cush in the original; I changed it because it did not seem to match the others in English.

POEM 6

Brody, *Dīwān*, 4:222–23 (poem 112). This poem plays a prominent role in Dinaburg's "ʿAliyato," 179–80, as the most explicit evidence for his argument that Halevi's pilgrimage was a summons to emigrate to the Land of Israel.

POEM 7

Brody, *Dīwān*, 4:232 (poem 121).

POEM 8

Brody, *Dīwān*, 3:161–62 (poem 87).

POEM 9

Jarden, *Shirei haqodesh*, 4:921–22 (poem 405). Brody, *Dīwān*, 4:293 (poem 158), is an even smaller fragment of the same poem.

POEM 10

Brody, *Dīwān*, 2:296 (poem 75); Scheindlin, *Gazelle*, 198–201; the translation offered here is new.

POEM 11

Brody, *Dīwān*, 2:302 (poem 86).

POEM 12

Brody, *Dīwān*, 2:160 (poem 4).

POEM 13

Brody, *Dīwān*, 2:159 (poem 3).

POEM 14

Brody, *Dīwān*, 2:167–68 (poem 8).

POEM 15

Brody, *Dīwān*, 2:155 (poem 1). The hesitation between forward and backward motion in this poem has also been noticed, partly on other grounds, by Brann, "Intertextual Irony in Judah Halevi." Levin, *Meʿil tashbets*, 1:267 n. 100, and Brann, "Intertextual Irony," 371, point out lines of Arabic verse that could have been the inspiration for the opening antithesis of East and West.

POEM 16

Brody, *Dīwān*, 2:155–58 (poem 2). See also the classic article by Heinemann, "Hafilosof vehameshorer," 187–89, which also stresses the sense of personal urgency in the poem; Heinemann also uses the poem to show how Halevi used what were then scientific arguments to justify the rabbinic traditions of love of the Land of Israel. For a thoughtful but surprisingly negative evaluation of the poem's rhetorical qualities, see Tsur, *ʿIyunim bashira haʿivrit biymei habeinayim*, 114–18.

POEM 17

Brody, *Dīwān*, 2:160–63 (poem 5). See also the superb reading of this poem by Andras Hamori, "Lights in the Heart of the Sea," which calls attention to the poem's use of Neoplatonic imagery and analyzes the end of the poem as representing the three stages of purification, illumination, and union originating in Plotinus and Proclus.

POEM 18

Brody, *Dīwān*, 2:164–66 (poem 6). See the commentary on the poem by Heinemann, "Hafilosof vehameshorer," 190–95.

POEM 19

Brody, *Dīwān*, 2:180–82 (poem 19). Halevi addresses Egypt as a city (*ʿir*); I have rendered it "land" because in premodern Hebrew *mitsrayim* (and Arabic *miṣr*) were used for both Egypt and Fustat. Although Halevi calls this place a city, he surely did not mean to say that all the events in Israel's sacred history occurred within the limits of the city itself. Rather, as in the case of Jerusalem, he must be using the city name as a synecdoche for the land as a whole.

POEM 20

Brody, *Dīwān*, 2:184–87 (poem 23).

POEM 21

Brody, *Dīwān*, 2:167 (poem 7).

POEM 22

Brody, *Dīwān*, 2:172–74 (poem 13). See Itzhaki, " 'Hetsiqatni teshuqati' liyhuda haleivi," who reads the poem in the light of William James's study of religious conversion; and Tsur, *ʿIyunim bashira haʿivrit biymei habeinayim*, 77–78, whose analysis underscores the ambivalence in the speaker's voice. Jonathan Decter translates and discusses the poem as part of his treatment of themes of estrangement in medieval Hebrew and Arabic poetry; see his *Iberian Jewish Literature*, 62–64. There is also a lengthy discussion of the biographical elements in this poem and in "Anxious or Secure, My Soul Is Yours" (poem 25) in Gil and Fleischer, *Yehudah haleivi*, 196–97.

POEM 23

Brody, *Dīwān*, 2:175–76 (poem 16).

POEM 24

Brody, *Dīwān*, 2:171–72 (poem 12). For a good analysis emphasizing the poem's motion from secular to religious, see Saperstein, "Halevi's West Wind." The last line of the translation makes explicit the remainder of the biblical verse (Amos 4:13) alluded to in the last line of the Hebrew.

POEM 25

Brody, *Dīwān*, 2:170–71 (poem 11).

POEM 26

Brody, *Dīwān*, 2:174 (poem 14).

POEM 27

Brody, *Dīwān*, 2:174–75 (poem 15).

POEM 28

Brody, *Dīwān*, 2:168 (poem 9).

POEM 29

Brody, *Dīwān,* 2:169 (poem 10).

POEM 30

Brody, *Dīwān,* 2:176–79 (poem 17).

Bibliography

Abramson, Shraga. "Mikhtav rav yehuda haleivi ʿal ʿaliyato leʾerets yisraʾeil." *Qiryat sefer* 29 (1952–53): 132–44.

Abū l-ʿAtāhiya. *Dīwān*, ed. Shukrī Fayṣal. Damascus: Maṭbaʿat jāmiʿat dimashq, 1987. Beirut: Dār Ṣādir, 1964.

Altmann, Alexander. "The Delphic Maxim in Medieval Islam and Judaism." In idem, *Studies in Religious Philosophy and Mysticism*, 1–40. Plainview, N.Y.: Books for Libraries, 1969.

Ashtor, Eliyahu. *The Jews of Moslem Spain*. 2 vols. Philadelphia: Jewish Publication Society, 1992; originally published 1960–66.

Assaf, Simḥa. "Toṣeʾot erets yisraʾeil." In idem, *Meqorot umeḥqarim*, 74–90. Jerusalem: Mosad Harav Kuk, 1946.

Baer, Yitsḥaq. "Hamatsav hapoliṭi shel yehudei sefarad bedoro shel rabi yehuda haleivi." *Zion* 1 (1935–36): 6–23.

———. *A History of the Jews in Christian Spain*, trans. Louis Schoffman. 2 vols. Philadelphia: Jewish Publication Society, 1961–66; originally published 1959.

Baḥya ben Joseph Ibn Paquda. *Al-hidāya ilā farāʾiḍ al-qulūb*, ed. Yosef Kāfiḥ. Jerusalem: Vaʿad hakelali liyhudei teiman, 1972–73.

———. *The Book of Direction to the Duties of the Heart*, trans. Menaḥem Mansoor. London: Routledge and Kegan Paul, 1973.

Barash, Asher. "Hanishʾar beṭoleda," by Asher Barash. Tel Aviv: Masadah, 1942–43; translation entitled "The Last in Toledo." In Asher Barash, *Though He Slay Me*, 114–47. Tel Aviv: Masadah, 1963.

Baron, Salo W. "Yehudah Halevi: An Answer to an Historic Challenge." *Jewish Social Studies* 3 (1941): 243–72.

Benjamin of Tudela. *Travels*, ed. and trans. E. N. Adler. London: Henry Frowde, 1907.

Ben-Sasson, Menaḥem. "Hamivne, hamegamot, vehatokhen shel ḥibur rav natan habavli." In *Tarbut veḥevra betoledot yisra'eil biymei habeinayim*, ed. Reuven Bonfil et al., 137–96. Jerusalem: Historical Society of Israel, 1989.

Ben-Yehuda, Eliezer. *Milon halashon haʿivrit*. 8 vols. New York: Thomas Yoseloff, 1960.

Bernstein, Shimon. "Shelosha shirim bilti yeduʿim shel rabi yehuda haleivi." *Hadoar* 19 (1939–40): 151–52.

Bonebakker, S. A. "Prejudice Against Poetry in Early Islam." *Medievalia et Humanistica* 7 (1976): 77–99.

Brann, Ross. *The Compunctious Poet: Cultural Ambiguity and Hebrew Poetry in Muslim Spain*. Baltimore: Johns Hopkins University Press, 1991.

———. "Intertextual Irony in Judah Halevi." In *Judaism and Islam: Boundaries, Communication, and Interaction*, ed. Benjamin H. Hary et al., 368–69. Leiden: Brill, 2000.

———. "Judah Halevi." In *The Literature of Al-Andalus*, ed. M. R. Menocal, R. Scheindlin, and M. Sells, 265–81. Cambridge: Cambridge University Press, 2000.

Braslavi (Braslavsky), J. "Madrikh yerushalayim min hageniza haqahirit." *Erets yisra'eil* 7 (1964): 69–80.

Brenner, Ann. *Judah Halevi and His Circle of Hebrew Poets in Granada*. Leiden: Brill, 2005.

Brody, Ḥayim. *Die schönen Versmasse*. Leipzig: Haag-Drugulin, 1930.

———, ed. *Dīwān yehuda ben shemuel haleivi*. 4 vols. Berlin: Mekize Nirdamim, 1894–1930.

———, ed. *Shirei haḥol: Moshe ibn ezra*. 2 vols. Berlin: Schocken, 1935–41.

Brody, Ḥayim, and Ḥayim Schirmann. *Shelomo ibn gabirol: Shirei haḥol*. Jerusalem: Schocken Institute, 1974.

Carmi, Ted. *Penguin Book of Hebrew Verse*. Harmondsworth, England: Penguin, 1981.

Cohen, Gerson D. *The Book of Tradition (Sefer ha-Qabbalah) by Abraham Ibn Daud*. Philadelphia: Jewish Publication Society, 1967.

———. "Messianic Postures of Ashkenazim and Sephardim Prior to Sabbethai Zevi," originally published 1967 and reprinted in idem, *Studies in the Variety of Rabbinic Cultures*, 271–97. Philadelphia: Jewish Publication Society, 1991.

Cohen, Mark R. *Poverty and Charity in the Jewish Community of Medieval Egypt*. Princeton, N.J.: Princeton University Press, 2005.

———. *Under Crescent and Cross*. Princeton, N.J.: Princeton University Press, 1994.

Corbin, Henri. *Avicenna and the Visionary Recital*, trans. Willard R. Trask. Irving, Tex.: Spring Publications, 1980; originally published 1954.

Davidson, Israel. *Otsar hashira vehapiyut*. 4 vols. New York: Jewish Theological Seminary, 1924–33.

Decter, Jonathan P. *Iberian Jewish Literature: Culture and Change from al-Andalus to Christian Europe*. Bloomington: Indiana University Press, 2007.

Diem, Werner. *Arabische Privatbriefe des 9. bis 15. Jahrhunderts: Textband*. Wiesbaden: Harrassowitz, 1996.

Dinaburg (Dinur), Ben-Zion. "ʿAliyato shel rabi yehuda haleivi leʾerets yisraʾeil vehatesisa hameshiḥit beyamav." In *Minḥa ledavid* (David Yellin Festschrift), ed. S. Assaf, 157–82. Jerusalem: Mass, 1935, reprinted in Yisraʾeil Zamora, *Rabi yehuda haleivi: Qovetz meḥqarim vehaʿarakhot,* 47–83. Tel Aviv: Maḥbarot lesifrut, 1964.

Dinur (Dinaburg), Ben-Zion. *Yisraʾeil bagola.* Vol. 3. Jerusalem: Dvir, 1968.

Einbinder, Susan L. *Beautiful Death: Jewish Poetry and Martyrdom in Medieval France.* Princeton, N.J.: Princeton University Press, 2002.

Elbogen, Ismar. *Jewish Liturgy: A Comprehensive History,* trans. Raymond Scheindlin. Philadelphia: Jewish Publication Society, 1993; originally published 1913 and revised again in 1972.

Elizur, Shulamit. "Vehayamim metsuvim meʾeloa: Goral ʿiver veʾemuna datit bashira haʿivrit bisfarad." In *Sefer yisraʾeil levin,* ed. Reuven Tsur and Tova Rosen, 1:27–43. Tel Aviv: Tel Aviv University Press, 1994.

Entsiqlopedya talmudit. Meir Bar-Ilan, ed. 24 vols. Jerusalem: Hotsaʾat Haʾentsiqlopedya Hatalmudit, 1949.

Fenton, Paul. *The Treatise of Pool.* London: Octagon, 1981.

Fierro, Maribel. "La Religion." In *Historia de España,* ed. Ramón Menéndez Pidal, vol. 8, part 2, 437–546. Madrid: Espasa Calpe, 1997.

Fleischer, Ezra. "Ḥomarim veʿiyunim liqrat mahadura ʿatidit shel shirei rabi yehuda haleivi." *Asupot* 5 (1990–91): 103–81.

———. "Rabi yehuda haleivi: Beiʾurim beqorot ḥayav vitsirato." In *Sefer yisraʾeil levin,* ed. Reuven Tsur and Tova Rosen, 1:241–76. Tel Aviv: Tel Aviv University Press, 1994.

———. "Tamtsit artseinu umashmaʿutah." *Peʿamim* 68 (1996): 4–15.

Franklin, Arnold. "Cultivating Roots: The Promotion of Exilarchal Ties to David in the Middle Ages," *AJS Review* 29 (2005): 91–110.

Frenkel, Miriam. "Qehilat yehudei aleksandria batqufa hafaṭimit uvatqufa haʾayubit: Deyuqana shel ʿilit manhiga." 2 vols. Diss., Hebrew University of Jerusalem, 2001.

al-Ghazzālī, Aḥmad. *Iḥyā ʿulūm al-dīn.* 4 vols. Cairo: Dār iḥyāʾ al-kutub al-ʿarabiyya, n.d.

Gil, Moshe, and Ezra Fleischer. *Yehuda haleivi uvenei ḥugo.* Jerusalem: World Union of Jewish Studies, 2001.

Ginzberg, Louis. *Legends of the Jews.* 2 vols. Philadelphia: Jewish Publication Society, 2003; originally published 1909–46.

Gluck, Andrew L. *Solomon Ibn Gabirol: The Kingly Crown.* Notre Dame, Ind.: University of Notre Dame Press, 2003.

Goitein, S. D. "Haʾim higiaʿ rabi yehuda haleivi el ḥof erets yisraʾeil?." *Tarbiz* 46 (1976–77): 245–50.

———. "Haparasha haʾaḥarona beḥayei rabeinu yehuda haleivi." *Tarbiz* 24 (1954–55): 21–47.

———. "A Jewish Addict to Sufism." *Jewish Quarterly Review* 44 (1953–54): 37–49.

———. "Leʾigarto haḥadasha shel rabeinu yehuda haleivi zq'l." *Tarbiz* 36 (1966–67): 299.

———. *A Mediterranean Society*. 5 vols. Berkeley: University of California Press, 1967–93.

———. "Mikhtav el rabeinu yehuda haleivi ʿal asifat shirav." *Tarbiz* 28 (1958–59): 343–61.

Golb, Norman. "The Topography of the Jews of Medieval Egypt." *Journal of Near Eastern Studies* 24 (1965): 264–66.

Goldreich, Amos. "Possible Arabic Sources for the Distinction between 'Duties of the Heart' and 'Duties of the Limbs.'" *Teʿuda* 6 (1987–88): 179–208.

Goldschmidt, Daniel. *Maḥzor layamim hanoraʾim*. 2 vols. Jerusalem: H. Koren, 1970.

———. *Seder haqinot letishʿa beʾav*. Jerusalem: Mosad Harav Kuk, 1968.

Goldziher, Ignatz. *Muslim Studies*. Vol. 1, trans. C. R. Barber and S. M. Stern. London: George Allen and Unwin, 1967; originally published 1899.

Graetz, Heinrich. *Geschichte der Juden*. 4th ed. Leipzig: Oskar Leiner, 1896.

Hamori, Andras. "Lights in the Heart of the Sea: Some Images of Judah Halevi's." *Journal of Semitic Studies* 30 (1985): 75–83.

Hazan, Ephraim. *Torat hashir bapiyuṭ hasefaradi*. Jerusalem: Magnes, 1986.

Heinemann, Yitsḥaq. "Hafilosof vehameshorer: Beiʾur shivʿa piyutim shel rabi yehuda haleivi." *Keneset lezekher ḥ. n. bialik* 9 (1945): 163–200; reprinted in *Rabi yehuda haleivi: Qovets meḥqarim vehaʿarakhot*, 166–236. Tel Aviv: Maḥbarot lesifrut, 1950.

Hirschberg, J. W. "The Sources of Moslem Traditions Concerning Jerusalem." *Rocznik Orientalistyczny* 17 (1951–52): 314–50.

Hughes, Aaron W. *The Texture of the Divine* (Bloomington: Indiana University Press, 2004).

Ibn ʿAbd Rabbihi, Aḥmad b. Muḥammad. *Dīwān*, ed. Muḥammad Riḍwān al-Dāya. Beirut: Muʾassasat al-risāla, 1979.

———. *Al-ʿIqd al-farīd*. 9 vols. Beirut: Dār al-kutub al-ʿilmiyya, 1983.

Ibn Abī Dunyā. *Kitāb al-tawakkul ʿalā l-lāh*, ed. Jāsim al-Fuhayr al-Dawsarī. Beirut: Dār al-bashāʾir al-islamiyya, 1987.

Ibn al-ʿArīf, Aḥmad b. Muḥammad. *Maḥāsin al-majālis*, ed. M. Asín Palacios. Paris: Geuthner, 1933.

Ibn Ezra, Moses. *Kitāb al-muḥāḍara wa l-mudhākara*, ed. A. S. Halkin. Jerusalem: Hotzaʾat Meqitsei Nirdamim, 1975.

———. "The Lamp Within," trans. Raymond Scheindlin. *Prooftexts* 17 (1997): 260–65.

Ibn Jubayr, Abū al-Ḥusain Muḥammad. *Travels*, trans. Francis E. Peters. In idem, *The Hajj*, 109–14. Princeton, N.J.: Princeton University Press, 1994.

Ibn Khafāja, Abū Isḥāq b. Ibrāhīm. *Dīwān*, ed. Muṣṭafā Ghāzī. Alexandria: Manshaʾat al-Maʿārif, 1960.

Ibn Parḥon, Solomon. *Maḥberet heʿarukh*, ed. S. G. Stern. 2 vols. Pressburg: Anton Edlen von Schmid, 1844.

Ibn Qudama, Muwaffaq al-Din Abū Muḥammad. *Kitāb al-tawwābīn*, ed. Abd al-Qādir al-Urnawut. Beirut: Dār al-kutub al-ʿilmiyya, 1974.

Ibn Yaḥya, Gedalia. *Shalshelet haqabala.* Jerusalem: Hadorot harishonim veqorotam, 1961–62.

Israeli, Isaac. "Book on the Elements." In Alexander Altmann and Samuel M. Stern, *Isaac Israeli,* 133–45. London: Oxford University Press, 1958.

Itzhaki, Masha. " 'Hetsiqatni teshuqati' liyhuda haleivi: ʿItsuv shiri leḥavayat haqonversia." *Teʿuda* 5 (1986): 29–37.

Jarden, Dov. *Dīwān shemuel hanagid: Ben tehilim.* Jerusalem: Hebrew Union College Press, 1966.

———. *Shirat haqodesh lerabi shelomo ibn gabirol.* 2 vols. Jerusalem: n.p., 1971–72.

———. *Shirei haqodesh lerabi yehuda haleivi.* 4 vols. Jerusalem: Dov Jarden, 1978–85.

Judah Halevi. *Kitab al-Khazari by Judah Hallevi,* trans. Hartwig Hirschfeld. 2nd ed. New York: Richards, 1927.

———. *Kitāb al-radd wa l-dalīl fī l-dīn al-dhalīl,* ed. David Baneth and Haggai Ben-Shammai. Jerusalem: Magnes, 1977.

———. *Sefer hakuzari lerabi yehuda haleivi,* trans. Yehuda Even-Shemuʾeil. Tel Aviv: Dvir, 1972.

———. *Sefer hakuzari,* trans. Yehuda Ibn Tibon; ed. by A. Tsifroni. Tel Aviv: Maḥbarot lesifrut, 1964.

Kāfiḥ, Yosef, ed. *Tehilim ʿim targum ufeirush hagaʾon rabeinu saʿadya ben yoseif al-fayyumi.* New York: American Academy of Jewish Research, 1965–66.

Katz, Sarah. *Benot hashir hanavot.* Jerusalem: Rubin Mass, 1997.

Kaufmann, David. "Jehuda Halewi," originally published 1877, reprinted in his *Gesammelte Schriften,* 2:99–151. Frankfurt am Main: J. Kauffmann, 1910.

———. "Torat haʾelahut shel rabi baḥya ibn paquda." In *Meḥqarim basifrut haʿivrit,* trans. Yisraʾeil Eldad. Jerusalem: Mosad Harav Kuk, 1961–62; originally published 1874.

Kogan, Barry S. "Al-Ghazali and Halevi on Philosophy and the Philosophers." In *Medieval Philosophy and the Classical Tradition in Islam, Judaism, and Christianity,* ed. John Inglis, 64–78. London: Routledge Curzon, 2002.

Komem, Ahron. "Bein shira linvuʾa: ʿIyunim beshirei yehuda haleivi." *Molad* 2 (1969): 676–97.

Kraemer, Joel. *Humanism in the Renaissance of Islam.* Leiden: Brill, 1992.

Laoust, Henri. *La Politique de Gazali.* Paris: Geuthner, 1970.

Levin, Yisraʾeil. "Biqashti eit sheʾahava nafshi." *Hasifrut* 3 (1971–72): 116–49.

———. "Haberiḥa min haʿolam el haʾelohim." In *ʿAl shira vesiporet,* ed. Zvi Malachi, 158–59. Tel Aviv: Tel Aviv University Press, 1976–77.

———. *Meʿil tashbets.* 2nd ed. 3 vols. Tel Aviv: Tel Aviv University Press, 1995.

Lobel, Diana. *A Sufi-Jewish Dialogue.* Philadelphia: University of Pennsylvania Press, 2007.

———. *Between Mysticism and Philosophy: Sufi Language of Mystical Experience in Judah Halevi's Kuzari.* Albany: State University of New York Press, 2000.

Luzzatto, Samuel David. *Betulat bat yehuda.* Prague: Landau, 1840.

———. *Dīwān rabi yehuda haleivi.* Lyck: Mekize Nirdamim, 1864.

Maimonides. *Igeret teiman,* ed. Abraham S. Halkin. New York: American Academy for Jewish Research, 1952.

Mann, Jacob. *The Jews in Egypt and in Palestine under the Fatimid Caliphs.* 2 vols. London: Oxford University Press, 1920–22.

———. *Texts and Studies.* 2 vols. New York: Ktav, 1972; originally published 1931.

al-Maqqarī, Aḥmad b. Muḥammad. *Nafḥ al-ṭīb min ghuṣn al-andalus al-raṭīb,* ed. Iḥsān ʿAbbās. 8 vols. Beirut: Dār Ṣādir, 1988.

al-Marrākushī, ʿAbd al-Wāḥid. *Al-Muʿjib fī talkhīs akhbār al-maghrib,* ed. R. P. A. Dozy. Leiden: Brill, 1888.

Massignon, Louis. "Essay on the Origins of the Technical Language of Islamic Mysticism," trans. Benjamin Clark. Notre Dame, Ind.: University of Notre Dame Press, 1997; originally published 1922.

McCarthy, R. J. *Al-Ghazali: Deliverance from Error.* Boston: Twayne, 1980.

Mekhilta derabi yishmaʿel. H. S. Horovitz and I. A. Rabin, eds. 2d ed. Jerusalem: Bamberger & Wahrmann, 1960.

Menocal, M. R., R. P. Scheindlin, and M. Sells, eds. *The Literature of Al-Andalus.* Cambridge: Cambridge University Press, 2000.

Midrash Tanḥuma. Solomon Buber, ed. Vilna: Widow and Brothers Rom, 1885.

Mirsky, Aaron. *Meḥovot halevavot leshirat halevavot.* Jerusalem: Magnes, 1992.

al-Mutanabbī, Abū Tayyib. *Al-ʿarf al-ṭayyib fī sharḥ dīwān abī l-ṭayyib,* ed. Nasīf al-Yāzijī. Beirut: Dār Sādir, 1964.

Nicholson, Reynold A. *The Mystics of Islam.* London: Routledge and Kegan Paul, 1963; originally published 1914.

Pagis, Dan. *Shirei levi ibn al-tabban.* Jerusalem: Israeli Academy of the Sciences, 1967.

Qushayri, Abū l-Qāsim. *Risāla.* Maḥmūd and Sharīf, eds. 2 vols. Cairo: Dār al-kutub al-ḥadītha, 1966.

Rahman, Faizlur. *Prophecy in Islam.* London: George Allen & Unwin, 1958.

Rasāʾil ikhwān al-ṣafāʾ. 4 vols. Beirut: Dār Ṣādir, 1957.

Ratzhaby, Yehuda. "Igeret meirabi yehuda haleivi lerabi ḥabīb." *Gilyonot* 25 (1953): 268–72.

———. "Miluʾim likhtovot ʿarviyot leshirei yehuda haleivi." *ʿAlei seifer* 18 (1993–94): 153–55.

———. "Yesodot sheʾulim befiyutei yehuda haleivi." *Molad,* n.s. 7 (1975–76): 165–75.

Reif, Stefan C. *A Jewish Archive from Old Cairo.* Richmond, England: Curzon, 2000.

Reiner, Elḥanan. "ʿAliya vaʿaliya leregel, 1099–1517." Diss., Hebrew University, 1988.

Reinert, Benedikt. *Die Lehre vom Tawakkul in der klassischen Sufik.* Berlin: Walter de Gruyter, 1968.

Rosen, Tova. "Hamahalakh hasṭrofi beshirat yehuda haleivi—poeṭiqa alternaṭivit?." In *Sefer yisraʾeil levin,* ed. Reuven Tsur and Tova Rosen, 1:315–28. Tel Aviv: Tel Aviv University Press, 1994.

Rosenzweig, Franz. *Jehuda Halevi: Zweiundneunzig Hymnen und Gedichte Deutsch.* Berlin: Lambert Schneider, 1927.

Saadia. *Book of Beliefs and Opinions,* trans. Samuel Rosenblatt. New Haven, Conn.: Yale University Press, 1948.

Safran, Bezalel. "Baḥya Ibn Paquda's Attitude Toward the Courtier Class." *Studies in Medieval Jewish History and Literature* 1 (1969): 154–96.

Saperstein, Marc. "Halevi's West Wind." *Prooftexts* 1 (1981): 306–11.

al-Sawisi, Rida. *Malik ishbīliya al-shāʿir al-muʿtamid ibn ʿabbād*. Tunis: Dār Bū Salāma, 1985.

Scheiber, Alexander. "Igeret lo yeduʿa miyhuda haleivi lishmuʾeil hanagid, negid mitsrayim." *Tarbiz* 36 (1967): 155–57.

Scheindlin, Raymond P. "Contrasting Religious Experience in the Liturgical Poems of Ibn Gabirol and Judah Halevi." *Prooftexts* 13 (1993): 141–62.

———. *The Gazelle: Medieval Hebrew Poetry on God, Israel, and the Soul*. Philadelphia: Jewish Publication Society, 1991.

———. "Ibn Gabirol's Religious Poetry and Sufi Poetry." *Sefarad* 54 (1994): 109–42.

———. "Islamic Motifs in a Poem by Judah Halevi." *Maghreb Review* 29 (2004): 40–52.

———. "Merchants and Intellectuals, Rabbis and Poets: Judeo-Arabic Culture in the Golden Age of Islam." In *Cultures of the Jews: A New History*, ed. David Biale, 313–86. New York: Schocken, 2002.

———. "Moses Ibn Ezra on the Legitimacy of Poetry." *Medievalia et Humanistica*, n.s. 7 (1976): 101–15.

———. "Old Age in Hebrew and Arabic *Zuhd* Poetry." In *Judíos y musulmanes en al-Andalus y el Magreb*, ed. Maribel Fierro, Collection de la Casa de Velázquez, vol. 74, 85–104. Madrid: Casa de Velázquez, 2002.

———. "Redemption of the Soul in Golden Age Religious Poetry." *Prooftexts* 10 (1990): 49–67.

———. "The Song of the Silent Dove: The Pilgrimage of Judah Halevi." In *Bringing the Hidden to Light: The Process of Interpretation—Studies in Honor of Stephen A. Geller*, ed. Kathryn F. Kravitz and Diane M. Sharon, 217–35. Winona Lake, Ind.: Eisenbrauns, 2007.

———. "*Tawakkul* in the Poetry of Judah Halevi." In Sasson Somekh Festschrift, forthcoming.

———. *Wine, Women, and Death: Medieval Hebrew Poetry on the Good Life*. Philadelphia: Jewish Publication Society, 1986.

Schimmel, Annemarie. *Gärten der Erkentniss*. Düsseldorf: Eugen Diederichs, 1982.

———. *Mystical Dimensions of Islam*. Chapel Hill: University of North Carolina Press, 1975.

Schirmann, Ḥayim. "Hameshorerim benei doram shel moshe ibn ʿezra viyhuda haleivi." *Yediʿot hamakhon leḥeqer hashira haʿivrit* 6 (1944–45): 319–22.

———. *Hashira haʿivrit bisfarad uvprovans*. 2 vols. Jerusalem: Mosad Bialik, 1954.

———. "Hashlamot leḥayei yehuda haleivi." In *Letoledot hashira vehadrama haʿivrit: Meḥqarim umasot*, 1:319–41. 2 vols. Jerusalem: Mosad Bialik, 1979.

———. "Ḥayei yehuda haleivi." *Tarbiz* 9 (1937–38): 35–54, 125, 219–40, 284–305; *Tarbiz* 10 (1938–39): 237–39, reprinted with significant revisions in his collected essays entitled *Letoledot hashira vehadrama haʿivrit: Meḥqarim umasot*, 1:250–318. 2 vols. Jerusalem: Mosad Bialik, 1979.

———. *Letoledot hashira vehadrama haʿivrit: Meḥqarim umasot*. 2 vols. Jerusalem: Mosad Bialik, 1979.

———. *Toledot hashira haʿivrit bisfarad hamuslimit,* published posthumously, with substantial intervention by the editor, Ezra Fleischer. Jerusalem: Magnes, 1995.

Schmelzer, Menahem. *Isaac ben Abraham Ibn Ezra: Poems* (Hebrew). New York: Jewish Theological Seminary, 1980.

Silman, Yohanan. *Philosopher and Prophet: Judah Halevi, the Kuzari, and the Evolution of His Thought,* trans. Lenn J. Schramm. Albany: State University of New York Press, 1995.

Silver, Abba Hillel. *A History of Messianic Speculation in Israel.* Boston: Beacon, 1959; originally published 1927.

Sivan, Emanuel. "The Beginnings of the *Faḍā'il al-Quds* Literature." *Israel Oriental Studies* 1 (1971): 263–71.

Stern, Samuel M. "Arabic Poems by Spanish-Hebrew Poets." In *Romanica et occidentalia,* ed. Moshe Lazar, 254–63. Jerusalem: Magnes, 1963.

———. *Hispano-Arabic Strophic Poetry.* Oxford: Clarendon, 1974.

Stern, Samuel M., and Alexander Altmann. *Isaac Israeli.* Oxford: Oxford University Press, 1958.

Stetkevych, Jaroslav. *The Zephyrs of Najd.* Chicago: University of Chicago Press, 1993.

Stroumsa, Sara. "On Jewish Intellectuals Who Converted in the Early Middle Ages." In *The Jews of Medieval Islam: Community, Society, and Identity,* ed. Daniel Frank, 179–97. Leiden: Brill, 1995.

Tanenbaum, Adena. *The Contemplative Soul.* Leiden: Brill, 2002.

Theodor, J., and Ch. Albeck, eds. *Genesis Rabba.* 3 vols. 2nd ed. Jerusalem: Wahrmann, 1965.

Tobi, Yosef. *Proximity and Distance: Medieval Hebrew and Arabic Poetry,* trans. Murray Rosovsky. Leiden: Brill, 2004.

———. *Qeruv udehiyya.* Haifa: University of Haifa Press, 2000.

Tsur, Reuven. *ʿIyunim bashira haʿivrit biymei habeinayim.* Tel Aviv: Daga, 1969.

Tsur, Reuven, and Tova Rosen, eds. *Sefer yisra'eil levin.* Tel Aviv: Tel Aviv University Press, 1994.

Vajda, Georges. *La Théologie ascétique de Baḥya ibn Paquda.* Paris: Imprimerie Nationale, 1947.

Weinberger, Leon J. *Twilight of a Golden Age: Selected Poems of Abraham Ibn Ezra.* Tuscaloosa: University of Alabama Press, 1997.

Wolfson, Elliot R. *Through a Speculum That Shines.* Princeton, N.J.: Princeton University Press, 1994.

Yahalom, Yosef. "ʿAliyato shel rabi yehuda haleivi le'erets yisra'eil: Bemar'e uveḥidot." *Shaleim* 7 (2001–02): 33–45.

———."Dīwān and Odyssey: Judah Halevi and the Secular Poetry of Medieval Spain in the Light of New Discoveries from Petersburg." *Miscelánea de estudios árabes y hebráicos: Sección de Hebreo* 44 (1995): 23–45.

———. "Maʿagalot erets yisra'eil." Forthcoming in *Shaleim.*

Index of Poems

The following is a list, by first line, of all the poems that appear in this book, in whole or in part.

- Poems marked * are the thirty key poems, which appear in Hebrew and English, accompanied by full discussion.
- Poems marked ° are other poems that are quoted in their entirety in the course of the discussion, in translation only.
- Poems not marked are quoted only in part and only in translation.

Index of Names and Subjects